New Orleans
in the Gilded Age

New Orleans in the Gilded Age

POLITICS AND URBAN PROGRESS
1880–1896

Joy J. Jackson

Published by
Louisiana State University Press
for the
LOUISIANA HISTORICAL ASSOCIATION

Copyright © 1969 by
Louisiana State University Press

Library of Congress Catalog Card Number 70–89828
SBN 8071–0910–X

Manufactured in the United States of America by
Thos. J. Moran's Sons, Inc., Baton Rouge, Louisiana

Designed by Jules B. McKee

To my parents

OLIVER AND ONEIDA JACKSON

Preface

THIS STUDY OF New Orleans was undertaken with a twofold purpose in mind. Its major objective is to analyze a period in the city's life that has been largely neglected. But complementing this primary task is another objective: to offer material which may be useful in placing New Orleans against the backdrop of the New South and in comparing it with other American cities in this era. Since most published material on city life in late nineteenth-century America deals mainly with northern cities, it is hoped that this examination of what was then the largest southern metropolis may prove useful to urban historians.

New Orleans during the Gilded Age was surprisingly similar to northern urban centers in many ways, while displaying at the same time some strictly southern characteristics and many distinctive qualities found only within its own limits. Truly cosmopolitan, it had many differences in its culture and population from the rest of the South and indeed from any other American city. This is a fact that should be strongly emphasized.

As C. Vann Woodward has pointed out, much attention has been given to Reconstruction, a relatively brief period, while the more significant decades in southern history, 1880 to 1900, have gone relatively unexamined. This is as true of New Orleans as it is of the South in general. The last twenty years of the century in the Crescent City were years of transition and reckoning when the municipality was forced to face many long-standing problems, some predating the Civil War. These problems affected current city affairs and their settlement paved the way for the sweeping municipal improvements of the early twentieth century.

The phrase "Gilded Age," which may be used rightfully to include the 1870's, has been interpreted in this study as beginning in 1880. Certainly Reconstruction might be considered a part of the Gilded Age on the national scene. But it has such a special political character that it is best studied by itself. New Orleans cannot really be said to have reflected the Gilded Age pattern of normal everyday life which northern cities displayed in the 1870's, until the 1880's. The terminal dates used here, 1880–96, are political in nature. When the occasion warrants, the treatment of certain subjects may go back in time or be carried beyond these years. Although this investigation deals mainly with politics and municipal administration and its problems, some attempt has been made to reflect the cultural pattern of Crescent City life as well.

The author wishes to acknowledge the generous financial support which was given by the American Association of University Women's Educational Foundation through the Irma E. Voigt Fellowship. It made possible a year of uninterrupted research and writing on this study. For their assistance in reading this manuscript and offering helpful criticism, sincere thanks are extended to Tulane University Professors Gerald M. Capers, William R. Hogan, and Charles P. Roland. Dean Philip D. Uzee of Francis T. Nicholls State College guided the editing and revising of the manuscript. His suggestions were of inestimable value and are deeply appreciated. Acknowledgment for their kind services must be given to Mrs. Connie Griffith of the Special Collections Division of Howard-Tilton Memorial Library, Tulane University, and to Patricia Catlett and Joseph T. Butler, Jr., of Linus A. Sims Memorial Library, Southeastern Louisiana College. Finally, for her tireless efforts as typist and copy reader, a loving tribute is paid to my mother, Mrs. Oneida D. Jackson.

Contents

Tables

*New Orleans
in the Gilded Age*

1

THE PERIOD IN
PERSPECTIVE

ALL SAINTS DAY, 1880, dawned clear and cool in New Orleans. It was the kind of sparkling day, one local scribe pointed out, that the French artist Claude had loved to paint. The temperature at ten o'clock in the morning was a bracing 58 degrees. By afternoon almost twelve thousand persons had come out to stroll down the garden-like cemetery aisles on Metairie Ridge and in the older cemeteries in the heart of the city. Rarely had the crowds been so large in recent years. The steady throng of visitors brought almost every type of flower grown locally—roses, chrysanthemums, lilies—and occasionally an artificial wax or glass flower wreath in the shape of a heart, a cross, or a crown.[1]

To New Orleanians, All Saints Day was more than a religious holiday or a time for personal remembrance of dead loved ones. It was a social occasion, the day on which one wore his or her best winter outfit for the first time. The Creole women called this outfit *la robe de la toussaint*. Fine velvets, heavy silks, crepes, and taffetas rivaled the flowers as friends stopped to exchange gossip with friends in the cities of the dead. Even children were included in this unusual fashion parade. On Canal Street outside the cemeteries grouped on Metairie Ridge were congregated hawkers of fruits, pastries, and liquid refreshments. Vendors usually offered for sale such delicacies as *estomac mulatte* (a flat ginger cake with icing), both coconut and pecan pralines, *candie Tiré, (pulled candy),* and rice cakes called *calas.* The favorite beverage sold was *La Biere*

1 All Saints Day, November 1, 1880, was described in detail in the New Orleans *Daily Picayune,* November 2, 1880.

3

Creole, a beer made from the juice and pulp of pineapple.[2]

The crowds which thronged to the cemeteries on November 1, 1880, could be particularly thankful that this had been a mild year for disease in the city. The terrible yellow fever epidemic of 1878 was only two years in the past. If they chanced to discuss current events, cemetery visitors must have talked about the municipal election which was to take place the following day. The *Daily Picayune* confidently predicted the victory of the reform group, which offered Joseph A. Shakspeare for mayor.[3]

In a way, this All Saints Day may be taken as an excellent vantage point from which to survey the past and future history of the city. Although local citizens had known poverty, sickness, debt, and the struggle to regain their city and state governments from carpetbaggers in the 1870's, they were finally beginning to recover and achieve a modest share of prosperity. The large turnout and modish apparel of the cemetery visitors this year was one small indication that life was returning to normal. On the next day the reformer Shakspeare was elected. His term of office as mayor was to be the opening chapter of a new era.

Slowly, painfully, since the removal of Federal troops from Louisiana in 1877, the city had been groping its way out of the miasma of Reconstruction violence and corruption. But the return to "normalcy" had been stymied in the last years of the 1870's by the devastating yellow fever epidemic of 1878 which claimed 4,046 lives, by the enormous municipal debt inherited from carpetbag regimes, and by the stagnation of the city's commercial life for the past decade.

Definite signs of recovery were evident, however, by 1880. A citizens' group, the Auxiliary Sanitary Association, had been formed in 1879 to help the local board of health combat disease and adverse sanitary conditions in the city.[4] The new municipal

---

[2] *Ibid.;* [Joy Jackson], "When All Saints' Day Saw the Fashion Parade," *Dixie Roto Magazine,* New Orleans *Times-Picayune,* October 28, 1951. Portions of this article were based on personal reminiscences of James J. Fortier in an interview with the author.

[3] *Daily Picayune,* November 1, 1880.

[4] George E. Waring, Jr., and George W. Cable, "History and Present Condition of New Orleans, Louisiana," *Tenth Census, Report on the Social Statistics of Cities,* XIX, Pt. 2 (Washington, 1887) , 286–87.

administration elected in 1880 was dedicated to working out a settlement of the nagging debt, and commerce began to give evidence of reviving. Some business property doubled in value between 1880 and 1881, and "For Rent" signs which had haunted many local houses for years began to disappear.[5] The completion of the jetties at the mouth of the Mississippi River by engineer James B. Eads in 1879 deepened the passes into the Gulf and opened the river to larger, oceangoing vessels.[6] By 1883, for the first time since the end of the Civil War, cotton receipts at the port of New Orleans equaled the receipts for the bumper cotton crop of 1859.[7] Equally as important was the completion in 1883 of the Southern Pacific Railroad which linked the Crescent City with California.[8] To the city fathers this long-awaited rail connection was like a rainbow stretching into a golden future.

This renaissance in business activity and civic optimism was noted by Mark Twain in 1882. He found New Orleans "well outfitted with progressive men—thinking, sagacious, long-headed men," and "a driving place commercially" with "a Great river, ocean and railway business." New Orleans was, furthermore, "the best-lighted city in the Union, electrically speaking," even surpassing New York in this respect. He praised its excellent men's clubs and its newly renovated pleasure resorts at West End and Spanish Fort on Lake Pontchartrain. Telephones existed "everywhere" and the city's newspapers were of a high caliber. As an example of local journalistic scope, Twain pointed to the *Times-Democrat* edition of August 26, 1882, which "contained a report of the year's business of the towns of the Mississippi valley, from New Orleans all the way to St. Paul—two thousand miles." [9]

Despite the obvious signs of better times, New Orleans in the 1880's could not boast of the population gains of Chicago, or the municipal improvements of Boston, St. Louis, or New York. While other American cities went into debt to pay for new waterworks,

[5] *Daily Picayune*, July 11, 1881.
[6] For a discussion of the jetties' construction, see John S. Kendall, *History of New Orleans* (Chicago and New York, 1922) , I, 438–40.
[7] *Daily Picayune*, May 13, 1883.
[8] *Ibid.*, January 13, 1883.
[9] Mark Twain, *Life on the Mississippi* (New York, 1960) , 200.

sewerage systems, or street paving, New Orleans had none of these to show for its indebtedness. Between 1882 and 1895 a considerable portion of city funds went to pay off old debts incurred by carpetbag regimes in the early 1870's. In staging a commercial revival it was also at a disadvantage in comparison with other American cities. By the 1880's the five railroad lines connecting it with various sections of the country did offer hopes of bringing back some of the trade lost since the Civil War. But building up new commercial ties took time, and other cities more centrally located in the Mississippi Valley, such as Chicago and St. Louis, had long had more extensive railroad systems. In addition, they were more favorably situated to serve as manufacturing centers.

New Orleans had always been chiefly a commercial center. By the early 1880's, with its commerce facing increasing competition from other cities, its industrial enterprises were still operating on a modest scale. In 1880 it had only 915 manufacturing industries, in which the average capital was $9,360.[10] Only about 30,000 persons (one seventh of the population of 216,090) were employed in manufacturing establishments in 1883.[11] To reach the general average of American cities of that time, the city would have had to find employment in factories for 15,000 more persons.

New Orleans' "new era" of the 1880's was thus one of mixed blessings. Larger cotton exports went hand in hand with a practically empty city treasury. Electric lights on the river front illuminated ramshackle wharves badly in need of repair. Amid the dazzling municipal growth which characterized American cities in the Gilded Age, New Orleans (like Alice in Wonderland) would have to run very fast if it wished to stand still. Between 1840 and 1880 it had dropped from third to ninth in national rank. The urge to expand the city's assets was, nevertheless, strong in the bosoms of its citizens no matter how difficult the task might be. A Whig city before the Civil War, New Orleans two decades later wholeheartedly endorsed the "New South" philosophy of an industrialized Dixie advocated by Richard H. Edmonds and Henry W. Grady.

10 *Report on the Manufactures of the United States at the Tenth Census* (Washington, 1883) , 416.
11 *Daily Picayune,* August 17, 1883.

This attitude was expressed succinctly by a local official address-ing a mass meeting to whip up enthusiasm for the Cotton Centen-nial Exposition, which was to be held in New Orleans. Speaking in June, 1884, seven months before the opening of the exposition, United States Marshal John R. G. Pitkin told his audience:

> Sectionalism is dead and peace reigns, and truly the reign of peace is a victory for both parties. This Exposition will show that a people who have been over borne by war and wreck, can still accomplish a great work, and it will prove that they are invincible in the face of any for-tune. All this, however, comes from our great resources. We must devel-op them. We must multiply sweat in steam and multiply muscle in machinery. When this is done there awaits us at the Passes our own Mediterranean, and beyond it the New World of the South invites. This is the province of your Exposition; this is its mission.[12]

One hastily put-together exposition could not accomplish all that its mentors such as Pitkin desired, but it could serve notice to the rest of the country that New Orleans was beginning a slow but sure economic comeback.

The city stretched about twelve miles along the east bank of a crescent-shaped bend in the Mississippi River. Its extension on the west bank reached out narrowly for about fifteen miles. But the major territory and population of the city were located on the east bank. Although the east bank limits of the municipality spread out as far as Lake Pontchartrain and Lake Borgne and the entire territory of the city totaled 187 square miles, less than one-tenth of the area was inhabited. As an aid to municipal administration New Orleans was divided into seven districts. The districts were subdivided into wards for political purposes.[13] Although Lake

12 *Ibid.*, June 3, 1884.
13 Waring and Cable, "History and Present Condition of New Orleans, Lou-isiana," 271; James S. Zacharie, *New Orleans Guide with Descriptions of the Routes to New Orleans, Sights of the City Arranged Alphabetically, And Other Information useful to Travellers; Also, Outline of the History of Louisiana* (New Orleans, 1893), 89–90, hereinafter cited as *New Orleans Guide;* Will H. Coleman (comp. and pub.), *Historical Sketch Book and Guide to New Orleans and Environs with Map, Illustrated with Many Original Engravings and Con-taining Exhaustive Accounts of the Traditions, Historical Legends, and Re-markable Localities of the Creole City* (New York, 1885), 3–4, hereinafter cited as *Historical Sketch Book.*

Pontchartrain was officially the eastern boundary of the six districts on the east bank, close urban settlement extended back from the river only to Claiborne Street. In the area between Claiborne and Broad streets, a section called "back-of-town," population was more thinly scattered, and beyond Broad Street in the direction of the lake the countryside took on a rural atmosphere. Cypress swamp and inpenetrable underbrush reached beyond Metairie Ridge and Gentilly suburb, a dairy and truck farm area, and this wilderness continued to the lake. The *Historical Sketch Book and Guide to New Orleans,* published in 1885 by Will H. Coleman, noted that "within the city limits are the best fishing and duck-hunting resorts in the South and there are probably sections of the Ninth Ward of New Orleans which have never been visited by man, and as unknown as the centre of Africa." [14] One could easily get lost in these morasses, and there had been several instances of men, near starvation, rescued after being stranded for days and weeks in the cypress swamps of the municipality.[15]

Of New Orleans' seven districts, the First District was bounded by Canal Street, Felicity Street, the river, and Lake Pontchartrain. This was the American sector where most of the main businesses, financial houses, and manufacturing concerns were located. The Second District had been created out of the original French city, or Vieux Carré, plus additional territory in the direction of the lake. Its boundaries were Canal Street, Esplanade Avenue, the river, and the lake. The Third District was bounded by Esplanade Avenue, by the lower limits of the city (which was also the boundary of Orleans Parish since the city and parish were synonymous), and by the river and the two lakes, Pontchartrain and Borgne. This area, in addition to the overflow of Creole population from the Vieux Carré, attracted many immigrants in the latter part of the nineteenth century.

The Fourth District consisted of the former small city of Lafayette. It was located between Felicity Street, Toledano Street,

14 Coleman, *Historical Sketch Book,* 3.

15 *Ibid.,* 3–4. The description of the seven municipal districts in the following two paragraphs is taken mainly from Coleman, *Historical Sketch Book,* 3–5, and Zacharie, *New Orleans Guide,* 89–90.

the river, and the lake. In this district between St. Charles and Camp streets was the fashionable Garden District of imposing new mansions, mostly built for American business leaders. By the standards of most crowded American cities, the grounds around these residences were unusually spacious, with broad green lawns, orange and magnolia trees, and heavy, ornate iron fences. The Fifth District, the only one of the districts located on the west bank of the Mississippi, had formerly been the independent town of Algiers. Its boundaries ran from the lower line of Jefferson Parish to the upper line of the parish of Plaquemines. It included the Negro suburb of Freetown. Commercially, it was the center of railroad repair shops and ship and steamer drydocks. The Sixth District was located between Toledano Street, Lowerline Street, the river, and the lake. It, like the neighboring Fourth District, was mainly a residential area. Upper City Park (later Audubon Park), site of the Cotton Centennial Exposition, and Tulane University were located in this area. The Seventh District, formerly the city of Carrollton, extended from Lowerline Street to the upper limits of the city bordering Jefferson Parish, and from the river to the lake. A sparsely settled area, it was a center for dairies, floral nurseries, and small truck farms.

Because its material progress was gradual, with no large-scale population changes, New Orleans managed to carry over into its late nineteenth-century life many of the customs, sights, and sounds of antebellum days. Because it had a French and Spanish heritage in addition to its bustling American business philosophy, the panorama it presented to visitors was unique. The architecture of the Vieux Carré and the French Market, the quaint street vendors, and the French patois of a sizeable part of the Negro population enthralled the visitor from the North, where conformity was fast overcoming individuality in cities.

The three sights of the city which seemed to capture most completely the fancy of the visiting stranger were the riverfront, the French Market, and Canal Street. By the 1880's the restless Mississippi had eaten away at certain points of the levee, while at other places it had deposited its burden of soil. The levee from Julia to St. Louis streets was a broad expanse of batture land on the east side of the river, all of it built up since the city's founding. The newcomer to New Orleans, therefore, saw narrow, abrupt banks and deep water the year around at those points which the river had eroded, and wide, sprawling battures where the water was shallow close to shore and where large log rafts were strung for fifty feet out from land.[16] It was on the batture levees that visitors arriving by rail generally detrained and got their first glimpse of New Orleans.

An English visitor, George Augustus Henry Sala, described the scene in the 1880's as a "labyrinth of sugar hogsheads, cotton-bales, coffee-bags, and barrels of pork and flour." The first sounds which greeted him as he stepped from the train onto the levee were the shrieks of hackmen contending for his patronage and the voices of small Negro boys chanting a popular jingle:

> When the butcher went around to collect his bill,
> He took a brace of dogs and a double-barrelled gun.

"To the noise made by the hackmen and negro boys," he explained, "should be added the jingling of the mule-bells, the rattling of the horse-cars, the warning grunt of the locomotive's steam horn, and the rumbling of innumerable drays bearing the rich products of Louisiana to the Levee for shipment." On the levee and the streets adjoining it, this Englishman was reminded that New Orleans was a seaport as well as a river port by such sights as "sailors of every nationality, sailors' boarding-houses and groggeries . . . slop-shops, or 'one-piece stores,' overflowing with guernseys, pea jackets, sou'wester hats, and overalls of oilskin; warehouses full of junk and jute, and sea-going tackle generally, and a pervading odour of pitch and tar, tobacco and garments saturated with salt." [17]

Another observer was impressed by the fact that the levee was the terminus for 150 streets, and was itself a vast, confusing, un-

16 Waring and Cable, "History and Present Condition of New Orleans, Louisiana," 268–69; [Emily Wright], *From the Lakes to the Gulf* (n.p., 1884) , 102–104.

17 George Augustus Henry Sala, *America Revisited* (London, 1883) , 11, 13, 14. The material on New Orleans in this book was originally published in a series of articles in 1880 in the London *Daily Telegraph*. Clippings of these articles are in a scrapbook, Howard-Tilton Memorial Library, Tulane University.

[Table 1]

*Comparison of Population, Rank, and Foreign Born
in Six Major Cities, Including New Orleans* [a]

Statistics for 1860

City	Population	Rank	Foreign Born
New Orleans	168,675	6	64,621
New York	808,651	1	383,717
Philadelphia	585,529	2	169,430
Chicago	109,260	9	54,624
Baltimore	212,418	4	52,497
St. Louis	160,773	8	96,086

Statistics for 1880

City	Population	Rank	Foreign Born
New Orleans	216,090	9	41,157
New York	1,206,299	1	478,670
Philadelphia	847,170	2	204,335
Chicago	503,185	3	204,859
Baltimore	332,313	6	56,136
St. Louis	350,518	5	105,013

Statistics for 1900

City	Population	Rank	Foreign Born
New Orleans	287,104	12	30,325
New York	3,437,202	1	1,270,080
Philadelphia	1,293,697	3	295,340
Chicago	1,698,575	2	587,112
Baltimore	508,057	6	68,600
St. Louis	575,238	4	111,356

[a] Joseph C. G. Kennedy (comp.), Superintendent of Census, *Population of the United States in 1860: Compiled from the Original Returns of the Eighth Census under the Direction of the Secretary of the Interior* (Washington, 1864), xxxii; *Statistics of the Population of the United States at the Tenth Census (June 1, 1880): Embracing Extended Tables of the Population of States, Counties and Minor Civil Divisions, with Distinction of Race, Sex, Age, Nativity, and Occupations* (Washington, 1883) I, 538–541; *Twelfth Census of the United States Taken in the Year 1900* (Washington, 1901) I, Pt. 1, lxix, cix.

paved thoroughfare of shifting humanity—"officeholders, merchants, sailors, policemen, travelers, dealers in fruit and vegetables, and last, though by no means of less importance, dockhands."
But no less impressive was the variety of vessels in port. As he
passed by the depots, warehouses, and canvas sheds on the board
levee, this visitor noted docked along the wharves "a mighty fleet
of ocean steamers, three-masted vessels and brigantines, boats of
every possible description, including hundreds of the famous Mississippi steamers, whose like the world does not elsewhere produce." [18] Although the golden age of steamboating was drawing
to a close, these stately queens of the river were still common
sights along the levee's edge.

After the levee front, the French Market was always one of the
first stops for tourists. All guidebooks of the period advised their
readers to arise early and visit the French Market between 5 AM
and 11 AM, the hours of its greatest activity. The market building
had been built in 1813 and was enlarged twice in the intervening
years. Its slate roof was supported by massive Doric columns of
brick plastered in imitation of stone. Its general appearance to one
writer was that of a "rookery." Within the structure were three
distinct markets. The first sold meat; the second, vegetables, fish,
game, fruit, and flowers; and the third, every possible article of
drygoods a housewife might need. Aside from shopping, no visit to
the French Market would be complete without a cup of coffee
served piping hot at one of the marble stands operated by Negro
women wearing colorful, elaborate tignons or head scarves.[19]

It is probably safe to say that every visitor to New Orleans in
the latter part of the nineteenth century made an appearance on
Canal Street, becoming for a short time, part of the colorful panorama which caught the eye of every chronicler of the period. The
street's broad expanse was still a dividing line between two different cultures—American above Canal (in New Orleans this means
upriver), and Creole below Canal (this means downriver), in the
Vieux Carré and along Esplanade Avenue. Even today Canal

18 [Wright], *From the Lakes to the Gulf*, 102–104.
19 *Sights and Sounds Along the Sunset Route* (New York, 1885), 6–7;
[Wright], *From the Lakes to the Gulf*, 102.

Street marks the division between "uptown" and "downtown" New Orleans.

Canal Street was a center of social as well as business activity, as any perceptive observer could see for himself. The Grand Opera House, the Art Union, the Customhouse, the exclusive men's clubs, and Christ Church Cathedral were all located there. "Here the gay carriage-parties turn northwestward scurrying away to the races," wrote George Washington Cable, in his *Creoles of Louisiana,* "here the funeral train breaks into a trot toward the cemeteries on Metairie Ridge. . . . Here the ring-politician mounts perpetual guard. Here the gambler seeks whom he may induce to walk around into his parlor in the Rue Royale or St. Charles Street." [20]

Confirming Cable's view of the Crescent City's main thoroughfare was the description given by Charles Henry White, a visitor shortly after the turn of the century. He found Canal Street to be "a great open street fringed by two and three story buildings of nameless architecture; crowded trolley-cars and two policemen; a wide expanse of hazy sky and yellow clouds of dust hovering over an idle crowd that shuffles slowly back and forth beneath the arcades." White's journalistic eye picked out race track touts, bookmakers, jockeys, commercial travelers, longshoremen, country folk in town for a day, clubmen on their way to an afternoon at the Pickwick or Boston clubs, and sightseeing naval personnel from visiting foreign vessels. "In short," he summed up, "one is apt to see here at some hour of the day anybody from a St. Louis capitalist to the man who came the night before with no change of linen, and seven dollars sewn in his waistcoat." [21]

Like most visitors to New Orleans, White was more intrigued by the Vieux Carré than the bustling American district above Canal Street. An artist and journalist, he struck up a friendship with a local Creole gentleman who invited him to sketch his courtyard, a dilapidated, picturesque Vieux Carré relic which had once been the private pleasure spot of a great family, but was now the com-

[20] George W. Cable, *The Creoles of Louisiana* (New York, 1910) , 268.
[21] Charles Henry White, "New Orleans," *Harper's Monthly Magazine,* CXIV (December, 1906) , 121.

mon court for an assortment of shabby boarders whom its Creole owner had to take in to support himself. "Here was a man," White noted, "whose antecedents entitled him to the highest considera- tion eking out an existence in the most humble position. He was waiting for something decent to turn up, he said. The family plate, mahogany, and crystal had long since passed through the dealers' hands in Royal Street, but he assured me that he still had a small legacy, some real estate. We visited it together. . . . It stands in the old St. Louis Cemetery and is as fine a tomb as any man could desire." [22] Cases like this, White added, were common among the Creoles.

Indeed from the 1880's on, the Creoles were a declining ethnic group and no longer a vital factor in politics as they had been be- fore the Civil War. But in its twilight years Creole society gave inspiration to George Washington Cable to write his tongue-in- cheek vignettes which attracted nationwide attention. The Creole past which he drew upon was evident everywhere in Vieux Carré architecture. It convinced visitors that there really were two cul- tures thriving on opposite sides of Canal Street. The fact that the older culture was all but overcome by the younger was not evident to the casual viewer. He saw the Vieux Carré and did not realize its way of life was only a museum piece which would pass out of general existence within thirty years.

Also, he accepted Cable's portrait of the Creole as completely valid, much to the annoyance of local upper-class Creoles. "Mr. Cable has made us an object of amusement to his American read- ers," one of them complained in the 1880's. "Northern people come here to New Orleans to study us as curiosities. They walk up and down Royal Street with 'Dr. Sevier' in one pocket, 'The Grandissimes' in another and 'Old Creole Days' in their hands trying to identify the localities and types of persons." [23] Cable used the word "Creole" to mean native born—including white, Negro, and those of mixed ancestry. Many of his characters were poor, illiterate, and spoke a delightfully broken English (which, though

22 White, "New Orleans," 125–26.
23 L. M. Harris, "The Creoles of New Orleans," *Southern Collegian*, XXX (January, 1898) , 210.

authentic, was resented by Creoles). In an effort to redress the grievances which they felt Cable had inflicted upon them, numerous Creole writers and their sympathizers attacked his interpretation of their background and culture.

The poet-priest Adrien Rouquette and the local French paper *L'Abeille* led this offensive. To them a "Creole" meant a white person of native French and Spanish stock. Unfortunately, the "myth of the Creole," which grew to full maturity as a result of this controversy, pictured the original Creoles as polished aristocrats, free from such human faults as greed and money-grubbing, a portrait which was far wide of the mark. Genteel literature on Creole life in its "golden age," such as the works of Grace King and Kate Chopin, was the result of this romanticizing of the Creoles in the last twenty years of the century.[24]

Such myth-making and fond recalling of the past were not limited to educated Creole elements. Indeed, while New Orleanians spoke in one breath of the commercial possibilities of the "New South," with the next breath they delivered dedication speeches for Confederate memorials. Between 1880 and 1911, monuments were erected to Robert E. Lee, Jefferson Davis, and Albert Sidney Johnston, among others. The United Confederate Veterans was organized in the Crescent City in 1889, and one of the city's most prominent matrons and wife of a mayor, Mrs. William J. Behan, became president of the Confederate Memorial Association of the South. She was also the guiding force in making Jefferson Davis' birthday the state Confederate Memorial Day.[25]

Sharing with the rest of the South, and indeed the entire nation, a romantic interest in the "Lost Cause" and the "Old South" tradition, upper-class New Orleanians kept at least a semblance of bygone manners while busily constructing new Gilded Age man-

[24] Cable and the Creole controversy is discussed in Arlin Turner, *George W. Cable: A Biography* (Durham, 1956), 101–102, 165–67, 197–207. The Creoles' grievance against Cable tended to become merged with the general Southern grievance against the freedman after 1885. For a reappraisal of the Creoles and the "Creole myth," see Joseph G. Tregle, Jr., "Early New Orleans Society: A Reappraisal," *Journal of Southern History*, XVIII (February, 1952), 20–36.

[25] C. Vann Woodward, *Origins of the New South, 1877–1914* (Baton Rouge, 1951), 146; Kendall, *History of New Orleans*, II, 785–88.

sions along St. Charles and its intersecting uptown avenues. In the 1880's society girls still married young—matrimony being the "grand, authorized aim, as publicly recognized as the Louisiana Lottery." One admirer noted in 1885 that the southern belles "read clever books, and discuss their fingernails; they are shocked at the conversational appearance of the word leg, but are enthusiastically devoted to the ballet." [26] A young lady could receive a gentleman alone or go for a drive in his carriage. But the couple had to be escorted by a chaperon to theaters, concerts, or balls. There were hardy souls, however, who resented such a sheltered existence. Throughout the last fifteen years of the nineteenth century occasional mention was made in local papers of suffragettes. They took quite an active part in the political campaign of 1896.

The private sanctum of society had been invaded in the 1880's through the society columns of the *Daily Picayune*. Its publisher and editor, Mrs. Eliza Jane Nicholson (who wrote under the pseudonym of Pearl Rivers) was responsible for pioneering the publishing of such news. She created a "Society Bee" whose buzzing and reporting began on March 16, 1879.[27] Scandalized at first by this invasion of their privacy, the city's elite soon came to be avid readers of the column and competitors for its attention. By 1892 there were thirty-five millionaires in the city, whose parties, marriages, and trips to Europe the society editor could report.[28]

The major portion of the population—English speaking and native born—had little to distinguish them from inhabitants of other American cities except that they were less likely to be engaged in factory work. Also, their death rate in 1880 was higher than that of New York, Boston, Chicago, St. Louis, or Baltimore.[29] Only one out of every five families owned their own homes by 1890. Almost half of these homes were owned by working class persons,

[26] *Sights and Sounds Along the Sunset Route,* 7–9.

[27] *Daily Picayune,* March 16, 1879; Thomas Ewing Dabney, *One Hundred Great Years: The Story of the Times-Picayune From its Founding to 1940* (Baton Rouge, 1944)), 307–308.

[28] Roger W. Shugg, *Origins of Class Struggle in Louisiana: A Social History of White Farmers and Laborers during Slavery and After, 1840–1875* (Baton Rouge, 1939) , 291.

[29] Stanford E. Chaillé, *Life and Death-Rates: New Orleans and Other Cities Compared* (New Orleans, 1888) , 15.

however, with an average mortgage of $1,000 or less.[30] Like urban residents of other cities, they worked long hours for small pay, joined the union movement in large numbers in the mid-1880's, and displayed occasional resentment against their employers through strikes.

Always a cosmopolitan city, New Orleans' mixture of European races set it apart from most of the South. It differed slightly from northern cities during the last half of the century in that its immigrant groups never reached such proportions that they could inhabit a large section of the city and remain isolated from the rest of the community for years.[31] Some semi-isolation did exist, of course, especially among the Irish in the so-called "Irish Channel," which spread along the riverfront streets mainly in the Fourth District; among the Creoles in the Vieux Carré; and among the Germans and Italians who had their own clubs, societies, and newspapers in the 1880's and 1890's. But the general tendency was toward integration, rather than clannishness. Such integration became much easier for Irish and German elements by the end of the century. There was only a fraction over a fifth as many foreign-born Irishmen in the city in 1900 as in 1860. The number of foreign-born Germans likewise decreased by 1900 to a little less than half the number recorded in 1860.[32] As these groups lost in newcomers, they gained in local acceptance. The bitter issue of the immigrant Irish (which had divided politicians before the Civil War into the Know Nothings and the Democrats) was a dead issue in Gilded Age politics. Good feeling toward the German segment of the population was amply displayed in 1889 and 1890 when the Germans were preparing to stage a national singing festival, the *Saengerfest*.

Forty thousand dollars was raised by New Orleans Germans, and a temporary concert hall was built facing Lee Circle to seat

30 Shugg, *Origins of Class Struggle in Louisiana*, 296.
31 See Tables 1 and 2 for statistics on the New Orleans foreign-born population.
32 Joseph C. G. Kennedy (comp.), Superintendent of Census, *Population of the United States in 1860; Compiled from the Original Returns of the Eighth Census under the Direction of the Secretary of the Interior* (Washington, 1864), xxxii; *Twelfth Census of the United States Taken in the Year 1900* (Washington, 1901), I, Pt. 1, clxxviii.

more than five thousand persons. Singers were engaged from the Metropolitan, the Mannheim, and Stuttgart opera houses. On October 6, 1889, local Germans had the satisfaction of seeing thousands turn out to watch their parade commemorating the laying of the concert hall cornerstone. Almost every element of the population participated in the affair. By the end of the century, nevertheless, those devoted to perpetuating German culture in New Orleans were facing the same decline as the French Creoles. Second-generation Germans thought of themselves as Americans and preferred English to the language of their immigrant parents.[33]

However, nativistic belligerence against newly arrived immigrants increased rather than decreased by the 1890's. Hostile cartoons against immigrants, particularly Italians, appeared in the local journal, the *Mascot, An Independent Journal of the Day,* which depicted them as the pawns of the municipal political machine. Although the Italian immigration never reached the proportions of the earlier Irish or German, there were almost three times as many of them living in New Orleans in 1900 as in 1880.[34] Hostility and suspicion were manifested against them as a result of the Mafia and Police Chief David C. Hennessy's murder in 1890. This prejudice disappeared only in the twentieth century with their gradual assimilation. Often the Italians were crowded into ramshackle Vieux Carré tenements, living under conditions which were common to other elements of the city's poor, white and Negro alike. If one followed such unfortunates home, a national magazine writer reported in 1898, he would find

a ten-roomed, leaky-roofed, tenement house where fifty families eat, sleep and have their being; old hags, drunken men, pale-faced young mothers and ghastly, bold-eyed children huddled together in penury and filth. A common court, the receptacle for rotten vegetables and cast-off clothing, does service as a common dressing room. A rusty pipe plays muddy water in a slime-lined basin, where sleep-begrimed eyes and crisp pink radishes are washed for the early market stalls. From this court a dozen rickety stairways lead up to as many unwhole-

33 John Frederick Nau, *The German People of New Orleans, 1850–1900* (Leiden, 1958), 141–43.
34 See Table 2 for exact figures.

some rooms, about whose upper galleries, out of reach of molding damp and hungry children, hang festoons of macaroni, peppers and garlic.[35]

The Negro portion of the population, which was about one fourth of the total population, lived mainly in dwellings of this kind, or in such squalid sections as Freetown in Algiers with its straggling row of cabins and mud-daubed chimneys, disjointed fences, truck patches, "yaller" dogs, cackling hens, and tethered goats.[36] The average life expectancy of a local Negro baby born in 1880 was 25.56 years as compared to 38.10 years for a white baby.[37] Because of their poor living conditions and reluctance to be vaccinated, Negroes, in general, suffered more fatalities from smallpox and from disease than whites. In contrast to the

[Table 2]

Population of Three Major Foreign-Born Groups in New Orleans[a]

Place of Birth	1860	1880	1900
Ireland	24,398	13,970	5,398
Germany	19,752	13,944	8,733
Italy	(not listed)	1,995	5,398

[a] Kennedy, *Population of the United States in 1860: Compiled from the Original Returns of the Eighth Census . . .*, xxxii; *Statistics of the Population of the United States at the Tenth Census*, I, 538–41; *Twelfth Census of the United States*, I, Pt. 1, clxxviii.

bulk of the Negro population, there was a small tight-knit, mainly French-speaking Negro elite with its own social clubs, debutantes, and business and professional men, some of whom even studied in France. Negro labor unions were also active in achieving recognition from business leaders and in cooperating with white unions in strikes. Despite their existence, however, the occupational opportunities for the New Orleans Negro gradually narrowed as

[35] Belle Hunt, "New Orleans, Yesterday and Today," *Frank Leslie's Popular Monthly*, XXXI (June, 1891), 642.
[36] *Ibid.*, 645–46.
[37] Chaillé, *Life and Death-Rates*, 13.

the century closed.[38] In addition, the rigid mores of segregation (in the making since the end of Reconstruction) were indelibly set on society by the late 1890's. When George Washington Cable spoke out against this developing southern pattern of discrimination, he was attacked sharply all over the South. His radical and unpopular views were one of the main reasons, by the 1890's, he found it more comfortable to live in New England than in his home town.[39]

The Negroes were participants in Crescent City politics throughout the 1880's and 1890's, despite their rigid social segregation. Both the Democratic-Conservative Ring and its reformer opposition vied for their votes until Negroes were disfranchised by the state constitutional convention in 1898. In the last twenty years of the nineteenth century, and as late as the Warren G. Harding administration in the 1920's, New Orleans Negroes even held high federal posts, such as surveyor of the port, register of United States lands, and comptroller of customs at New Orleans. Although the colored population was always the underdog of local society, there were few overt signs of bitterness against it until the 1890's. Violence broke out between white and Negro strikers on the docks in 1894. Disfranchisement came in 1898—both the local Ring and the reformers participating in this movement which was rationalized by its advocates as a means to end corrupt elections. The Charles riot in 1900 climaxed this anti-Negro feeling. In tracking down a Negro fugitive, Robert Charles, race warfare broke out. Negroes were beaten and two of their schools set on fire. Twelve persons were killed, five of them, Negroes.[40]

A full explanation for the heightened tension between white and Negro in the 1890's would be difficult to reach. But one factor which may be considered was the increase in Negro population in the decade between 1890 and 1900. The urban-born Negro, sometimes speaking a gumbo French, was part of the city's life. But new-

[38] See Chapter 8 of this book for more details on Negro labor.

[39] Cable was attacked particularly after the publication of "The Freedman's Case in Equity," in *Century Magazine,* January, 1885, and "The Silent South" in the same journal, September, 1885. A list of other articles by Cable on the Negro question is in the bibliography of Turner, *George W. Cable,* 358–66.

[40] *Daily Picayune,* July 26–29, 1900.

comers from the country were likely to get into trouble more easily and inspire resentment among the poor whites with whom they
competed for jobs. Such newcomers must have invaded the ranks
of the local black residents in the 1890's, because the Negro population increased 20.5 percent between 1890 and 1900, although it
had only increased 11.9 percent in the previous decade.[41]

From the viewpoint of health, New Orleans was stigmatized in
this period as a "pest hole." One poetical writer called the city "a
Garden of the Hesperides, intersected by horse-car tramways, and
guarded by a dragon hight Yellow Jack." [42] The threat of yellow
fever was a potent factor in the reluctance of northern capital to
invest in industrial concerns in the city, and the clumsy methods
of quarantine were equally distasteful. In addition, typhoid, smallpox, malaria, and diphtheria were year-round diseases which affected the population. Some of the chief causes for the high inci-
dence of disease, it was felt, were the faulty system of garbage collection and the innumerable smelly, refuse-cluttered ditches and
canals throughout the city.

In contrast to such eyesores and health nuisances, New Orleans
could boast an abundance of trees and flower gardens. Charles
Dudley Warner found in the 1880's that "flowers pervade the town,
old women on the street corners sit behind them, the florists' windows blush with them, friends dispatch to each other great baskets
of them, the favorites at the theatre and the amateur performers
stand behind barricades of roses which the good-humored audience piles upon the stage, everybody carries roses, and the houses
overflow with them." [43]

After the Civil War, the celebration of the carnival season culminating in Mardi Gras had become increasingly elaborate, with
more parades, carnival balls, and visitors flocking into the city to
share in the frivolity. George A. H. Sala, the English visitor in
1880, attended the carnival season in 1880 and observed that an estimated forty thousand out-of-towners saw the Mardi Gras festivities that year.[44] To accommodate such a number of guests, there

41 *Negro Population, 1790–1915* (Washington, 1918) , 782.
42 Sala, *America Revisited,* 42.
43 Charles D. Warner, *New Orleans* (New York, 1888) , n.p.
44 Sala, *America Revisited,* 91.

[Table 3]

Negro Population in New Orleans[a]

Year	Negro Population
1880	57,617
1890	64,419
1900	77,714
1910	89,262

Year	Percentage of Negroes in Total City Population
1880	26.7%
1890	26.6%
1900	27.1%
1910	26.3%

Decade	Rate of Increase by Decades
1880–1890	11.9%
1890–1900	20.5%
1900–1910	14.9%

[a] *Negro Population, 1790–1915* (Washington, 1918), 782.

were then at least half a dozen major hotels in New Orleans, in addition to several smaller ones. The most famous were the St. Charles and the Hotel Royale (formerly the St. Louis and during Reconstruction, the notorious State House of the carpetbag state government). In addition, visitors could find lodging in one of the innumerable boardinghouses. In the Vieux Carré such establishments usually had a sign *Pension Privée* which denoted room and board a la Creole cuisine. *Chambres Garnies* or *Chambres a Louer* indicated simply a furnished room. Such rooms were frequently rented to white men by quadroon or octoroon landladies.[45] While integrated housing was never in the majority in New Orleans, some integration always existed on the fringes of declining neighborhoods.

[45] For a listing of hotels in 1885, see Coleman, *Historical Sketch Book,* 82–83.

In the boom of organized recreational activities which marked the Gilded Age, New Orleans retained the reputation it had enjoyed before the war as a city of wide-open fun. Along with its gambling houses and Fair Grounds race track, one could find diversion at the theaters or the glittering French Opera, from baseball games, neighborhood dances, "walking contests," at the amusement garden at Carrollton, and at its Lake Pontchartrain parks, Spanish Fort and West End.

During the 1880's and 1890's New Orleans had three major legitimate theaters, the St. Charles Theater, the Academy of Music, and the Grand Opera House (formerly the Varieties Theater). For a number of years in the 1880's all three were managed by one man, David Bidwell, known as the "Napoleon of Managers" because of his extensive and lucrative operations in theater management and theatrical bookings in New Orleans, several other southern cities, and Havana, Cuba. Since Bidwell and other theater managers who followed him in the 1890's had financial interests in road companies which played a circuit of their theaters in the South, road companies were destined to undermine local stock companies by the end of the century. The Bidwell era of theater dominance in New Orleans saw such celebrated players on the local stage as Edwin Booth, Joseph Jefferson, Sarah Bernhardt, and Fanny Janauschek, the queen of the German theater. It also saw the introduction of Wagnerian opera at the Grand Opera House and the permanent installation of matinees, an innovation Bidwell first tried during the Civil War era. In addition to the major theaters, several minor playhouses offered everything from legitimate plays at the modest Avenue Theater to circus acts interspersed with Shakespeare at Faranta's tent show. Faranta, who was really Frederick William Stempel, built two inexpensive theaters out of his profits—the Iron Theater, constructed of wood scaffolding covered with corrugated iron, and the Elysium Theater. Numerous amateur theater groups were active at local schools and church halls. The two Lake Pontchartrain pleasure resorts, Spanish Fort and West End, could be reached by train or shell road in the 1880's. Both offered hotels, seafood restaurants, gardens, German bands, nightly fireworks and vaudeville acts. Occasionally a lakeside attraction might be a celebrity such as Oscar Wilde, who

lectured at Spanish Fort in 1882. By the close of the century, Spanish Fort lost its elegance and became mostly a favorite spot for
Negro picnickers. But another resort, Milneburg, which had always been a site of private camps and a trading base for hamlets
across Lake Pontchartrain such as Mandeville, began to become
popular by 1900.[46] Before the local introduction of the Society for
the Prevention of Cruelty to Animals in 1888, dogfights and cock-
fighting arenas existed within the city and in neighboring parishes.
Any Sunday afternoon an observant rider on one of the streetcars
which led to the city's outskirts could see gentlemen carrying bags
whose contents were obviously game cocks.[47] A Sunday closing
law was passed by the state legislature in 1886. But it was deeply
resented and often ignored by New Orleanians.

In assessing the city on this point, Warner astutely noted that
although New Orleans had never been straitlaced and its residents
viewed Sunday as a day of amusement as well as worship, it was
free of the "socialistic agnosticism" that he had observed in Cincinnati, St. Louis, and Chicago. Also, harmony and good feeling
appeared to exist between the Protestant and Catholic communities. He felt its citizens, both Protestant and Catholic, were imbued
with an old-fashioned religious simplicity. "If any one thinks
that faith has died out of modern life," he concluded, "let him
visit the mortuary Chapel of St. Roch." [48]

This chapel, located in St. Roch Cemetery, was built by a young
priest who invoked the help of St. Roch with a promise to build

[46] On New Orleans theater in the Gilded Age see John S. Kendall, *The
Golden Age of the New Orleans Theater* (Baton Rouge, 1952) , 550–605. References to amusements in New Orleans may be found in every issue of the daily
papers of the period. Oscar Wilde's appearance at Spanish Fort is mentioned in
Daily Picayune, June 26, 1882. West End, Spanish Fort, and Milneburg are discussed in Coleman, *Historical Sketch Book,* 3, 68, 148; Waring and Cable, "History and Present Condition of New Orleans, Louisiana," 275; Zacharie, *New
Orleans Guide,* 97–98; Rightor, *Standard History of New Orleans, Louisiana,*
477–78; Warner, *New Orleans.*

[47] The struggle against cruelty to animals was spearheaded by publisher Mrs.
Eliza Jane Nicholson (Pearl Rivers) in the *Daily Picayune.* On the local formation of an S.P.C.A., see Dabney, *One Hundred Great Years,* 311–13. On cock-
fighting see New Orleans *Mascot, An Independent Journal of the Day,* April 8,
1882, hereinafter cited as *Mascot.*

[48] Warner, *New Orleans.*

the edifice during a yellow fever epidemic in 1868 when his con-
gregation was swept by the disease. It became a shrine for the de-
vout, and its walls in time were covered with discarded crutches
and marble plaques testifying to cures or help the donors felt they
had received through the intercession of St. Roch. Candles lit by
the faithful constantly burned before its little, carved-wood al-
tar.[49]

Catholicism was the major religion in New Orleans, proof that
the French and Spanish religious tradition of the original settlers,
plus the devotion of the immigrant Irish and Italians, was potent.
Out of an approximate 95,716 church members in New Orleans in
1890, 67,156 were Catholics.[50] Much to the dismay of Catholic
church officials, during this period local Negroes began to leave
the Catholic Church, however. Paradoxically, its lack of segregation in the 1880's worked against its appeal to Negroes who were
more attracted to the rigidly segregated Baptist and Methodist
churches where they could organize and shape their separate black
congregations. Many of them also associated the Catholic faith
with slavery days or with the anti-Negro Irish laborers.[51] Only a
small activist group called the *Comite des Citoyens*, composed of
antisegregationist Negroes who were mainly descendants of free
persons of color, protested vigorously when a Catholic Church, St.
Katherine, was created for Negroes. Despite their protests the
church was opened in 1895. In his sermon at the dedication service
for St. Katherine, Archbishop Francis Janssens expressed satisfaction that Negro Catholics would now have a church in which they
could participate in all the varied activities of the laity. But he
added, as if to allay the fears of the *Comite des Citoyens*, that "the
church was not built to exclude the colored people from other
churches, but on the contrary they were just as welcome to come
to worship in the other churches as they had always been." The

[49] *New Orleans City Guide, Written and Compiled by the Federal Writers'
Project of the Works Progress Administration for the City of New Orleans* (Boston, 1938) , 197–98.
[50] *Report of Statistics of Churches in the United States at the Eleventh Census, 1890* (Washington, 1894) , 98–99.
[51] Dorothy Rose Eagleson, "Some Aspects of the Social Life of the New Orleans Negro in the 1880's" (M.A. thesis, Tulane University, 1961) , 7–9.

trend of segregation and separate Negro Catholic churches grew, nevertheless, and by the 1930's there were nine such churches.[52]

Local Protestants totaled over 25,000 in 1890 with the German Evangelicals, the Methodists, the Presbyterians, and the Episcopalians as the leading denominations. Although the German Evangelicals had the highest total of members, 4,750, of any Protestant group, they were divided into only four congregations. On the other hand, the other three denominations mentioned were more highly organized and established; each had at least a dozen churches or more. Other Protestant groups represented by congregations in New Orleans in 1890 included Baptists, Lutherans, Congregationalists, Disciples of Christ, and Adventists.[53] There was also one Unitarian Church in the city. To serve the local Jewish population there were nine Jewish congregations with a total membership of 2,750.[54]

The major newspapers in New Orleans by 1880 included the *Daily Picayune,* the *Daily States,* the *City Item,* the *Times* and the *Democrat.* In 1881 the *Times* and the *Democrat* merged into the *Times-Democrat* which published daily instead of the six days a week of the two original components. Other publications were the weekly *Mascot,* the French paper *L'Abeille,* the German publication *Deutscher Zeitung,* and the *Louisianian,* the weekly organ of the Negro Republicans in the city. There were numerous other

---

52 Charles T. Rousseve, *The Negro in Louisiana, Aspects of His History and His Literature* (New Orleans, 1937) , 138–40.

53 *Report of Statistics of Churches,* 94–99. The large number of German Evangelicals may tend to be misleading without an explanation. Most German Protestant immigrants to New Orleans in the nineteenth century had come under the influence of the Prussian Union in their fatherland. This was a governmental attempt to unify the three branches of Protestantism in northern Germany: Reformed, Evangelical, and Lutheran. It was mainly an administrative union and did not attempt to change the doctrinal views of individual congregations. In New Orleans, Germans from all three persuasions were often found forming a church and worshipping together until their different views forced them to separate. Thus the term "German Evangelicals" is a broad one and most certainly covered some who were only temporary affiliates of this church group. See Nau, *The German People of New Orleans,* 69–70, for an explanation of the Prussian Union and its effect upon German immigrants in New Orleans.

54 *Report of Statistics of Churches,* 94–95, 98–99.

business, professional, religious, and social publications as well.[55]

The newspapers contained signs that New Orleanians realized they had to meet the challenge of progress and of poverty which economist-reformer Henry George criticized. Editors talked eagerly of furthering business and encouraged more manufacturing establishments, yet sympathized with striking laborers. Many improvements, which were only dreams but eventually became realities in the twentieth century, were also discussed—such as a bridge across the river in the heart of New Orleans, a public belt railroad for the city docks, and a union terminal station for all railroads entering the city. Between 1880 and 1896 the city passed through a crucial era, one of transition and reckoning in which it was forced to face problems which had been accumulating for twenty years. The major problems were the revival of commerce, the municipal debt, and the struggle for political ascendency between the city's Ring and reformer elements in the Democratic-Conservative Party. The sweeping changes of the early twentieth century in New Orleans could not have come without the initial efforts at their solution in the turbulent 1880's and 1890's.

[55] J. C. Waldo, *Visitors' Guide to New Orleans* (New Orleans, 1879) , 103–105; Dabney, *One Hundred Great Years*, 257–58, 313–14.

2

BOSSES AND BUSINESSMEN

To UNDERSTAND politics in New Orleans in the last quarter of the nineteenth century, one must go back to the troubled days of Reconstruction when the pattern of local Gilded Age politics began to take shape. Carpetbag tenure of the mayor's office had come to an end in 1872. But carpetbaggers retained control of the state government and continued to wield much power in the city through their state-operated municipal police force, the Metropolitans, until 1877.

In the gubernatorial races of 1872 and 1876, both the Republicans and the Democratic-Conservatives (the revitalized Democratic Party that was currently the organ of the local Redeemers) claimed victory. In the latter race the issue was settled in favor of the Democratic-Conservatives when President Hayes ended political Reconstruction in Louisiana by removing the Federal troops in 1877. But the earlier race was more complicated. In 1872 two rival governors, Republican William Pitt Kellogg and Democrat John McEnery, set up office and called two rival state legislatures into session in New Orleans, each side claiming to be the legal government. For two years this situation dragged on, with the edge of power on the side of the Republicans, who were backed by Federal force. Then an incredible thing happened.

On September 14, 1874, occurred a second "Battle of New Orleans" which was destined to have an influence on city politics for the next twenty-five years out of all proportion to its actual accomplishment. Known as the Battle of September 14, this running

28

gunfight between the Metropolitan Police and the White League
ended in a carpetbag rout and the carpetbaggers' surrender of the
statehouse to the victorious citizens' "militia." The barricade fighting was somewhat reminiscent of that which launched the Second
Republic in France. But the bold coup of the New Orleans citizens was to prove far less fruitful in immediate gains. Democratic-
Conservative control of the statehouse lasted only a few days, since
President Grant looked upon what was strictly a local struggle for
power as a possible outbreak of general civil war. In response
to the pleadings of the ousted Republican officials in Louisiana,
Grant ordered Federal troops to intervene in the matter and rein-
state the deposed carpetbag legislature and governor.[1] Faced with
resisting Federal troops, the White League evacuated the statehouse.

Although this shortlived victory of the Redeemers may seem in
retrospect to have been futile and hollow, it appeared in an entirely different light to its conservative contemporaries. True, it
did not make McEnery the *de facto* governor. McEnery retired
from the gubernatorial contest after the White League forces retired from the field. But it did cause Kellogg to keep a weather
eye on public opinion. Throughout the rest of his term he tried
not to incite the hostile citizenry to another such violent outbreak.
Equally significant, it served as a stimulant to the morale of a
browbeaten people. The Battle of September 14 came to symbolize
the eventual victorious cause of the Redeemers—even though it
led paradoxically to an immediate defeat.

As a symbol it was to have additional repercussions in later
years. It had been a joint effort on the part of divergent groups
and individuals. Merchants, laborers, Confederate veterans, and
boys too young to have participated in the Civil War gathered together that fateful day at Henry Clay's statue on Canal Street in

---

[1] For a lively account of the Battle of September 14, see Kendall, *History of
New Orleans*, I, 359–75. For a detailed discussion of Reconstruction in Louisiana, see J. R. Ficklen, *History of Reconstruction in Louisiana* (Baltimore,
1910) ; Ella Lonn, *Reconstruction in Louisiana After 1868* (New York and London, 1918) ; W. M. Caskey, *Secession and Restoration in Louisiana* (Baton
Rouge, 1938) ; Garnie McGinty, *Louisiana Redeemed: The Overthrow of Carpetbag Rule, 1875–1880* (New Orleans, 1941) .

response to the White League's call to arms. In politics, as in this battle, New Orleanians united in the late 1870's behind the banner of the Democratic-Conservative Party, no matter what their political affiliation had been before the war. For the next twenty-five years this political union of white citizens, brought on by the Republican extremes of Radical Reconstruction and most dramatically displayed in New Orleans by the Battle of September 14, was to be held up as a *sine qua non* of white conservative rule in both state and city.

At the city level, complete unity within the Democratic-Conservative Party was impossible during the 1880's and 1890's. But the growth of a strong opposition party which would hold together its local organization from one municipal election to the next was also impossible. Fear of the Republican Party, fear of the Negro vote, and appeals to the "spirit of September 14" for white unity kept opposition to the city's regular party limited. Splinter groups were formed regularly before an election in protest to the "Ring," as the Democratic-Conservative machine in the city was called, but even when successful they fell apart shortly after the ballot counting.

As this indicates, the Battle of September 14 was a potent rallying cry for the Democratic-Conservative regulars and for the one-party system. Any notherner who might have chanced to attend a political rally in the Crescent City in the 1880's would have found that southern orators could wave the local version of the "bloody shirt" as well as any Yankee. Since New Orleans had been an occupied city throughout most of the Civil War, the Battle of September 14 was actually the only organized large-scale armed clash within the city limits in the entire Civil War and Reconstruction period. Its memory was to live on in the speeches of politicians and in the lessons of schoolboys until the close of the century.

A natural result of this esteem for the carpetbag rout of September 14 was the tendency to reward political favor to those who had been fortunate enough to have taken part in the battle on the Redeemers' side. Other factors might be more pertinent in one's climb to political prominence in the New Orleans of the 1880's, but to say that one had fought with General Frederick N. Ogden against the "carpetbag rascals" was to complete the local picture of

a perfect candidate. General Ogden himself, the leader of the Redeemer forces in the September 14 struggle, was prominent for
years in the local Democratic-Conservative Party, although he held
no municipal office. Two mayors, William J. Behan and Joseph
Valsin Guillotte, were both veterans of this battle for white supremacy. Finally, there was that political wizard Major Edward
A. Burke, state treasurer in the 1880's and also a potent influence
in city affairs, who had used his authority as a railroad official in
1874 to delay the arrival of Federal troops in the city until after
the Battle of September 14. This had assured the Redeemers of
military success and saved them any danger of having to oppose
federal troops.[2]

In addition to the strong tendency to support the one-party system and glorify the memory of the September 14 struggle, late
nineteenth century New Orleanians had inherited from Reconstruction a legacy of violent and corrupt election practices, the
problem of the Negro vote, and the strange custom of "fusion" between usually incongruous factions.

Disorder and corruption were by no means solely the result of
the Reconstruction experience. Local politics before the Civil War
had known its share of stuffed ballot boxes, the intimidation of
immigrant voters by the Know Nothings, and the spectacle of
armed men at the polls ready for violence and sometimes finding
it. But the scope of violence and election frauds was heightened
and intensified by the Reconstruction era. Their pattern also
changed.

In antebellum elections, rivalry had been first between the
Whigs and the Democrats, and later between the Know Nothings
and the Democrats. By the 1850's the Know Nothings had attracted the American element of the population, while the Creoles
championed the newly arrived Irish and German immigrants in
the Democratic Party.[3] By the end of Reconstruction the struggle

[2] An interesting account of Burke's part in the Battle of September 14 may
be found in Waldo, *Visitors' Guide,* 220–22.

[3] Although a few prominent Creoles, such as Charles Gayarré, joined the
local Know Nothings in the antebellum period and are sometimes mentioned in
political histories because of their novelty in this party, the rank and file of
Creole voters belonged to the Democratic Party and became a potent force when

of native American versus immigrant had been completely sub-merged by the introduction of the Negro into southern politics. Most white southerners in New Orleans, as elsewhere in the South, now united behind the Democratic-Conservative Party to oppose the Republicans and their Negro protégés and to make white su-premacy a solid reality. Whenever reform groups were organized to oppose the city's Democratic Ring, they had to fight against charges that they were former associates of carpetbag officials, or that they were in league with the Republicans and jeopardized the state or national power of the Democratic Party by their local rebellion.

To stave off any tide in favor of such reformers, the Ring felt justified, therefore, in taking drastic action. In the municipal elec-tion of 1882, the reformers investigated the voting returns and came up with an estimate of about six thousand fraudulent votes. After a formal investigation several election officials were indicted. But the case against them was dropped, and the allegedly fraudulent votes allowed to stand in the official election totals.[4]

Frauds were even more blatant in the election of 1884—an esti-mated fifteen thousand votes, according to reformer charges. In Poll Five in the Eleventh Ward the inspectors for the reform can-didate were thrown out by Ring stalwarts when the voting closed. The ballots were then dumped out of the box onto a table. Each one found to be unfavorable to the Ring was thrown into a wash kettle under the table. However, this manipulating was discovered by reform sympathizers and all ballots were hastily returned to the box by the Ring representatives with some consternation.[5] At an-other polling place the name of a famous deceased evangelist, Brother Haskell, who was buried in another city, appeared on a

---

backed up by the vote of recently naturalized immigrants. Gayarré himself withdrew from the Know Nothing Party after being rejected as a delegate by the party's 1855 national convention because he was a Catholic. On this point see Leon C. Soulé, *The Know Nothing Party in New Orleans: A Reappraisal* (Baton Rouge, 1961), Chapters 3 and 4, pp. 39–84.

4 See scattered references in *Daily Picayune* and *Times-Democrat*, November through December, 1882, and New Orleans *Daily States,* March 31, 1883.

5 *Daily Picayune,* April 29, 1884.

voting list. The *Daily Picayune* guessed that the "ghost" of Brother Haskell probably voted for the Ring.[6]

Such incidents were typical of New Orleans elections in the Gilded Age and led in 1888 to the appearance at the polls of armed men pledged to see that their reform candidates would get a fair count. Their physical strength, coupled with universal disgust at the inefficiency of the former administration, spelled victory for the reformers. At every election the newspapers reported fistfights, the discharging of guns, drunkenness, and attempts of Negroes to vote under fraudulent registration papers.

Although whites of both Ring and reformer persuasion claimed to stand for white supremacy, they were not adverse to using Negro votes. In the 1882 city election, the New Orleans *Mascot,* which dealt out savage criticism to local politicians, felt that one of the vital factors in the Ring victory had been the Negro voters who, after voting for the Republican Congressional candidates, had sold their local vote to the Ring.[7] Just how many Negroes voted in the 1880's in New Orleans is impossible to estimate; but they were a factor in politics which had to be considered. The black population in Louisiana in 1880 was 463,655, the white, only 454,954; but in New Orleans, Negroes made up just one fourth of the population.[8] Such a difference meant that New Orleans politicians could tolerate a modest Negro vote without fear of its consequences much more easily than could those in the rest of the state.

In the early 1880's according to the *Mascot,* the Ring got most of the local Negro votes for municipal offices. But in 1888 and again in 1896 Negro groups backed the reformers. By the 1890's in the state as a whole, the Populists sought to nullify the Negro vote which usually went to the Democratic Bourbons. In the dispute over the election of Governor Murphy J. Foster in 1896, they final-

6 *Ibid.,* May 9, 1884.

7 *Mascot,* November 11, 1882.

8 George Reynolds, *Machine Politics in New Orleans, 1897–1926* (New York, 1936), 18; Warner, *New Orleans.* For an interesting account of how the black belt of southern states has influenced the attitude toward Negro suffrage in other areas with less Negroes, see V. O. Key, Jr., *Southern Politics in State and Nation* (New York, 1949) , 3–18.

ly got Foster and his following to agree to a revision of the suffrage requirements through a constitutional convention. In return they did not contest his election. The disfranchisement of the Negro in the new state constitution of 1898 was the result.[9]

As in other southern communities, the phenomenon of "fusion" was present in New Orleans politics in this era. In their efforts to defeat the city Ring, rebellious reform Democrats sometimes considered joining locally with such parties as the Republicans, the Greenbackers, or the Populists. In 1882 the chances of the dominant reform group, which called itself the Independent Party, were probably spoiled by its clumsy attempts to fuse with the Republicans and Greenbackers. No actual agreement was reached among these groups. But the placing of two congressional candidates in the field along with a city ticket made the *Daily Picayune,* usually sympathetic to reform attempts, turn against the Independents. Putting up congressional candidates appeared to mask a deal with the Republicans and might threaten Democratic control of all state offices, the *Picayune* feared.[10]

After the election was won by the Ring, the *Times-Democrat* noted that if the Independents had been completely free of "guilt by association" with the Republicans, this reform group might have proved the winner.[11] Fourteen years later, in the city contest of 1896, fusion was successfully used by the reformers' Citizens League to join to their forces the city's Republicans and Populists. This time the reformers were victorious. But their cooperation with the Republicans did not outlast the election.

Political fraud, violence, manipulation of the Negro vote, and fusion were features of New Orleans Gilded Age politics that were easy to see on the surface. They were commented on vigorously by contemporary newspaper writers. The exact nature of the reform groups, which sprang to life before each municipal election and died just as quickly after election day, was a different matter. To the partisan political observers of their time, they were either

9 On Negro disfranchisement, see Mary Elizabeth Phillips Robert, "The Background of Negro Disfranchisement in Louisiana" (M.A. thesis, Tulane University, 1932).

10 *Daily Picayune,* November 7, 1882.

11 *Times-Democrat,* November 8, 1882.

high-minded idealists set out to banish Ring corruption and extravagance, or Republican wolves decked out in reformers' fleece to fool the public.

It is evident from studying the makeup of these groups that most of them did contain a few Republican elements or their collaborators during Reconstruction. The president of the Independent Party in 1882 was Harry H. Walsh, who had been suggested as city attorney by Governor Kellogg during the 1870's against the wishes of the Democratic-Conservative mayor. Walsh had not been successful in getting the position, even with Kellogg's help. But he had incurred a great deal of bitterness from Redeemer forces which was hurled back at him in the campaign of 1882. His reputation as an associate of Kellogg substantially hurt the Independent Party.[12] In 1888 and again in 1896, there were Republicans among the ranks of the reform parties. Since they were shut off from the Democratic-Conservative machine their only hope for participation in municipal politics lay in joining with its opposition. But the strength which kept reform parties cropping up with each city election and allowed them to elect their candidates for mayor in 1880, 1888, and 1896 was drawn primarily from the commercial and professional elements in New Orleans. Merchants, businessmen, and lawyers were the backbone of these organizations.

In 1880 a reform group, organized by prominent businessmen, was the People's Democratic Association, or the "People's Party." All its candidates, except two, were citizens with a business background who had never before held office. Of the two who had served in public life, one was the distinguished Judge Ernest Miltenberger of the Second Municipal District. He had been Governor Henry W. Allen's aide-de-camp during the Civil War and one of the three commissioners sent to France by the Confederacy to seek recognition from Napoleon III. Another nominee, Theodore G. Hunt, had been a member of Congress in 1853 and the colonel of a Confederate regiment.[13] Such men might be said to belong to the true Bourbon class, if that word may be used to characterize

12 *Ibid.*, October 24, 1882.
13 Kendall, *History of New Orleans,* I, 422.

some public figures in this era. The ticket was headed by one of the city's most popular young businessmen, Joseph A. Shakspeare, who was the only successful candidate among the reformers. His victory over the machine candidate, Jules Denis, was a slim one of about five hundred votes.

In 1882 two reform parties appeared, the People's Party and the Independent Party. Both again put up candidates conspicuous for their impeccable business reputations and material success. The People's Party offered Robert S. Howard, one of the city's outstanding businessmen, as its mayoral candidate. The Independents put up Colonel Abel W. Bosworth, another man prominent in the city's commercial life. Howard later withdrew and the People's Party also backed Bosworth.[14] In 1884 a reform party grew up around the outgoing mayor, William J. Behan, a former Confederate officer and a well-known wholesale grocer and sugar planter.[15] Behan had been given the nomination for mayor in 1882 on the Ring ticket as a concession by that realistic organization to the commercial community to keep it from going *en masse* for the Independents. After election he refused to follow Ring instructions in his appointments and was, in general, vigorous in maintaining his independence of action as mayor.[16] By 1884 he was back where he belonged, running for reelection on a reform ticket drafted by the Citizens Party, a group of merchants and lawyers who opposed the Ring. Machine politics proved too much for these fledgling reformers. Behan lost to his Ring opponent, J. Valsin Guillotte.

In 1888, with strong support from many members of the Produce Exchange and other commercial groups in the city, another opposition group, the Young Men's Democratic Association (Y.M.D.A.) , scored a heavy victory over the Ring, again running Shakspeare as mayor. Its campaign committee read like a blue book of the city's commercial elite and included such names as that

14 *Times-Democrat*, October 13, 18, 20, 29, 1882.

15 A brief biography of Behan may be found in "Administrations of the Mayors of New Orleans, 1803–1936" (Typescript compiled and edited by Works Progress Administration in New Orleans Public Library) , 189–90.

16 For additional details, see Chapter 3 of this study.

of John M. Parker, an outstanding civic leader.[17] In 1892 the
Young Men's Democratic Association again put up Shakspeare.
But he was defeated by the Ring candidate John Fitzpatrick. By
1896 the reform elements came back stronger than ever in the
Citizens League, composed of the same types of important mer-
chants and lawyers who had supported other reform movements.
Their candidate, Walter C. Flower, defeated the regular machine's
choice, Charles F. Buck.

To comprehend fully the reason for the composition of the reform movements, the Ring itself has to be carefully analyzed. The
most important ward leaders in the Democratic-Conservative Party in New Orleans were professional politicians, almost exclusively
of laboring class origin. John Fitzpatrick, the "Big Boss of the
Third Ward" and the perennial commissioner of improvements,
had been an orphan reared in St. Mary's Asylum. A newsboy at a
tender age in the best Horatio Alger tradition, he became a car-
penter and later entered politics. Fond of gambling and prizefighting, he was handsome, impulsive, generous, toweringly ambi-
tious, and wholly self-made. By the 1880's Fitzpatrick controlled his
own ward and many workers' votes through the patronage of the
Department of Improvements. The papers of the day and the reformers complained bitterly of featherbedding in city jobs, particularly in his department. But Fitzpatrick ignored his critics and
hired as many laborers as his budget would allow.

In commenting on the Irish spade-and-shovel voters in Fitzpatrick's department, the *Mascot* observed that such Irishmen "seem
to think God made the Democratic party as immaculate and infal-
lible as the Blessed Virgin Mary. They would stand up and vote
the Democratic ticket straight if the devil and all his angels were
at the hell-m." [18] There was a reason for the city workers' position
which the *Mascot* did not mention. Fitzpatrick gave them jobs
which the reform elements claimed should be pared down to balance the budget. In the strikes of 1892 and 1894, which occurred
while Fitzpatrick was mayor, his sympathies were overwhelmingly

17 Kendall, *History of New Orleans,* I, 470.
18 *Mascot,* July 15, 1882.

[Table 4]

Mayoral Election Returns[a]

Year	Party	Candidate	Vote
1880	Democratic-Conservative	Jules Denis	9,362
	People's Party	Joseph A. Shakspeare	9,803
1882	Democratic-Conservative	William J. Behan	14,897
	Independent Party	Abel W. Bosworth	5,346
1884	Democratic-Conservative	J. Valsin Guillotte	18,278
	Citizens Party[b]	William J. Behan	6,512
1888	Democratic-Conservative	Robert C. Davey	15,635
	Young Men's Democratic Association	Joseph A. Shakspeare	23,313
1892	Democratic-Conservative	John Fitzpatrick	20,547
	Young Men's Democratic Association	Joseph A. Shakspeare	17,289
1896	Democratic-Conservative	Charles F. Buck	17,295
	Citizens' League	Walter C. Flower	23,345

[a]*Daily Picayune*, November 3–6, 1880; April 29, 1884; April 21, 1888. *Times-Democrat*, November 9, 1882; T. W. Campbell (comp.), *Manual of the City of New Orleans* (New Orleans, 1901), 33–43.
[b] Full name of this group was the Citizens' Democratic Parochial and Municipal Party.

with the strikers, a fact bitterly held against him by the business community.[19]

Another powerful ward leader, Patrick Mealey, was intimately connected with the labor movement in New Orleans. He was a leader in the Cotton Yard Men's Society No. 1 and acted as their representative on the arbitration board which settled the 1881 strike.[20] As commissioner of police and public buildings, he was, like Fitzpatrick, in an excellent position to offer patronage to his laboring class followers. Others of importance in the party, such as J. Valsin Guillotte and Tom Duffy, were also self-made men and professional politicians. Even Edward A. Burke, who attained

[19] Biographical material on Fitzpatrick may be found in Kendall, *History of New Orleans*, II, 506, and in *Mascot*, February 25, July 1, 15, 1882.
[20] *Daily Picayune*, September 14, 1881; *Mascot*, October 21, 1882.

prominence among the commercial elite of the city while remaining a Democratic-Conservative stalwart in both the state and city machines, was of humble origin.

A charming and extraordinarily brilliant man, Burke claimed to be a native of Louisville, Kentucky, but his place of birth remains doubtful. At the outbreak of the Civil War he was railroading in Texas. Although only nineteen at the beginning of the conflict, his four years in the Confederate Army were eventful. He is credited with setting up the first wagon factory in Texas to supply the Confederate Army and came out of the war with the title of major.[21] After Appomattox he drifted to New Orleans where he began at the bottom of the local economic ladder, first taking a job chipping stone in a marble yard alongside Negro workers. Later he became the head of the freight department of the Great Jackson Railroad and one of the heroes of the White League.[22] In 1872 he was the unsuccessful candidate of the regular Democratic Party for Administrator of Improvements in New Orleans. In 1874 he finally won this municipal post by a large majority.[23] This proved to be a banner year for Burke. As already stated, he played a pivotal role in avoiding a clash of Federal troops with the White League in the Battle of September 14, 1874, and that same year was one of the Democrats on a joint Democratic-Republican committee entrusted with the task of revising the state registration rolls.[24]

During the hotly contested national and state elections of 1876, Major Burke was chairman of a Democratic investigating committee which canvassed the state to uncover fraudulent votes and argue in favor of a Democratic victory both for local candidates and the national ticket.[25] After the election he was sent to Washington, D. C., by Francis T. Nicholls, whom the Democrats had sworn in as governor, to urge the removal of Federal troops from Louisiana. Such troops had become the mere palace guard of the Repub-

21 Coleman, *Historical Sketch Book*, 315–16; Woodward, *Origins of the New South*, 70.

22 Waldo, *Visitors' Guide*, 220–22.

23 Coleman, *Historical Sketch Book*, 316.

24 John Edmond Gonzales, "William Pitt Kellogg, Reconstruction Governor of Louisiana, 1873–1877," *Louisiana Historical Quarterly*, XXIX (April, 1946), 437–39.

25 Coleman, *Historical Sketch Book*, 316.

licans. Nicholls could not be secure in the governor's chair until
their removal, which would put an end to claims of victory from
the Republican gubernatorial candidate, Stephen B. Packard.[26]
In Washington, with the aid of Louisiana's Democratic members
in Congress, Burke instigated the "Wormley House conference," a
farcical bit of horse trading at which the Louisianians were assured by friends of Rutherford B. Hayes that he would remove federal troops from Louisiana if the contested election were decided
in his favor. This assurance was given to persuade the Louisianians to drop their filibustering plans to obstruct the count of presidential votes. Although Burke later admitted that the Louisianians were mainly bluffing, he was given lavish credit in the 1880's
for ending Reconstruction in Louisiana as a result of this incident.
The result would probably have been the same in regard to the
removal of troops from the state if Samuel Tilden had been declared the winner. But Burke and at least another member of the
Wormley House conferees, Congressman E. John Ellis, were avidly
interested in internal improvements. Hayes certainly seemed more
likely to favor such a policy in Louisiana than the reformer Tilden.
This seems to have been a decisive factor in their decision not to
oppose Hayes's election.[27]

In 1877 Burke was appointed state tax collector. The following
year he was elected state treasurer. When the Louisiana Constitutional Convention met in 1879 to revise the state government machinery fashioned during carpetbag days, Burke's position of state
treasurer was the only one not eliminated. On the contrary, his
term of office was extended until 1884.[28] The day after the convention closed, Burke and some associates including Charles T.
Howard, head of the Louisiana Lottery Company, acquired the

26 By arranging the Wormley House conference Burke apparently acted in
contradiction to Nicholls's instructions to him on this mission which were to do
nothing to jeopardize the Tilden claims to the presidency while pleading Louisiana's case for removal of Federal troops. See Barnes F. Lathrop (ed.) , "An
Autobiography of Francis T. Nicholls, 1834–1881," *Louisiana Historical Quarterly*, XVII (April, 1934) , 257.

27 For a detailed account of the Wormley House conference see C. Vann
Woodward, *Reunion and Reaction* (Garden City, 1956) , 5–10, 206–19, 221–27;
Woodward, *Origins of the New South*, 44–45; Robert Cinnamond Tucker, "The
Life and Public Service of E. John Ellis" (M.A. thesis, Louisiana State Univer-
sity, 1941) , 76–82.

28 Coleman, *Historical Sketch Book,* 316.

Democrat, a New Orleans newspaper founded to oppose Republicans and carpetbaggers in the 1870's. The *Democrat* had also opposed the lottery faction in politics. Now this opponent of Burke and the lottery was converted into their agent through clever but unscrupulous tactics which pushed the paper's owners into a financial crisis and forced them to sell out.[29] By 1880 Burke became sole proprietor and editor of this paper and purchased the *Times* in 1881. He consolidated these two into the *Times-Democrat,* which quickly became one of the leading dailies in the South and specialized in commercial news of the Mississippi Valley and of possibilities of trade with Latin America.[30]

During the early 1880's Burke was one of the most powerful men in the state. He was a law unto himself in politics. Usually favoring the machine politicians in New Orleans and at the state level, he could humble them by backing the reformer element when he felt inclined, as in 1880 when he backed Shakspeare for mayor.[31] John Fitzpatrick was the one Crescent City politico who seemed likely to challenge Burke's popularity with local voters. But no open break ever came between them. In 1884 and 1885 Burke reached the height of his prestige as director-general of the Cotton Centennial Exposition, largely his own brainchild. When his term as state treasurer ended in 1884, he was easily reelected for four more years.[32]

At the end of his second term as treasurer, Burke turned his attention to high finance and to Honduran mining and fruit investments which he had acquired through the president of that republic while that official was visiting New Orleans during the exposition.[33] Burke was in England arranging for the financing of his Honduras projects when a storm of scandal arose in Louisiana. In September, 1889, the *Daily Picayune* broke the story of possible bond frauds in the state treasurer's office.[34] In the weeks that followed, a dark picture of the dapper major's dishonesty was revealed to his friends and foes by the local papers. The state auditor

29 For the full story on how the *Democrat* changed hands see Edward Larocque Tinker, *Creole City: Its Past and Its People* (New York, 1953) , 193–94.

30 Dabney, *One Hundred Great Years,* 378–79.

31 Kendall, *History of New Orleans,* I, 421–24.

32 Coleman, *Historical Sketch Book,* 316–17.

33 Woodward, *Origins of the New South,* 71–72.

34 Dabney, *One Hundred Great Years,* 302.

and Burke's successor in the treasurer's office found that a calculated bond fraud had been going on since 1880 in which Burke had allowed state bonds which should have been retired to continue circulating and paying interest. The total amount lost to the state by Burke's action was $1,777,000, not counting interest, though enough bonds were found in his bank box to reduce the loss to $793,600. Charges of embezzlement and fraud were brought against him on nineteen counts.[35]

At first Burke promised to return as soon as his business was concluded in London. Even his avowed opponents such as the *Daily States* (whose editor Henry J. Hearsey had left the *Democrat* when Burke acquired it and founded the *States* as a paper independent of Ring control) cautioned its readers not to judge the ex-treasurer until he returned to tell his side of the story.[36] But by October 28 when it was obvious that Burke would not return, the *States* rebuked Burke for claiming innocence and for giving out a statement that the bond fraud must have been perpetrated by his trusted assistants while he was busy with the Cotton Centennial Exposition. The *States* pointed out that the fraud dated back to 1880, years before the Exposition. Also, Burke had claimed he was being persecuted for political reasons. On this point the *States* observed: "He was the creation of no Democratic administration but of the people, and he's not the first man who has won the confidence of the people, and then grossly betrayed them." [37]

Attempts at extradition failed and Burke eventually fled to Honduras where his vast land holdings made his exile a comfortable one. Even as a fallen hero, Burke's value was still high. In July, 1890, Governor Nicholls, who had been elected again in 1888, offered a ten-thousand-dollar reward for Burke's apprehension and return to Louisiana.[38] But the major's luck held. He remained safe

35 All the New Orleans newspapers carried full coverage of the Burke scandal from the end of September through the end of October, 1889. After that, occasional stories appeared. See particularly *Daily Picayune,* September 27, 29, 1889; *Times-Democrat,* October 19, 20, 22, 24, 26, 31, 1889; *Daily States,* September 17, 21, 26, October 26, 27, 28, 1889. Also see Woodward, *Origins of the New South,* 72.
36 *Daily States,* September 17, 1889.
37 *Ibid.,* October 28, 1889.
38 Alcée Fortier, *Louisiana: Comprising Sketches of Parishes, Towns, Events, Institutions, and Persons, Arranged in Cyclopedic Form* (n.p., 1914), I, 134–35.

in his new home and outlived most of his contemporaries, dying in his eighties in 1928. Two years before his death, a small group of his friends persuaded the state to drop the charges against him so that he could return home in his last years.[39] Although Burke remained in Honduras, he certainly won the last hand in this lengthy game of political poker.

Aside from Burke, several prominent members of the city Ring administration under Fitzpatrick in the 1890's (including several aldermen, the city engineer, and a retired tax assessor) were indicted for malpractices. Fitzpatrick himself was impeached but found innocent of any actual crime. Among charges against him was allowing a city contract to go to a firm in which his wife was an investor.[40] The Ring leaders, on the whole, were hotheaded and prone to violence to settle their personal arguments. The gentlemen's duel of antebellum days had degenerated into rowdy, Wild West shoot-outs. Along with politicians, journalists were frequent carriers of firearms under their coats. The flamboyant Major Burke engaged in a formal pistol duel with a rival editor who succeeded in wounding him slightly. But more characteristic of the age was his encounter with Governor Kellogg in 1874 when Burke stopped the governor's carriage on Canal Street between Rampart and Basin streets and tried to pull Kellogg out of the vehicle. Kellogg retaliated by starting up the carriage and firing at Burke with his silver pistol, "Swamp Angel." Burke returned the fire; but the intentions of the two were more deadly than their aim, and no one was injured.[41] Guns were not always necessary in this age devoted to bare-knuckled prize fighting. Politicians protected their honor with any weapon that was handy.

Fitzpatrick once had a fistfight in City Hall with another politician, during which he was hit on the head with a cuspidor. The next day Fitzpatrick's brother sought revenge by shooting at and wounding his brother's attacker.[42] The city treasurer, Blayney T. Walshe, got his name in the papers by engaging in an umbrella

39 Dabney, *One Hundred Great Years,* 303.
40 Kendall, *History of New Orleans,* II, 512–13; *Daily Picayune,* March 15, 1895.
41 Gonzales, "William Pitt Kellogg," 439.
42 *Daily Picayune,* January 29, 30, 31, 1881.

fight with a disenchanted office-seeker on Canal Street.[43] Fiery J.
Valsin Guillotte, during his term as comptroller, slapped the face
of a councilman who questioned some of the purchases in his office.[44] Not all Ring antics were as comic, colorful, or minor. Patrick Mealey was shot to death on New Year's Day, 1888, when he
attempted to intervene in a saloon brawl.[45] In another case the
judge of one of the city courts, Recorder Thomas J. Ford, was
convicted of manslaughter in the murder of a House of Detention
guard. The guard was shot in broad daylight with numerous witnesses looking on.[46] Before his unfortunate resort to mayhem, Ford
had been seriously considered by the Ring as its next candidate for
mayor.[47]

The Ring and the reformers opposed each other, as is evident,
with basically different backgrounds and interests to protect. The
Ring politicians had sprung mainly from the working classes and
catered to this group to keep themselves in power through city
jobs, sympathy to strikers, outdoor rallies, and social gatherings
during election time. No one gave more generously to the needy in
times of flood than John Fitzpatrick. The reformers were mainly
gathered from the commercial and professional classes and were
devoted to their interests, a fact which meant balancing the city
budget by reducing the number of city employees. The many
needs of all classes in the city for better schools, streets, and protection from criminal hoodlums, some of whom were minor city
employees under Ring protection, were dramatized by the reformers in their bids for power. But the fact that they were "silk stocking" reformers went against them in bidding for the poor man's
vote. City laborers who had to wade home ankle-deep in water after a summer downpour probably resented the fact that the city's
first asphalt-paved street was St. Charles Avenue, the address of
the town's elite.

In short, what could the reformers offer the city that the Ring
could not? Honest government? A balanced budget? Perhaps. But

43 *Ibid.*, March 18, 1881.
44 *Ibid.*, February 12, 14, 28, 1883; *Daily States*, March 1, 7, 1883.
45 *Daily Picayune*, January 2, 1888.
46 *Ibid.*, December 2, 3, 13, 14, 1884; February 14, 1885; May 20, 1886.
47 Kendall, *History of New Orleans*, I, 452.

the vision of good government that the reformers conjured up was usually a rich man's good government: one which was penny-pinching in operating city departments and benevolent to business and commerce. The machine was equally anxious to attract new business, but let a balanced budget go in favor of patronage to its faithful.

The independent voters not indebted to the Ring for any gratuities were largely indifferent to elections. Newspaper editorials at election time suggested that the painful experience of Reconstruction had made many turn their backs on politics after white rule had been restored at the end of the 1870's. The *Times-Democrat* pleaded in vain with its readers to register, noting that thousands held back because they believed the names of jurors were picked from the registration rolls. This was not the case, the paper explained, and urged a larger turnout of voters.[48]

Aside from elections, the struggle between the Ring and the reformers was clearly reflected in the drafting of a new charter for the city in 1882. The council form of government adopted for the Crescent City in 1870 had several features which many New Orleanians viewed as objectionable and hoped to eliminate. It combined executive and legislative power in one body, consisting of the mayor and seven administrators whose departments were independent entities. Each administrator was the boss of his department and neither the mayor nor any group of citizens could interfere with his conduct of the department. The mayor was indeed without any power to control his subordinates except for the veto, which could easily be overcome by a small number of administrators. This system had been deliberately devised by the carpetbaggers and had served their purposes well in the early 1870's. The various departments were merely divisions of the spoils and sources of political patronage. In the 1879 state constitution, recognition was given to the fact that New Orleans desired a new charter. An attempt had been made in the legislative session of the next year to frame a suitable charter, but it was such a slipshod and hastily drawn-up document that the governor vetoed it.[49]

48 *Times-Democrat,* September 21, 1882.
49 Kendall, *History of New Orleans,* I, 433–37.

Recalling this fiasco of 1880 the city members of the legislature, who were also Ring stalwarts, and various civic groups, which represented the reformer viewpoint, began separate discussions of possible charter provisions early in 1882. The Cotton Exchange, the Chamber of Commerce, the Produce Exchange, and the Mechanics', Dealers', and Lumbermen's Exchange each had committees considering revision. They eventually merged their efforts and cooperated through one interorganizational committee, which drew up what became known as the "citizens charter." Concurrent with their efforts, the city members of the legislature appointed a committee from their group to draft a "legislative charter." [50]

By the time the legislature convened in Baton Rouge, two bills embodying the rival charters were submitted to the representatives and senators. The major differences between the two lay in the selection of the executive officers other than the mayor (whose post both agreed should be elective). The citizens' charter called for appointment of these municipal officers by the mayor, a proposal urged by the ultraconservative Cotton Exchange.[51] The legislative charter, on the other hand, provided for their election by popular vote.[52]

The philosophy behind these two points of variance is obvious. The exchanges, representing conservative business interests, felt that their best chance of securing a city government sympathetic to their point of view was to have only one elective executive, the mayor. It might be possible for a citizens' reform group, which really meant a consolidation of conservative business, to elect as mayor a man whose Confederate war record or philanthropic interest in the masses would pull the popular vote away from the Ring candidate. But the exchanges knew that they had little chance of electing an entire slate of executive officers. The ward bosses, Mealey, Fitzpatrick, and Guillotte, had too tight a control

[50] *Daily Picayune,* January 31, March 8, 9, 14, April 3, 5, May 4, 12, 16, 1882.

[51] Such strengthening of the mayor's power was beginning to occur in major American cities at this time. The mayor of Brooklyn in 1882 had power to appoint the main department heads. By 1884 the mayor of New York City also was given this power. Boston and Buffalo conferred the same trust upon their mayors within the next decade. Frank Mann Stewart, *A Half Century of Municipal Reform* (Berkeley and Los Angeles, 1950), 6.

[52] *Daily Picayune,* scattered references throughout April and May, 1882.

of their constituencies to let anyone wrest their offices away from them.

The legislative committee, which approved a charter calling for popular election of all executive officers, was solidly behind the incumbents of City Hall. The Ring bosses had successfully elected their candidates to the legislature and thus were in a position to influence the charter. Popular election of all executive officers was the safest way to stay in power. The bosses knew that should a conservative business candidate be elected mayor, he certainly would not appoint them to administrative posts. Popular election could be upheld as more democratic than appointment by the mayor. But in practice this system came to serve the Ring, whose superior organization meant that its ward bosses could dictate the election of their choices to most executive posts.

With a few minor amendments, the Ring's legislative charter was approved in the state house and senate by the middle of June, 1882.[53] It provided for an executive branch consisting of the mayor, comptroller, treasurer, commissioner of public works, and commissioner of police and public buildings, all popularly elected. The legislative power was invested in one aldermanic council of thirty members, some to be chosen from specific districts and others as councilmen-at-large. All were elected at the same time as the executive officers. The council was to hold weekly meetings, at which the mayor presided; the other executive officers could take part in debate but could not vote. Along with the legislative and executive branches, the charter provided for four recorders also elected by popular vote to preside over city magistrate courts.[54]

With the inauguration of this new form of government (under which New Orleans remained until 1900), the Crescent City adopted as many bad government techniques as it had tried to abolish. The aldermanic system, defended as truly democratic and representative, resulted in ring control and chicanery in most American cities during this period.

In New Orleans the aldermanic system fitted perfectly into the

[53] *Times-Democrat,* June 15, 1882; *Daily Picayune,* June 15, 1882.
[54] *Charter of the City of New Orleans* (New Orleans, 1882), 1–36.

Ring's municipal operations. Thirty aldermanic seats meant more officers for the party members, although the aldermen were not paid for their services. But it also meant endless squabbling and debating between the members of the unicameral council. One newspaper noted that some alderman were "as proud of their position as a Spanish Don of his pedigree," and entirely too much haggling was the result.[55] Since New Orleans was thoroughly debt-ridden, and little opportunity arose to sell contracts to builders of public buildings or for physical improvements in the city, the aldermen's scope of activity in such directions was limited. Nevertheless, they did make the most of their opportunities.

One of their most publicized escapades was the appropriation of $5,000 to pay the expenses of a large delegation sent to Philadelphia in 1885 to accompany the Liberty Bell back to New Orleans for exhibition at the Cotton Centennial Exposition.[56] The council was also criticized for its contract with the Water Works Company, under which the city government began paying for its water instead of getting it free as formerly. The Water Works Company, in return, had to pay taxes from which it had been exempt. Under this new arrangement the company paid only $11,000 in taxes, while the city's water bill amounted to $68,000.[57] Other such deals were attempted by the council, some successful and some blocked by court action of irate reforming elements. By the end of the 1880's the budget was in such a state of chaos from mismanagement that the municipal government was almost paralyzed. The aldermen lost interest and for weeks at a time failed to meet for lack of a quorum.

In the 1890's the council's worst mistake was an attempt to grant a monopolistic franchise to a railroad to run tracks down some of the finest residential streets and to cut off other railroads from the levee. This caused a public uproar. Under the pressure of hundreds of citizens gathered outside of City Hall in protest, the council hastily repealed the ordinance.[58] The climax to such malpractices

[55] *Daily Picayune*, May 31, 1883.
[56] *Ibid.*, scattered references, May, 1885.
[57] *Ibid.*, January 18, 19, 1886.
[58] *Ibid.*, May 16, 23, 30, 1894.

came in 1894 when ten aldermen were indicted for bribery.[59] The aldermanic council was thus no improvement over the administrative government it replaced. It actually offered more opportunity for political intrigue, since it held most of its important debates in private committee meetings, where the real purpose of legislation might be withheld from public scrutiny if its framers so desired.

Politics in New Orleans in the Gilded Age was probably no better or no worse than in other major American cities. In their tendencies toward violence, petty politicians in the Crescent City definitely were not surpassed by any others in the nation. In its utilization of immigrant votes, on the other hand, the local machine was limited by the comparatively small number of newcomers in the Louisiana metropolis. It did champion the Sicilians, whose growing numbers by the 1890's caused the Democratic-Conservatives in the city to make sure that disfranchisement bills in the state legislature aimed at Negroes did not also take away the vote of poor white immigrants.[60]

In other issues, such as home rule versus state control, New Orleans faced the same problems as Philadelphia, Atlanta, and New York City. The urban Orleanians in the state legislature often found themselves facing a hostile rural majority unsympathetic to city interests. This was a chronic American problem which was deplored by many in this era, but not solved.[61] One indication of rural hostility to the Crescent City was the affirmative vote in 1880 to move the state capital from New Orleans to Baton Rouge. In state politics between 1880 and 1892, the two strongest Democratic factions were more or less grouped around Francis T. Nicholls on one side and Samuel D. McEnery on the other. The governorship practically shifted back and forth between these two gentlemen, both of whom had professional and residential connections in

[59] *Ibid.*, June 9, 10, 12, 14, 15, 20, 21, 24, 27, 28, July 23, 24, 25, August 3, 23, 27, and "Grand Jury Report" in September 1, 1894; *Mascot*, August 18, 1894.

[60] Reynolds, *Machine Politics in New Orleans,* 36–37.

[61] For an up-to-date discussion of this urban-rural clash in southern politics, see Rupert B. Vance and Nicholas J. Demerath (eds.) , *The Urban South* (Chapel Hill, 1954) , 230–51.

New Orleans during this era, although originally from other sections of the state.[62] The Ring, as a rule, cooperated with the McEnery faction. But such figures as Burke, who served under both Nicholls and McEnery, and Congressman Ellis, who backed the Ring stalwarts in the city while allying with the Nicholls politicians on the state level, were independent in their political endorsements. The 1892 gubernatorial and mayoral election in New Orleans which was really a death struggle between the Louisiana Lottery and its opponents, who emerged victorious, ushered in a period of strained relations between the state government leaders and the New Orleans municipal officials. Murphy J. Foster, the antilottery candidate backed by Nicholls, became governor while John Fitzpatrick, the prolottery candidate was elected mayor.[63] By 1896 Governor Foster, reelected for a second term, has established cordial relations with local Ring leaders, but ignored City Hall's reformer mayor, Walter C. Flower, who had opposed his second term and was therefore excluded from state patronage.

On the national level during the last twenty years of the nineteenth century, New Orleans was well represented in Congress. Between 1879 and 1894 the Crescent City had almost a monopoly on the two Senate seats. Six United States senators, born elsewhere, were residents of New Orleans at the time they took office. They were ex-Governor Kellogg, Benjamin F. Jonas, Randall L. Gibson, James B. Eustis, Edward Douglass White, and ex-Governor Samuel D. McEnery.[64]

Congressmen from New Orleans between 1880 and 1900 included Randall L. Gibson, E. John Ellis, Carleton Hunt, William P. Kellogg, Louis St. Martin, ex-Governor Michael Hahn, Nathaniel D. Wallace, Matthew D. Lagan, Hamilton D. Coleman, Adolph Meyer, Robert C. Davey, and Charles F. Buck.[65] Although a few

[62] Governors of Louisiana in this period were as follows: Francis T. Nicholls, 1877–80; Louis Wiltz, 1880–died 1881; Samuel D. McEnery, 1881–84, then elected to continue in office, 1884–88; Francis T. Nicholls, 1888–92.

[63] See Chapter 5 of this study for further material on the lottery issue and the Fitzpatrick administration.

[64] "Biographical Directory of the American Congress, 1774–1961" *House Documents,* 85th Cong., 2nd Sess., No. 442, pp. 217, 222, 227, 232, 237, 242, 248, 253, 263.

[65] *Ibid.,* pp. 217, 222, 227, 232, 237, 242, 248, 253, 263, and 258–59.

Republicans such as Kellogg, Hahn, and Coleman were scattered among the New Orleans representatives in the Louisiana Congressional delegation, the majority were Democrats.

The career of one Congressman, E. John Ellis, serves to illustrate the experience of a Gilded Age southerner who tried to do a conscientious and meaningful job in public life. His youth had been taken up with the Civil War and Reconstruction struggle in which he had played a prominent role. In the post-Reconstruction years, he was an embittered man, sometimes politically threatened by the factional struggles within the Democratic Redeemer ranks in Louisiana. He bemoaned the dishonesty and lack of ability of many in high political office. Commenting on the times in Washington, he once wrote to his brother Thomas that "it is a day of small men." [66] At another time he noted that even those considered great seemed to shrink down to almost ordinary size when one got up close enough to observe them carefully.[67] Like so many others in that age of illusion, Ellis alternated between the realities of debt and dreams of wealth through shrewd investments. Realizing that business, not politics, was the high road to making one's fortune, Ellis tried again and again to reap a financial bonanza from his modest investments, but to no avail.

A native of Covington, Louisiana, Ellis settled in New Orleans a few years after returning from service in the Confederate Army and internment in a Union prisoner-of-war camp. A participant in the Battle of September 14, he was first elected to the House of Representatives from the Second Congressional District in the election of 1874. He served in Congress until March, 1885, when personal finances forced him to devote full time to private law practice in Washington.[68] In his role as congressman, he was a participant in the Wormley House conference, staunchly fought for improvements for his state and adopted city (such as levee construction, creation of the National Board of Health, and a Navy yard in Algiers), and took an extremely active part in cam-

[66] E. John Ellis to Thomas C. W. Ellis, April 13, 1884, in E. John Ellis Collection, Department of Archives and Manuscripts of Louisiana State University, Baton Rouge.
[67] Tucker, "The Life and Public Service of E. John Ellis," 85.
[68] Ibid., 1, 12–39, 40–48, 50, 59–64, 66, 105.

paigning for General Winfield S. Hancock, the Democratic presidential nominee in 1880.[69] A man noted for his spellbinding oratory and spotless integrity, Ellis was as dismal a failure in business ventures as the nefarious Burke was successful. Ellis invested in railroad land grant bonds and railroad construction, tried to charter a lottery to rival the Louisiana Lottery, and became president and part owner of a company which manufactured machines to process ramie, an Asiatic plant whose fibers were capable of being woven into a coarse, lightweight fabric similar to linen. None of these quixotic enterprises brought the profits Ellis dreamed of attaining.[70] Between his retirement from Congress in 1885 and his death in 1889, he returned to the law. But even in this profession $23,000 in legal fees were due him in 1888.[71] Ellis and Burke were antagonists through much of their public life. The year 1889 marked the exit of both of them from the local scene. Ellis went to an early grave, a poor but honest and honored man. Burke, to Honduras to live to a ripe and rich old age in baronial but tarnished exile. The Gilded Age was filled with such pungent contrasts.

Burke and Ellis were not the only politicians who exercised "rugged individualism" in their political decisions. The mayor was sharply limited in the power he could wield over other executive officers. In addition, although they were part of the Ring organization, the ward bosses, such as Fitzpatrick and some of the more influential aldermen, had a personal following which would support them even if they decided to oppose the regular party organization. In 1884 Behan, formerly a Ring mayor, ran on an opposition ticket, and in 1896 former Mayor Guillotte practically repudiated his career as a Ring leader by backing the reform group

69 *Ibid.*, 77–82, 90–92, 95; *Ceremonies Attending the Presentation of the Portrait of the Hon. E. John Ellis Deceased To the Supreme Court of Louisiana* (January 5, 1914), 17, 19. This volume is in Thomas C. W. Ellis and Family Collection, Department of Archives and Manuscripts of Louisiana State University.

70 Tucker, "The Life and Public Service of E. John Ellis," 93–96, 98–99.

71 E. John Ellis to Thomas C. W. Ellis, September 18, 1888, in E. John Ellis Collection, Department of Archives and Manuscripts of Louisiana State University.

in the election of that year. This tendency to bolt for personal reasons was typical of Gilded Age politics.

The rise of reform groups in municipal politics, often drawn from the same party as the Ring they opposed, also happened in other cities. Between 1870 and 1895 no less than fifty-seven reform groups existed in cities other than New Orleans.[72] That they did not appreciably improve city government may be blamed on their ineffective methods, rather than their lack of zeal. Their only remedy for corruption, as Lincoln Steffens has pointed out, was to throw the rascals out and put in new rascals. Such weapons against corruption as the secret ballot, referendum, recall, centralized purchasing, and boards of estimate and apportionments for city budgets had to wait for the Progressive Era to meet fulfillment.

Graft in the granting of franchises and contracts existed in New Orleans as elsewhere. But, as already pointed out, its scope was limited by the fact that the city debt prohibited large-scale improvement projects. The bonded debt left over from Reconstruction days was indeed the key to the local political situation. Tied down to the redemption of this debt between 1882 and 1895, the various city administrations could not afford to engage in vitally needed improvements such as new drainage, sewerage, and water purification systems. The struggle between the Ring and the reformers was one which seesawed back and forth, with power going first to one and then to the other. The Ring, without being able to expand municipal activities into such fields as drainage and sewerage, could not build up a strong enough machine vote of municipal employees to drive the reformers completely from the field of competition. The very existence of faulty drainage, lack of sewerage, and an understaffed police force—which the Ring would have remedied to its own advantage if it could have—gave the reformers ammunition for an attack upon the regulars.

Only with the final redemption of the main Reconstruction debt in 1895 did politics begin to take on a new complexion. By the early twentieth century the almost evenly divided struggle be-

[72] See the list of reform organizations listed in William Howe Tolman, *Municipal Reform Movements in the United States* (New York and Chicago, 1895), 12–13.

tween the old Ring and the reformers was over. The long-term control of a new Ring, the Choctaw Club and its boss, Martin Behrman, had replaced it. The Choctaw Club was founded in 1897 after the old Ring's formal organization, the Crescent Democratic Club, was wrecked by the lottery fight in 1892 and Ring regulars had drifted uneasily along under the direct leadership of the Fitzpatrick administration until the defeat of its candidates in the 1896 city election.[73]

There was also a new city debt by the early 1900's, one of the highest in the United States, but it was incurred to pay for long-awaited drainage, sewerage, water purification, and dock improvements. The old Ring thrived on personal patronage in modest proportions; the new Ring, on vast impersonal programs of civic improvement which transformed the face of the city. Ironically, no one benefited more from this "Ring benevolence" than its former opponents, the city's businessmen.

[73] Reynolds, *Machine Politics in New Orleans,* 32.

3

THE VIEW FROM CITY HALL
1880–1884

DIRECTLY ACROSS Lafayette Square from City Hall stood Odd Fellows Hall, where the Ring held its nominating conventions for municipal elections. The physical distance between these two buildings was negligible. But the vantage point of City Hall almost inevitably offered to each new mayor a very different view of the city from the one he had enjoyed as a party spectator in the structure across the square. While formerly he may have accepted with indifference the appointment of incompetent men to local administrative posts for political reasons, as mayor he was faced with the responsibility for their incompetence if he appointed them. Also, the passage of pork barrel bills and blatant corruption in the city council could be dismissed with a smile and a wink by the Ring's rank and file. But the mayor would have to share in any retribution which descended upon scoundrel councilmen if he kept quiet about their actions for the sake of party loyalty.

When a man became the city's head administrator, he took on a three-dimensional job in which partisan politics was only one consideration, and his personal reputation and civic conscience might emerge as equally important factors. In addition to Joseph A. Shakspeare and Walter C. Flower, the reformers who became mayors, all but one of the men who held the highest office between 1880 and 1896 eventually found themselves, to some degree, in public opposition to corrupt or power-usurping Ring forces within their administrations. John Fitzpatrick was the lone example of the complete party stalwart. The reward for his misplaced trust in crooked councilmen was a charge of impeachment which narrowly missed toppling him from office.

Two other things should be kept in mind about the mayors of New Orleans in this period: (1) the mayor was never the "boss" of his party, but only a compromise candidate chosen by equally powerful ward leaders; and (2), just as important, his administrative power was weakened by the decentralized system of government created by the charter of 1882. Each municipal department was virtually a small island ruled over by its head. The city council, often hostile to advice from the mayor, was made up of men whose petty jealousies and ambitions for their own precincts almost always took precedence over their interest in the metropolis as a whole. Politically and legally, therefore, the mayor was sharply limited—although, as the city's titular head, he had to face the praise or abuse which the local papers saw fit to heap upon his administration. How each man elected mayor reacted to this dilemma determined the success or failure of his term of office.

The victory of reform candidate Shakspeare in the mayoral election of 1880 marked one of the first setbacks for the local Democratic-Conservative machine since its rise to prominence in the 1870's as the adversary of carpetbaggers. In the 1878 municipal election five factions had participated. Fear of the Republicans no longer forced all dissenters within the Democratic ranks to unite under one banner and program. The opposition to the budding machine was too divided, however, and the Democratic regulars retained control of the city government.[1]

But by 1880 scandals in city government, bribery in the 1879 election of parish officials, and the refusal of the parish committee to allow reorganization of city Democratic ward clubs forced the formation of a strong reform group, the People's Democratic Association. Shakspeare was chosen as their reform candidate for mayor. The campaign was bitter and conceded to be primarily between the regulars and "the people's party," although six other factions participated. Shakspeare got the support of all the city newspapers except the *Daily States*. The *Daily Democrat* was actually a regular paper, but its proprietor, E. A. Burke, had quar-

1 Kendall, *History of New Orleans,* I, 409–14.

reled with his party's bosses over patronage and supported Shak-speare out of spite. The result of the election on November 2 was a narrow victory for Shakspeare—with 9,803 votes as compared to 9,362 for the regular candidate, Jules Denis. But every one of the regular candidates for administrative posts on the city council was elected.[2]

A legal barrier to Shakspeare's assuming the mayor's office was raised by the incumbent, Mayor Isaac W. Patton. Patton con-tended that the state constitution drawn up in 1879 had called for a new charter to be granted the city of New Orleans. No elec-tion could be held, argued Patton, until another city charter was approved. This last-ditch fight of the "ins" lasted from November 15, 1880, when Shakspeare presented himself formally at City Hall to state his claims, until December 13, when the state supreme court substantiated the findings of the lower court in his favor.[3]

The *Daily Picayune* wrote about the Shakspeare inauguration on December 14:

> The old city administration has gone out and the new come in, not like the metamorphosis of the old and new year with clanging of bells, lavish libations of eggnog and distribution of gifts, but with much tribulation and perturbation of spirit. Throngs of citizens began to collect at an early hour around the City Hall and in the damp corridors of that building, so that by half-past eleven enough patriotic persons were as-sembled to fill all the positions in the gift of the municipal administra-tors.[4]

This small army of job-seekers and the inscrutable smiling faces of the administrators seated across the council table from the new

2 *Ibid.*, 421–24.

3 *Ibid.*, 424; *Daily Picayune,* December 14, 1880. The consolidated cases of *State of Louisiana* v. *I. W. Patton* et al. and *State of Louisiana* ex rel. *J. A. Shakspeare* et al. v. *Isaac W. Patton* et al. appear in *Reports of Cases Argued and Determined in the Supreme Court of Louisiana* (St. Paul, 1908) , XXXIX (reprint of XXXII of *Louisiana Annual Reports*) , 759–67.

4 *Daily Picayune,* December 15, 1880. See also the account in New Orleans *Democrat,* December 15, 1880. Shakspeare's inaugural speech was not given at this first meeting, but at the third meeting of the new city council on December 16, 1880. It appears in "Minutes of the City Council of New Orleans, July 20, 1880–March 31, 1881" (MS in Archives of the City of New Orleans, New Orleans Public Library) , 81–85.

mayor were ample proof that his victory had been a personal one. The only reform candidate elected, he faced seven administrators picked from the ranks of his opposition, the Ring. This meant that he would be handicapped throughout his administration. In council proceedings, the mayor voted only in case of a tie, and ordinances he objected to could be passed over his veto.[5] A tall, handsome man of forty-three, with dark hair that fell into waves to frame a clean-shaven, strong-jawed face, Shakspeare was the proprietor of a local ironworks and had a reputation for being public-spirited.[6] But he was totally inexperienced in government, while his board of administrators were, as a whole, politically adept. Balanced against this disadvantage, the mayor did have one thing in his favor—most of the administrators, while members of his political opposition, were newcomers like himself to their specific jobs and were anxious to make a good record. This enthusiasm for office was the link which brought the mayor and the other city executives together.

The city's board of administrators which, with the mayor, was usually referred to as the city council, consisted of seven officials. John Fitzpatrick had been elected administrator of public works. His department was charged with the upkeep of the city streets, canals, wharves, and bridges.[7] Two other key administrators were Patrick Mealey, administrator of police, and J. Valsin Guillotte, administrator of waterworks and public buildings. Mealey had been reelected to his post, having served under the outgoing Mayor Patton. His department had responsibility for public order, for the care of houses of refuge and correction, and for supervision over the city lighting contractors.[8] Guillotte had served as chief clerk in the Department of Water Works and Public Buildings in 1875.[9] At the time he was elected administrator of that depart-

5 *The Amended Charter of the City of New Orleans* (New Orleans, 1871) , 6.

6 Kendall, *History of New Orleans,* I, 429–30.

7 Semiannual report of the Department of Improvements, in *Daily Picayune,* July 27, 1881; Fortier, *Louisiana,* II, 234.

8 Lon Soards (pub. and comp.) , *Soards' New Orleans City Directory for 1879* (New Orleans, 1879) , 472; Fortier, *Louisiana,* II, 234.

9 Lon Soards (pub. and comp.) , *Soards' New Orleans City Directory for 1875* (New Orleans, 1875) , 334.

ment in 1880, he was employed as a clerk in Sixth District court.[10] The title of his department was ludicrous in view of the fact that the waterworks had passed from city control to private interests in 1877.[11] But he did have supervision over the waterworks franchise, over schoolhouses, hospitals, and asylums.[12]

The administrator of commerce, William Fagan, was a member of a wholesale butcher firm, Wilson and Fagan. His department had general supervision of all matters relating to markets, railroads, the volunteer fire department, weights and measures, manufacturing, and canals.[13] A former clerk in a wine importing firm, George Delamore, filled the post of administrator of assessments with control over city taxation and the issuing of licenses.[14] Two administrators who were newcomers to full-time political activity were businessmen Blayney T. Walshe, administrator of finance, and William E. Huger, administrator of public accounts. They had been nominated by the Ring because of their war records and business background.[15] Walshe had migrated to New Orleans from Ireland at the age of thirteen. He served under General "Stonewall" Jackson in the Irish Brigade which was part of the Confederates' Sixth Louisiana Regiment. After the war he opened a men's clothing store in New Orleans and quickly became a success.[16] A small, conscientious man with a mercurial temper, Walshe as administrator of finance had control of the city treasury and played a significant part in the eventual settlement of the city debt problem.[17] Huger, like Walshe, was a Confederate vet-

[10] Lon Soards (pub. and comp.), *Soards' New Orleans City Directory for 1880* (New Orleans, 1880), 359.

[11] Rightor, *Standard History of New Orleans,* 127.

[12] Fortier, *Louisiana,* II, 234.

[13] Soards, *Soards' New Orleans City Directory for 1880,* 295; Fortier, *Louisiana,* II, 234.

[14] Soards, *Soards' New Orleans City Directory for 1880,* 251; Lon Soards (pub. and comp.), *Soards' New Orleans City Directory for 1881* (New Orleans, 1881), 245.

[15] Kendall, *History of New Orleans,* I, 422–23.

[16] Edwin L. Jewell (ed. and comp.), *Jewell's Crescent City Illustrated (The Commercial, Social, Political and General History of New Orleans including Biographical Sketches of its Distinguished Citizens)* (New Orleans, 1874), 119.

[17] Fortier, *Louisiana,* II, 234.

eran and had lost a leg at Murfreesboro.[18] He was a broker whose duties as administrator of public accounts were those of city auditor and comptroller.[19]

The municipal problems which faced this new administration in 1880 were formidable. The condition of the streets was the worst in forty years. Canals and ditches were usually filled to the brim with green, slimy water and floating refuse. Wharves on the river front were dilapidated, overcrowded, and often the hangouts of criminals. The police force was badly demoralized, understaffed, and subject to political maneuvering. School teachers and city employees, likewise, were political pawns, whose salaries were paid sporadically and usually by certificate instead of cash.

The key to all of these problems was the municipal debt. As long as the city labored under a huge deficit, no amount of good will on the part of the incumbent government could bring about improvements. Shakspeare's first term is significant for the debt settlement which was reached in 1882, largely through the determination of the mayor and Administrator of Finance Walshe. The total city debt of approximately $24,000,000 was a combination of floating and bonded indebtedness plus back interest, which had begun its snowballing growth under carpetbag control and increased with each subsequent administration. This vicious debt was complicated by the different types of city bonds held by creditors.

The city had adopted the Premium Bond Plan in 1876, and the state legislature created the Board of Liquidation in 1880. Both were attempts to scale down the debt and fund it over a long period at reasonable interest rates. But creditors holding high-interest-rate bonds, such as 7 percent, would not negotiate. By 1880 New Orleans faced a crisis in its development. Public improvements were sorely needed, and business capital could not be encouraged to invest further in a run-down, debt-ridden city.[20]

18 Kendall, *History of New Orleans,* I, 422–23.

19 Fortier, *Louisiana,* II, 234.

20 For a complete explanation of the Premium Bond Plan and the Board of Liquidation, see R. S. Hecht, *Municipal Finances of New Orleans, 1860–1916* (New Orleans, 1916) , 4–10; a more general history of the city debt is given in Kendall, *History of New Orleans,* I, 430–31; and the city budget and debt are

With this in mind, the mayor and the board of administrators early in their term created a committee of city debt, made up of prominent citizens connected with the Board of Liquidation and including the mayor and Walshe. The committee was to ascertain the full extent of the indebtedness, thus clearing the way for a compromise with the creditors. Although it took a year for the committee to untangle the details, the mere acceptance of its intervention invigorated the financial life of New Orleans during 1881 and stopped all talk of giving up the municipal charter as Memphis had done in its debt struggle.[21]

Unfortunately, in January, 1882, trouble returned to plague the city fathers. By federal court order, they were forced to include in the budget a special tax to meet orders under judgments and writs of mandamus for $1,600,000 awarded to creditors.[22] These judgments brought the local tax for 1882 up to the highest point it had ever reached: a burdensome 3.175 percent, of which 1.675 percent was for the judgment tax.[23]

Gloom descended upon City Hall, which officially protested this federal court action while carrying it into operation.[24] The public in general was demoralized by the added tax burden. Business, which had been enjoying a heartening expansion, fell off. Unemployment rose, and many taxpayers threatened to ignore their 1882 taxes.[25] The *Mascot,* in a biting cartoon, contrasted the collections

---

discussed in Mayor Shakspeare's inaugural address in the "Minutes of the City Council of New Orleans, July 20, 1880–March 31, 1881," pp. 81–85 and in *Daily Picayune,* December 17, 1880.

21 *Daily Picayune,* December 23, 1880; *Democrat,* December 23, 1880; New Orleans *Times,* December 23, 1880. For information on the Memphis debt, see Gerald M. Capers, Jr., *The Biography of a River Town (Memphis: Its Heroic Age)* (Chapel Hill, 1939), 202–204, 211–12.

22 *Daily Picayune,* January 5, 1882. The state legislature had set 10 mills as the limit for municipal taxes in 1880. But in the case of *Saloy* v. *the City of New Orleans,* the state supreme court ruled 5 additional mills could be added to this for city debts. The judgment tax of 1882, the result of a United States Supreme Court decision in the Southern Bank case, brought the total city tax up to 31¾ mills (3.175 percent). Many taxpayers resented this federal court action which nullified state tax limits and doubled taxes. *Daily Picayune,* December 28, 1880, and scattered references in December, 1881, and January, 1882.

23 Rightor, *Standard History of New Orleans,* 101.

24 *Daily Picayune,* January 5, 1882.

25 *Tax Payers' Organ and Journal of Reform,* February 11, 1882.

of taxes in 1882 with Butler's confiscations in 1863.[26] When the committee on city debt finally reported to the mayor in February, 1882, that their estimate of the debt was $24,329,839.04, their findings were denounced by the Tax Payers' Association, a special group formed to fight additional taxes through court action and through its newspaper, the *Tax Payers' Organ and Journal of Reform*.[27] Dissatisfied citizens in the Sixth District (which had been added to New Orleans in 1870) attempted to stir up sentiment in their district to secede from the city in late April, 1882. A bill to secede was actually introduced into the legislature that year, but it was pigeonholed and never considered seriously.[28] While citizens grumbled over heavy taxes and the estimate of the debt, creditors threatened even more judgment taxes in the future and the possible garnishment of city property.

To find a middle way between the taxpayers and the creditors required all the tact, vigor, and good nature of which Shakspeare was capable. Ignoring the attacks he received from both sides, he strove conscientiously to reach a debt compromise by May, so that it could be presented to the state legislature for enactment into law. Shakspeare's gift for getting men to work together, plus the financial acumen of Administrator of Finance Walshe achieved this difficult goal. With the aid of a committee of private citizens, composed of three bank presidents and two large property holders, the administration arrived at a debt solution which was incorporated into state law by the end of June, 1882.[29] Under this plan, the final details of which were worked out by Walshe, coupon 6 percent bonds were extended for forty years with an option for redemption after 1895.[30] Walshe was convinced that the city would be solvent enough by that year to redeem most of these bonds, thereby opening the way for bond issues at much lower rates for civic improvements. His conviction was to prove correct.

26 *Mascot*, May 27, 1882.
27 *Tax Payers' Organ and Journal of Reform*, March 4, 1882.
28 *Daily Picayune*, April 27, 28, 1882, and scattered references in May, 1882, for bill in legislature.
29 *Ibid.*, February 16, 24, 26, March 5, 14, May 31, June 28, 1882. The complete act appears in *Acts Passed by the General Assembly, State of Louisiana, Regular Session, 1882* (Baton Rouge, 1882), Act No. 58, pp. 66–70.
30 *Daily Picayune*, March 14, 1882; Hecht, *Municipal Finances*, 4–11.

The success of the first Shakspeare administration in the debt settlement was repeated in other endeavors. Although he was a political novice, the mayor showed a high degree of common sense and creative imagination in meeting municipal problems. One of the most fascinating experiments he launched was the "Shakspeare Plan," which was an extralegal gentlemen's agreement between the local government and gamblers.

Gambling could be found almost everywhere, from the notorious Negro barrelhouses at the foot of Canal Street, where frequent fights and stabbings took place, to the plush exclusive gambling casinos on Royal Street. Roustabouts from the *Robert E. Lee* frequently fought over a game of dice.[31] Four youngsters were picked up on Carondelet between Canal and Common for throwing dice on the public streets in the main business district.[32] Such congregations of youths, in mixed groups of white and colored, were fairly common. Fashionable ladies played "set back euchre" for money, reported the *Picayune's* society column, although they did not consider it gambling and held up "their little jeweled hands in holy horror against gambling and gamblers." [33] Even a part of the city debt tied up in premium bonds was paid off in a gambling fashion—a wheel of fortune was used to pick the numbers of the lucky bonds which would be redeemed at that drawing. The Louisiana Lottery Company did a booming business all over the country with New Orleans as its headquarters. The most powerful gambling syndicate in the United States, its roster of employees included such notables as General Pierre G. T. Beauregard and General Jubal A. Early.

In April, 1881, a visiting nobleman was bilked of $150 in a card game in a St. Charles Street saloon. Convinced that he had been cheated, Count Dadun de Kereman complained to the mayor, who immediately had the saloon closed.[34] This incident brought Shakspeare's attention to the high number of card sharks and bunko artists who operated small games of chance on a crooked basis in

31 *Daily Picayune,* December 29, 1880; January 31, February 1, 1881; Cable, *The Creoles of Louisiana,* 267.
32 *Daily Picayune,* January 31, 1881.
33 *Ibid.,* December 19, 1880.
34 *Democrat,* April 22, 23, 1881; *Daily Picayune,* April 23, 1881.

the city. The mayor was fully conscious of the popularity of gambling in New Orleans and realized that trying to stop all gambling was outside the realm of possibility at that time. The Louisiana Lottery Company held a charter from the state legislature, and the city police force was too small to patrol the back rooms of saloons or break up every floating crap game. Regulation seemed a better solution. Shortly after the Count de Kereman episode the mayor quietly closed the most obnoxious bunko houses, allowing only the most fasionable to stay open in the area bounded by Camp, Chartres, St. Louis, Bourbon, Carondelet, and Gravier. He made an arrangement with the big gambling houses by which they paid a donation to the city of $150 per month for keno and $100 a month for faro. Since the law did not allow licensing, this was not a legal arrangement. But it worked well in driving shady operators out of the gambling fraternity. The gamblers received protection from the mayor against police molestation as long as they ran honest games. A corps of private detectives was paid out of the donation money to keep watch and make sure the gamblers lived up to this stipulation. The first collections were made in May and June of 1881 and yielded between $1,200 and $2,400 each month. Under this "Shakspeare Plan" the number of gambling establishments dropped from eighty-three to sixteen.[35] By September, 1881, the plan was producing such good results that the grand jury commended the mayor for his action and conceded that the state's antigambling laws were almost impossible to enforce.[36] The major share of the gamblers' fund, which averaged in its entirety around twenty thousand dollars annually, was dedicated by Shakspeare to the building and maintenance of a new almshouse which was desperately needed. By the time he left office, he had the satisfaction of seeing it partially completed.[37]

In several matters the mayor received the wholehearted cooperation of his administrators. Walshe's contribution to the debt settlement had been vital. Fitzpatrick was vigorous in his efforts to repair as many streets as his slim budget in the Department of Improvements would allow. Administrator of Police Mealey fully co-

35 Kendall, *History of New Orleans*, I, 432–33.
36 Grand jury report as published in the *Daily Picayune*, September 2, 1881.
37 See Chapter 7 of this book for additional information on the almshouse.

operated in prodding the police to exercise more rigorous control over rowdy barrooms and houses of prostitution and to curtail the city-wide practice of allowing goats to run loose in the streets and on public squares.[38] During the rioting that accompanied the cotton draymen's strike and the disastrous flooding of sectors of the city after an 1881 storm, the administrators worked tirelessly with the mayor to meet these emergencies.

But Shakspeare's relations with his administrators were not always cordial. Whenever an ordinance had political implications, they consistently sided against him. The police were a prime source of patronage to Ring politicians. It was no surprise, therefore, that soon after taking office several administrators drew up an ordinance "reorganizing" the entire squad. Since this bill involved mass dismissals, the mayor vetoed it. Passed over his veto, the ordinance was immediately challenged in Civil District Court by Chief of Police Thomas N. Boylan. Boylan won his case on the grounds that only the Board of Police Commissioners could remove policemen, and the reorganization ordinance was repealed.[39]

While this controversy was being tested in the courts, the administrators created the office of "chief of aids," replacing the incumbent chief of detectives (or aids as they were also called). The new chief of aids was given wide authority, a fact which was to cause a clash with Chief Boylan. Thomas Devereaux, a man not connected with the force, was appointed. He had been largely responsible for securing the nomination of William Fagan to the post of administrator of commerce, according to the *Mascot*.[40] Now he was to claim his reward. Shakspeare also vetoed this act,

[38] "City Ordinances, No. 4280 Administration Series in the Year 1878 through No. 7336 Council Series in the Year 1887" (clippings from the *Official Journal of the City Council of New Orleans* in a ledger book in the Archives of the City of New Orleans, New Orleans Public Library), pp. 4548, back of page 4553, 4561, 4556; Edwin L. Jewell (comp.), *Jewell's Digest of the City Ordinances Together with the Constitutional Provisions, Acts of the General Assembly and Decisions of the Courts Relative to the Government of the City of New Orleans* (New Orleans, 1882), 310, 314, 328, 329, 330, hereinafter cited as *Jewell's Digest*. See also *Daily Picayune,* February 17, May 4, 24, June 7, 8, 1881.

[39] *Daily Picayune,* January 8, 19, 20, 26, February 2, 13, 22, April 27, May 4, 1881. A thorough editorial review of the controversy is in *Democrat,* September 27, 1881. The ordinance and its repeal may be found in "City Council Ordinances, No. 4280 A. S. through No. 7336 C. S.," pp. 4545, back of page 4553.

[40] *Mascot,* April 1, 1882.

but once again it was passed over the veto.[41] Bad feeling at once sprang up between Devereaux and a number of his staff. It reached its climax with a three-way gun battle in which the chief of aids was killed by two of his detectives.[42]

The immediate effect of Devereaux's death upon City Hall was a complete about-face by the shocked and frightened administrators. Hurriedly, they met with the mayor and dissolved the office of chief of aids. They also repealed several other recent police ordinances which transferred control from Chief Boylan to Administrator Mealey.[43] What had begun as a campaign to weaken Boylan ended as a movement to give him full authority.

One long-range effect of this tragedy was a change in the local form of government. For years many local observers had felt that the board of administrators, which made and enforced city ordinances, was an arbitrary oligarchy. Now, viewing the violent results of the administrators' handiwork, the public demanded the change in the system they had been promised for several years. A new charter was drawn up and approved by the same state legislative session which passed the debt compromise bill in 1882. The Ring, as already shown, protected its interests by having the prevailing voice in drafting the new charter.[44]

One of the features of the new charter which affected the incumbent city administration dealt with the next municipal election, to be held on the first Tuesday after the first Monday in November, 1882. This would be November 7, 1882. The officials elected at that time would serve until the third Monday in April, 1884. From that date, municipal elections were to be held every four years on the Tuesday following the third Monday in April.[45] With the prospect of a new form of government and a new slate of municipal officers to be chosen in the fall, the city council was naturally slow to inaugurate any new projects or legislation. Another cause of city council inaction was the difficulty Administrator Walshe encountered in collecting taxes for 1882. By August 23

41 *Daily Picayune*, April 1, 5, 8, July 2, 1881.
42 A full account of the Devereaux murder is in Chapter 9 of this volume.
43 *Daily Picayune*, October 20, 27, November 3, 1881.
44 See discussion of the charter in Chapter 2 of this volume.
45 *Acts Passed by the General Assembly, 1882*, Act. No. 20, p. 37.

Fitzpatrick had to dismiss 801 employees from his department because of an empty treasury.[46] With an uncertain source of income the council lost all interest in new projects.

But one piece of administrative business proved the exception to this rule: the selling of the Carrollton railroad franchise. Since it involved approximately $200,000 or more for the city coffers, the administrators were their old enthusiastic, ingenious selves whenever the franchise was discussed. The New Orleans and Carrollton Railroad Company actually operated the St. Charles streetcar from Canal to Carrollton. But in this period the line was called the Carrollton railroad. (All streetcar lines were referred to as city railroads in the 1880's.) The franchise was scheduled to expire in early 1883, so both the city government and the current holders of the franchise wished to see the matter settled in 1882. The New Orleans and Carrollton Railroad Company legally contested the city's stipulations in the franchise that its holder must repair the streets along its route. They also contested the city's right to resell the franchise in 1883.[47]

But on both points they lost out. In March, 1882, the state supreme court recognized the city's right to sell the franchise, although it refused to consider whether the present stockholders of the Carrollton company had the right to first consideration.[48] The city council believed they did not. The company's president, Watson Van Benthuysen, stated that the company's rights in the matter were still open to litigation. He pointed out the franchise for the Carrollton route might be sold by the city, but the tracks and mule cars currently in operation belonged to his company. If the route were sold to another corporation, the public would be inconvenienced while his company's tracks were pulled up and their successor's were put down. Also, his company was in a position to make a higher bid than outsiders since it did not have these expenses to consider. He claimed further that his company actually owned portions of the neutral ground over which it ran, hav-

46 *Daily Picayune*, August 23, 1882.
47 *Ibid.*, March 8, 1882.
48 *Ibid.; Reports of Cases Argued and Determined in the Supreme Court of Louisiana* (St. Paul, 1907), XXXXI (reprint of XXXIV of *Louisiana Annual Reports*), 284–96.

ing acquired this property previously from several small munici-
palities which existed uptown before the city spread out and
swallowed them.[49] This preposterous claim was scoffed at and de-
flated by the *Picayune* and the *Mascot,* but it had the intended
propaganda effect of worrying the administrators.[50]

In the battle of wits which ensued between Van Benthuysen
and the city council in the next few months, the protagonists
used tactics more in keeping with horse trading than with administrative negotiations over a streetcar line. Complicating the situation was the fact that all money the city received from the sale of
franchises was supposed to be turned over to the Board of Liquidation to help pay the city debt. In early 1882, with prospects favorable for a debt compromise and a new city charter to pass the
legislature, the administration began to look longingly at the valuable franchise and wish that its revenue could be set aside for
improvements, particularly repair and paving of streets, instead of
going into the pockets of ancient creditors.

With this thought always in the back of their heads, the council worked indefatigably, carefully wording the specifications in
order to get the highest price possible for the franchise. On April
14 the council announced that sealed bids on the franchise would
be opened on April 28. The specifications called for the sale of the
St. Charles Avenue line right of way from Canal Street to Carrollton Avenue, for the sale of right of way on Napoleon and Jackson avenues, and the right to construct a new streetcar line from St.
Charles Avenue to Lake Pontchartrain on any suitable thoroughfare between Jackson Avenue and Madison Street.[51]

Before the bids could be opened, a sensational sidelight to the
franchise sale pushed the main issue out of the headlines. On
April 22 the outspoken *Mascot* published a cartoon which covered its front page and was headlined: "The Great Railroad
Trickster and His Automatons." The president of the New Orleans and Carrollton Railroad, Watson Van Benthuysen, was presented as a puppeteer who was manipulating his puppets, the city

49 *Ibid.,* April 9, 1882.
50 *Ibid.,* April 9, May 6, 1882; *Mascot,* scattered references in June and July,
1882.
51 *Daily Picayune,* April 15, 1882.

council, to finagle the franchise for his company. Shortly after the paper reached the streets, Van Benthuysen and his son Edward entered the *Mascot* office at Camp Street and Commercial Alley and demanded to know who was responsible for the cartoon and accompanying article. George Osmond, *Mascot* business manager, claimed he could not tell them, but if they would call back in two hours they would be given the information. At this evasion the angry Van Benthuysens drew revolvers, and the son raised his walking cane as if to hit Osmond. The *Mascot* manager stood his ground and refused to talk. Putting their revolvers away, the Van Bethuysens left and went to police headquarters. Edward made out an affidavit against the unknown *Mascot* editors charging malicious libel.[52] The next day Watson Van Benthuysen appeared before the city council and asked permission to "prosecute the scoundrels who publish the libels in the *Mascot*. They are guilty of malicious libel, the penalty of which is fine and imprisonment." He pointed out appropriately that the *Mascot* had also attacked the city council and suggested that "this paper should be suppressed. It seems to me it is within the province of the Mayor to suppress it." [53]

The mayor agreed with Van Benthuysen, informing the council that he had examined city ordinances and inquired of the city attorney if any law prohibited such scandalous publications. He was satisfied that such a law did exist in article 663, which prohibited the sale and distribution of obscene, scandalous, or libelous material. Backed by this ordinance he issued an order to Chief Boylan to seize and destroy the print termed the *Mascot* and to notify all connected with its publication that after April 26 they would be subject to fine and imprisonment if they tried to continue publication.[54]

Van Benthuysen was gratified by this action. In his heated appeal to the council, he had predicted: "If this sheet continues to exist it will assail every female in the community, our mothers, sisters and daughters, with scandalous charges. If the people are

52 *Ibid.*, April 23, 1882; *Times-Democrat*, April 23, 1882.
53 *Daily Picayune*, April 23, 1882.
54 *Ibid.*

such cowards as to stand it, I think they deserve it." [55] Although his oratory had awakened the desired response from the mayor, the administrators were singularly unmoved. No strangers to political criticism, Fitzpatrick and Guillotte both tried to dissuade the mayor from suppressing the *Mascot*. Guillotte pointed out logically that such action would only give the paper an importance which it did not deserve. Fitzpatrick remarked that the suppression order might be construed as personal revenge by the mayor, since he and the council had been repeatedly lambasted in the weekly *Mascot*. But the mayor remained firm in his decision.[56]

This stubborn refusal to view the practical side of things and face the bigger issue of freedom of the press, as opposed to the few libelous liberties the *Mascot* had taken, was Shakspeare's gravest mistake as mayor. It reflected one weakness in an otherwise sterling executive: a mulish determination to follow his own feelings no matter what the consequences, a belief that right had only one side—the one he could see. Ironically, the *Mascot* had discovered this facet of the mayor's character and always caricatured him as a long-eared mule, referring to him as "Our Mare." [57] When Shakspeare reigned as Rex on Mardi Gras in 1882, the *Mascot* criticized him for borrowing a piano from Werlein's to liven up City Hall. A barrel organ would be more in keeping with the atmosphere, the paper said.[58] All of the administrators, particularly Fitzpatrick, were assailed time and again by this journal. When they went to Mississippi City, Mississippi, to attend the John L. Sullivan-Paddy Ryan fight in February, 1882, the *Mascot* criticized them as spendthrifts.[59] Later it intimated they were thieves and compared Fitzpatrick to Boss Tweed.[60]

Shakspeare's highhanded order was never put into operation, for the *Mascot* publishers got an injunction from court restraining Chief Boylan from carrying it out.[61] Van Benthuysen countered

55 *Ibid.*
56 *Ibid.*
57 See the *Mascot* from the middle of May through October, 1882.
58 *Mascot*, March 4, 1882.
59 *Ibid.*, February 25, 1882.
60 *Ibid.*, March 4, July 1, 1882.
61 *Daily Picayune*, April 28, 1882.

this action by getting another injunction restraining the *Mascot* from referring to him or printing any libelous cartoons in reference to him.[62] The *Mascot,* considering this injunction as an unconstitutional attempt to censure a paper before it went to press, ignored the court's order. On April 29 it featured a cartoon showing Van Benthuysen and son threatening George Osmond, titling it "The Jesse James of New Orleans." The result of this disobedience of court orders was a ten-day jail sentence for the manager and publishers, George Osmond, Joseph S. Bossier, and Joseph Liversey. Francis T. Nicholls, former governor who was a member of a New Orleans law firm at that time, served as attorney for the *Mascot* and made an impassioned plea against the sentence, but to no avail.[63] Meanwhile Osmond had preferred charges against the Van Benthuysens for assault and intent to kill. Also one of the paper's printers was arrested and followed to jail by a large crowd.[64] Public interest was so aroused that the circulation of the *Mascot* shot up tremendously.[65]

The entire affair was settled when the state supreme court reversed the decision of the lower court and branded the original injunction against the *Mascot* as improvident. By the time this decision closed the *Mascot* incident, the city council had twice turned down bidders for the Carrollton franchise.[66] A third set of bids from Van Benthuysen and another rival bidder was also rejected on May 16.[67] At this point the administrators decided to postpone the opening of any new bids until after the legislative session.

With the debt settlement and the new charter about to become realities, they felt the present legal restrictions which required that all franchise revenue be applied to the city debt might be lifted by the legislature. This would clear the way for them to ap-

62 *Ibid.*

63 *Mascot,* April 29, 1882; *Daily Picayune,* April 30, May 5, 1882.

64 *Daily Picayune,* April 30, May 9, 1882.

65 *Ibid.,* April 30, 1882.

66 See the case of the *State* ex rel. *Liversey* et al. v. *Judge of Civil District Court* in *Reports of Cases Argued and Determined in the Supreme Court of Louisiana,* XXXXI (reprint of XXXIV of *Louisiana Annual Reports*) , 490–95. See also *Daily Picayune,* April 28, May 11, 1882.

67 *Ibid.,* May 17, 1882.

ply the franchise money to improvements.[68] The reason that three bids were so hastily considered during April and May was Van Benthuysen's threat to get a renewal of his franchise from the legislature, which would leave the city with nothing to sell. The *Picayune* believed this could not be done. But the city council hated to take a chance on such a possibility. In the end they decided to gamble and see what the legislature would do. They also knew full well that they would probably have to sell to Van Benthuysen eventually. The hubbub over the other bidders, however, was desirable for the administrators' purpose of trying to drive the best possible bargain with the New Orleans and Carrollton Railroad Company. By summer the city council's hopes were realized when the legislature, as part of its revamping of city debt laws, passed an act permitting the use of revenue from franchise sales to be used for municipal improvements.[69]

The final bids were opened on August 1. All three bids were from Van Benthuysen's company; two were for a sum of cash and a certain amount of street paving, and the third was a straight cash bid of $275,000. The council accepted the cash bid.[70] But during the next five days the Board of Liquidation claimed it for the debt and other creditors tried to garnish it. A long legal battle seemed certain. On August 7 the mayor, after long private conferences with the administrators, called a meeting of the city council and read his veto of the ordinance adopting the cash bid for the franchise. The administrators solidly sustained the veto and then rapidly moved to consider a new bid from Van Benthuysen. This bid called for a straight paving contract in exchange for the franchise. The Carrollton railroad company was to pay for $275,000 worth of paving on St. Charles Avenue and several adjoining streets. The work was to be under the direction of the administrator of improvements. After months of discussion, this contract was ap-

[68] *Ibid.,* May 12, 1882.
[69] *Ibid.,* April 18, 1882; *Times-Democrat,* July 11, 1882; *Acts Passed by the General Assembly, 1882,* Act No. 81, p. 103; J. G. Flynn, *Flynn's Digest of the City Ordinances Together with the Constitutional Provisions, Acts of the General Assembly and Decisions of the Courts Relative to the Government of the City of New Orleans* (New Orleans, 1896) , 60–61, hereinafter cited as *Flynn's Digest.*
[70] *Times-Democrat,* August 2, 1882.

proved and signed within twenty minutes.[71] The next day the
Times-Democrat observed: "As the bid made and accepted is for
paving, the judgment creditors will have nothing to seize and the
garnishment process already issued falls to the ground by the May-
or's veto of the ordinance under which the purchase money for
the railroad was seized. Everybody seemed to be gratified that such
a conclusion had been reached and there was a general gratifica-
tion over the prospect of having St. Charles avenue paved." [72]

During the closing months of the Shakspeare administration, attention was focused on the coming municipal election in November, 1882. The reformer group which had backed the mayor in
1880, the People's Democratic Association, had to turn to another
candidate, Robert S. Howard, because Shakspeare was not interested in a second term. But that party had been a temporary organization composed of such divergent elements and allies in 1880
that two years later it could not depend on a strong following. Another self-styled reform group had taken the lead in the opposition to the Democratic Ring. It was the Citizens' Independent
Movement or simply the Independents. Its executive group,
known as the Committee of Ninety, drew up a slate of nominees
with Abel W. Bosworth heading the list as candidate for mayor.
Eventually after much acrimony and confusion the two reformer
groups merged to back Bosworth.

A third opposition party was the local branch of the National
Greenback-Labor Party. This group was made up of former Republicans and a rough-and-ready labor force. At their convention
held in October, the laborers in the party almost came to blows
with former Republicans over the suggestion that they cooperate
with the Republican Party in putting up a common municipal
ticket. This suggestion was rejected after the party president restored order by waving his walking cane and shouting at the dis-
turbers that he desired "those infernal rats to sit down." [73] The
Greenback-Labor Party sponsored Judge William M. Burwell as
mayor.[74] But although this group was colorful copy for the papers, it offered no threat at the polls.

71 *Ibid.*, August 8, 1882.
72 *Ibid.*
73 *Times-Democrat,* October 18, 1882.
74 *Ibid.*

The regular organization of the Democratic-Conservative Party held its municipal nominating convention at Odd Fellows Hall in an atmosphere of harmonious apathy. The nominees had been decided upon beforehand and every nomination received a unanimous vote. The slate of candidates included William J. Behan as mayor; John Fitzpatrick as commissioner of public works; Patrick Mealey, commissioner of police; Blayney Walshe, treasurer; and J. Valsin Guillotte, comptroller.[75] These last four posts had been created by the new charter to replace the seven administrators. Of the four men chosen by the Ring to run for these new positions, three were professional ward bosses—Fitzpatrick, Mealey, and Guillotte. But their performance of their duties in the Shakspeare administration had been conscientious and sometimes outstanding. The attempt to reorganize the police had been their only significant blunder. Walshe, nominated for treasurer, had certainly proved his financial ability through his contribution to the debt settlement. Behan, at the head of the ticket, was a socially prominent wholesale grocer. It was correctly estimated by the Ring leadership that he would embody the same image of business respectability as the outgoing mayor.

The major newspapers, the *Daily Picayune* and the newly-merged *Times-Democrat*, both supported the Ring candidates. The *Times-Democrat*, as already noted, was operated by Major Burke who had returned to the Ring after straying over to the reform side in 1880. The *Picayune* backed the Ring because it feared reformer fusion with the Republicans and the loss to the Democratic Party of congressional seats which were also at stake in this election.[76] Certain of their victory, the Ring candidates, nevertheless, held mass meetings in the various wards to "ratify" the selections of the nominating convention.[77] The demoralized reform elements held no rallies at all.

Election day proved to be one of the quietest in years. The vote was small, probably since the public belief was that the Ring

[75] *Ibid.,* October 17, 1882; *Daily Picayune,* October 17, 1882.

[76] *Daily Picayune,* November 1, 7, 1882. See scattered references in editorials throughout October and early November, 1882 in this newspaper.

[77] *Times-Democrat,* October 29, 31, November 1, 3, 1882; *Daily Picayune,* October 29, 31, November 3, 1882.

would win, and the slate of Ring nominees and their past performance were acceptable to the electorate. Ring candidates did win with a substantial vote. Behan received 14,897 votes while his opponent Bosworth received only 5,346. Fitzpatrick received the highest vote of any municipal candidate, 16,975.[78] The Independents, stung by their defeat which they felt had been abetted by fraudulent votes, initiated an investigation. This investigation, as pointed out earlier, did bring indictments, but these were later dropped.

On November 15 the Shakspeare city council held its final meeting. Its last official act was to create Liberty Place on Canal Street and authorize the erection of a monument there to the men who had taken part in the carpetbag rout of September 14, 1874. After its official business was concluded, "there was a general hand shaking over the close of the term of service of the old Council and soon the hall was deserted." [79]

At noon on November 20, the old administration, represented by Blayney Walshe, handed over the city government to the new regime. In contrast to the pessimistic, somber atmosphere which had prevailed on Shakspeare's inaugural day, there was a gala, festive air about this inauguration. Symbolic of this new optimism was a huge bouquet of roses prominently displayed on the mayor's desk for the inaugural ceremonies. In the general excitement which surrounded last-minute preparations for the change of administrations and of municipal reorganization under the new charter, the old regime had not been entirely forgotten. The *Daily Picayune* had publicly praised Shakspeare for his service as mayor and added congratulations to him on retiring from a thankless job. Whatever his feelings might have been under ordinary cir-

78 Almost all thirty Democratic-Conservative regular candidates for the council were elected. See returns in *Times-Democrat,* November 9, 1882, and in *Daily Picayune,* November 9, 1882.

79 *Times-Democrat,* November 16, 1882. For ordinance on Liberty Place see "City Council Ordinances, No. 4280 A. S. through No. 7336 C. S.," p. 4553. This ordinance, No. 8151, was the last signed by Mayor Shakspeare on November 18, 1882, and thus was the last ordinance to become law under the old Administration Series. When the new council form of city government took over two days later, one of their first acts was to establish a new ordinance series called "Council Series." *Daily Picayune,* November 21, 29, 1882.

cumstances at the end of his term, Shakspeare left the mayor's office at a highly emotional moment in his life. His only son, twelve-year old Joseph, lay dying in the new mansion his father had recently built on Carondelet Street. This tragedy prevented Shakspeare from attending the inauguration of his successor. The child died four days later on November 24.[80]

Following the procedure prescribed in the new charter, the thirty-member council at its inaugural meeting checked the voting returns for mayor and other executive officers, and installed these men after the official count had been accepted. The new mayor delivered his inaugural address to a packed chamber of councilmen and visitors. According to their prearranged plan, the councilmen elected Matthew D. Lagan (later a United States Congressman) as the council's president pro tempore and Michael McNamara as its secretary. Charles F. Buck was chosen to continue as city attorney, and Daniel M. Brosnan was reelected to the post of city surveyor. Twelve permanent committees were created at the council's first meeting. They were concerned with public order, finance, estimate of expenses, public health, public schools, police, the fire department, streets and landings, water, public improvements, charities, and prisons.[81]

Made up of young business and laboring men, who had to be over twenty-five and residents of the city district they represented for five years, the council served without pay.[82] It met at least one night a week (usually more often, however), starting at 7 P.M. Its meetings had to be open to the public, but most of its work was done in the committees. Reporters sometimes attended committee meetings, but not as often as they had covered the old committee of the whole meetings under Shakspeare. To safeguard against hasty or rash action, the new charter required that no ordinance could be passed at the same meeting at which it was introduced, but had to lay over until the next week. The cautious note in this

[80] *Daily Picayune,* November 21, 25, 1882.

[81] *Ibid.,* November 21, 29, 1882. See Appendix to this study for full roster of city officials and councilmen.

[82] *Charter of the City of New Orleans* (1882), p. 14; Kendall, *History of New Orleans,* I, 433.

provision had commendable features, but it also hindered the council when sudden floods or other disasters called for quick action.[83] Added to the council's natural tendency to talk too much and act too seldom, this requirement only bogged down the legislative process instead of furthering its efficiency. In fairness to this first council elected under the new charter, it must be pointed out that its members were well-intentioned, conscientious men offering their services free to the city. The large size of the council and the inexperience of the councilmen in government contributed substantially to the petty quarrels and delays which sprang up at every meeting. The council's ardent desire to retrench in city finances and place the city on a solvent, businesslike basis was the motive behind their arguments over budgets and appropriations, no matter how petty the items involved might be.

Leaders in the council amply displayed the cautious, businesslike attitude which was characteristic of the new legislative body. The three pillars of strength in the council upon whom the mayor relied to back up his efforts at municipal economy and solvency were Matthew D. Lagan, the president pro tempore; Edward Booth, a wholesale hat dealer and chairman of the finance committee; and Otto Thoman, chairman of the budget committee.[84] The new mayor, an enthusiastic, jovial man of military bearing whose neatly groomed mustache gave him the air of an elegant boulevardier, served as president of the council as well as chief executive of the city.[85]

A native New Orleanian, Mayor Behan had been the youngest Confederate artillery officer under General Lee during the Civil War, holding the rank of lieutenant. He commanded what was probably the last action of the Battle of Appomattox. In 1874 he had taken a prominent part in the White League and its famous battle on September 14. In 1877 he was made commander of the state militia with the title of major-general. In that capacity he helped preserve order during the New Orleans labor riots of 1881,

[83] See *Daily Picayune's* discussion of this problem in issue of November 14, 1882.
[84] Kendall, *History of New Orleans*, I, 443.
[85] *Ibid.*, 433; *Charter of the City of New Orleans* (1882), pp. 14–16.

even acting as chairman of the arbitration committee which settled the strike. In private life he had had a varied career as a merchant, whiskey manufacturer, and sugar planter. At the time he became mayor, he was a partner in the wholesale grocery firm of Zuberbeir and Behan.[86]

High hopes were entertained for Mayor Behan's term. The debt settlement meant that the urban credit was established on a more solid basis than it had been since the Civil War. The municipal government would begin to operate under the revised charter, and the new mayor was a powerhouse of energy. Elected by the party in power, he also did not enter office with the discomfiture of being a "minority mayor" like his predecessor. But party moguls had outdone themselves when they chose him as their candidate because of his character and business background, which were similar to that of Shakspeare. Perhaps it was poetic justice for the conniving Ring politicians—but Behan was like Shakspeare when called upon to make a choice between his personal convictions and political expediency. He proved this early in his administration to the chagrin of his recent campaign managers, Major E. A. Burke and James D. Houston, a powerful, behind-the-scenes politician.

This test case in which the mayor's conscience was triumphant involved the choice of a new police chief after Chief Boylan resigned at the beginning of the new administration. Naturally conscious of his debt to the men who had run his campaign, Behan offered to appoint anyone with the proper qualifications whom Burke and Houston would suggest, provided the nominee was not affiliated with any local political organizations. This unorthodox view of appointments obviously did not please Burke and Houston, who argued heatedly for their choice, Michael J. Sheehan, recorder of the Fourth Recorder's Court. Sheehan, however, had been indicted for illegally putting up bail for persons appearing before his own court. The indictment had been dropped, and the recorder, promptly reelected. Behan refused to accept him and appointed instead a police captain, Richard B. Rowley, whose

86 For biographical material on Behan see Kendall, *History of New Orleans,* I, 441; "Administrations of the Mayors of New Orleans, 1803–1936," pp. 189–90.

claims to the position were an outstanding record on the force and no political influence whatsoever.[87] This episode divided party regulars in the council, but the appointment was ratified.

Defiance of the Ring in choosing a police chief was to mark the break between Behan and his recent political allies. The mayor chose to keep his independence of action in all future matters, even though it meant he would never again be considered seriously for a political post by the regular Democratic-Conservative machine.

The appointment of Rowley was the first step in Behan's campaign to improve the city's law enforcement agency. Next he set about a real police reorganization, accomplished without large-scale dismissals, however. He tightened discipline, delivered personal pep talks, encouraged crackdowns on confidence men, and ordered the enforcement of an ordinance forbidding merchants to clutter the sidewalks with merchandise.[88] Both criminals and so-called law-abiding citizens were made to feel the impartial justice of Behan's squad. By August, 1883, the mayor, through careful personal supervision, had made more judicious use of the $185,000 appropriation for police expenses than had Mealey when he was in complete control of the force under Shakspeare. Proof of this was the fact that he had been able to add about 100 men to the pitifully inadequate force, bringing its total up to 358.[89]

Behan attacked the problem of irregular pay to city employees with equal vigor. It had been common practice for years to pay them each month in certificates which would be redeemed when their municipal agency had ready funds. Such payment in cash might come only once in four or five months—and then never in

[87] Kendall, *History of New Orleans,* I, 443–44. For announcement of Boylan's retirement, see *Daily Picayune,* November 19, 1882, the day before the new administration took office. For background on Sheehan's indictment, see *Daily Picayune,* October 29, 1881. For Rowley's appointment, see *Daily Picayune* and *Times-Democrat,* November 18–25, 1882.

[88] On police reforms, see *Daily Picayune,* January 5, June 6, 1833. Campaign against confidence men is discussed in *Daily Picayune,* February 6, 27, 1883; *Daily States,* April 16, 1883. The sidewalk nuisances are mentioned in *Daily Picayune,* February 1, 1883.

[89] *Daily Picayune,* August 7, 1883.

full. The custom grew up, therefore, of selling one's certificates at a discount to brokers who could afford to wait for the total payment. Mayor Behan desired to end the parasitic hold of the brokers over municipal employees by guaranteeing the latter payment of monthly salaries. He had the council pass a bill calling for such payments and began carrying it out faithfully in 1883.[90] He attempted to have bills passed outlawing the selling of certificates to brokers, but these were always defeated.[91] Many unfortunates had sold their certificates for a year in advance, and the mayor's new policy of cash salaries did them no good. Despite this, his sincere effort lifted the morale of most municipal workers.

Coupled with this success was his crowning achievement of balancing the budget in 1883, with the help of the council which kept a tight check on the budgets of the various municipal departments. The city government was just beginning to take on the semblance of a businesslike operation when Treasurer Walshe sabotaged Behan's efforts. An undercurrent of resentment against the council had existed among the commissioners since the beginning of their term. The latter had difficulty adjusting to the new situation, in which they took orders from a body of thirty councilmen whom they considered political novices. A showdown was deliberately forced by Walshe to determine who had the most authority—the commissioners or the council. In this struggle for power the mayor's salary reforms were seriously damaged, and the entire city government almost came to a standstill.

Walshe claimed that the municipal budget was illegal, since it set aside one fourth of the revenue from taxes alone for public improvements. The revenue from market notes, licenses, and franchises should also be included in this one-fourth appropriation, he felt. In August of 1883 he announced that he would not pay out a cent of money henceforth, because he did not want the responsibility for handling funds which were being misappropriated. Behan and the council stood firm in their belief that their interpretation of the one fourth appropriation clause in the new charter was the correct one. To break the impasse, Walshe was quickly suspended

90 *Ibid.*, November 29, 1882; February 2, 11, 14, August 8, 1883.
91 *Ibid.*, February 21, 1883.

from office by the mayor and escorted from City Hall by a police detachment.[92]

Four different court cases were initiated over this matter, and the city, solvent for the first time in years, could not touch its own money. Walshe was reinstated to office by court order and then removed again by the mayor, while the council began impeachment proceedings against the treasurer.[93] By the end of the year, the council and Walshe agreed to drop the whole matter, which had reached a stalemate. But in forcing this controversy, Walshe had gravely hindered the mayor's attempts to free city employees from the brokers. Although the mayor personally stood responsible for the salaries of workers during the months in which revenues were tied up, many panicked and sold out to brokers.[94]

Nevertheless, Behan persisted in this policy, so that by the time the quarrel with Walshe was ended, monthly payment of salaries had become an established fact. Although this was probably the most personally satisfying achievement to Behan in his brief year-and-a-half term as mayor which ended in April, 1884, the next administration was to lapse back into paying city workers with certificates. In appointing the police chief he wanted and fighting to upgrade the police, and break the hold of brokers over city employees, Mayor Behan had shown the same dogged determination which had made him one of the last active soldiers on the field at Appomattox. The analogy is a suitable one since, like at Appomattox, he was destined ultimately to meet defeat. This time it was in the political arena in the 1884 municipal election.

[92] *Daily Picayune*, September 4, 9, 10, 11, 13, 1883; *Times-Democrat*, September 10, 11, 1883.

[93] See both *Times-Democrat* and *Daily Picayune* for September, October, November, 1883.

[94] Kendall, *History of New Orleans*, I, 444; *Daily Picayune*, September 22, 1883.

4

THE VIEW FROM CITY HALL
1884–1892

IN MOST CHRONICLES of New Orleans the year 1884 is usually associated with the opening of the Cotton Centennial Exposition. But the exposition did not open until December of that year and actually had little permanent or significant influence upon the lives of New Orleanians. The most important event of 1884, one which shaped the city's destiny for the next four years and influenced it long after, was the municipal election. This took place in April and resulted in a complete victory for the Democratic-Conservative machine.

The machine victory was significant for two reasons. It brought one of the most patronage-minded politicians in town into the mayor's office, and it filled every one of the other executive offices with professional politicians. Gone were the concessions to business which in the past had been expressed in the nominations of Walshe, Huger, and Behan. The machine was now well enough "oiled" to work without making concessions. The year 1884 was a year of decision in which the issue was "machine" or "no machine." The machine won not merely because its lieutenants stuffed ballot boxes and intimidated voters, as its enemies claimed, but also because of a combination of factors which may best be seen by a close examination of this fateful election.

Behan's term as mayor, cut short by the new charter, lasted only a year and a half. Because of this, protocol required that the Democratic-Conservative city organization should offer the mayor the top spot again on their ticket. But Burke and his colleagues tied a firm string to the proffered nomination: Behan would have to agree to appoint all persons whom the party leaders recommended. The unhappy episode of the police chief appointment in 1882 was still a sore point with party diehards. The Ring knew very well that Behan would decline under these circumstances, and they would be free to choose a "safer" candidate. After he declined, the nominating convention which met on March 24, 1884, chose Comptroller J. Valsin Guillotte, as the "regular" candidate for mayor.[1]

Noted for his frank cynicism and Gallic wit, Guillotte's candid public remarks had made him the *enfant terrible* of the Ring stalwarts and the favorite of a large following of voters in the Ninth Ward, his home territory. In 1881 he had forced the city to pay him a full salary of five hundred dollars a month, despite the protests of Shakspeare and Fitzpatrick that all candidates had pledged themselves to accept only three hundred dollars monthly to help curtail expenses for the city's slim budget. Guillotte denied making such a personal pledge.[2] He had, however, run on the Democratic-Conservative platform which did contain such a pledge. In the 1882 campaign when he had been running for comptroller, Guillotte had amused an outdoor audience at a political rally by stating: "I don't intend to say anything tonight. I am on the ring ticket, and after all that has been said against the ring, the less I say about myself the better." He had added that those candidates who claimed that they were moved by patriotic impulses and cared nothing for the salary involved in public service were confounded liars. He admitted he himself wanted all the ease, comfort, and money that being in office could bring, and in political campaigns would always ask the public to vote for him first and for the rest of the ticket afterward.[3] In 1881, during a heated discussion

1 See *Times-Democrat,* March 25, 1884, for details of Ring nominations. See discussion of the Ring's offer of renomination to Behan in Kendall, *History of New Orleans,* I, 444–45.

2 *Daily Picayune,* February 2, 3, 16, 17, March 16, 1881. Shakspeare, Fitzpatrick, and Fagan, however, drew only three hundred dollars even after Guillotte began collecting five hundred dollars per month.

3 *Times-Democrat.* November 3, 1882. Biographical material on Guillotte may be found in Kendall, *History of New Orleans,* I, 451, and in "Administrations of the Mayors of New Orleans, 1803–1936," p. 191.

among council members of the advisability of converting the volunteer fire service into a paid city department, Guillotte's retort to
one administrator's statement that such a reorganization would appear politically orientated was that he saw nothing wrong in voting for an ordinance which aided one politically. As a matter of
fact, he bluntly concluded, he would always support any ordinance
which benefited him in politics.[4] Despite this "professional" and
essentially negative attitude toward his various municipal posts,
Guillotte had a deep sense of personal honor which had driven
him as comptroller under Behan to slap the face of a councilman
who mistakenly accused him of misappropriating stationery funds
in his department.[5]

Guillotte's popularity in some quarters as a witty cynic and
sharp-tongued, able politician, and his share of city patronage as
comptroller were not sufficient to gain him the nomination for
mayor. The two most powerful men in Crescent City politics in
1884 were obviously Major E. A. Burke and Commissioner of
Public Works John Fitzpatrick. They were natural rivals and an
uneasy truce had existed between the two since the last election.
Burke was not interested in the role of mayor. His position as state
treasurer was too lucrative and he was also about to turn his at-
tentions to the promotion of the Cotton Centennial Exposition as
its director-general. If Burke were to back Fitzpatrick for mayor,
he would not have as much influence over this political strong
man as he would have if he backed a politically weaker, and therefore, more easily influenced politician. Patrick Mealey had always
been closely allied with Fitzpatrick, and Walshe had ruined his
political career through his stubborn fight over the budget. Burke's
only choice, and the obvious one, was Guillotte. There was another influential local politician who probably aided Burke in securing the nomination for Guillotte. He was James Houston, who
after a term as administrator of public works in the 1870's, had
settled comfortably into the job of tax collector for the upper districts of the city and was credited with wielding much power behind the scenes in local Ring politics. He and Burke had been
Behan's campaign managers in the 1882 election. Now in 1884 it

4 *Daily Picayune,* August 3, 1881.
5 *Ibid.,* February 12, 14, 28, 1883; *Daily States,* March 1, 7, 1883.

appears that they teamed up once again to secure the mayoral nomination for Guillotte.[6]

The rest of the Democratic-Conservative ticket was composed of John Fitzpatrick for commissioner of public works, Patrick Mealey for commissioner of police and public buildings, former Mayor Isaac W. Patton for treasurer, and Joseph N. Hardy for comptroller.[7] The newcomer Hardy had been a salesman in a wholesale drug and grocery firm and later a partner in a photography studio before running for municipal office.[8]

Following the selection of the regular party candidates, an independent movement sprang up to endorse the reelection of Mayor Behan. This group composed predominantly of businessmen called itself the Citizens' Democratic Parochial and Municipal Party.[9] A bitter contest ensued between this citizens' group and the Ring, in which the events were strangely parallel to those of the Behan-Bosworth campaign. Once again the cry of collaboration with the Republicans was raised against the reformer group by the regular Democrats. This was brought about by the uninvited endorsement of Behan by the Republican State Executive Committee, which merely wished to cause dissension and confusion within the Democratic ranks.[10] The citizens' groups retaliated by leveling charges of bossism and inefficiency against the regular incumbents running for reelection—Mealey, Fitzpatrick, and Guillotte.[11]

[6] The author feels it is significant as an indication of the rivalry between Burke and Fitzpatrick, and of Burke's ability to check Fitzpatrick's driving political ambitions, that Fitzpatrick did not become mayor of New Orleans until 1892—after Burke had fled into exile in Honduras.

[7] *Daily Picayune,* March 25, 1884.

[8] Lon Soards (pub. and comp.) , *Soards' New Orleans City Directory for 1883* (New Orleans, 1883) , 365; Lon Soards (pub. and comp.) , *Soards' New Orleans City Directory for 1884* (New Orleans, 1884) , 333.

[9] *Daily Picayune* and *Times-Democrat* both ran advertisements listing the citizens' ticket, April 17–22, 1884.

[10] Kendall, *History of New Orleans,* I, 447. The *Daily Picayune* on April 19, 1884, denied that Behan was the puppet of the Republicans. Kendall agrees with this view. However, Behan left the Democratic ranks and became a Republican during the second Grover Cleveland administration in protest against Democratic proposals to put sugar on the free tariff list. He served as chairman of the Republican State Executive Committee from 1900 to 1912, and had been the Republican candidate for governor in 1904. "Administrations of the Mayors of New Orleans, 1803–1936," pp. 189–90.

[11] *Daily Picayune,* April 18, 19, 1884.

The climax was election day, Tuesday, April 22, 1884. The Ring sent eight hundred to a thousand specially appointed deputy sheriffs to the polling places. These "deputies" forcibly removed many of the commissioners of the Citizens' Party. When the votes were tabulated and presented to the president pro tempore of the city council that night, many were listed in alphabetical order, although the votes were supposed to be listed exactly as they had been cast. Also, several persons absent from the city and others who were deceased were listed on the returns. The official vote was 18,278 for Guillotte and 6,612 for Behan.[12]

As in 1882 the question of vote frauds was raised by the *Picayune*. Major Burke's *Times-Democrat*, as a supporter of the regular Democratic ticket, was satisfied with the results. But the "old woman of Camp Street," as the *Picayune* was called by her fellow newspaper the *Mascot*, declared that "the election was a mockery. . . . The people cast the ballots but the ring counted them." [13] It demanded that the people of New Orleans hold a mass meeting and consider how to nullify the false election. For a brief time, Behan, the brusque soldier, even considered taking forceful action against his opposition. But his temper cooled after several days, and he contented himself with writing vigorous protests to the mayor incumbent. Guillotte quietly advised Behan to go to court if he had a grievance. He knew that litigation would be long and tedious and might very well end in a stalemate, just as it had for Bosworth in the vote fraud trials of 1882. Behan was well aware of the ironic similarity between his present situation and that which had faced his defeated opponent in 1882. Ultimately he dropped the matter and retired to private life.[14]

The reasons for Guillotte's election are more complex than a mere explanation of fraudulent votes. It is probably true that thousands of the votes counted were fraudulent. But it is also true that the Democratic-Conservative regular party organization had a real following in the city. As the party of the former White

12 *Election Laws of Louisiana* (New Orleans, 1884), 20; Kendall, *History of New Orleans*, I, 449.
13 *Daily Picayune*, April 23, 1884.
14 For discussion of election results and frauds see *Daily Picayune* for the month following election.

League which had struggled against scalawags and carpetbaggers in the 1870's, its emotional appeal to white voters in the Crescent City was potent as has already been pointed out. Also, as in other American cities of the period, the city machine politicians appealed to the common man at his own level with "shirt-sleeve" political tactics—outdoor rallies at which barbecued meats and beer were served along with florid speeches, or dances sponsored by the various ward clubs.

Some of the city's labor population had expressed themselves politically in the late 1870's and early 1880's through the Greenback-Labor Party.[15] But by 1884 this group had ceased to exist as a real local party, although there were at least twenty unions in the city. Laborers had to turn either to the Ring or the reformers. Opportunity for their political advancement was easier in the Democratic-Conservative Party than in the sporadic reform opposition ranks. Men of laboring class origin came to be the main leaders in the regular party organization, a fact previously noted. Patrick Mealey retained his leadership in the Cotton Yard Men's Association No. 1 even after becoming an administrator and later commissioner of police and public buildings. Fitzpatrick was considered one of the best friends of organized labor in local politics. The workingman's point of view was expressed more often by machine politicians than reformers and this paid dividends on election day.

Aside from its appeal to the workingman, the Ring in 1884 had the advantage of Cotton Centennial "fever" on its side. One of the machine's leaders, Major Burke, was the chief promoter of this fantastic daydream which by early 1884 was fast becoming a reality. It was mainly through Burke's efforts that the exposition was able to open in a blaze of electric lights by December, and he became its director-general. New Orleans merchants anxious to regain some of their prewar prosperity looked eagerly to the exposition as the "open sesame" to more business and trade. The fact that Burke was a leader in the Democratic-Conservative local organization probably helped the party's cause among the business and mercantile population. At the very least, the reformers could

15 The mayoral election of 1882 seems to have been the last one in which the Greenback-Labor Party put up a candidate, Judge William M. Burwell. See *Times-Democrat,* October 18, 1882.

not deny that machine politicians in the Behan administration had been energetic and prompt in their furtherance of the exposition.[16]

Although the exposition was not destined to be the boon to New Orleans commerce that its enthusiasts expected, its brief existence was to give the city a chance to turn away from the hard times of the past decade and look expectantly to the future. It was a tangible manifestation of the new hope which affected the city's business and commercial life like a slow but steady fever. The popular desire of the city's capitalists was to venture into new projects, to expand the city's economic assets. In this new climate of opinion, Behan, who had achieved the difficult feat of balancing the city's budget, was not as representative a figure as the ingratiating, imaginative adventurer, Major Burke. Ironically, Behan's good record as mayor could be used against him in this election. After all he had been a Democratic-Conservative regular when he was elected, and his administration had been solidly made up of Ring men. Thus the Ring could and did claim Behan's achievements as its own.

The first year of Mayor Guillotte's tenure in City Hall revealed a downhill course in municipal administration. The mayor's individual honesty was not enough to insure good government in New Orleans. As mayor he seldom directed or challenged the actions of the council and commissioners. The city council, unfortunately, declined from the earnest, hard-working, budget-minded body it had been in the former administration to a confused, quarrelsome collection of spendthrifts. In his appointments, the mayor always followed the wishes of his party. As a result, the spoils system completely dominated municipal affairs. Personal tragedy and ill health dogged Guillotte during this first year as mayor. He was frequently absent from City Hall, often because of illness in his family. An infant son died. His wife became seriously ill. Even Guillotte himself had to take sick leave when one of his hands became severely infected and almost had to be amputated.[17] Such a

16 For specific cases of their interest in the exposition see *Daily Picayune,* February 21, July 4, October 10, 1883.

17 *Daily Picayune,* September 2, 1884.

combination of circumstances which grew chronic in succeeding years brought the city to the brink of anarchy by the end of his term.

Petty bickering in the council was common as some members tried to push through legislation favorable to their sections over protests of "jobbery" and "favoritism" from others. The mayor vetoed an ordinance calling for a street lighting contract with a local electrical company because it favored uptown neighborhoods to the detriment of those downtown, his own territory.[18] The paving contract for St. Charles Avenue, which was to be paid by the New Orleans and Carrollton Railroad Company in return for its streetcar franchise, caused a three-way fight among the council, the streetcar line, and the paving contractor. The streetcar company refused to pay for what they considered defective work. The contractor appealed to the council and the council threatened to cancel the franchise. President Watson Van Benthuysen of the streetcar line, thereupon, revealed that he had hired private detectives to check the backgrounds of councilmen, one of whom he publicly accused of embezzlement from a former employer.[19] Neither was the executive branch of the government free from trouble. Fitzpatrick exploded in a tirade of injured pride against a council member who had criticized his handling of funds in his department.[20] More serious was the council's censure of the city surveyor for his cavalier conduct in departing from specifications after these had been approved by ordinance. He was also charged with accepting too many private assignments, while at the same time asking for additions to his staff.[21]

Trivialities could cause a tempest in the council chamber. But such vital matters as garbage disposal, the almshouse, and the effectiveness of the police found few sincere champions. One member of the council tried to have the garbage, or nuisance wharf, turned into a commercial one. (It was not currently in use because the garbage barge, on which refuse was towed downriver and dumped, was in need of repairs.) This conversion of the garbage

18 *Ibid.*, December 27, 1884.
19 *Ibid.*, May 21, 24, 25, December 17, 1884; *Daily States*, December 15, 1884.
20 *Daily States*, October 18, 1884.
21 *Ibid.*, September 17, 1884.

wharf was opposed successfully by a doctor in the council who claimed that the garbage piling up on neutral grounds and empty ground on the city's outskirts was a health hazard.[22] But garbage disposal did not improve. The Shakspeare Almshouse had been completed during Behan's term. But it received so little notice under Guillotte that in November, 1884, a notary advised the mayor that through some error the ground on which it stood had been advertised for taxes.[23]

The police, after their brief revitalization under Behan and Rowley, were plunged deeper than ever into politics in 1884. Guillotte had noted in his inaugural address that more patrolmen were needed. But in appointing them he showed indifference to their fitness or effect upon the morale of the force. These "specials" were rowdy hoodlums who acted as strong-arm boys for the Ring. Many never wore a policeman's uniform or did regular duty on a beat. Lounging in City Hall corridors or brawling in saloons or streetcars were their main pastimes. Crime rapidly grew worse under these conditions.[24] One of the most notorious of Guillotte's appointees to the force was Theodore J. Boasso, a known companion of gamblers and confidence men, whom the mayor, nevertheless, named chief of aids. In addition to being constantly in trouble with his superiors on the police force, Boasso became involved in a scandalous seduction of the daughter of a friend of Mayor Guillotte. The affair ended with the shooting of the philandering chief by his wronged woman friend, who had been led to believe she was married to Boasso. He survived his wounds, however, to face charges of forging a false marriage certificate and received a fourteen-year sentence in the state prison.[25]

Violence and murder were not limited to minor politicians. A series of brazen murders during Guillotte's administration involved some of the most prominent men in local politics. In December, 1883, a gun battle erupted between two groups of feuding

22 Ibid., December 24, 1884.
23 Ibid., November 18, 1884.
24 Ibid., April 29, June 14, 1884; Times-Democrat, April 29, 1884; Kendall, History of New Orleans, I, 451–52.
25 Herbert Asbury, The French Quarter, An Informal History of The New Orleans Underworld (Garden City, 1938), 398–99.

politicians. Three were killed and eight were wounded. Taking
part in this shooting were Criminal Sheriff Robert Brewster and
Tax Collector James D. Houston who was one of the top men in
the local Democratic-Conservative Party. Thirteen months later,
in January, 1885, Sheriff Brewster was shot to death when he and
Houston tried to attack the editor of the *Mascot* with a horsewhip
in response to scurrilous material which had appeared in that paper about Houston's brother.[26] The most sensational of these
murders was the fatal shooting of Andrew H. "Cap" Murphy, a
cousin of Congressman E. John Ellis, by seven assailants, one of
whom was Thomas J. Ford, judge of the Second Recorder's Court
in the city. The origin of the trouble between Murphy and Ford
dated back several months before the murder which occurred on
December 2, 1884. Murphy, who served as a house of detention
guard and deputy clerk in Civil District Court, had a noisy and
bellicose nature and had been an amateur boxer in his youth. But
his good humor and generosity made up for his rough manners as
long as he was sober. When drunk, Murphy became a wild man
who wanted to fight anyone in sight and frequently wrecked theaters or barrooms before he could be subdued and dragged off to
the police station to regain his sobriety.

It was as a result of one of these drunken rampages that Murphy was brought before Recorder Ford's court. Murphy and the
recorder exchanged bitter words, and the recorder ordered that
Murphy be listed in the court records as "a hoodlum, a deadbeat
and a city official." This was published in the papers much to the
amusement of Murphy's acquaintances; but Murphy himself
vowed vengeance. He tried to publish a card in a daily paper criticizing Ford—but it was turned down. He then seized upon the
idea of having posters run off in which he called Ford a perjurer
and poltroon and made specific charges against the recorder to
back up these accusations. Shortly after the posters appeared on
walls and fences, Ford brought the matter before the grand jury
and had Murphy indicted for criminal libel. Murphy was out on
bond awaiting trial and boasting that he was going to prove his
charges, when the murder took place. The cold-blooded brutality

26 *Ibid.*, 396–97.

of the crime in the middle of the day before numerous witnesses shocked New Orleanians who felt it reached a new low in local violence.[27]

Murphy was sitting on the stoop of a lottery shop supervising a gang of House of Detention prisoners working on the drainage canal in the middle of North Claiborne Street, when he noticed several officers attached to Ford's court approaching. Several companions, who had been discussing a coming election of officials in Murphy's volunteer fire company with him, spotted other men with drawn guns coming from two other directions. Recorder Ford was one of them. There were seven men in all, one a police officer. Without warning, the approaching men began firing at Murphy who jumped to his feet and struggled to reach his revolver in his hip pocket covered by his long gray overcoat. One of Murphy's friends was slightly wounded; his prisoners were cowering frightened on the slimy bank of the canal, and Murphy himself returned the fire of his assailants while attempting to get away. His pursuers were relentless. They chased him until his revolver was empty and shot him down. One of the gunmen then walked over to Murphy's inanimate body and fired two more bullets into him. Recorder Ford meanwhile had noticed two sailors in the work gang whom he knew could identify him and suggested to them that they just walk away free. They declined. By night Ford and the others involved in the shooting were arrested for murder.[28] The trial was long and 140 witnesses were examined by the grand jury in connection with it.[29] Political pressure was extended as far as the governor's office to try to get a pardon for the two men who were sentenced to death, Recorder Ford's brother, Patrick Ford and John Murphy. But the district attorney was determined to get justice. The two were eventually hanged after litigation and delays. Recorder Ford and two others were convicted of manslaughter and received prison terms.[30]

The "Cap" Murphy murder took place about two weeks before the opening of the Cotton Centennial Exposition in upper City

27 *Daily Picayune,* December 2, 31, 1884.
28 *Ibid.,* December 2, 1884.
29 *Ibid.,* December 13, 1884.
30 Asbury, *The French Quarter,* 397.

Park. In addition to stirring up local tempers, it caused shocked reactions from numerous out-of-town newspapers which warned that such incidents would hurt the exposition.[31] Unfortunately, the opening of the exposition not only coincided with the Murphy publicity, but with a local streetcar strike during which fights, threats, and the overturning of a car occurred. The police were miserably ineffective in this crisis and scores of sightseers were frightened away.[32]

The exposition itself, forced to begin in 1884 by Act of Congress, was incomplete on opening day, December 16, and was sharply criticized for its lack of cohesion by some visiting journalists. It ran from December 16, 1884, through June 1, 1885. Then, with new management, it reopened as the American Exposition in November, 1885. But it failed to yield a profit and was closed in March, 1886, its property being sold at auction to pay creditors.[33] It was a cruel twist of fate that such an exhibition should have been attempted in New Orleans during the Guillotte administration. How could the city sustain a successful commercial project of this scope when ordinary public services were fast deteriorating and its budget slipping into the red?

The deterioration of law and order and the general ineptness of municipal government roused the public sufficiently that a citizens' reform group, the Committee of One Hundred, was organized in May, 1885, to cope with the sad state of civic affairs.[34] This committee, which came into being during the exposition and outlived it by only a few months, was to prove a gadfly to the local body politic. Beginning in 1885, the Ring felt its stings, but these proved to be only an annoyance to it rather than a deterrent to administrative abuses. The committee tried to get injunctions to prevent the carrying out of several objectionable ordinances. One allowed a private individual to collect back taxes on a percentage basis, although officials for this purpose already existed. Another leased the police telephone to private parties, and a third made a contract with the Water Works Company extremely unfavorable to the

[31] *Daily Picayune,* December 13, 1884.
[32] *Ibid.,* December 28, 29, 30, 1884.
[33] See Chapter 8 of this study for a detailed account of the exposition.
[34] *Times-Democrat,* May 26, 1885.

city.[35] The Committee of One Hundred was unsuccessful in all three of these cases.

Another matter which received scrutiny from both the Committee of One Hundred and the grand jury was the Shakspeare Plan. The council had made an appropriation of ten thousand dollars for the almshouse. As a result of this action, much of the gamblers' fund in 1885 was used for other purposes, such as funeral expenses for a deceased councilman, an official junket to St. Louis, cabs for policemen during a strike, and for entertaining exposition visitors. Out of the estimated twenty thousand dollars collected yearly, only about four thousand dollars was expended on the almshouse in 1885. A grand jury investigation in 1886 recommended that the fund be continued but turned over exclusively to the charity for which it was intended. A year later, however, another grand jury branded the gamblers' collections as a secrect service fund whose existence only encouraged its misuse. It further took a stern stand against gambling, indicted several gamblers, and refrained from indicting local officials only because they could not be touched for compounding a misdemeanor. The result of this action in February, 1887, meant the demise of the Shakspeare Plan.[36]

Aside from its court actions, the Committee of One Hundred petitioned the legislature to investigate New Orleans politics in 1886, but to no avail.[37] They also failed to get a revision of election laws stiffening penalties for ballot box stuffing, or an act requiring a new registration of voters in Orleans Parish.[38] As a result of its constant failure by 1887 the committee had fallen apart. Its place was taken first by the Law and Order League, organized in November, 1886, with the same objectives as its predecessor; and in 1887 by the Young Men's Democratic Association, a political coalition of diverse elements destined to accomplish what the others had sought only in vain.[39]

35 *Daily Picayune,* January 19, April 11, 14, 21, May 19, June 23, 1886.

36 *Ibid.,* January 27, 28, February 27, 1886; Kendall, *History of New Orleans,* I, 451–56.

37 *Memorial of the Committee of One Hundred to the General Assembly of the State of Louisiana* (New Orleans, 1886).

38 *Daily Picayune,* May 27, June 1, 2, 9, 11, 14–17, 1886.

39 Kendall, *History of New Orleans,* I, 455–56; Howe, *Municipal History of New Orleans,* 187.

The Young Men's Democratic Association, as one historian has noted, was not made up strictly of young men, or of Democrats.[40] In addition to its basic reformer composition, it included a few Republicans who always followed in the wake of any local movement, and a surprising number of persons who had previously voted the straight Democratic-Conservative ticket. The conduct of the Ring councilmen had alienated many of the younger "regulars." Even Mayor Guillotte was disgusted with the council members who had become so disinterested in their roles as city legislators by 1888 that they failed to meet for weeks at a time for lack of a quorum.[41]

The mayor had been pictured by the grand jury in 1886 as an estimable gentleman who was helpless, under the limitations placed upon him by the charter, to control the unsavory actions of his colleagues. This analysis does not take into consideration, however, that he actually favored such a system when he first took office. On the other hand, he was probably under promise to the other Ring leaders to secure their consent for all appointees. (Such a promise had been demanded of Behan, and there is no reason to think that Guillotte had avoided it.) Some of these appointments had turned out disastrously—such as that of Theodore J. Boasso as chief of aids and of Louis Clare as a special policeman. Clare, who had been arrested thirty times in one year for petty offenses, murdered Patrick Mealey seven months after joining the police force. Such appointments came back as specters to haunt the mayor, even though they may have been dictated by others in the Ring hierarchy. Embittered by all of the criticism heaped upon him, Guillotte was content to retire in 1888 and let someone else struggle with the problem of patronage and corruption in city government.

40 Howe, *Municipal History of New Orleans*, 187.
41 *Times-Democrat*, March 22–April 13, 1888. John S. Kendall states that Mayor Guillotte backed Joseph Shakspeare, the reform candidate, in 1888 rather than the Ring candidate, Robert C. Davey. But he gives no reference to verify this statement. In a day-by-day search of several local dailies for five weeks before the 1888 election no mention was found of such an endorsement. In 1896 Guillotte did bolt the Ring to join the Citizens League and back its mayoral candidate. At that time, a *Picayune* reporter who interviewed him showed great surprise at the former mayor's actions, which would seem to indicate that he had been a faithful Ring associate up to that time. On Kendall's statement, see Kendall, *History of New Orleans*, I, 471; on Guillotte's affiliation with the Citizens League, see *Daily Picayune*, March 25, 1896.

The 1888 municipal election was the second time in a decade that a reform movement beat the regular Democratic-Conservative organization. The Young Men's Democratic Association protected its interests by patrolling the polling places on election day with shotguns. The members did not intend to let Ring "deputies" turn voters away or manipulate the ballots after the polls closed. As before the Republicans backed the reformer ticket, and just as predictably, the campaign manager for Shakspeare was a leader in business and professional circles, William S. Parkerson.[42] The vote for mayor was 23,313 for Joseph Shakspeare, and 15,635 for the regular candidate, Judge Robert C. Davey.[43] But whereas Shakspeare had been the lone victorious reformer in the 1880 campaign, he now entered office with a complete slate of reformers or regulars who had crossed over to his ticket in the other executive posts and in most of the council seats. The greatest upset of the election was the defeat of Fitzpatrick by the Confederate luminary, General Pierre G. T. Beauregard, for the post of commissioner of public works. Thomas Agnew was elected commissioner of police and public buildings. Joseph N. Hardy won the post of treasurer, and Otto Thoman was chosen comptroller.[44]

Naturally, there were joyous celebrations at the various commercial exchanges and in the fashionable, gaslit mansions along St. Charles Avenue. The Bourbon businessmen seemed to have inherited City Hall. A surprising exception to the general conservative sponsorship of the reformers was the attitude of the *Picayune*, which argued during the campaign that the Ring ticket was superior to the Y.M.D.A. slate. Judge Davey, who headed the Ring ticket, was certainly one of the most qualified men in public life to run for mayor of New Orleans in the last twenty-five years of the nineteenth century. He had been elected to the state senate in 1879 and 1884, and had served as president pro tempore of the senate during the sessions of 1884 and 1886. He was judge of the First Recorder's Court in New Orleans from 1880 to 1888. Following his defeat in the mayor's race in 1888, he was later elected to

42 Henry Clay Warmoth, *War, Politics and Reconstruction: Stormy Days in Louisiana* (New York, 1930) , 252.
43 *Daily Picayune*, April 20, 21, 1888.
44 *Ibid.*

the House of Representatives from the Second Congressional District.[45] Most of the city's newspapers, however, felt confident that the reform regime would do a far better job than its opposition. Perhaps the press expected too much of the second Shakspeare administration. It was supposed to avoid the errors of its predecessor and solve all the vexing problems which had been accumulating for years. What actually happened was an old political story —after their victory some of the reformers lost their zeal and began to act like the former Ring councilmen, while others fought among themselves over the proper way to carry out their plans. When attempts were made to change or improve municipal services with the intention of removing them from politics, Shakspeare always alienated some block of voters whose interests were hurt. Reform, under these circumstances, proved a rather difficult business which sometimes could not be distinguished from Ring rule. The *Mascot*, noting the dissension which the new administration plunged into immediately over control of the police force, guessed that the politically-weary ex-Mayor Guillotte must be laughing over his beer at City Park.[46]

One of the few things which the new government could agree on was an investigation of the executive departments under the former administration. Two sources of scandal were allegedly discovered. The Board of Assessors was accused of gross favoritism to certain property holders, and a payroll book from the department of public works when Fitzpatrick had been commissioner was alleged to contain four hundred deadheads. Since several months' wages, amounting to about $3,100, were outstanding to some of these laborers, the council refused to pay, claiming the list of employees was fraudulent. Fitzpatrick demanded an investigation to clear his name. But the council considered the matter closed after

45 Fortier, *Louisiana*, I, 336; *Who Was Who in America, 1897–1942* (Chicago, 1942) , 297; "Biographical Directory of the American Congress, 1774–1961" *House Documents*, 85th Cong., 2nd Sess., No. 442, p. 780.

46 After he left the mayor's office, Guillotte was admitted to the bar by examination before the state supreme court and practiced law as a member of the firm of Kerr, Duvigneaud, and Guillotte. He served in the state Senate during the administrations of governors Murphy J. Foster and Jared Y. Sanders. At the time of his death in 1917, he was assistant secretary of the New Orleans police department. "Biographies of the Mayors of New Orleans, 1803–1936," 134–35.

they announced the payroll was padded. As a result of this unfavorable publicity, the "Big Boss of the Third Ward" lost an appointment as United States marshal which President Grover Cleveland had sent to the Senate but later withdrew, undoubtedly under pressure from Y.M.D.A. men in New Orleans.[47]

The attempt to discredit Fitzpatrick backfired, however, when the matter of the unpaid salaries was brought to court. The deadheads turned out to be live men who had actually worked for the city, and the court ordered the council to pay their delinquent wages.[48] Although the witch hunt in the department of public works failed, the assessors' board definitely was proven to be corrupt. But this was an embarrassment to the reformers, since the former president of the board, Edgar T. Leche, was one of their leaders and succeeded General Beauregard when that gentleman resigned the post of commissioner of public works after clashing with the city council over cuts in his budget.[49]

In addition to investigations of old misdeeds, the Y.M.D.A. faction tried to guard against future malpractices by getting several reform measures passed by the state legislature in 1888. These included an act sharply defining certain powers of the city council. It could not make a contract of purchase without previous authorization from its members and had to accept the lowest bid. All department heads were required to make reports to the council twice a year. Wharves could not be leased without public advertisement and free competition. Streetcar franchises had to be advertised for three months before officially accepted. Unauthorized absenteeism of city councilmen or employees was forbidden, and stringent terms were set down under which tax collecting might be farmed out. Another act defined the crime of extortion in city office. Anyone accepting gratuities for performing their official duties, or hiring or allowing deadheads to remain on the payroll unchallenged was subject to a one thousand dollar fine and up to five years in prison. The crowning reform passed by the legislature was the Police Board act, which placed the local force under a

47 *Daily Picayune,* June 16, 26, 1889; *Mascot,* August 18, September 22, 1888.
48 *Daily Picayune,* June 16, 1889.
49 *Mascot,* July 5, 1890.

board, required all patrolmen to pass certain tests, and forbade them to take part in politics.[50] The creation of the Police Board split the reformers into two hostile camps, one faction backing the board and the other, the mayor.[51] Shakspeare was violently opposed to the Police Board act since it took away his sole authority to appoint officers and gave this prerogative to the board. After the passage of the act early in his term the mayor branded it unconstitutional, and the council, sharing his view, refused to put it into operation by appointing the six police commissioners. Ignoring the demands of the board's advocates, the mayor proceeded to reorganize the police himself and chose as his chief, David C. Hennessy, one of the most brilliant and dedicated law-enforcement officers the city had ever known.

Adherents of the board act, however, were not to be ignored. The state attorney general, Walter Rogers, appealed to the Civil Courts to compel the municipal officials to enforce the provisions of the bill. This request was denied. But in an appeal to a higher court, the act was declared constitutional, and the city authorities were directed to abide by its terms. This ruling came in February, 1889, almost a year after the Police Board act had been passed. The council, therefore, appointed the board's six commissioners. Two were to serve for four years, two for eight years, and two for twelve years. When their terms expired, all other appointees would serve twelve-year terms. The mayor was an ex officio member of the board, which held its first meeting in his parlor on March 9, 1889.

In their reorganization of the police according to the terms of the Police Board act, the commissioners were as circumspect as possible. All officers had to undergo physical examinations and civil service tests. Only those who failed to pass were removed. In trying cases of police discipline the board was strict, but impartial.

50 Flynn, *Flynn's Digest,* 61–64, 569–70, 638–44.

51 References for the following discussion of the Police Board struggle may be found in *History of the New Orleans Police Department, Benefit of the Police Mutual Benevolent Association of New Orleans* (New Orleans, 1900) , 37–49; Rightor, *Standard History of New Orleans,* 116–17; Kendall, *History of New Orleans,* I, 476; *Daily Picayune,* scattered references in July, 1888; February 13, 20, March 10, 1889; June 10, 12, 19, July 3, 6, 7, 8, 15, August 5, 12, 1890; January 6, 8, 1891.

As a result it held over most of Shakspeare's appointees, who had been conscientiously selected in the first place.

For a year relations between the commissioners and the mayor seemed amiable. Shakspeare was astute at handling himself in the midst of a united opposition. But by the spring of 1890, when the legislature met, the politeness on both sides had worn thin. Two rival bills were introduced into the legislature—one to increase the mayor's power over the police and decrease that of the board, and the other to increase the board's authority. Under the tension of this situation, relations between the mayor and the police commissioners were dramatically severed. The commissioners called a meeting to discuss the bills. In retaliation the mayor, who felt he alone could call meetings, highhandedly removed four of the six commissioners from office on July 7 for holding this meeting and for approving its minutes at the next session.

Since the board was now without a quorum, Governor Francis T. Nicholls appointed four new commissioners. The ousted board members carried their fight against the mayor into court. Meanwhile, the two bills which had caused the crisis were both defeated. This was the tangled state of affairs in October, 1890, when Police Chief Hennessy was assassinated.[52] Uncertain of their jurisdiction, the rump Police Board refrained from appointing a new permanent chief. Instead they made the ranking captain, John Journes, temporary head of the force until their legal status could be settled in court.[53] The last act of the petty, vainglorious drama involving the mayor and the Police Board came on January 5, 1891, when the state supreme court restored the four original commissioners to office.[54]

The Police Board, and indirectly the principle of civil service, had triumphed over the mayor. All that came of this lengthy struggle for power was the discrediting of the Shakspeare regime, which appeared anxious to shun reform and embrace the practices of for-

[52] See Chapter 9 of this volume for an account of Hennessy's murder and of the lynching of the Italian immigrants accused of his murder.

[53] When the Police Board case was finally settled, a permanent successor to the slain chief was chosen by the reinstated board. The new superintendent of police elected unanimously on January 21, 1891, was Detective Dexter S. Gaster. *History of the New Orleans Police Department,* 49.

[54] *History of the New Orleans Police Department,* 49.

mer Ring administrations in its attitude toward the police. The fact that the mayor seriously believed himself a better guardian of police efficiency and morals than a board, did not impress many prominent businessmen. Boards of civil service were coming into vogue at both the national and state levels, and Shakspeare was struggling against a rising tide of public opinion in favor of such boards. This controversy, which seriously weakened the city's law enforcement during the critical time following Hennessy's murder, was the major blot on the reform regime's record and probably one of its main sources of defeat at the polls in the next election.

Shakspeare's objection to the Police Board was in sharp contrast to his wholehearted support of the Orleans Levee Board, created by the legislature in 1890 to handle local drainage and levees, and his vigorous campaign to create a paid fire department under the supervision of a board.[55]

In the first instance, the city had never received adequate aid from the state and did not have funds sufficient to keep the levees and drainage system in good condition. Since the Levee Board was invested with the power to tax, something the municipality could not do without holding a property owners' election, the nagging problem of drainage seemed closer to solution. Shakspeare was happy to have this responsibility partially shifted from his administration.

His reasons for refusing to renew the contract of the volunteer fire service, the Fireman's Charitable Association, were compounded of a civic desire to catch up with the progressive methods of other American cities, most of which had paid municipal fire departments, and a reforming zeal to take the firemen out of politics. The Fireman's Charitable Association had been quite a political power in past elections, forming a "ring" of its own. Former Governor Louis A. Wiltz, had been an active member of this association and was its vice-president at the time of his death in 1881, the first year of his term as governor.[56] Many other local politicians

<hr />

55 Further details on the Orleans Levee Board are in Chapter 6 of this study.
56 Thomas O'Connor (ed.), *History of the Fire Department of New Orleans: From the Earliest Days to the Present Time, Including the Original Volunteer Department, the Fireman's Charitable Association, and the Paid Department Down to 1895* (New Orleans, 1895), 253–54.

belonged to the nineteen volunteer companies which made up the association by 1891 and were vigorously supported in politics by their fellow firemen.

The wish to convert the firemen from members of a volunteer service to employees of a full-time municipal department had been expressed in Shakspeare's first administration. Administrators Fagan and Delamore had offered ordinances proposing such a change in 1881. But the city was not financially prepared at that time to meet the cost of such a changeover, and Mayor Shakspeare had vetoed the Delamore ordinance after its passage.[57]

The organization and contractual agreements between the city and the Fireman's Charitable Association dated back to 1855. In that year the volunteer fire companies were reorganized with a chief engineer created to coordinate their efforts. A contract with the city was agreed upon in which the companies of the association would fight fires in return for a yearly lump fee. The contract was to be renewed every five years. In 1858 the contract had set a fee of $70,182.[58] By 1887 it was $253,699.[59] But the firemen frequently had difficulty in getting their money on time and in full during the hard times of the late 1870's and early 1880's. Following the terrible yellow fever epidemic of 1878, the Fireman's Charitable Association had to accept only partial payment for the years 1878–79. They also attempted to meet this crisis by sponsoring a nationwide drive for relief funds which brought in $16,650.54 from over two hundred organizations all over the country. To guard against a return of the pestilence in 1879, the newly formed Auxiliary Sanitary Association enlisted the aid of firemen in using their hose equipment to flush out gutters and do general cleanup work around the city.[60]

57 Delamore revised his ordinance to create a paid department which would be under private contract. This passed the council on September 8, 1881, but the only bidder for the contract was the Fireman's Charitable Association. Thus nothing was really accomplished. *Daily Picayune,* July 31, August 3, September 7, 9, 22, October 11, 1881. See also O'Connor, *History of the Fire Department of New Orleans,* 257–58.

58 *Biennial Report of the State Superintendent of Public Education, 1886–87, To the General Assembly* (Baton Rouge, 1888) , 238; Rightor, *Standard History of New Orleans,* 122.

59 *Biennial Report of the State Superintendent of Public Education, 1886–1887,* p. 238.

60 O'Connor, *History of the Fire Department of New Orleans,* 248, 251.

The time element so vital in firefighting was profoundly affected when the Gamewell fire-alarm telegraph system was introduced into the Crescent City in 1860.[61] Only thirty seconds were needed for the alarm to get from the fire alarm box to the engine houses. Fire bells would then be tolled to alert the firemen. Any fire company within a city district could answer the call. Extremely large fires might call for a city-wide general alarm. The first company to arrive and connect its hose to the nearest hydrant received extra compensation from the association. Stories are told of firemen who arrived at a fire before the rest of their company and put a barrel over the hydrant so that other fire companies would not find it before their own engine appeared on the scene.[62] This sort of unprincipled behavior was rare. But unfortunately it stood out in the columns of the newspapers, while the many volunteers burned, injured, or killed fighting fires far outnumbered the truants in their midst.

The two most persistent difficulties New Orleans firemen encountered in the 1880's were impassable streets which caused engines to overturn or bog down and men and horses to be injured or killed, and a deplorable lack of water pressure which the independently operated Water Works Company refused to remedy. Also frustrating was the city's lack of enforcement of fire ordinances. While some reformers in City Hall might fume about firemen in politics, dedicated firefighters such as the chief engineer of the association, Thomas O'Connor, were exasperated over City Hall's lack of concern that wooden buildings were being constructed in the business district of the metropolis in violation of the city building code.[63] Chief O'Connor further complained to the mayor and city council in his annual report for 1883 that many factories and commercial houses in the heart of the city had no fire escapes.[64] The use of iron shutters on many buildings as a precaution against robbery proved one of the greatest problems firemen had to cope with. Since these shutters could be opened only from the inside, they acted as effective deterents to firemen trying to

[61] Rightor, *Standard History of New Orleans*, 124.
[62] Lura Robinson, *It's An Old New Orleans Custom* (New York, 1948), 311.
[63] *Daily Picayune*, May 31, 1883.
[64] *Annual Reports of the Officers and Committees of Fireman's Charitable Association for the year 1883* (New Orleans, 1884), 32.

reach a blaze inside of a building. They did not yield to axes, crowbars, or hammers. Usually when a building protected by such shutters caught fire, the frustrated firefighters would have to wait for the roof to cave in before they could reach the interior with sprays of water from the roofs of adjoining buildings.[65]

Although the camaraderie of the volunteer fire companies was eyed with suspicion by Mayor Shakspeare, to the men who belonged to a particular fire company it offered an important social outlet. The Orleans Steam Fire Engine Company, No. 21 may be used to illustrate this point. The minute book of this company between 1881 and 1892 reveals that in 1881 the company had a total membership of ninety-eight. Its president was a man well known in Ring politics, Victor Mauberret. The ill-fated Judge Thomas Ford was also a member.[66] A graphic picture of its assets is given in this itemized list: $316.60 in cash; $677.25 in relief funds; ten city certificates valued at $800; one silver fire cap worth $300; one lot of ground valued at $300; one gold medal worth $25; three excellent horses, $700; one roll case, $150; furniture in the engine house valued at $500; stock in the Fireman's Insurance Company (a local group started by the Fireman's Charitable Association), valued at $500; one steam engine, $4,500; one good hose carriage, $500, and five hundred feet of hose; and one vault in St. Louis Cemetery, value not specified.[67]

Company No. 21 imposed its own discipline upon members. Any man not reporting to a fire, being out of uniform at a fire, or leaving a fire before it was extinguished had to answer to the membership's grievance committee. A doctor's note had to accompany any explanation of illness as an excuse for missing a fire. Once a year a gold medal was presented to the man who had reported for the most night fires. A leather medal was handed out to the member who had the poorest record of firefighting.[68] If a man resigned

65 O'Connor, *History of the Fire Department of New Orleans*, 260, 263–65; *Times-Democrat*, August 1, 1882; *Daily States*, March 30, 1883.

66 Minute Book, Orleans Steam Fire Engine Company, No. 21, From 1881 to 1892 (MS in Special Collections Division, Howard-Tilton Memorial Library, Tulane University), 2–3.

67 *Ibid.*, 3.

68 *Ibid.*, 5, 6, 9.

from the company, he usually asked for a letter of recommendation stating that he was in good standing at the time of his resignation.[69] Like its counterparts, Company No. 21 paid for medicine its members needed, took up subscriptions for widows and orphans of firemen killed in the line of duty, and had a standing "wake committee" whose job was to attend the wakes and funerals of firemen.[70]

Intense rivalry existed over the elected offices in a volunteer fire company. Sometimes as many as four ballots had to be taken before a post was won.[71] One unsuccessful candidate for the post of housekeeper of Company No. 18 deliberately set off a false fire alarm to discredit his rival who had won the post and whose job it was to rouse the company to answer the alarm. To make certain that No. 18 would not reach the scene first and be eligible for extra compensation, the plotter tipped off another housekeeper in Company No. 20. When the scheme was finally uncovered by detectives Dave and Mike Hennessy, the conspirators were arrested and also ousted by their respective fire companies.[72]

Once a year on March 4 the Fireman's Charitable Association sponsored a fireman's parade. The engines and equipment were polished and decorated with floral garlands and hand-embroidered banners. The horses sported such finery as gilded hooves, white satin harnesses, and saddles with silver bells. On the day of the parade members of a fire company were invited by various well-wishers to call at their homes and receive a floral wreath and a toast in champagne punch. Every company had a "godmother" upon whom they called on Fireman's Day. Company No. 21 had chosen their captain's daughter, Elise Philips, as their godmother and named the company fire engine for this young lady.[73]

By the mid-1880's as solvency began to return to the city government, there were signs that the heyday of the volunteer fire companies was coming to an end in New Orleans. In 1886 the city council created a Board of Control which was to have jurisdiction

69 *Ibid.*, 238, 239, 242, 243.
70 *Ibid.*, 9, 11, 354.
71 *Ibid.*, 293–96.
72 *Daily Picayune*, April 12, 1881.
73 Minute Book, Orleans Steam Fire Engine Company, No. 21, 13–16.

over the contract with the Fireman's Charitable Association. In 1889 the volunteer fire company in the city's Sixth District was converted into a paid city department. This fire company was independent from the Fireman's Charitable Association and its contract expired earlier than that of the larger organization.[74]

Financial conditions in the city government were more stable than they had been since the Civil War. The cost of buying the equipment of the various volunteer fire companies and of paying salaries to a full-time smaller fire department was at least feasible. Much discussion and argument over the possibility of a paid fire department filled the newspapers and the conversation of citizens in 1891, the year of the transition. The expiring contract of the Fireman's Charitable Association was not renewed by the city council. Since the reformer faction controlled the mayor's office and the council, the Ring adherents in the volunteer fire companies were unsuccessful in their efforts to resist a paid fire department. On December 15, 1891, the final transfer took place. The long-time president of the Fireman's Charitable Association, Isaac Marks, met Shakspeare in the mayor's parlor at noon on that day and concluded the transfer.[75] The city council appropriated $247,-000 to meet the expenses of setting up the new fire department. A Board of Fire Commissioners was created first by city ordinance and several years later through an act of the state legislature.[76] It consisted of nine members, plus the mayor and the commissioner of police and public buildings, and had control over the procedure and personnel of the fire department.[77] The mayor appointed the members of this board.

74 There were actually four separate volunteer fire departments prior to 1889. The First through the Fourth District made up the major department, the Fireman's Charitable Association; the Fifth, Sixth, and Seventh Districts each had their own volunteer companies. Since the last three districts were the newer, least populated areas of the city, their fire companies were fewer and less influential than those of the powerful Fireman's Charitable Association in the heart of town. By 1900 all of the four departments were under city control and integrated into one system. Rightor, *Standard History of New Orleans*, 102–103, 123.

75 *Daily Picayune*, December 15, 16, 1891.

76 T. W. Campbell (comp.), *Manual of the City of New Orleans* (New Orleans, 1901), 36; O'Connor, *History of the Fire Department of New Orleans*, 419–20, 432, 435; Rightor, *Standard History of New Orleans*, 107.

77 Rightor, *Standard History of New Orleans*, 107.

Thomas O'Connor was retained as the fire chief of the new city department, and the city was redistricted for fire purposes with some changes in the location of fire houses and personnel.[78] By 1900 the paid fire department consisted of 255 firemen. Its equipment included 27 steam engines, 12 chemical engines, 7 hook-and-ladder trucks, 144 horses, and 1 water tower.[79] One indication that the public was satisfied with the changeover was the concerted effort of the commercial exchanges, prominent businessmen, and fire insurance underwriters to improve and enlarge firefighting facilities during the last decade of the century.[80]

Although creating the city fire department might be considered Shakspeare's most memorable achievement in his second term as mayor, certainly his administration's accomplishments in the realm of finance were considerable. Taking over the city in a chaotic financial condition, his administration straightened out the budget and balanced it by 1890.[81] In that year, the Shakspeare regime also worked out a new debt settlement to replace the 1882 6 percent bonds when these became eligible for refunding in 1895. Their plan, which was incorporated into an act and passed by the legislature, provided for the refunding of the local bonded debt, other than premium bonds, into an issue of constitutional 4 percent bonds. A 1 percent tax was levied upon all property in New Orleans to back up the bondholders' principal and interest. Of the surplus tax money which remained after the bonds were provided for, one half was to go to public improvements and the other, to the School Board.[82]

This entire debt act became an amendment to the constitution when it was approved by the voters in 1892. Shortly afterward, the first bonds were issued, and in 1895, when the 1882 6 percents became eligible for refunding, practically all of the city debt was turned into 4 percents, totaling $10,000,000. From 1895 on, the city's credit rose rapidly, and its finances assumed a steady, solvent pattern.[83] If Shakspeare had done nothing else as mayor but offer

78 O'Connor, *History of the Fire Department of New Orleans*, 420.

79 Rightor, *Standard History of New Orleans*, 124.

80 O'Connor, *History of the Fire Department of New Orleans*, 436.

81 Kendall, *History of New Orleans*, I, 473.

82 Hecht, *Municipal Finances*, 11–13; *Progressive New Orleans* (New Orleans, 1894), 14–15; Flynn, *Flynn's Digest*, 227–29.

83 Hecht, *Municipal Finances*, 13.

the leadership for the 1882 and 1890 settlements, he would have more than repaid the voters for their trust in him. No other municipal accomplishment in the last half of the century was as important to the Crescent City's future as these two acts.

As both the executive and legislative branches of the city government were controlled by men who had been elected on the reform ticket, it was assumed at the outset of their terms that harmony and strict adherence to reform principles would exist in City Hall. But by the end of Shakspeare's administration, he found himself in the same position he had occupied in the early 1880's —facing a group of legislators who consistently tried to push through scandalous special privilege bills and franchises over his vetoes. The reformers had pictured Fitzpatrick as a local "Boss Tweed" and had eliminated him for the time being from power. But after castigating the "city boss" as an evil figure who should be suppressed, the reformers found themselves facing a far more sinister and powerful influence—the ruthless financier who controlled numerous utility and construction companies and seemed to hold the city council in the palm of his hand.

The businessman most cited in this role was Maurice Hart, who had come to New Orleans as an obscure stranger some years earlier and swiftly had achieved economic prominence. By the late 1880's he controlled a local electric light company, the smallpox hospital, a paving firm, an excavating business, and a handsome share of the city's streetcar lines, plus numerous other smaller investments.[84] His shadowy, but nonetheless real, control of the council did not come to an end when the reformers took over the government in 1888. If anything, it grew more bold and demanding. His rosetta gravel, which was more like red clay than gravel, was chosen by the council to surface street after street against the wishes of irate property owners. He also received the council's consent to set up high towers topped by clusters of electric lights, which were supposed to illuminate larger areas than standard street lights. These towers proved to be ridiculous failures.[85]

In late September, 1889, when the Burke scandal broke, Hart

84 *Mascot,* April 6, 1889; December 5, 1891.
85 See Chapter 6 of this volume.

was cited jointly in the indictment against Burke for fraudulently manipulating state bonds. Although the financier claimed he was the innocent victim of the former state treasurer, $55,000 of his property was sequestered as a result of his trial.[86] Hart evaded a prison term and seemed by 1891 to be more powerful than ever. By the end of the Shakspeare regime, a sizeable number of reform councilmen were discredited by their compliance with Hart's wishes. The mayor, however, did not truckle to the wily financier, preferring instead to fight a losing battle against his schemes in the council.

By the time a new administration was chosen in April, 1892, a host of grievances handicapped the reformers' chances to keep control of the government and reelect Shakspeare. For one thing the reform ranks had thinned out. Many former enthusiasts resented Shakspeare's stand on the Police Board, which had divided the force between two masters and demoralized it. The 1891 lynching of the Italians accused of Hennessy's murder was an indication to the more responsible citizens of New Orleans that the police department was as ineffective as ever in keeping order under extraordinary circumstances. Naturally, the conduct of the council toward Hart alienated many voters from the reform ticket. In addition, others resented the favor which the mayor had shown to Negroes. The Negro vote had been a vital factor in his 1888 victory, and Shakspeare, mindful of his obligation to them, promised a delegation of Negro businessmen and labor leaders that they would get their share of patronage.[87]

One proof that he kept his word was his appointment of fourteen Negroes to the police force to serve in colored neighborhoods.[88] The *Mascot*, loyal to white supremacy and to the Democratic-Conservative Ring, took the mayor to task on another occasion for showing partiality to "low negro dance halls" while forcing white barrooms to close at midnight.[89] It also criticized him for recommending two local Negroes to President Benjamin

86 *Daily Picayune*, September 27, 28, 1889; Januanry 25, 1890; *Mascot*, September 21, 28, December 21, 1889; January 25, 1890; December 5, 1891.

87 *Daily Picayune*, April 28, 1888; *Mascot*, July 21, 1888.

88 *Daily Picayune*, May 26, June 16, 1888.

89 *Mascot*, October 13, 1888.

Harrison for important federal positions.[90] Conscious of these attempts by Shakspeare to curry Negro favor, the *Mascot* reported with great glee of an official snub of City Hall by the mayor of New York City on a local visit. Instead of visiting Shakspeare the Gotham chief executive went to a Negro dance hall on South Franklin Street, where the colored stevedores congregated, and watched the patrons perform a local honky-tonk dance called "Hog Face." [91]

Shakspeare's crushing of the Fireman's Charitable Association had naturally lost him the votes of many of its members and their cohorts. Also, while he was viewed with suspicion by many laborers, his Ring opponent in the 1892 election, John Fitzpatrick, was the greatest champion of labor rights in the city.[92] No one could have wrested their votes away from him.

The most crucial issue, however, on which the election was decided more than any other was the fight to crush the Louisiana Lottery Company which came to a climax in 1892. This struggle dominated the municipal election of 1892 just as it did the governor's race that year. In the brief, bitter campaign that preceded the municipal election on April 19, 1892, the personalities of both Shakspeare and his opponent Fitzpatrick—probably the two most well-known men in the city—were usually forgotten or ignored by political orators and newspaper editors. The questions of the day were simple. Is the lottery an evil? Should it be destroyed? Can the state and city survive without its revenue? It seems a paradox that Shakspeare, the man who had devised a plan for regulating gambling since he felt it could not be stopped, sided with the antilottery faction. Fitzpatrick, who had grave misgivings about the sinister influence of the Louisiana Lottery, was forced to espouse the prolottery cause since the municipal Ring was aligned with the state McEnery faction which backed the lottery. Thrown into such an awkward situation, both men must have found the spring campaign of 1892 one of the most painful experiences of their lives.

90 *Ibid.*, March 30, 1889.

91 *Mascot*, February 14, 1891.

92 Fitzpatrick's bias toward labor during the strike of 1892 and 1894 is discussed in Chapter 8.

5

THE LOTTERY CONTROVERSY
AND ITS AFTERMATH

IN THE FALL of 1891 Shakspeare was serving his last year in the mayor's office and the struggle over the rechartering of the Louisiana State Lottery Company was causing more than ordinary interest in the election of delegates to the Democratic State Nominating Convention for governor to be held in Baton Rouge that December. At that point in time *Century Magazine* writer Clarence C. Buel visited New Orleans to do a feature article on the lottery.

"When the traveler turns his face toward New Orleans," he later wrote, "a still voice asks if Fortune has ever done anything for him. If not, why not? And may not Fortune have been waiting for this very visit to the capital of lottery gambling? Visiting actors forget their cues in devising lucky numbers; conventions of bankers compliment the local bankers, many of whom favor the lottery, by making a losing investment; boards of serious business directors, when they meet, often contribute to a common fund for lottery tickets." [1]

The humbler natives of New Orleans were just as avid lottery players as were visitors or business tycoons. Visitors might purchase one-dollar fractional tickets for the monthly drawings at a cigar store near their hotel. Servants, bootblacks, draymen, hackmen, and children crowded the neighborhood policy shops to buy twenty-five-cent fractional tickets in the daily drawings. There

---

[1] Clarence C. Buel, "The Degradation of a State: or, the Charitable Career of the Louisiana Lottery," *Century Illustrated Monthly*, XLIII (1892), 619.

were 108 policy shops or branch offices of the lottery company in the city. These usually were leased out to state legislators or minor city politicians and offered employment for their poor relations and constituents. In addition, innumerable lottery tickets were sold by individual agents, at cigar stands, in barbershops, or in other small places of business.[2]

Confirmed lottery addicts, Buel discovered, were liable to use any method at hand to increase their chances of winning. In citing examples, he noted that "inveterate players stop children in the streets and ask their ages; they consult voodoo doctors; if they see a stray dog, they play 6; a drunken man counts 14; and a dead woman 59, an exposed leg plays the mystic number 11; and to dream of a fish is a reminder to play 13."[3]

In walking through the main sections of town, Buel found reminders of the lottery everywhere. The headquarters of the Louisiana State Lottery Company at St. Charles and Union streets, with its courtyard in which an alligator sunned himself in a shallow pool, appeared sinister to him, and the alligator seemed a fitting symbol of the predatory nature of the lottery. In every direction he walked from his hotel, his attention was attracted by "neatly printed slips of paper hung on strips in the windows of shops." These were fractional lottery tickets, a dollar apiece. Twenty of them equalled a monthly lottery ticket. Every month 100,000 whole tickets (or 2,000,000 fractional ones) amounting to $2,000,-000 were offered for sale in New Orleans and other major cities in the United States. The monthly drawing would feature $1,054,600 in 3,134 prizes ranging from $100 to $300,000.[4]

In addition to ten monthly drawings with a major prize of $300,000 each, there were two semiannual drawings each featuring a $600,000 grand prize for a $40 whole ticket (sometimes divided into $1 fractional tickets). The semiannual drawings brought into the Louisiana Lottery coffers money from foreign countries as well

---

2 *Ibid.*, 619, 620, 627; Berthold C. Alwes, "The History of the Louisiana State Lottery Company," *Louisiana Historical Quarterly*, XXVII (October, 1944), 1022–1024; John C. Wickliffe, "The Louisiana Lottery: A History of the Company," *Forum* (January, 1892), 570.

3 Buel, "The Degradation of a State," 620.

4 *Ibid.*, 619.

as the United States. The daily drawing for which twenty-five-cent fractional tickets were sold offered $4,275.40 as its highest prize. Players might purchase tickets with three printed numbers or buy a "policy" ticket on which they indicated what three numbers they wished to play. Drawings were at 4 P.M. with from seventy-five to seventy-eight numbers put into the wheel and eleven to fourteen drawn out and written on a blackboard at the lottery headquarters in the sequence of their drawing. If three of the numbers drawn corresponded to the numbers on one's ticket, a prize of about $4.36 was awarded the lucky ticket holder. For twenty-five cents extra, a player could put "gig and saddle" on his ticket. This paid him a prize of $2.45 if two out of three of his numbers were drawn. The mathematical chances of winning as much as $4.25 were estimated at 1 in 1,237. The chance of winning the grand prize of $4,275.40 for $1 was 1 in 67,525.[5]

Monthly drawings, which were presided over by Confederate luminaries General P. G. T. Beauregard and General Jubal A. Early, attracted more attention than the daily drawings and were held in a theatrical setting. Two descriptions by reporters who attended such drawings in 1890 and 1891 vividly recreate the events. "Women venders of tickets were making their last calls at offices," *Century* reporter Buel wrote of the morning of the drawing, "and street brokers were thronging hotel lobbies and barrooms. As eleven o'clock approached, dealers rushed with their unsold tickets to the main office, preferring their fifteen percent commission on the tickets they had sold to the chance of winning a great sum by becoming responsible for the unsold tickets. Opposite, in a theater, the drawing promptly began." [6] Buel, in glancing around the theater at the crowd in attendance for the drawing, found some of the balconies occupied by ladies who took a "homelike interest" in the proceedings, but the "sparse company of men, in the body of the theater, were redolent of rum and tobacco and poor bathing facilities, and had no taste or money for clean raiment." They reminded Buel of Cable's 'Sieur George "who was respected for a

[5] *Ibid.;* Alwes, "The History of the Louisiana State Lottery Company," 985–86, 1021–1024; Garnie W. McGinty, "The Louisiana Lottery Company," *Southwestern Social Science Quarterly,* XX (March, 1940) , 341.

[6] Buel, "The Degradation of a State," 619–20.

supposed trunk full of money, that proved to be a trunk full of unlucky lottery tickets." [7]

Another visitor, Dr. William Shaw Bowen, penned an almost photographic impression of what he saw upon the stage. "The superfluous scenery was cleared away so as to expose the entire stage area. A parlor set in black and gold was spread. The floor was . . . very suitably covered with a plain green cloth like the table of a faro game." [8] On one side of the stage was a large mahogany and glass drum, about six feet long with a hand crank attached on each side. It was filled with several sacks of black and white rubber cylinders containing slips of paper with the numbers of lottery tickets. On the other side of the stage was a smaller wheel into which were placed similar cylinders containing slips indicating the amounts of money that might be won. Several chairs for the commissioners stood on the stage to the rear of the wheels. General Early, who presided over the biggest wheel, was of large stature, but bent over by age. Dressed in Confederate gray, he seemed to take an eager proprietary interest in the proceedings and never left his place during the long, tedious hours of the drawing. General Beauregard, dressed in a dark suit, was found by both observers to be dignified, of handsome military bearing, and seemed more detached and less intimidated than Early by his surroundings. Occasionally during the drawing, he relinquished his post to an assistant. When Beauregard first seated himself behind the small wheel, waiting for the game to begin, he "complacently pulled his immaculate linen wristbands down over his hands"—a gesture of preciseness and perhaps aloofness, which contrasted sharply to the slovenly appearance of the men in the audience.[9]

The procedure followed was simple: two blindfolded boys (usually orphans) in knickerbockers pulled numbers out of the wheels, one from the large wheel, the other from the small one. General Early took the cylinder from the large wheel and read the number it contained. An assistant with his hat "cocked rakishly on one side" repeated the number in a loud voice. Then Beauregard

[7] *Ibid.*, 620.
[8] Alwes, "The History of the Louisiana State Lottery Company," 1016.
[9] *Ibid.*, 1016–20; Buel, "The Degradation of a State," 620.

opened the cylinder from the small wheel handed him by one of the boys and announced the amount of money to be won. His assistant repeated this number in tones loud enough to be heard outside in front of the theater. At the rear of the stage a clerk sat at a table recording the winning numbers and the amounts they won. After every ten to twenty numbers drawn, time was called while the wheels were revolved. The drawing went on in this fashion for several hours.[10]

Since the lottery itself held all tickets unsold, it could and did win prizes in its own drawings. In one of the monthly drawings, only about $90,000 of the $300,000 grand prize ever left the company. It held tickets for the other $210,000. The highest amount the lottery would pay out of every $100 it took in was about $52. European lotteries paid out 21 to 33 percent more of their proceeds than the Louisiana Lottery.[11] The *Democrat* had produced similar statistics in 1878 when it was still an antilottery paper. Foreign lotteries, it found, were keeping 15 percent of the money they collected. But the Louisiana Lottery was keeping over 47 percent of its receipts.[12]

Despite the obvious wealth and political power which it commanded, the Louisiana State Lottery by 1891 was fighting for its life. In April, 1892, the renewal of its charter was to be voted upon as a constitutional amendment in the same general election which decided the governor's race and the mayoral contest in New Orleans. All over the state, Louisianians were split into two fanatically hostile camps of prolottery and antilottery followers. In probing into the history of this controversial enterprise, writers such as Buel and Bowen found that the lottery had a stormy history in which bribery, broken faith among gamblers, incessant court suits, and political corruption were outstanding.

The Louisiana State Lottery, like so many of New Orleans' problems in the last two decades of the nineteenth century, was a child of Reconstruction. The all-white legislature of 1866, however, had prepared the way for its incorporation by passing Act No. 21

10 Alwes, "The History of the Louisiana State Lottery Company," 1017–20; Tinker, *Creole City*, 294–96.
11 Buel, "The Degradation of a State," 619, 621.
12 Alwes, "The History of the Louisiana State Lottery Company," 986.

of 1866 which permitted licensed lottery vending and assigned
$50,000 from the license fees for the Charity Hospital in New Or-
leans. This act brought in an average $36,000 in 1866 and 1867
and $28,000 in 1868. By 1868 when carpetbaggers and Negroes
gained admittance to the legislature, the poverty of the state and
the susceptibility of many legislators to bribes, allowed a remarkable individual, Charles T. Howard, to push through the act
chartering the Louisiana State Lottery Company. The company,
whose charter was to run for twenty-five years in return for a
$40,000 annual fee, was granted a monopoly on the lottery business
in the state. It was exempt from all taxes or licenses, and its capital
stock was to be $1,000,000 with ten thousand shares valued at $100
each. The lottery was authorized to begin operations when a tenth
of its stock was subscribed.[13]

At least three different versions of how and from whom Howard
secured the $100,000, which would amount to the subscription of
one-tenth of the stock, were recounted (several times in affidavits)
in the 1870's and 1880's.[14] Such testimony figured in a number of
court suits instituted by parties who claimed to have a legal right
to share in the profits of the lottery. Two facts stand out in regard
to the lottery's creation: (1) Charles T. Howard originated the idea
of a monopolistic Louisiana lottery and was the prime mover in
pushing the lottery franchise through the legislature, and (2)
John A. Morris, a wealthy resident of Westchester County, New
York, and the dominant stock holder in the C. H. Murray Lottery
Company of New York, was the major financial angel behind the
scenes.

Charles T. Howard lobbied assiduously in the 1868 legislature
for the lottery bill which became Act No. 25, and his name was
among the seven "dummy" incorporators listed in the final act.
These seven, however, were replaced nine days after the bill's

13 *Ibid.*, 969–71, 973–75; McGinty, "The Louisiana Lottery Company," 330–
31; Wickliffe, "The Louisiana Lottery: A History of the Company," 569; *Acts
Passed by the General Assembly of the State of Louisiana, at the First Session of
the First Legislature, Begun and Held in the City of New Orleans, June 29, 1868*
(New Orleans, 1868), Act No. 25, pp. 24–26.
14 Alwes, "The History of the Louisiana State Lottery Company," 976; Buel,
"The Degradation of a State," 622–25.

passage by the name of Zachariah E. Simmons, Charles H. Murray, and John A. Morris, all of whom were out-of-state men involved in lottery, gambling, and horse racing enterprises in New York.[15] Simmons, who seems to have served often as a straw man in the business manipulations of the affluent Morris, was eliminated from the Louisiana company shortly afterward. His stock was acquired by Howard, who as an agent for the Murray lottery in New Orleans had alerted that company to the easy terms under which a lottery might be chartered in Louisiana and the mania for gambling in New Orleans which offered a favorable climate for the headquarters of such an undertaking. Howard was named president of the Louisiana State Lottery Company and held that post until his death in 1885.[16]

Born in Baltimore, Maryland, in 1832, Howard had drifted south from Philadelphia to New Orleans in 1852 and found employment in the steamboat business. When an opportunity arose to be named the local agent of the Alabama State Lottery Company, his restless ambition jumped at this chance to become an executive. During the Civil War, according to the biographical sketch in *Jewell's Crescent City Illustrated* in 1874, he served the Confederacy in three different roles: in the fledging Confederate Navy, then as orderly sergeant in the Crescent Regiment from which he was discharged on account of illness, and last as a cavalryman. Years later, after he had become the lottery king of New Orleans, some of his enemies doubted the veracity of his war record, and two members of the Society of the Army of Tennessee resigned when he was elected to that group. At the war's end Howard secured the post of New Orleans manager of the Kentucky State Lottery and also formed a connection with the C. H. Murray Lottery Company of New York.[17]

[15] Buel, "The Degradation of a State," 623; Alwes, "The History of the Louisiana State Lottery Company," 975–76; T. Harry Williams, *P. G. T. Beauregard: Napoleon in Gray* (Baton Rouge, 1955) , 292; McGinty, "The Louisiana Lottery Company," 331–32.

[16] Buel, "The Degradation of a State," 622–23; Williams, *P. G. T. Beauregard*, 291–92.

[17] Jewell, *Jewell's Crescent City Illustrated*, 113–14; Buel, "The Degradation of a State," 622; *National Cyclopaedia of American Biography* (New York, 1907), IX, 173–74.

In disposition, Howard was dynamic to the point of ruthlessness, but could be charming and generous to those he favored, and was always liberal to charitable causes. General Beauregard recalled after Howard's death that he was rough but goodhearted.[18] Buel found from interviewing persons who had known Howard that "those who knew him well say he was fitted to be the hero of such a great epic as Milton's 'Paradise Lost.' He aimed at success, not glory." [19] *Jewell's Crescent City Illustrated* verified this last statement. It had noted in 1874 that Howard's residence in New Orleans was "pleasantly situated in the most delightful portion of the city and is surrounded by all the elegance, luxury and comfort wealth can afford." [20]

In 1854 Howard had married Floristelle Boulemet, a native New Orleanian whose family was descended from a French officer who served under Napoleon and migrated to the New World after Waterloo. They had four children. Howard fancied himself a sportsman and helped to found the Fair Grounds Racing Track and became a guiding force in the Louisiana Jockey Club. The most famous story told about Howard was that upon being rejected for membership in the Metairie Racing Club, he vowed to turn their famous track into a cemetery—which he did. In addition to racing, Howard engaged in yachting and as owner of the yachts *Protos* and *Xiphias* took part in the activities of the Crescent City Yacht Club and in national races. Howard's leisure activities even included membership in the Louisiana Hose Company of the Fireman's Charitable Association. In recognition of his membership, the company named its engine Annie Howard, after his daughter. Howard's administration of the lottery came to an end in 1885 with his death following a fall from a horse at his summer home in Dobbs Ferry, New York.[21]

Between 1885 and 1893 two other men served as lottery president, first Maximilien Dauphin and then Paul Conrad. But John A. Morris, who spent his winters in the Crescent City and mingled socially with the city's elite without calling attention to his con-

18 Williams, *P. G. T. Beauregard,* 291.
19 Buel, "The Degradation of a State," 626.
20 Jewell, *Jewell's Crescent City Illustrated,* 114.
21 *Ibid.;* Buel, "The Degradation of a State," 626; Alwes, "The History of the Louisiana State Lottery Company," 1013–14.

nections with Howard and the lottery, took a more prominent and open role in the lottery's affairs after Howard's death.[22] Between 1890 and 1892, the most hectic years of the lottery's existence, he became the lottery's chief spokesman. Unwittingly, he also became the *deus ex machina* of its downfall. Through his insistence upon forcing through the 1890 legislature, three years before the lottery company's charter expired, a bill to recharter it, he goaded his opposition into frenzied crusading action.

The course of the Louisiana State Lottery Company's existence was never smooth nor unchallenged. In the 1870's other prospective lotteries had attempted to operate sub rosa in Louisiana. The Louisiana Lottery got special legislation passed in 1874 to prosecute stiffly such intruders in its domain.[23] In 1876, Edward Booth, as a New Orleans representative in the state legislature, had tried unsuccessfully to get a bill passed abolishing the Louisiana Lottery. In 1878 the "Big Boss of the Third Ward," John Fitzpatrick, was serving a term in the legislature and again introduced two bills similar to Booth's aimed at abolishing the Louisiana State Lottery Company. Both bills died without causing a stir. In 1879, during the first term of Governor Nicholls, another attempt was made to break the monopoly of the lottery. Once again a New Orleans representative, Louis Arnauld, introduced House Bill No. 20, eventually Act No. 44, which abolished the Louisiana Lottery. This bill was passed by both houses and after an uneasy delay of two months, Governor Nicholls signed it on March 27, 1879.[24] This action of the governor brought a swift answer from the lot-

---

22 Alwes, "The History of the Louisiana State Lottery Company," 1014; Buel, "The Degradation of a State," 626. John A. Morris, born in 1836 in Jersey City, New Jersey, had ties to Louisiana before the incorporation of the Louisiana Lottery. Son of a wealthy shipping magnate whose avocation was raising and racing thoroughbreds, he graduated "summa cum laude" from Harvard in 1856. In London, England, in 1857, he married Cora Hennen, daughter of Judge Alfred Hennen of Louisiana. His wife later inherited a vast estate in Tangipahoa Parish which Morris stocked with game as a hunting resort for his family and friends. The Morrises had two sons and a daughter. Like his father, Morris loved horse racing and maintained three breeding farms for thoroughbreds. In 1889 he constructed Morris Park, the first loop track in the United States, in Westchester County, New York at a cost of $1,250,000. *National Cyclopaedia of American Biography*, XX, 336.

23 Alwes, "The History of the Louisiana State Lottery Company," 980–81.

24 *Ibid.*, 982, 991, 994–97; McGinty, "The Louisiana Lottery Company," 337.

tery whose spokesmen claimed lottery money had been used to persuade the members of the Packard legislature in 1877 to come over to Nicholls's assembly and thus insure it of a quorum and strengthen Nicholls's claim to be the head of the rightful government. They felt this had been a public service and were disappointed at such repayment.[25] When the next quarterly payment of the lottery's fee came due, the state auditor refused to accept it. In New Orleans, John Fitzpatrick had been elected criminal sheriff in 1878 and in this capacity it was now his duty to enforce Act No. 44 and close down the lottery. To prevent such action, the lottery lawyers went into federal district court. As a result of the case of the *Louisiana State Lottery* vs. *John Fitzpatrick* et als., the lottery emerged triumphant when the court decided that Act No. 44 was unconstitutional as a breach of contract.[26]

Throughout the legislative session of 1879 the New Orleans crusading journal, the *Democrat* had thundered denunciations of the lottery and upbraided its fellow papers, the *Picayune* and the *Times,* for not emulating its example. By the beginning of 1879 as the long awaited constitutional convention met in New Orleans to rewrite the carpetbag state constitution of 1868, the lottery moved to silence the *Democrat*. As state printer, the *Democrat* was paid in state scrip. Through the instigation of the Louisiana Lottery, complaints were lodged in the federal courts against the scrip and it was judged unsound, causing its value to drop. The *Democrat,* unable to meet its obligations with devalued state warrants, went bankrupt and its proprietor, Major Hearsey, was forced to sell the paper to E. A. Burke and his associates, one of whom was Charles Howard. Shortly after this transaction, a second federal court decision found the state scrip to be sound after all and it went back up to its former value.[27]

25 Estimates of exactly how much money was used to win over members of the Packard legislature range from a little over $34,000 to $250,000. Alwes, "The History of the Louisiana State Lottery Company," 997–98; Woodward, *Origins of the New South,* 11–12; Dabney, *One Hundred Great Years,* 342–43; *Times,* March 29, 1879; *Daily Picayune,* February 1, 1879.

26 "Biographies of the Mayors of New Orleans, 1803–1936," p. 142; Richard H. Wiggins, "The Louisiana Press and the Lottery," *Louisiana Historical Quarterly,* XXXI (July, 1948) , 763–64.

27 For examples of the *Democrat's* editorial barbs against the *Picayune* and

The next hurdle which the lottery had to overcome in its struggle to protect its charter was the constitutional convention. Fearful of future legislative attempts to rescind its charter, the lottery faction was determined to get its charter written into the new constitution. This maneuver was successful, but the lottery had to compromise. In Article 167 of the 1879 Constitution, the Louisiana State Lottery Company was allowed to continue operating, but was forced to relinquish its monopoly on lottery vending in the state. After January 1, 1895, all lotteries were to be suppressed.[28]

During the 1880's the Louisiana Lottery enjoyed its most prosperous decade. It paid dividends of 110 percent in 1887, 120 percent in 1888, 170 percent in 1889, and 125 percent in 1890.[29] Its influence and patronage were widespread. Among its many business connections, it was known to control the waterworks, Metairie Cemetery, several cotton mills, and the Cafferey sugar mill—which had been the brainchild of Donelson Cafferey who had withdrawn from any connection with its operation when the lottery took over.[30] Some of the leading banks in Louisiana which dominated the reserve capital of the state were lottery allies. The four banks which advertised as sponsors of the lottery were the Louisiana National Bank, the State National Bank, the Union National Bank, and the New Orleans National Bank. Albert Baldwin of the New Orleans National, who was the "leading merchant and banker in New Orleans," was a major stockholder in the lottery.[31] The French Opera House, the rendezvous of the city's

<hr>

Times, see Democrat, September 4, 1878; January 11, 1879. Articles advocating the abolition of the lottery's charter and the holding of a state constitutional convention appear almost daily in the Democrat between January and the end of April, 1879 when it changed hands. On the bankrupting of the Democrat, see Wiggins, "The Louisiana Press and the Lottery," 773–86; Tinker, Creole City, 192–93; Woodward, Origins of the New South, 13.

[28] Alwes, "The History of the Louisiana State Lottery Company," 999–1001; Henry E. Chambers, A History of Louisiana: Wilderness, Colony, Province, Territory, State, People (Chicago and New York, 1925), I, 707.

[29] Alwes, "The History of the Louisiana State Lottery Company," 1014–15; McGinty, "The Louisiana Lottery Company," 339.

[30] Buel, "The Degradation of a State," 627.

[31] Ibid.

society set, was supported by the lottery's money. After the death of Howard, his family provided the Confederate Memorial Hall as a meeting place for the Louisiana Historical Association and a museum for Confederate trophies. Next to it on Camp Street was constructed the Howard Memorial Library, the gift of his daughter, Annie Howard, to the city in her father's memory.[32] A number of futile attempts were made in the early 1880's to introduce bills into the legislature attacking the lottery's franchise or, on the other hand, to charter rival lottery companies.[33] These were quickly dispensed with through the lottery's influence in the legislative halls. A much graver threat to its welfare came from the federal government through the attempts of the post office to deny the use of the mails to the Louisiana Lottery. Basing his action on an 1872 law revised in 1876 which empowered the Postmaster General to deny the use of the mails to any fraudulent lottery, Postmaster David M. Key in 1879 instructed the New Orleans postmaster not to deliver any registered mail or pay any money order to lottery president, Maximilien Dauphin. Dauphin brought suit against the postmaster in the United States Supreme Court. Key, meanwhile, was forced to rescind his order and resigned from office. Thus the case was dropped.[34] Although it was true that the chance of winning in the Louisiana Lottery's drawing were slim, its drawings had a firm reputation for their honesty. Since 1877 when Generals Beauregard and Early came into the fold of the lottery family, the company's main line of advertising had been to stress the integrity of its two commissioners and their watchful presence at the major drawings. In 1883 another Postmaster General, Walter Q. Gresham, tried to restrain mail or money orders from being delivered to the New Orleans National Bank because he had evidence such mail was directed to the lottery.

This resulted in a lawsuit which the lottery won in the United

32 Williams, *P. G. T. Beauregard*, 293; *New Orleans City Guide*, 317–18; Buel, "The Degradation of a State," 626.

33 Alwes, "The History of the Louisiana Lottery Company," 1003–1007.

34 *Ibid.*, 1007–1008; a summary discussion of this case appears in Jubal A. Early to Walter Q. Gresham, in Washington *Post*, October 7, 1883. (A clipping of this letter is in a scrapbook in the Louisiana State Museum Library, New Orleans, Louisiana.)

States Circuit Court for the Eastern District of Louisiana.[35] While this case was being considered, General Early dutifully wrote an open letter in answer to Gresham's attack upon the lottery which appeared in the Washington *Post*. In his well-phrased, lengthy letter, he pointed out the legal weaknesses in Gresham's case against the lottery and then waxed poetic in defending the lottery as an institution. He wrote: "By the Divine command, the promised land was divided by lot among the tribes of Israel. An apostle was chosen by the casting of lots in the place of the one who had betrayed the Saviour; . . . General George Washington was president of a lottery company . . . Thomas Jefferson wrote a defense of lotteries . . . and applied for and obtained the passage of a bill to dispose of his lands by lottery to pay his debts. James Madison, the father of the Constitution, approved and signed an act of Congress authorizing a system of lotteries for the purpose of improving the city of Washington." [36] From Westchester, New York, John A. Morris, well aware that all eyes were on the lottery during this trying period wrote a private letter to General Beauregard to smooth over bad feeling between the general and the lottery officials in New Orleans. Beauregard's absence from daily drawings had been criticized since he was part of the assurance of honesty on the part of the company. Morris entreated Beauregard not to get into any controversy with the lottery company at this crucial time and assured him that he would personally guarantee the general's salary whether or not he attended all ordinary daily drawings. However, he added: "I must beg of you, just at this time, while the Post Office authorities are acting so badly and so wantonly to further their own disgraceful purposes that you will be absent as seldom as possible, because every blackmailer in the United States is watching his opportunity to pounce on us . . . ." [37] The lottery case attracted a statement from another general and political figure, Frederick N. Ogden, who was being considered by some politicians as a possible candidate for governor

[35] Wiggins, "The Louisiana Press and the Lottery," 339–40.
[36] Jubal A. Early to Walter Q. Gresham, in Washington *Post*, October 7, 1883.
[37] John A. Morris to Pierre G. T. Beauregard, August 30, 1883, in Beauregard Manuscripts, Special Collections Division, Howard-Tilton Memorial Library, Tulane University.

in 1884. In answer to a request from Donelson Cafferey that he speak out on the lottery issue, General Ogden replied in the *Picayune* by strongly denouncing the lottery. He ended by expressing the hope that "in place of rings, monopolies and lotteries, which are fast absorbing all the treasure of the State, there will spring up manufactories and honest industries, which will command the energies and the capital of our citizens and fill their homes with plenty and peace." [38]

In addition to the post office controversy in the 1880's, the lottery met resistance in New York City, one of its most lucrative fields of activity. In 1880 William Russell Grace, a shipping magnate who made his fortune in the carrying trade between United States and South America, became the first Roman Catholic mayor of New York City. He launched a reform administration, attacking the spoils system in city government, police scandals, and organized vice, and the open operation of the Louisiana Lottery. Reformer Anthony Comstock helped to spearhead the antilottery drive.[39]

In Philadelphia, the *Times* also waged a vigorous campaign against the lottery's newspaper advertising which amounted to $50,000 a year in Pennsylvania. This resulted in an 1883 act passed by the Pennsylvania legislature which forbade such lottery advertising in that state. The Louisiana Lottery retaliated by initiating two libel suits against the Philadelphia *Times* and its editor. These cases were eventually dropped, but they set in motion a crusade against the lottery by members of Congress from Pennsylvania. The result was an act of Congress passed in 1890 which made it illegal for any lottery, fraudulent or honest, to use the mails.[40] Since the lottery spent about $10,000 a month on postage and received thousands of incoming letters weekly, this was a serious

38 Frederick N. Ogden to Donelson Cafferey, in *Daily Picayune*, November 4, 1883.
39 Dumas Malone (ed.), *Dictionary of American Biography*, (New York, 1931), VII, 463. Lottery in New York City was so widespread that Grace's campaign was not able to eradicate it completely. See Herbert Asbury, *Sucker's Progress, An Informal History of Gambling in America from the Colonies to Canfield* (New York, 1938), 86–87.
40 Alwes, "The History of the Louisiana Lottery Company," 1010–11, 1074–77, 1109–10.

blow. It switched to using express companies; but this was never as successful as postal service had been.[41]

The year 1890 was a time of troubles—not only for the lottery— but for the entire state. By March, the Mississippi River was at flood stage with a record-breaking high-water mark. By April 6, there were sixteen crevasses in the levees of the Mississippi and its tributaries in the state. Ironically, the state and federal governments had spent more money on levee construction in 1889–90 than ever before. But this did not seem to be sufficient. Panic seized inhabitants of threatened or already flooded areas. Lottery president Dauphin offered to meet the emergency with $100,000 which Governor Nicholls could use as he desired to fight the flood. The governor turned down the offer. But the Louisiana State Lottery Company then offered to divide the money directly among the various levee districts in the state, almost all of whom accepted it. The lottery boat *Dakotah* was also put into service to rescue flood victims and their stock and to feed and house workers on the levees.[42]

To protect New Orleans levees, Mayor Shakspeare accepted $50,000 from the lottery. He was severely criticized by the Reverend Beverly Carradine, pastor of the Carondelet Street Methodist Church and a rabid antilottery fighter. Carradine asked the mayor, "Do you realize the harm the acceptance of such a gift from a gambling institution will do in the eyes of the world?" Shakspeare's reply was blunt and filled with City Hall wisdom. "If every dollar stained with wine or crime was cast out." he retorted, "sweet charity's treasure-box would be very empty." The minister persisted, "Shouldn't the citizens at a mass meeting decide whether or not they wish to accept the gift?" Shakspeare's answer was the classic statement of a politician trying to explain his actions to the public. "I have done my best," he said.[43]

While the flood was ravaging the Louisiana countryside and the New Orleans dailies were almost unanimous in their praises

---

[41] *Ibid.*, 1024, 1077.

[42] *Ibid.*, 1026–29; Wiggins, "The Louisiana Press and the Lottery," 787–91; *Daily States,* March 15, 16, 17, 18, 1890; *Daily Picayune,* March 16, 17, 19, 1890; *Times-Democrat,* March 16, 1890.

[43] Alwes, "The History of the Louisiana State Lottery Company," 1028.

of the lottery's aid to flood victims, John A. Morris announced that the lottery would seek a renewal of its charter, set to expire on January 1, 1894, in the 1890 legislature. The lottery was willing to raise its annual license fee from $40,000 to $500,000. Morris suggested that the money be used by the state to support public schools, charitable institutions, and levee maintenance.[44]

The rumor that Morris was going to ask for a new charter had brought reaction from antilottery forces in New Orleans even before his official announcement in April. As early as February 28, twelve citizens met in the law office of Charles Parlange to found the Anti-Lottery League of Louisiana. On March 6 the group, expanded to thirty, adopted a constitution and elected Colonel William G. Vincent, president. Head of an auctioneer firm, Colonel Vincent was a veteran of both the Mexican and Civil Wars. By April a thousand persons attended the first public meeting of the Anti-Lottery League. Local branches of this club sprang up all over the city and the state. On the day the legislature opened in Baton Rouge, May 12, the league held a second public meeting at which Senator Edward Douglass White was the principal speaker. It also brought out the first issue of its newspaper, the *New Delta,* which its members felt was a necessity since all of the major papers in the city were in sympathy with the lottery. C. Harrison Parker served as editor-in-chief of the new paper, and John C. Wickliffe, who was its most fiery and articulate spokesman, was associate editor.[45]

The 1890 session of the legislature was one of the most dramatic in Louisiana history. Governor Nicholls' opening message opposed Morris' plan to get the lottery rechartered by a constitutional amendment which would be submitted to the voters in the general election of 1892. Morris' reply to the governor's speech was to raise the amount of the annual license fee that his company was willing to pay to $1,000,000. By the beginning of June the struggle

44 *Daily States,* April 18, 1890; *Daily Picayune,* April 18, 1890.

45 Alwes, "The History of the Louisiana State Lottery Company," 1054–55; Grace King, "The Higher Life of New Orleans," *Outlook,* LIII (1896) , 759–61; Wickliffe, "The Louisiana Lottery: A History of the Company," 571; *Daily Picayune,* May 13, 1890; *Times-Democrat,* May 13, 1890; *Daily States,* May 13, 1890.

in the legislature between the pros and antis on the lottery recharter began in earnest. Advocates of the lottery bill argued that the
people of the state should have the right to decide about the lottery for themselves by voting on its charter as a constitutional
amendment in 1892. They also felt that the revenue its license fee
would bring into the state would do inestimable good for education and charitable institutions. The opponents of the bill branded
the lottery a monopolistic octopus which would strangle the state
through bribery and corruption if allowed to continue in existence. As to the need for the lottery's license fee, antilottery legislators pointed out that there would be a surplus in the state's general fund in 1890.[46]

During the course of the lottery bill's passage through the house
and senate, other rival lotteries, particularly the Mexican Lottery,
offered to outbid the Louisiana Lottery for a charter. This forced
Morris to raise his company's annual fee to $1,250,000. Twice
when the bill was coming up for a vote in the house, a house member was taken ill and the vote postponed. When the rollcall vote
was allowed to proceed, a storm raged outside the State Capitol
and lightning struck the building as the final vote was cast giving
the lottery bill its two-thirds majority. After a rough passage
through the Senate in which it passed by the bare two-thirds majority, it went to the governor who vetoed it. In what was to become his most famous statement, Governor Nicholls, who had lost
an arm at Winchester and a leg at Chancellorsville, explained why
he would not sign the bill: "At no time and under no circumstances
will I permit one of my hands to aid in degrading what the other
was lost in seeking to uphold . . . the honor of my native State." [47]

In an attempt to pass the bill over the governor's veto, the house
voted 66 to 31 for the bill, but the prolottery forces in the senate
faced a stalemate. One of their men became critically ill and could
not be present to vote. Since his one vote was vitally necessary,
they pigeonholed the bill into the judiciary committee. There a

[46] McGinty, "The Louisiana Lottery Company," 342–43; *Daily States,* May
13, 1890; *Daily Picayune,* May 13, 1890.
[47] Alwes, "The History of the Louisiana State Lottery Company," 1032–44;
Wickliffe, "The Louisiana Lottery: A History of the Company," 572; Lathrop,
"An Autobiography of Francis T. Nicholls," 264–66.

decision was reached that since this bill was a proposed constitutional amendment which had to be submitted to the voters there was no necessity to secure the governor's signature. Since it had already passed both houses once, the senate judiciary committee pronounced it valid without Nicholl's signature. This line of reasoning was approved by the prolottery majority in the house and the bill was sent to the Secretary of State. This official refused to promulgate the bill because of its irregular passage. But Morris went into court and once again emerged victorious when the state supreme court sided with the senate judiciary committee's interpretation of the bill's legality. Now all that remained was its submission to the electorate in 1892.[48]

The next year and a half before the election which would settle the lottery's fate was one long campaign in which the prolottery forces formed the Progressive League to rival the Anti-Lottery League, and the antis added a women's league to their ranks, of which Mrs. William Preston Johnston, the wife of Tulane's president, was the top official. The widow of E. John Ellis was a vice-president.[49] The *Mascot*, which followed the lead of other New Orleans dailies in attacking the antilottery forces, was more vociferous than any in its charges. It claimed that at least one member of the executive board of the Auxiliary Sanitary Association, which had voted to reject the lottery's offer of $30,000 to aid in flushing city gutters and in building public bathhouses, was a holder of Mexican lottery stock. Members of Governor Nicholls'

48 Sidney James Romero, Jr., "The Political Career of Murphy James Foster, Governor of Louisiana, 1892–1900," reprint from *Louisiana Historical Quarterly*, XXVIII (October, 1945), 22–23; Buel, "The Degradation of a State," 629–30; Tinker, *Creole City*, 304–305; Supreme Court of Louisiana, No. 10,794, *State ex rel. John A. Morris, Appellant, versus L. F. Mason, Secretary of State. Appendix to Brief on Behalf of Defendant and Appellee* (New Orleans, n.d.), bound together with other legal papers and articles on the lottery and titled "Frank McGloin Papers, Anti-Lottery League, 1890–1892." (This compilation of McGloin papers is in the New Orleans Public Library.)

49 Alwes, "The History of the Louisiana State Lottery Company," 1061–63. Robert S. Day, a cotton merchant, was president of the prolottery Progressive League. Its secretary, Thomas A. Marshall, Jr., was manager of the *Spirit of the South Weekly*, a sporting paper in which the Louisiana Lottery ran extensive advertising. On the first formal meeting of the Progressive League, see *Daily Picayune*, September 2, 1890.

staff it also cited as owners of such stock. Edward Douglass White, it charged, owned property which he rented out to the lottery for a policy shop, and two prominent antilottery leaders had won $75,000 in the lottery, which, it noted, they pocketed while pledging their condemnation of the source of their enrichment.[50]

Antilottery rallies were frequently held in church halls and a *Mascot* reporter attending one of these gatherings was merciless in his description of what he saw. It was more of a mild revival service than a political rally, he commented, with women outnumbering men. Among the men, he noticed one gentleman whom he suspected was against the lottery since he thought it had helped to defeat his father for political office. Another member of the audience was connected with the Mexican Lottery faction. About a dozen young men who were employees of the lottery attended out of curiosity. The girls at the meeting, the reporter found as "homely as a consumptive cow" but still intent upon attracting male attention, their main object in attending the meeting. "The meeting may have been a subdued affair," he concluded, "but the apparel of the choir members was the opposite. Turkey Red and Ultramarine Blue are not the mildest colors in the world when coupled with black head gear trimmed with red poppies." [51]

Church leaders in New Orleans were in the vanguard of the fight against the lottery. In addition to the Methodist clergymen, Reverend Carradine, who wrote a tract against the lottery, *The Louisiana State Lottery Company Examined and Exposed*, Episcopal Bishop David Sessums, Presbyterian minister Benjamin Palmer, Rabbi Max Heller of the local Jewish community, and Catholic Archbishop Francis Janssens all opposed the lottery. Archbishop Janssens forbid the blessings of lottery tickets in local Catholic churches and turned down a lottery offer to contribute handsomely to the reduction of the church debt in his archdiocese.[52] The most stirring oratory in the antilottery campaign was delivered by Reverend Palmer at a rally of the Anti-Lottery

[50] *Mascot,* May 10, 16, 24, 1890.
[51] *Mascot,* April 12, 1890.
[52] Alwes, "The History of the Louisiana State Lottery Company," 1070–71; Buel, "The Degradation of a State," 628; King, "The Higher Life of New Orleans," 760.

130   New Orleans in the Gilded Age

League held in the Grand Opera House on June 25, 1891. Speaking without notes, the bearded, patriarchal divine condemned the lottery as an undermining influence which tempted its patrons to get money without working. In a pitch of emotion he alluded to the lynching of the Italians accused of Hennessy's murder just a few months in the past and warned "if this lottery cannot be destroyed by forms of law, it must unquestionably be destroyed by actual revolution." His speech brought hysterical cheers and applause from his audience, but scathing criticism from the local newspapers who found it demagogic and an invitation to civil disorder.[53]

In the summer of 1891, the Anti-Lottery League called a statewide convention in Baton Rouge, timed to meet along with the Farmers' Alliance. Later at Lafayette, representatives from the two groups worked out a compromise ticket they would support at the Democratic state nominating convention for governor in December. It was to consist of Thomas Scott Adams, president of the Farmers' Alliance, as governor, with the Farmers' Alliance naming also the treasurer and superintendent of education. The Anti-Lottery Leaguers would select the rest of the ticket.[54] Within two months some members of the Farmers' Alliance were rejecting this coalition. By the time of the Democratic nominating convention, prolottery forces had rallied enough votes to assure nomination of their candidate, Samuel D. McEnery. One historian has pointed out that McEnery "represented essentially the alluvial, black-belt parishes, the old New Orleans Ring, and the lottery." [55] McEnery had been one of the state supreme court justices who had saved the lottery bill in 1890.[56] Unwilling to accept McEnery and

53 Thomas C. Johnson, *The Life and Letters of Benjamin Morgan Palmer* (Richmond, 1906) , 553–63; *Daily Picayune,* June 26, 1891; *Item,* June 27, 1891.
54 For a complete account of the Anti-Lottery League convention, see *Official Report of the Proceedings of the Anti-Lottery Democratic Convention Held in the Hall of the House of Representatives, Baton Rouge, Louisiana on Thursday and Friday, August 7 and 8, 1890* (New Orleans, 1890) , bound with other papers under the title "Frank McGloin Papers, Anti-Lottery League, 1890–1892." On the collaboration of the Anti-Lottery League with the Farmers' Alliance see Romero, "The Political Career of Murphy J. Foster," (reprint) , 24–27; Henry Dethloff, "The Alliance and the Lottery: Farmers Try for the Sweepstakes," *Louisiana History,* VI (Spring, 1965) , 147–49.
55 Dethloff, "The Alliance and the Lottery," 150.
56 Romero, "The Political Career of Murphy J. Foster," (reprint) , 23.

the lottery, which they felt were inseparable, the antilottery faction broke away from the nominating convention and held their own convention in the statehouse. Fearful that Adams did not have enough vote-getting power, the Anti-Lottery League pressured him into rejecting the top spot on their ticket and into taking instead the lucrative job of secretary of state. For governor they chose a dynamic young senator from St. Mary Parish who had spearheaded the antilottery drive in the 1890 legislature, Murphy J. Foster.[57]

This split of the Democrats into two factions alarmed the dailies in New Orleans who feared the Republicans might use this discord to their political advantage. The Republicans themselves, however, were divided by the lottery issue. Former acting Governor Pinckney B. S. Pinchback was a major stockholder in the Louisiana Lottery. Former Governor Henry Clay Warmoth was the leader of the antilottery Republicans. Their gubernatorial nominating convention ended in a split, just as the Democratic one had done. Each faction of the Republicans entered a candidate in the governor's race.[58] The People's Party of Louisiana, organized in October, 1891, at Alexandria, entered a fifth candidate who was against the lottery but stressed Populist reforms more than the burning issue of the lottery's charter.[59] Obviously the real race was between the two Democratic candidates. The bitterness that this campaign engendered was evident in the statement of one of Senator Foster's close associates: "We are in this fight and we are in it to win. As Mr. Foster has said, it will be 'war to the knife and the knife to the hilt.' " [60]

[57] Ibid., 28–32. Romero points out that Foster had been the "logical choice to lead the fight against the recharter" in the 1890 legislature since "there was never any charge of bribery directed against him, which could not be said of all of those who opposed the recharter. Even Governor Nicholls and Senator Edward D. White were accused of receiving money from the Lottery Company." This seems also to have made him the strongest gubernatorial candidate for the antilottery forces.

[58] Daily Picayune, December 20, 1891; Romero, "The Political Career of Murphy J. Foster," reprint, 33–34; Wickliffe, "The Louisiana Lottery: A History of the Company," 576. The Warmoth Republican candidate for governor was John A. Breaux. The anti-Warmoth, or Kellogg prolottery, Republican candidate was Albert H. Leonard.

[59] The Populist gubernatorial candidate was Richard L. Tannehill. Dethloff, "The Alliance and the Lottery," 152–53.

[60] Daily Picayune, December 22, 1891.

At this heated point in the campaign, a dramatic turn of events transpired in a courtroom in Washington, D.C. The 1890 congressional act denying the use of the mails to lotteries had also covered newspaper advertising as well as letters or parcels. The lottery had taken to the use of newspaper advertising more heavily as the doors of express companies had begun to slam shut on them. Now in February, 1892, a test case on the right of Congress to exclude lottery advertising from newspapers, which New Orleans journals branded a violation of freedom of press, came before the United States Supreme Court. The court ruled that Congress did have the right to set up such regulations and the act stood firm. At last the Louisiana Lottery had lost a legal battle which proved to be a fatal one. Lottery employees were advised not to try to violate the law by mailing lottery advertisements, and John A. Morris conceded defeat in an open letter on February 3, 1892, in which he stated that his company would not accept rechartering, even if the lottery amendment was passed by the electorate in the coming election.[61]

This turn of events seemed to offer some hope of bringing the two factions of Democrats back together again. But the hope was a vain one. The antilottery faction did not believe Morris' statement. The two factions finally agreed to a Democratic white primary to be held on March 22. The winner was to become the Democratic nominee in the April general election. A committee of seven was set up as a returning board for the primary—three McEnery men (one of whom was John Fitzpatrick), three Foster men, and one neutral chosen by both sides. The vote in this primary was so close that several days elapsed before the returning board could report its findings. The "neutral" member sided with the Foster followers and after eliminating certain returns, the majority of four declared Foster the winner by 549 votes. Naturally such a decision was not acceptable to the McEnery forces. McEnery decided to enter the general election anyway.[62]

[61] *Cases Argued and Decided in the Supreme Court of the United States,* (143, 144, 145, 146 U.S.) (Rochester, 1920), 93–103; Wiggins, "The Louisiana Press and the Lottery," 827–32; *Daily Picayune,* February 4, 1892; *Times-Democrat,* February 4, 1892.
[62] Romero, "The Political Career of Murphy J. Foster," 34–37.

With the lottery still an overwhelming issue despite Morris' statement to the contrary, it was inevitable that it would also affect the selection of a new mayor for New Orleans in the April general election. Many members of the reforming Y.M.D.A. which had elected Shakspeare in 1888 were now ardent antilotterites. Shakspeare's former campaign manager, William S. Parkerson, was one of the leaders in the Anti-Lottery League. Meeting in a closed conference at Grunewald Hall on March 26, 1892, Parkerson and a group of Foster followers endorsed Mayor Shakspeare for reelection and drew up an entire slate of municipal candidates they would offer the voters on election day, April 19, 1892. Parkerson spoke enthusiastically of the solvent finances of the incumbent city administration and felt another term of office was necessary for Shakspeare to wipe out the municipal debt entirely and complete some other planned reforms. Shakspeare, who had sponsored the Shakspeare Plan for gambling and taken fifty thousand dollars from the lottery to aid in levee repairs, was not the avid antilottery figure his supporters could have chosen. But his second term of office had produced solid achievements.[63]

The Ring organization in the city realized that the state and city races were delicately tied together. A candidate for mayor who attracted local votes might also pull them over to the side of his favored entrant in the governor's race. With Burke in exile in Honduras, Fitzpatrick was the most powerful and popular Democratic leader of the regular organization in the city. In the 1870's, when the Democrats were struggling to overthrow the Republicans in Louisiana, Fitzpatrick had been a close friend of Nicholls and of such Nicholls associates as E. John Ellis. He had twice introduced bills into the legislature to abolish the Louisiana Lottery and as criminal sheriff had been opposed in court by lottery officials in the key case which struck down Act No. 44 of 1879. Now the strange path of politics had led him to the opposite side from Nicholls and made him the ally of the lottery. At the nominating Democratic convention of the city Ring organization on April 11,

[63] *Daily Picayune,* March 27, 1892; Kendall, *History of New Orleans,* II, 502–503. On Parkerson's connection with the Anti-Lottery League, see Buel, "The Degradation of a State," 631.

Judge Davey, himself a former mayoral candidate, put Fitzpatrick's name in nomination for mayor. Although most of the newspapers in the city backed McEnery enthusiastically for governor, they found the Fitzpatrick ticket less to their taste. Fitzpatrick himself was conceded to be competent—but the *Item* felt his entrance into the mayor's office would be an invitation for deadheads to crowd into the city's departments. The *Picayune*, whose publisher Mrs. Nicholson was a personal friend of the John A. Morris family, loyally backed the McEnery candidacy, but refused to endorse Fitzpatrick or Shakspeare. The Republicans in the city race split just as they had on the state level. Warmoth's faction backed Shakspeare, while the anti-Warmoth faction supported Fitzpatrick.[64]

Three nights before the election, the Ring held a rally in Lafayette Square with four platforms for speakers and bands. Fitzpatrick, remembering happier days when he had been part of Shakspeare's first administration, told the crowd in a generous gesture: "I have nothing to say against my worthy competitor, Mr. Shakspeare. ... I honor and esteem him, and if on Wednesday next your votes show him to be your choice as the incumbent of the great office for which we both are candidates, I will take his hand and say to him: 'It has been a fair and square contest. You have won and I am with you.' "[65]

Fitzpatrick never had to deliver that speech to Shakspeare. On election day he was elected mayor of New Orleans with 20,547 votes to 17,289 for Shakspeare. In the state contest, Murphy J. Foster was elected governor with a landslide vote of 79,388 to McEnery's 47,037. The lottery amendment which was really a dead issue by the time of the election, was rejected by 157,422 votes. Only 4,225 votes were cast in its favor.[66] The Louisiana Lottery eked out a greatly reduced livelihood until its charter expired on January 1, 1894. By that time it was losing money. Its

<hr>

[64] *Daily Picayune*, April 11, 17, 1892; *Item*, April 12, 18, 1892; Kendall, *History of New Orleans*, II, 504; John S. Kendall, "Journalism in New Orleans Between 1880 and 1900," *Louisiana Historical Quarterly*, VIII (October, 1925), 561.

[65] *Daily Picayune*, December 20, 1891; Kendall, *History of New Orleans*, II, 504–505.

[66] *Daily Picayune*, April 17, 1892.

operations were transferred to Honduras from where it continued to operate an illegal business underground in the United States. By 1907 further federal legislation and stringent law enforcement forced its demise.[67]

The political aftermath of the lottery fight was a deep and lingering bitterness between those who had fought the lottery and those who had supported it. With the antilottery ticket triumphant on the state level, its New Orleans backers were particularly unreconciled to their defeat at the city level. Governor Foster was painfully aware of the necessity of reconciliation between the two factions of Democrats, if his party was to remain dominant in the state over the Republicans and the newly-formed Populist Party.[68] Therefore, he soon made overtures of friendship to Fitzpatrick and the Ring in New Orleans. Since Fitzpatrick had been a Nicholls associate in the past, this rapprochement was welcomed by the new mayor. But the Anti-Lottery League faction in the city, most of whom had been Y.M.D.A. men in 1888, were adamant in their hostility to Fitzpatrick. They simply watched their chance to strike a political body blow at him.

The major accomplishments of Fitzpatrick's first two years in office centered in public improvements and the carrying out of projects begun under Shakspeare. As a former commissioner of public works, he was especially conscious of the city's needs for better streets and drainage. By 1894 Fitzpatrick could state proudly that "fine drives and roads now encircle our city, where was formerly mud and impassable streets. . . . Carrollton avenue, Broad and Canal streets, both sides are graveled roads, while most all the cross streets are likewise paved, much to the credit of the city's enterprise and progressiveness. Square block granite pavements have also been laid on Rampart, Burgundy and St. Philip streets." The total amount expended for these improvements was $232,000, which had been paid in full by 1894.[69]

In addition, much work was done in cleaning out and culverting

---

[67] Campbell, *Manual of the City of New Orleans*, 36; Romero, "The Political Career of Murphy J. Foster," 37; Alwes, "The History of the Louisiana State Lottery Company," 1097–1102.

[68] Romero, "The Political Career of Murphy J. Foster," (reprint), 38–39.

[69] John Fitzpatrick, *Mayor's Message to the City Council of New Orleans* (New Orleans, 1894), 8.

canals and ditches and in repairing the drainage machines. The culverting of the Camp and Melpomene canals eliminated two smelly nuisances of which citizens had complained for twenty years. Of its approximate $384,000 cost, all but $48,000 was paid for by the Fitzpatrick administration.[70] Several attempts were made to create a completely new and more effective drainage system, but this proved such an extensive task that, by the end of his term, the mayor suggested it should be submitted to the voters or incorporated into state law by the next administration. The first topographical survey of the city, however, was completed as a result of these deliberations.

The two major projects which the mayor inherited from his predecessor were the construction of a new courthouse and jail, and the completion of fire equipment purchases from the Fireman's Charitable Association. Shakspeare had let out the contract for the new courthouse, but it was built during Fitzpatrick's term. Completed by July, 1894, it cost $350,000 and was to be paid for in installments running through 1897. However, the administration was able to wipe out this debt by the end of 1894.[71] Conversion of the fire department to a municipal agency proved costly. Since the changeover came in December, 1891, the major share of payment for equipment to the former volunteer organization fell upon the new city government elected in 1892. The purchase price, $165,608.94, was taken from the revenue of 1892, 1893, and 1894. In addition, Fitzpatrick's regime built new fire stations at a cost of $25,000.[72]

To complete these improvements and to pay for them within two years was an accomplishment which would not have been possible if the city debt had not been settled advantageously.[73] The gradual reduction of this debt allowed a corresponding reduction in taxes. But in contrast to 1880, when about one quarter of the taxes was not paid and had to be collected years later, over 82

70 *Ibid.*, 7.
71 Fitzpatrick, *Mayor's Message*, 6–7; Kendall, *History of New Orleans*, II, 506–507.
72 Fitzpatrick, *Mayor's Message*, 13; Kendall, *History of New Orleans*, II, 506–507.
73 Also a help in furnishing funds for these projects was the share of revenue set aside for public improvements from the surplus of the debt tax after 1892.

percent of the 1893 taxes were paid on time and most of the balance, within the next six months.[74] This modest improvement takes on more significance when one realizes that this was a year of nationwide panic and business failure. New Orleans suffered a recession, but it was not as severe as in northern cities. By the beginning of 1894 the mayor could point out that the collection of license fees from trades and businesses had reached $315,000, the largest sum in local history.[75]

With its credit established on a solid basis at last, the local government met most of its obligations much more promptly than in the early 1880's. By July, 1894, the council was able to pass an ordinance providing for semimonthly payments of salaries to employees.[76] An era of "hard times" passed away with this act as the financial solvency of the city finally freed its workers from the toils of brokers.

[Table 5]

New Orleans Tax Rates and Assessments[a]

Year	Tax Rate (%)	Assessment
1881	1.78.40	$ 97,340,605.
1882[b]	3.17.5	103,975,662.
1888	2.02	119,361,801.
1892	2.02	129,638,500.
1896	2	140,567,443.

[a] T. W. Campbell, *Manual of the City of New Orleans*, 34–42.
[b] The tax rate rose sharply in 1882 as a result of the judgment tax. It then slowly fell, while assessments increased.

If Fitzpatrick had left office in early 1894, his administration would have appeared to be one of the most successful since the Civil War. With a balanced budget, a surplus in the treasury, and

[74] *Progressive New Orleans*, 14; Fitzpatrick, *Mayor's Message*, 6.
[75] Fitzpatrick, *Mayor's Message*, 5–6.
[76] Flynn, *Flynn's Digest*, 295.

public improvements for all to see, the Third Ward's favorite son was at the peak of his career. He could even look forward to the possible capture of the governorship at some future date. But his opponents among the business and commercial interests had been biding their time since their investigation of his payrolls had collapsed in 1889–90 and the bitter lottery fight and election of 1892. Now with Maurice Hart still hovering over the council like Banquo's ghost, and a spending spree on public works between 1892 and 1894, the reform element got their chance to renew their attacks on the mayor.

The extraordinary wave of reform which swept over the City Hall incumbents in late 1894, like a hurricane following a stretch of unbroken sunny days, might not have occurred, despite the reformers' zeal, if the administration had not committed a fatal blunder. It pushed through two pieces of legislation, one of which was hotly opposed by the commercial classes, and the other by the public in general, including many of the Ring's own following.

In an effort to improve the slipshod collection of garbage, the mayor and council had asked for proposals in August, 1893, on new methods of garbage removal and disposal. Within a month they accepted a contract calling for disposal by burning.[77] Elaborate machinery was set up in the garbage plant to convert a part of the refuse into grease or fertilizer. But in April, 1894, the grand jury report criticized the garbage contract in stern language. It felt the financial terms were too lenient to the contractor. This new method cost the city $90,000 annually, while the old one had cost $57,000. But its main objections were the same which could be heard on the streets throughout the city—the definition of "garbage" which the contractor would pick up was too limited. He refused to cart off old shoes, bottles, broken glass, or tin cans. A special type of receptacle had to be used for garbage, or it would be left to rot on the sidewalk. The incinerator plant itself was not completed in April, and as a consequence huge piles of garbage were accumulating on the dumping grounds surrounding it.[78]

Several weeks after the grand jury report, when the burning of

[77] *Ibid.*, 370, 377.
[78] *Daily Picayune*, April 11, 1894.

refuse did begin, the smoke proved as obnoxious to the adjacent neighborhood as the reeking garbage heaps had been. The mayor, who could be arbitrary when he felt he was right, argued that this new method was more sanitary and should be accepted by the populace. To accomplish this, he issued an order to arrest any householder who did not properly sort his garbage and put it in the designated type of container.[79]

While tempers and noses were inflamed over the garbage problem, the council awarded a franchise to construct a belt railroad along the riverfront to Cooney B. Fischer, who was actually only an agent for the Illinois Central Railroad. The Fischer franchise would have allowed this railroad to run a line around the city and down State Street to the river, then along the river to the lower end of town, using or closing whatever streets were most convenient or desirable to its purposes. Such a railroad would have monopolized the commerce on the river front and forced the other lines in New Orleans to use its facilities on its terms. The *Picayune* indignantly noted that the franchise was granted for ninety-nine years to almost unknown parties with no pledge, no bond, nor restrictions of any kind demanded in return.[80]

Cries of protest were raised in every commercial exchange in town over the swift and highhanded manner in which this franchise had been passed and signed by the mayor. At the time it was granted to Fischer, a joint committee of members from commercial exchanges was trying to bring together interested industries and railroads in order to discuss securing a belt line which could be used equally by all.[81] The council's monopolistic grant to the Illinois Central's man Fischer put an end to these plans. But it set into motion the formation of another reform organization, the Citizens' Protective Association, which drew its leadership from the irate commercial element and former antilottery men. Ward clubs bearing this new group's name formed daily.[82] The repeal of the Fischer franchise and future protection against such grants by the council were its chief aims. It also announced that it would

79 *Ibid.*, April 17, 1894.
80 *Ibid.*, May 16, 1894.
81 *Ibid.*, May 15, 1894.
82 *Ibid.*, May 29, 1894.

fight the unpopular garbage contractor, a stand which considerably widened its following.

Events moved quickly after the passage of the franchise on May 15, 1894. On May 21 three thousand persons attended a mass meeting at St. Charles and State streets, called by the citizens' group to demand the repeal of the Fischer franchise. A simultaneous meeting of downtown residents was held at Rampart Street and Bayou Road to protest the excessive use of rosetta gravel in paving jobs in that area. Speakers claimed this form of street surfacing was defective, but was foisted unwillingly upon property owners to the benefit of Maurice Hart, the president of the gravel company. Hart had also been mentioned in the press as a lobbyist in the Fischer franchise affair, and resentment against him and the council was beginning to run high.[83]

Two days after these meetings, two such widely different sources as the Texas and Pacific Railroad and the screwmen's union issued official protests to the Fischer franchise.[84] Under the increasing pressure of public opinion, the council decided to retrace its steps and repealed the franchise in a night session on May 29. A meeting had been called for that night at Washington Artillery Hall, up the block from City Hall, by the Citizens' Protective Association to offer the council "moral support." About five thousand turned out for the franchise's repeal and the citizens' rally. After the announcement of its repeal, the cheering crowd spilled out into the street and led by a band marched to the various newspaper offices to serenade them for their help in the fight against City Hall.[85]

Once they tasted victory, the citizens' organization was determined to launch a full-scale investigation of "the Boodle Council," as they called the local legislative body. It was through their efforts that between June and September the grand jury was supplied with evidence and witnesses which led to the indictment of ten councilmen, the city engineer, and an ex-tax assessor for vari-

[83] *Ibid.*, May 21, 22, 1894; *Times-Democrat*, May 22, 1894; *Daily States*, May 22, 1894.

[84] *Daily Picayune*, May 23, 1894.

[85] *Ibid.*, May 30, 1894; *Times-Democrat*, May 30, 1894; *Daily States*, May 30, 1894.

ous degrees of misconduct in office. Three of these twelve were convicted.[86] During the course of these investigations and indictments, a shocking string of minor and major scandals was uncovered. Some of the charges against individual councilmen included the taking of a five-hundred-dollar bribe to secure council approval for a coal landing on the levee, the receipt of $1,400 from a dredge company for council permission to construct a portable trestle in the company's yard, and the acceptance of $2,500 to approve the laying of a switch track into a warehouse. One policeman identified a councilman whom he claimed had tried to extort $8,000 from a prominent sporting man in 1892 under threat of closing gambling houses and the race track. These were a few of the smaller deals in which councilmen were involved.[87] Patient probing and questioning revealed that the price for the City and Lake Street Railroad franchise had been $800,000, but only $700,-000 had been officially announced. The sum of $100,000 was left unaccounted for, a mystery which the grand jury was unable to solve.[88] The Citizens' Protective Association added to the growing evidence against the council by calling attention to the fact that paving contracts had been juggled frequently. Time after time the paving price at which a contract was let out would be advertised in the newspaper at 90¢ per running foot, but the property owners would be charged $1.50 by the city government.[89]

The major scandal which the grand jury investigated was the taking of bribes and giving of special privileges during the construction of the courthouse. This episode was intensified by the disappearance of one of the star witnesses, a partner in the construction firm which built the edifice. Within two days he was discovered in Texas, and returned after admitting that a councilman had paid him $1,000 to leave town.[90] The courthouse investigation revealed that one of the contractors had been a plumbing firm in

86 Almost daily references on the council investigation and trials of councilmen appeared in the local papers, June–November, 1894.

87 Daily Picayune, June 9–20, 1894; Times-Democrat, June 9–20, 1894; Item, June 9–20, 1894.

88 Daily Picayune, August 21, 1894.

89 Ibid., August 4, 1894.

90 Ibid., July 20, 23, 25, August 3, 1894.

which Mayor Fitzpatrick's wife was a partner. The *Daily States* took Fitzpatrick to task for such a practice, intimating that he might also have been involved in bribe-taking. The mayor immediately sued the paper for libel.[91]

Fitzpatrick's attitude throughout the council investigation was one of staunch loyalty to his associates. He advised the council that indictment did not prove guilt and refused to remove any of the indicted men from their seats, leaving them in a position to continue legislating for the city after being accused of taking bribes.[92] The newspaper organ of the Ring machine, the New Orleans *Post*, lashed out at the grand jury as "packed" and violently attacked the judges and officers of the Criminal Court as prejudiced and motivated by politics in the investigation. It was strongly criticized for this impudence by the *Picayune*.[93] But the weekly *Mascot*, which was now also a Ring organ, struck out at the dailies as sensation seekers. It claimed they were scaring the public and intimidating the juries trying the councilmen by recalling the lynchings which followed the acquittal of the Italians in the Hennessy case. Such emotion-charged journalism was robbing the accused men of a fair trial.[94] Under the shadow of impeachment themselves, the council had to hear the impeachment case of a city recorder for extortion. The verdict they brought in was "not guilty," a pathetic gesture toward saving some of the honor of their besmirched administration.[95]

On September 14, the investigation reached the mayor's office. The district attorney asked for his impeachment in Civil District Court on charges of nonfeasance, malfeasance, favoritism, corruption, and gross misconduct. Since the citizens' organization could unearth no criminal charges against the mayor, they had contented themselves with this vague suit in civil court. The specific acts which were used as evidence against him included the following: his signing the Fischer franchise, failure to suspend indicted councilmen, granting of pay during suspension to the recorder who

91 *Daily States,* July 23–26, 1894.
92 *Daily Picayune,* June 15, 27, 1894.
93 *Ibid.,* June 24, 1894.
94 *Mascot,* August 18, 1894.
95 *Daily Picayune,* May 6, June 29, 30, 1894.

had been impeached, the connection of his wife's firm with the courthouse construction, his signing of contracts for labor and supplies with private firms without public advertisement, and his attempt to remove the Police Board for its appointments of patrolmen in courts.[96]

The prosecution argued that the Fischer franchise had been illegal, since it was not publicly advertised as required by law. The mayor, therefore, had broken the law by signing it. The defense met this charge by pointing out that law covered only street railroads (streetcar lines), not railroads. It also added that in the last administration Shakspeare had approved ordinances providing for the building of a belt railroad, but the parties involved had been unable to carry through the project. In challenging the mayor's struggle with the Police Board as a usurpation of power, the citizens' case against Fitzpatrick was weak. He had done nothing more than Shakspeare, whom no one would have thought to impeach for his long stubborn battle with the police commissioners.[97]

Judge Fred D. King handed down his verdict in this case in March, 1895, although the evidence had been heard by the beginning of January. His verdict favored the mayor on all points.[98] The daily papers were disgusted with the verdict. But the *Mascot* re-ran a cartoon it had used when Fitzpatrick was elected, showing working men carrying him on their shoulders to City Hall.

The big boss of the Third ward had beaten the reformers again. But it was a personal victory. The old Ring organization was in trouble—badly shaken up by the lottery fight, it was falling to pieces as a result of the scandals in the Boodle Council. Only the

---

96 *Ibid.*, September 15, 1894.

97 *Ibid.*, January 10–13, 1895; State of Louisiana, Parish of Orleans, Civil District Court, Division B, No. 43,762, *State* ex rel. *Charles A. Butler, District Attorney* vs. *John Fitzpatrick, Mayor, Argument of Counsel for Citizens in the Proceedings asking for a Removal of Mayor of New Orleans* (New Orleans, 1895) , 3–63.

98 *Daily Picayune*, March 15, 1894; *Times-Democrat*, March 15, 1894; *Daily States*, March 15, 1894. Judge King had been a member of the Anti-Lottery League and, therefore, not a political ally of Mayor Fitzpatrick in the election of 1892. Thus he could not be charged with political bias in deciding this case in the mayor's favor.

personality of the mayor kept it intact through the election of 1896. Also the reform drive against the Fitzpatrick administration was more than a mere bid for power by a silk stocking clique, as the friends of the Ring claimed. It was part of a general stirring of the community's conscience which had begun with the crusade against the lottery. By the election of 1896, the old Ring was dissolving and new reformers, who wanted more than a businessman for mayor and a balanced budget, were emerging.

6

MUNICIPAL SERVICES
AND TECHNOLOGICAL CHANGES

IN 1884 UPPER CITY PARK blossomed out in gardens and lovely buildings for the Cotton Centennial Exposition. The city government spent $100,000 for an exposition horticultural hall. But at the same time municipal sanitary conditions were allowed to continue in the most outdated fashion. This sharp contrast of beauty and baseness certainly could have found parallels in other American cities of its time. It illustrated one of the biggest problems in the United States after the Civil War: the discrepancy between the expansion of urban centers and the development of proper municipal facilities to meet the needs of their rapidly growing populations.[1]

New Orleans was decidedly backward in offering such services. It had no sewerage system and no adequate garbage collection. Drinking water was secured from cisterns, because the waterworks supplied a muddy brown water fit only for industrial uses. The streets were mainly unpaved, littered with stinking debris, and pock-marked with ruts. Drainage pumping machines were outmoded and never able to carry off the sudden semitropical rainfall characteristic of the Crescent City. Flooding of the streets was frequent, particularly in the area between Claiborne Street and Lake Pontchartrain, and in Algiers, which had no drainage apparatus. Even in relatively dry spells the deep gutters and drainage canals usually reeked with slimy, stagnant water.

[1] See Table 6 for a comparison of local expenditures on municipal services with those of other cities in 1880.

[Table 6]

Comparison of New Orleans
and Six Other Cities in Expenditures in 1880 [a]

City	Total expenditures	Per capita	Approximate population
Philadelphia	$23,360,872	$ 27.60	847,000
Chicago	4,138,906	8.20	503,000
Boston	18,327,870	50.00	362,000
Louisville	2,008,105	16.30	123,000
San Francisco	3,184,120	13.60	234,000
Baltimore	5,902,899	14.70	332,000
New Orleans	1,889,627	8.70	216,000

City	School expenditures	Per capita	Sanitary expenditures	Per capita
Philadelphia	$1,090,718	$1.17	$191,756	$ .22
Chicago	726,883	1.43	53,475	.11
Boston	1,652,245	4.58	535,031	1.48
Louisville	158,000	1.29	4,500	.04
San Francisco	817,173	3.50	(not given)	(not given)
Baltimore	599,997	1.80	246,300	.74
New Orleans	200,000	.92	10,000	.05

(NOTE: Sanitary expenditures do not include sewerage costs which are listed below.)

City	Police Department	Per capita	Fire Department	Per capita
Philadelphia	$1,141,824	$1.34	$387,318	$ .45
Chicago	444,186	.86	310,275	.81
Boston	810,154	2.24	567,444	1.56
Louisville	95,000	.77	80,805	.65
San Francisco	433,848	1.85	276,700	1.18
Baltimore	584,719	1.75	165,035	.50
New Orleans	185,000	.66	121,500	.56

City	Charities	Streets	Sewerage
Philadelphia	$421,876	$ 455,162	$ 78,911
Chicago	(not given)	255,993	219,467
Boston	232,031	1,257,021	752,034
Louisville	60,675	163,000	8,200
San Francisco	160,497	(not given)	471,890
Baltimore	160,244	107,474	28,003
New Orleans	57,632	182,860	(no sewerage)

ª These statistics are taken from "A Tale of Six Cities," *Daily Picayune*, January 11, 1881. George E. Waring, Jr., who compiled the statistics on cities for the Tenth Census (1880), may have supplied this data since he was a frequent visitor to New Orleans during the winter of 1880–1881 in connection with the proposed Waring System of sewerage.

Because of its saucerlike shape between the Mississippi River and Lake Pontchartrain, New Orleans had a more severe drainage problem than almost any other city in the nation. Its inability to solve this problem kept its soil saturated. The water table was only about four to six feet below the ground's surface.[2] Until the metropolis could be drained more thoroughly, the laying of pipes for large-scale drinking water or sewerage systems was risky and exorbitant in cost. The realization of these two vital public needs, therefore, depended upon the solution of the drainage problem. The disease rate of the population was also intimately connected with drainage. Most prominent local physicians realized that the city's smelly ditches, canals, and mud puddles were unhealthy. But, unaware that the disease-carrying mosquitoes breeding in these places were the chief danger, doctors complained of the harmful effect upon health which the rotting garbage in the canals and ditches might have.

During Reconstruction a tendency had appeared to "farm out" certain sanitary services, mainly the drainage system, to private contractors. With the ousting of the municipal carpetbag regime, the Redeemers continued this practice. Burdened with the huge Reconstruction debt, the municipality could not afford to continue

2 In 1884 when the Robert E. Lee monument was erected, the water table at Lee Circle was about four to six feet below ground level. By 1936, when a survey was made of the statue's foundation, the water table had fallen to twenty feet below ground level. Joy Jackson, "How They Erected Lee's Statue the First Time," *Dixie Roto Magazine, Times-Picayune*, January 18, 1953.

operating the water works, which it leased to a private company in 1877. The dumping of garbage in midstream downriver was handled by private contractors, as was the disposal of contents from privies. Drainage came back under the direct control of the city by the early 1880's. But the local government willingly accepted the help of a volunteer civic group, the Auxiliary Sanitary Association, in keeping gutters flushed, cleaned, and repaired. This abdication of their responsibilities for the sanitary welfare of the city was one of the most unfortunate weaknesses of the city fathers in this period. Imbued with a laissez-faire philosophy which made them feel private enterprise was best, they were subjected to extreme pressure from powerful business tycoons and always badgered by the city's old debts and empty treasury. This combination of influences forced them to give out contracts for municipal services.

In fairness to the administrations of this era it must be admitted that the public was hostile to any improvements that meant raising taxes. Accustomed to the shortcomings of their sanitary facilities, they did not appreciate attempts to force compulsory services upon them. This attitude doomed a private sewerage company in 1881. Householders would have been compelled to accept its service if it had been put into operation. But as opposition was too strong, the idea was abandoned. In addition to the hostility of the public to municipal sponsorship of public works projects, the technological difficulties that would have to be overcome to achieve proper drainage, sewerage, and water purification for New Orleans seemed almost insurmountable, or so costly as to be unobtainable. This is why the 1880's and 1890's were years of frustration, rather than achievement, in the field of municipal services. Only a rise in prosperity in the late 1890's, a concurrent lowering of the municipal debt and of taxes, and the mild yellow fever epidemic of 1897 finally assured public backing for an extensive program of improvements, beginning in 1899.

The haphazard drainage system serving the community throughout the last twenty-five years of the nineteenth century consisted of open canals receiving water from higher portions of the city via street gutters and conveying it to four drainage pumping machines. The pumps delivered the water into Lake Pontchartrain.

The *Mascot* cartoon of April 22, 1882, which was responsible for an injunction against the weekly.

A Rex parade reaches the Henry Clay statue at the foot of Canal Street.

The New Orleans levee during the cotton season.

That the *Mascot* was strongly pro-Lottery is
evident in this cartoon of February 15, 1890.

Three of the pumping stations were located in the bottom of the basin between the river and the Metairie and Gentilly ridges: the Dublin drainage machine at 14th and Dublin streets, the Melpomene drainage machine at Claiborne Avenue and Melpomene Street, and the Bienville drainage machine at Hagan Avenue and Toulouse Street. The London Avenue drainage pump was situated on Gentilly at London Avenue. The entire east bank of the city was divided into three drainage districts by the two navigation canals, the Old and New basins. The area drained did not extend farther than the Gentilly and Metairie ridges, and the section between Claiborne Street and the ridges was very poorly drained. Working at their full capacity the four drainage pumps were capable merely of disposing of the runoff from 1/100 of an inch of rain in five minutes, or 12/100 in an hour. This was totally inadequate to meet the emergencies of sudden heavy storms. Rapid rainfall always meant the inundation of large areas of the city which took days to drain off. In Algiers the situation was worse since this section had no drainage apparatus at all.[3]

Storm and subsequent flood were almost yearly occurrences in low-lying areas of New Orleans. Although the river levees were never in first-class condition, inundations from levee crevasses did not occur in the city limits. It was the inability of the drainage equipment to carry off rainfall and the occasional backing up of waters from Lake Pontchartrain upon the city that caused flooding. The scenes of misery at such times were pathetic to behold. Some streets were covered with as much as three feet of water. Streetcars continued operating as long as possible; often when the mule could no longer see where he was going in the water-covered street, the driver would get out and lead him carefully along the track. Skiffs, however, were more common than streetcars.

George Washington Cable, describing such inundations, wrote: "Skiffs enter the poor man's parlor and bedroom to bring the morning's milk or to carry away to higher ground his goods and chattels. All manner of loose stuff floats about the streets; the

[3] *Report on the Drainage of the City of New Orleans by the Advisory Board (Appointed by Ordinance No. 8327, Adopted by the City Council, November 24, 1893)* (New Orleans, 1894) , 51–52.

house-cat sits on the gatepost; huge rats come swimming, in mute
and loathsome despair, from that house to this one, and are pelted
to death from the windows. Even snakes seek the same asylum." [4]

To meet these emergencies, citizens' committees were always
hastily formed by the mayor and other prominent residents to dis-
pense food and dry clothing to the flood victims. But the modest
vegetable and dairy farmers on the outskirts of the city suffered
dreadful losses despite all well-intentioned efforts at relief. Their
small crops were destroyed. Their cattle starved in water up to
their bellies since wagons with hay could not reach them.

After one vicious flood in 1881 a displaced old woman and her
nine cows were found perched hungry and homeless in the upper
room of the Melpomene pumping station. In Algiers, where flooding was common, Negro residents complained that white residents,
by damming up certain ditches and canals to protect their sections from overflow had caused a deluge of the Negro section. In
contrast to deeds of unselfishness in distributing food to the needy,
there were also many acts of vandalism and theft. To discourage
such conduct, Mayor Shakspeare expressed the public sentiment
that anyone looting an abandoned flooded home should be shot
on sight. After the water receded from local homes and thoroughfares, New Orleanians had to do a mammoth job of cleaning up
the remaining mud, debris, and dead animals that littered streets
and private property. Unfortunately, this type of devastation occurred every few years.[5]

Although funds were lacking to remedy the faulty drainage
system, there was no lack of proposed plans to correct the trouble.
Various schemes to improve or completely reorganize the system were suggested between 1880 and 1890 by Joseph Jouet, John
L. Gubernator, and Samuel D. Peters.[6] Attempts were also made
to set up a drainage board with the power to tax. In 1888 Judge
William H. Howe introduced into the state legislature a bill that
would have created such a board; it did not have the approval of

4 Cable, *The Creoles of Louisiana*, 271–72.

5 *Daily Picayune*, January 16, 22, February 11, 12, 16, 1881; April 14, May 6,
1882; June 29, 1888; January 7, 8, 1889; August 14, 15, 16, 1894; *Final Report of
the Citizens' Central Storm Relief Committee* (New Orleans, 1894).

6 *Report on the Drainage of the City of New Orleans*, 50.

the city council and was defeated.[7] The following year the city government presented its own drainage bill to the public in a special election, authorizing a special tax for drainage and paving. This too was rejected by a majority of 932 votes out of a meager total of 4,852.[8] (The *Mascot* had opposed the tax since paving contracts were involved. It felt paving companies would be the only benefactors if the tax were passed.) [9]

In the spring of 1890 a severe storm hit New Orleans. Agitation quickly revived for the establishment of a drainage board, with the result of the immediate creation of the Orleans Levee Board by the legislature. Composed of the mayor, the commissioner of public works, and seven other members, it had full control of local levees and the drainage of the city. No large funds were allowed for drainage, but the board did have the right to collect a one mill tax for levee purposes and to issue bonds for levee construction.[10] The banks of the Old and New Basin canals were particularly in need of repair. In former years when mules and horses had pulled vessels through these waterways, the banks had been kept in perfect condition. But with the widespread adoption of tug boats to pull loads through the canals, the banks had been allowed to decay and to become riddled with crawfish holes.[11] Some of the inundations after heavy rains were the result of breaks in the canal levees.

Soon after its creation the board decided that a complete revamping of the drainage system had to be accomplished. It offered a prize of $2,500 for the best plan of drainage submitted. But none of the proffered plans were acceptable, because no scientific knowledge existed of the city's topography, exact area to be drained, or hydrography. There was no way, therefore, to tell if any of them were practical. A topographical survey of the city was necessary.[12] Unsuccessful endeavors were made to secure money for such a survey from the state legislature, the city council, and private sub-

---

[7] *Daily Picayune*, May 26, June 6, 1888.

[8] *Ibid.*, May 26, 1889.

[9] *Mascot*, May 11, 18, 1889.

[10] Flynn, *Flynn's Digest*, 432–35; Rightor, *Standard History of New Orleans*, 108.

[11] *Daily Picayune*, February 1, 1882.

[12] *Report on the Drainage of the City of New Orleans*, 50.

scription. Finally in 1892 the city council appropriated $17,500 for surveying purposes. Bitter opposition forced a search of city archives to ascertain whether or not such data already existed, but none was found. In February, 1893, the ordinance authorizing the work and appropriating the funds for its completion was adopted. Although a few opponents of the survey contested its legality, the courts fortunately held it was a legal act of the city government, and work was begun to compile the much needed information.[13]

To conduct the survey, Mayor Fitzpatrick appointed an Advisory Board on Drainage. Three members of the board were engineers who prepared a topographical map of New Orleans, with the aid of the city engineer, Linus W. Brown. By 1895 the Advisory Board had formulated a scientific drainage plan which was approved by the council. Within another year the specifications of this plan had been completed. Fitzpatrick vetoed an ordinance calling for bids to execute the new drainage system since he felt it could not be adequately financed through the regular sources of revenue. It was left to the Walter C. Flower administration in 1896 to secure passage of a legislative act creating a drainage commission to supervise the construction of the new system and providing for its special financing. Work began in 1897 to build modern pumping stations, set up allied electrical equipment, and extensively repair the canals. The old drainage machinery dating back to the 1870's was finally abandoned in 1900 when the entire new system began operating.[14]

Plans were discussed and several ordinances passed between 1880 and 1900 in regard to a sewerage system for New Orleans. In 1880 the New Orleans Drainage and Sewerage Company had been organized and had asked the city council to grant it the privilege of laying a sewerage system similar to the Waring System operating in Memphis. The chief difference between Memphis' sewerage plan and its modification proposed for New Orleans was the utilization of natural drainoff in Memphis to pump waste into the river, while New Orleans, below the river level, would have to drain its sewage toward Lake Pontchartrain and then pump it back into the Mississippi. Its promoters assured the council that it could be done.

13 *Ibid.*, 51; Kendall, *History of New Orleans*, II, 507, 573.
14 Campbell, *Manual of the City of New Orleans*, 38–41; Rightor, *Standard History of New Orleans*, 124–26; Kendall, *History of New Orleans*, II, 574.

Since the system was to be compulsory, it was opposed by many property owners and by the Tax Payers' Association. Although eleven hundred citizens signed a petition against it, it was endorsed by the Auxiliary Sanitary Association and by the state board of health. After sending a delegation to Memphis to inquire about its success in that city in 1881, the council approved the ordinance granting the company the right to lay its pipes. But public disapproval and the high cost of construction doomed the project to failure within a year.[15]

A second group, the New Orleans Sewerage Company, headed by Dr. Joseph Holt, former president of the Board of Health, secured a franchise in 1892. Specifications were drawn, property acquired for a pumping station, and iron pipe purchased. Five miles of pipe were laid in the central part of the city. But once again the cost proved far in excess of the contractor's estimate, and hostility arose to the privately owned system. By 1895 this company, like its predecessor, had failed.[16]

Public awareness of the city's urgent need for sewerage was fearfully sharpened in 1897 with the outbreak of a mild yellow fever epidemic which claimed 298 victims. In 1898, fifty-seven died from this disease, and in the last year of the century, twenty-three victims were recorded.[17] City finances were now in a solvent state—the local government could no longer pass on its responsibilities to private concerns. Undoubtedly influenced by Populist advocacy of public ownership of vital community facilities, the reform Flower administration effected the purchase of the sewerage company's franchise and also that of the waterworks. These two municipal facilities were placed jointly under the Sewerage and Water Board, created in 1899. The laying of the sewerage pipes was initiated in 1903, and the system began operating on a partial basis in 1907. By the following year it was fully completed.[18]

The lack of pure drinking water in nineteenth century New Or-

15 *Daily Picayune,* December 15, 19, 1880; January 16, 18, February 12, March 11, 23, 30, April 5, 14, 19, 20, 1881.

16 Kendall, *History of New Orleans,* II, 577; Flynn, *Flynn's Digest,* 1001–10.

17 Rightor, *Standard History of New Orleans,* 210.

18 *Eighteenth Semi-Annual Report, New Orleans Sewerage, Water and Drainage Board* (New Orleans, 1908) , 60–61. See also Martin Behrman, *The History of Three Great Public Utilities—Sewerage, Water, and Drainage and Their Influence Upon the Health and Progress of a Big City* (New Orleans, 1914) .

leans adversely affected the health of the population. Malaria, typhoid, and dysentery (all tied in with the water supply) were far more common than the more spectacular plagues that occasionally swept over the metropolis. But their causes were not completely understood, and the public stoically accepted "wiggletails" in the water. The major source of drinking water came from cisterns, which were required by law to have covers. This, however, did not prevent mosquitoes from entering them.[19] During long dry spells, when the dregs of the cisterns had to be drained, many residents turned instead to drinking beer. Breweries did a booming business after several weeks of drought.[20] During such water famines the fire plugs were usually turned on to allow thirsty citizens to collect buckets of water for their own use and that of their stock. This muddy water came from the Water Works Company by agreement with the city government. But in 1889, during a particularly long dry period, the waterworks vigorously objected to distributing its water to the public in this manner. It claimed that hydraulically operated elevators in the business district would be unable to function if the water pressure were dissipated by the widespread opening of hydrants.[21]

The waterworks dated back to 1833 when it had been incorporated as part of a banking firm. At the expiration of the company's franchise in 1869, the city had taken over and enlarged the plant. In 1878, however, the poverty of the municipal government forced the state legislature to give the waterworks franchise to a private firm with monopolistic rights over the water supply.[22] Although the waterworks allowed the nonprofit Auxiliary Sanitary Association to pump water out of the river to aid in flushing gutters and canals, it aggressively challenged the attempts of some industrial firms along the river to pipe water into their plants.[23] Most of the

19 For cistern ordinances, see Flynn, *Flynn's Digest*, 209, 392. On mosquitoes, see Thomas Ewing Dabney, *The Indestructible City* . . . (New Orleans, n.d.) , 9.

20 *Mascot*, October 27, 1894.

21 *Daily Picayune*, June 10, 1889.

22 Dabney, *The Indestructible City*, 9; Kendall, *History of New Orleans*, II, 527.

23 See *Daily Picayune*, September 23, 1884, for an account of the substantial supply of water furnished the city by the Auxiliary Sanitary Association. See the May 18, 1886, issue of *Daily Picayune* for "The Water Monopoly," a discussion

waterworks' customers were industrial users, as the high cost of its product and the muddy sediment it contained made it unfit for drinking purposes.[24] In the early 1880's the waterworks had furnished water free to the city's buildings and hydrants in return for tax exemption. But during the administration of Guillotte, the council made a bargain with the company in which the latter agreed to pay taxes if the city would pay its water bill. As already noted, the municipal water bill was far in excess of the taxes involved.[25] This arrangement was challenged in court, but was upheld. As a result, the city paid yearly approximately sixty dollars for every fire plug in use, although much of the water supplied to these outlets came from the water pipes of the Auxiliary Sanitary Association.[26]

Because it was interested mainly in its industrial customers and placed the operation of elevators above the needs of drought-stricken citizens, the Water Works Company ultimately met its downfall. When the Flower administration decided to attempt the combination of drainage, sewerage, and water under public

---

of the waterworks' claim to a monopoly of river water. The waterworks' fight to keep local industries from taking water from the river may be traced in its annual reports. See the *Fifth Annual Report of the Water Works Company* (New Orleans, 1883), 4; *Ninth Annual Report of the Water Works Company*, (New Orleans, 1887), 3–4; *Nineteenth Annual Report of the Water Works Company* (New Orleans, 1897), 3–5.

[24] Anyone desiring to drink the water furnished by the company had to purify it by placing it in large earthen jars and adding alum. Dabney, *The Indestructible City*, 9. A comparison of the waterworks' statistics for 1887 and 1897 reveals the following: In 1887 this company had 73.67 miles of pipes, served 1,117 hydrants, and supplied to its customers a total of 2,209,075,710 gallons of water. By 1897 the company had made only a modest increase with 119.30 miles of pipes, 1,757 hydrants served, and 3,917,941,248 gallons of water supplied to its users. *Ninth Annual Report of the Water Works Company*, 15; *Nineteenth Annual Report of the Water Works Company*, 11–12.

[25] The water bill amounted to approximately $68,000 a year while taxes paid by the waterworks were about $11,000. *Daily Picayune*, January 18, 19, 1886. Details of the contract between the city and the waterworks concerning municipal purchasing of water are in *Seventh Annual Report of the Water Works Company* (New Orleans, 1885), 3–4.

[26] For court fight against the company's contract with the city, see *Eighth Annual Report of the Water Works Company* (New Orleans, 1886), 3–4; *Daily Picayune*, January 19, 1886; May 23, 1889. On cost of five fire plugs, see *Daily Picayune*, June 9, 1889.

control in 1898, the city attorney in conjunction with the state attorney general initiated a suit against the water company for breach of contract, claiming it had grossly abused its privileges. One of the major complaints against it was the raising of rates in defiance of its contractual restrictions. Appealed to the state high court, the case was settled in favor of the city and state, and the Water Works Company was forced to forfeit its franchise. As a result of this civic victory, a new city-owned water plant dedicated to purification and service to private homes began operating in 1908–09, roughly the same time as did the sewerage system.[27]

In addition to facing the challenge of its faulty sanitary facilities, the Crescent City struggled vainly in the Gilded Age to maintain its muddy, unpaved streets. The Department of Improvements, renamed the Department of Public Works in 1882, had one of the largest staffs of any local government agency. John Fitzpatrick served as head of this department from 1880 to 1888 and was often criticized for creating a political machine within its confines by hiring more men than needed. Although politics naturally played a major role in city employment, Fitzpatrick must be cred-

27 For suit against the company to force surrender of its charter see these documents: Civil District Court, Parish of Orleans, Division E. *The State of Louisiana versus New Orleans Water Works Company. Printed Compilation of Pleadings* (New Orleans, n.d.) ; Civil District Court, Parish of Orleans, No. 345. *The State of Louisiana versus The New Orleans Water Works Company. Defendant's Reply, J. R. Beckwith, Farrar, Jones & Kruttschnitt, E. Howard McCaleb, Counsel for Defendant* (New Orleans, n.d.) ; Civil District Court, Parish of Orleans, Division E, No. 58, 345. *The State of Louisiana versus The New Orleans Water Works Company. Defendant's Reply to the Brief of the State by J. R. Beckwith of Counsel for Defendant* (New Orleans, n.d.) ; Supreme Court of Louisiana, No. 13,701. *State of Louisiana, Appellant versus New Orleans Water Works Company, Appellee. The City of New Orleans, Intervenor. Appeal from the Civil District Court For the Parish of Orleans* (New Orleans, n.d.) ; Supreme Court of Louisiana, No. 13,701. *State of Louisiana, Appellant versus New Orleans Water Works Company, Appelle. The City of New Orleans, Intervenor, Appeal From the Civil District Court For the Parish of Orleans. Reply to Supplement Brief of Appellant by Counsel for Appellee* (New Orleans, n.d.) . Discussion of the new water purification plant may be found in Behrman, *History of Three Great Public Utilities;* R. S. Weston, *Sewerage and Water Board Report on Water Purification Investigation and on Plans Proposed for Sewerage and Water Works System* (New Orleans, 1903) ; G. G. Earl, *Proceedings of the Thirtieth Annual Convention of the American Water Works Association* (New Orleans, 1910) 23–37.

ited with a genuine dedication to his job as commissioner of public works. His staff and available funds were actually far below what was needed to keep the streets in good condition. But he stubbornly pursued the job of filling holes, grading as many streets as possible, cleaning out canals, and hastily adding fill to the city's upper and lower protection levees in times of inundation. He also did not hesitate to prod streetcar lines into repairing streets they were responsible for by the terms of their charters, or which they had torn up in laying new tracks.[28] An investigation of his stewardship, following his defeat for reelection in 1888, failed to discredit him. His successor, General Pierre G. T. Beauregard, was appalled at the overwhelming responsibilities of this department and resigned shortly after taking office in disgust at the lack of cooperation received from the council.

When Fitzpatrick first took office in the early 1880's, the condition of the streets, ditches, and footbridges in New Orleans was at the lowest point they had known since antebellum times. Constant rainfall during the winter of 1880 had burrowed out huge ruts in all city streets. The continual passage of drays and carts to and from the levee had made the riverfront streets almost impassable. When a dock watchman's shanty caught fire on the wharf at the foot of Robin Street, the volunteer fire wagon could not get closer than one square to the blaze.[29] Holes in the streets caused havoc to four other volunteer companies during a fire at Broadway and Levee streets: the engine of Pioneer Company broke down, Babcock Company broke several spokes in a wheel, a horse of Young America Company was crippled, and the second assistant of Protector No. 2 was thrown from the engine and severely injured. As a result of this fiasco, the chief engineer of the Sixth Fire District refused to answer any more calls in this neighborhood.[30]

Broken bridges across gutters and canals were reported by the dozens every day. Newspaper readers chuckled over the story of one young woman who caught her foot in a broken bridge plank

[28] For examples of Fitzpatrick's correspondence with streetcar companies concerning their obligations to repair streets, see Letterbook of Administrator of Department of Improvements of the City of New Orleans, 1881-83 (MS in Archives of the City of New Orleans, New Orleans Public Library).
[29] *Daily Picayune*, December 21, 1880.
[30] *Ibid.*, January 11, 1881.

and drew quite a crowd before she was extricated.[31] Stark tragedy was chronicled in the case of a two-year-old girl who fell through a broken bridge into a gutter filled with boiling lye and was burned to death. A nearby soap factory was discharging the lye into the open gutter.[32] This was a common practice and residents often complained to the Board of Health of offensive matter discharged into city gutters from the gas works, the ammonia works, and Charity Hospital.[33] In addition to dilapidated bridges, numerous decayed and listing flagpoles, private fences, sheds, and buildings were reported in the papers.

Within ten months after Fitzpatrick took office, his department had repaired 145 blocks of cobblestone streets, 26 miles of shell roads, 39 blocks of ballast roads, and built 1,228 bridges and 51 blocks of plank roads. A total of 645,093 feet of lumber was used in the work.[34] This represented a sizeable improvement over street work in preceding years. But of the approximate 566 miles of streets in the city, 472 were unpaved.[35] No matter how diligently the Department of Improvements worked, it could never repair all the streets. Those which it did work on were likely to be impassable again after the next hard rain. Throughout the Gilded Age in New Orleans, the problem of bad streets and broken bridges continued to nag local residents.

Materials used in street repair and paving varied. Ordinary mudholes were patched up with ballast stone from the holds of ships which discharged it at Port Eads. It was picked up by a ballast company, hauled to the city, and sold as street filling.[36] Paving materials included cobblestone, stone blocks, planking, gravel, and

31 *Ibid.*, December 15, 1880.
32 *Ibid.*, April 8, 1881.
33 *Ibid.*, December 24, 1880.
34 Semiannual report of the Department of Improvements in *Daily Picayune,* July 27, 1881. See also a more complete record in Department of Improvements Record Book of Bridge Gangs and Repairs to Bridges, 1881–83 (MS in Archives of the City of New Orleans, New Orleans Public Library) .
35 Waring and Cable, "History and Present Condition of New Orleans," 272.
36 For information on the ballast company which had a monopoly on its product, see grand jury report in *Democrat,* April 1, 1881.

shells.[37] The first asphalt-paved street in the city was St. Charles Avenue, completed in 1884–85. This paving was paid for with the funds from the St. Charles Avenue streetcar franchise.[38] Asphalt was not as popular, however, as rosetta gravel, which was used to surface many streets during the second Shakspeare and Ftizpatrick administrations. The highhanded way in which the council usually decided to use this gravel along a particular street (without consulting the property owners involved) caused much bitterness in the late 1880's and early 1890's, especially since Maurice Hart was president of the gravel company. Citizens complained that the graveled streets did not hold up and soon sank back into their former state of mire.[39] Undoubtedly one of the main difficulties was the lack of proper drainage which quickly undermined such soft surfaces as gravel and shells. However, these soft surfaces were preferred to hard ones, such as asphalt and cobblestones, as they made a cushioned foundation for carriage and dray cart wheels. Only in the late 1890's when bicycles became very popular locally and in the early twentieth century with the advent of the automobile did hard paving, such as asphalt, begin to come into common use on local thoroughfares.

One of the main street nuisances was garbage, which was sporadically collected. Department of Improvements carts were supposed to haul it to the garbage wharf. There it was loaded on the barges of a private contractor, towed downriver, and dumped. But garbage collection never covered the entire metropolitan area adequately. Smelly refuse was allowed to stand for days on some streets. Furthermore, the garbage boats broke down several times

[37] Waring and Cable, "History and Present Condition of New Orleans," 272. Materials used most frequently in the 1890's are itemized in Fitzpatrick, *Mayor's Message*, 1894, pp. 9–10. "Paving" meant any type of surfacing other than dirt.

[38] Since the council was afraid city creditors might garnish the $275,000 paid in the New Orleans and Carrollton Railroad for this streetcar franchise, they made an agreement whereby the company received the franchise in return for paying the cost of the St. Charles Avenue paving and that of several other streets. With the money coming directly from the company, rather than the city treasury, there was nothing for the creditors to garnish. *Daily Picayune,* August 2, 8, 1882.

[39] *Daily Picayune,* May 22, August 4, 1894.

and lay idle for months. This led to the practice of merely dumping the garbage on some neutral grounds in sparsely settled sections. Frequently, when repairs were done on canal banks, garbage was used as filling.[40]

The unsightly litter of refuse on local thoroughfares spurred Mayor Fitzpatrick to call for a new method of garbage disposal in 1892. A garbage contract was awarded in 1893 to a company that built a combination incinerator-fertilizer plant. As previously pointed out, this new method of garbage disposal was bitterly resented by New Orleanians, since the contractor refused to pick up any garbage not set out in a special type of container and would not pick up glass and old shoes at all. During 1894, the year of the council scandals and Fitzpatrick's impeachment, garbage was allowed to stand in noxious heaps all over the city by the stubborn contractor, who insisted it was not being put out according to the required regulations. This was one of the main causes of public hostility toward the incumbents of City Hall. During the next administration the ordinance concerning garbage regulations was repealed.[41] The practice of dumping garbage on neutral grounds or in the area surrounding the incinerator continued, however, into the twentieth century.

Aside from the holes and garbage that marred the streets, stray goats, mules, horses, dogs, and cattle roamed loose on a city-wide scale. Goats infested the public squares, particularly Annunciation Square, where one resident counted thirty-two of the "pleasing animals" grazing across from his house.[42] An ordinance was passed in 1881 making it illegal for goats to run loose. But this could not be enforced.[43] Other ordinances aimed at mules and horses were partially enforced. One forbid the driving of loose horses or mules through the city streets.[44] A second made it illegal to hitch horses in front of private or public places to the inconvenience of the property owners.[45]

Controlling the number of dogs roaming the streets was a much

40 *Ibid.*, May 11, 1881.

41 See Chapter 5 of this book for a discussion of public opposition to the garbage contractor in 1894.

42 *Daily Picayune*, January 18, 1881.

43 Jewell, *Jewell's Digest*, 310; *Daily Picayune*, February 17, May 4, 1881.

44 Jewell, *Jewell's Digest*, 312; *Daily Picayune*, March 9, 1881.

45 Jewell, *Jewell's Digest*, 312; *Daily Picayune*, July 19, 1881.

more difficult task. The most common method of removing them was to distribute poisoned sausage to such strays. This harsh practice resulted in occasional heartrending stories in the papers in which children struggled futilely to keep their pets from eating the fatal morsels. A rise in the number of rabid dogs in the early 1880's drove the city fathers to purchase two covered wagons and four horses to aid in catching, impounding, and destroying stray mongrels. These dog wagons, the first ever used locally, proved too costly for the impecunious city. Within a year they were abandoned, but by 1890 dog wagons were again put into operation on a permanent basis.[46]

Stray cattle were found mainly on the outskirts of the city where the sparse population was usually engaged in dairy farming. The greatest friction with the city authorities came in the area surrounding lower City Park. In 1880 this area was undeveloped and dairymen let their cattle roam freely. When a fence was put up by the city in an attempt to begin beautifying the park, the enraged dairymen tore it down.[47] As this section was improved, however, the cattle had to retreat to other pastures.

The difficulty of traversing the muddy, hole-ridden city streets sharply restricted the number of private carriages. Only the most wealthy, or those to whom it was a business necessity, traveled in this fashion. A rented carriage with two horses cost two dollars an hour in 1880.[48] By 1893 the price had risen to three dollars an hour. After midnight, the cost was more, sometimes double the daytime rate.[49] As a result, many persons traveled by streetcar instead of private vehicles. One English visitor in 1880 observed: "Gentlemen go out to dinner; ladies go to balls per horse-car. It is the great leveller. It is the Temple of equality on wheels." [50] But this "great leveller," despite its modest fare of five cents, was still too

46 *Daily Picayune,* June 7, 14, 1882; June 24, 1883; *Times-Democrat,* July 1, 1882; Flynn, *Flynn's Digest,* 97–101; a copy of the report of the superintendent of the dog pound may be found in Department of Police and Public Buildings Register of Pounds for Dogs, 1890–92 (MS in Archives of City of New Orleans, New Orleans Public Library).

47 *Daily Picayune,* July 26, 1881.

48 "On Canal Street," Pt. XXIV of "America Revisited," London *Daily Telegraph,* February 19, 1880. See also Sala, *America Revisited,* 16.

49 Zacharie, *New Orleans Guide,* 24.

50 "On Canal Street," Pt. XXIV of "America Revisited" London *Daily Telegraph,* February 19, 1880. See also Sala, *America Revisited,* 19.

expensive for the poorer citizens. Shop girls walked to work because they would have had to spend about one-eighth of their weekly salary for carfare.[51]

New Orleans had one of the most extensive systems of streetcars in the country, as various visitors and local writers liked to point out. Canal Street was the meeting place for lines radiating up and down town. The cars were drawn by mules and had no conductors. Passengers deposited their fares in a box upon entering. If they needed change, drivers could provide it up to two dollars. Service was regular with a car coming along on most lines every five minutes during the daytime.[52]

A streetcar ride could sometimes turn into an unpleasant experience. Occasional accounts appear in the local dailies about drunken petty politicians who picked fights on streetcars. Frequently the driver got into these brawls. Strikes of car drivers also meant trouble. At such times blockades were set up by the strikers to stop cars, passengers were turned out, and the cars pulled off the tracks.[53] One constant annoyance which bothered passengers was the widespread habit of smoking and chewing tobacco on the mule cars. A visitor to the cotton exposition in 1885 noted that "even when ladies and children are fellow-passengers the men smoke and expectorate all over the place. . . . The matter is now under discussion in the public journals, many of which, while talking fustian about the 'native chivalry' of the Southerner, urge him not to offend on this one point. . . . The City Council have debated whether to make smoking in public cars a punishable offense. Meanwhile . . . the 'chivalric' one smokes and spits regardless alike of threats and remonstrances." [54] Obviously the streetcar companies were as insensitive to such criticism as most of their male customers. The *Mascot* complained that the streetcars were covered with accumulated filth, and it urged the officials of the car companies to start a cleanup campaign.[55]

Since the streetcars were the most vital means of transportation,

51 Shugg, *Origins of Class Struggle in Louisiana,* 281.
52 Zacharie, *New Orleans Guide,* 37.
53 *Daily Picayune,* December 23, 28, 30, 1884.
54 "New Orleans Exhibition," London *Daily Telegraph,* February 2, 1885.
55 *Mascot,* April 8, 1882.

the street railroad companies (as they were called) and their executives wielded great power. They were respected and praised in some quarters, while hated and attacked in others. During a feud between the management and labor of one line, the president narrowly missed being hit by a shot fired at him from ambush.[56] Another president of a car company went to jail twice for contempt rather than answer questions on whether his firm gave a fifty-thousand-dollar bribe to city officials to secure a franchise. One member of the grand jury that considered this case was a rival street railroad head, Watson Van Benthuysen. It was rumored that he had been challenged to a duel by the accused man because of his part in the investigation.[57] A colorful, dynamic personality, Van Benthuysen had a hot temper and a predilection for speaking his mind, which often brought him into conflict with council members, with striking employees, and with Commissioner Fitzpatrick over the responsibility of his streetcar line for repairing certain streets. Van Benthuysen's most publicized escapade, described in the discussion of the Shakspeare administration, was his threatening of the *Mascot* business manager after that paper ran a cartoon insinuating that he was manipulating the city council to get a favorable renewal of the franchise of his company, the New Orleans and Carrollton Railroad. As already pointed out in discussion of the Shakspeare administration, this incident resulted in the mayor attempting unsuccessfully to suppress the *Mascot,* and in an injunction which Van Benthuysen secured to prevent the *Mascot* from referring to him in future publications. This injunction was eventually overruled by the state supreme court.[58]

The corporate actions of streetcar companies paralleled the cavalier conduct of their executives. In a railroad "war" in the early 1880's, two companies fought over the right of way on Carondelet Street. The original line along this route resented attempts by a second company to build tracks next to its own. The mayor and

[56] *Daily Picayune,* January 17, 1882.
[57] *Ibid.,* December 30, 1880.
[58] The cartoon which started this trouble appeared in *Mascot,* April 22, 1882. Details of the resulting chain of events which culminated in the appeal to the state supreme court are in *Daily Picayune,* April 23, 28, 30, May 5, 9, 11, 1882; *Mascot,* April 29, 1882.

the Cotton Exchange got into the squabble when the second company began tearing up street paving in order to lay its tracks and also threatened to cut off the entrance to the exchange's new building.[59] Several months later another streetcar line was reprimanded by the mayor for pulling up gutter curbing and sidewalk on Camp Street to lay new tracks.[60]

Electric trolley cars were comparative latecomers to New Orleans. The first successful electric railway operated for profit in an American city had been installed in 1887–88 in Richmond, Virginia, by Lieutenant Frank J. Sprague. By 1890 fifty-one cities had such electric trollies.[61] Several times during the 1880's suggestions had been laid before the New Orleans streetcar companies and the city council concerning the merits of electric streetcars. But it was 1893 before electrical power was put into full-time operation on a local streetcar line. On February 1, 1893, that aristocrat of streetcars—the St. Charles Avenue line—inaugurated the city's first electric cars.

The *Picayune,* describing the inauguration scene, noted that Carrollton Avenue, where the cars were drawn up for opening ceremonies, was crowded with spectators. Ladies drove up in private carriages, and teachers and their students stood in rapt attention in front of McDonogh [public school] No. 23, which was decked with flags for the occasion. At the signal to begin, the first car started "as gently as a leaf drifting on a summer river" and made its way from Carrollton down St. Charles to Canal Street as "pompously as any Carnival king." In the business district from Poydras to Canal the sidewalks were lined with cheering citizens.[62] The lethargic, long-eared mules did not disappear immediately, however. In Algiers especially they could be found pulling streetcars until 1907.[63]

[59] *Daily Picayune,* March 18, 22, 23, 1881.

[60] *Ibid.,* June 11, 1881.

[61] Arthur M. Schlesinger, *The Rise of the City, 1878–1898* (New York, 1933), 92.

[62] *Daily Picayune,* February 2, 1893.

[63] Louis C. Hennick and E. Harper Charlton, *Louisiana: Its Street and Interurban Railways* (Shreveport, 1962), I, 22–23. For a detailed description of local streetcar lines see Louis C. Hennick and E. Harper Charlton, *The Streetcars of New Orleans, 1831–1965* (Shreveport, 1965).

Despite the late appearance of electric streetcars in the Crescent City, electric lights had been in use on public streets since 1881. Between 1880, when they were exhibited as a novelty, and November, 1882, about five hundred outdoor electric lights were installed, mostly on prominent streets in the business area. They were in operation on city wharves and in several public squares and markets. Private groups of businessmen shared the cost of lights along their thoroughfares.[64]

The company experiencing this electrical boom was the Southwestern Electric Light and Power Company, which had been organized in New Orleans in 1881. The next January it started operations with one generator capable of supplying forty lights. By the end of October, it had twelve generators capable of furnishing five hundred lights, all of which had been contracted for before they were set in place.[65] These first electric lights in New Orleans were Brush open arc lamps on series circuits, perfected by Charles F. Brush in Cleveland, Ohio, in 1879. They were used indoors only in such large areas as the *Times-Democrat* composing room and under the galleries of commercial houses.[66] On Canal Street, however, Cusach's Drug Store had had electric lights since early January, 1882. In this store, one of the first indoor photographs using electrical illumination was taken on January 10. The glass plate negative required a time exposure of nineteen minutes to get a perfect picture.[67] On September 11, the *Times-Democrat* reported that New Orleans was in advance of other cities its size in the number of electric lights it displayed. Mark Twain on a local visit also praised the city's many electric lights.[68]

In 1884 the council authorized the city to contract with the Brush Electric Company for 113 lights on numerous streets in the business district.[69] This was the first time the city had awarded a lighting contract to an electric company. Gas, although not yet

64 *Daily Picayune,* January 8, 11, 24, April 7, 1882; *Times-Democrat,* July 2, 29, September 11, November 2, 1882.

65 *Times-Democrat,* September 11, 1882.

66 *Ibid.,* Hugh M. Blain, *A Near Century of Public Service in New Orleans* (New Orleans, 1927), 59–60; Schlesinger, *The Rise of the City,* 99.

67 *Daily Picayune,* January 11, 1882.

68 Twain, *Life on the Mississippi,* 200.

69 *Daily Picayune,* November 14, 19, December 24, 1884.

generally used for cooking, was the major source of street illumination. But the New Orleans Gas Light Company, which served
most of the city, and the Jefferson City Gas Light Company, operating in the Sixth and Seventh Districts, offered far from ideal service.
Numerous gas lights were reported unlighted every night. Incentive for better service was lacking since the municipal government
was lax in paying its own light bill. Shortly before the election of
1882 the long-suffering gas company threatened to turn off all gas
lights on election night if its bill did not receive prompt attention.
Officials had to transfer money from another account to pay the
New Orleans Gas Light Company and avoid such a calamity.[70]

With the opening of the Cotton Centennial Exposition in 1884,
Maurice Hart and several associates formed the Louisiana Electric
Light and Power Company to operate the lighting system for the
main building at the exposition. This meant more competition for
the harassed gas companies and the fledgling Brush concern. Hart's
company was best known to local residents for the half dozen towers with clusters of five electric lights on top of each which it erected
in March, 1885, at various spots around town. It was Hart's
conviction that these towers would throw a wider beam of light
since they were higher than ordinary street lamps. They proved to
be a miserable failure, unfortunately, and were bitterly denounced
by editors and the reformer-business faction which missed no opportunity to criticize the actions of the incumbent Ring council.[71]

In 1886 a charter was granted to a third electric company, the
Edison Electric Illuminating Company. This firm, using incandes-
cent lights, was the first to specialize locally in interior lighting.
In the 1890's it was succeeded by the Edison Electric Company.
Although the Louisiana Electric Light and Power Company was
awarded a five-year lighting contract in 1886, the Edison Electric

[70] *Ibid.,* scattered references between November 1 and 11, 1882. See also
Times-Democrat, November 11, 1882; *Mascot,* November 11, 1882. A brief history of the gas companies is in *A Near Century of Gas in New Orleans* (New Orleans, 1926) , a publication of the New Orleans Public Service, Incorporated. On
both electricity and gas, see W. E. Clement, *Over a Half Century of Electricity
and Gas Industry* (New Orleans, 1947) .

[71] For privileges of Louisiana Electric Light and Power Company, see Flynn,
Flynn's Digest, 281–84. A brief history of the company is given in Blain, *A Near
Century of Public Service in New Orleans,* 60–61.

Company eventually absorbed it in 1897. The Brush company also was eliminated from competition. Eventually, in the twentieth century, the control of the three public utilities—streetcars, gas, and electricity—was consolidated in the New Orleans Public Service, Incorporated.[72]

Telephones, like electric lights, were introduced into New Orleans shortly after their national appearance. A local resident, William H. Bofinger, was so impressed with the exhibition of the telephone at the Philadelphia Centennial Exposition in 1876 that he entered into a contract to exploit the invention in Louisiana. With his associates in the American District Telegraph System, he formed a company which built and equipped special telephone lines for business firms beginning in 1877, after attracting public attention by several demonstrations. Each line could connect only two points at its opposite ends. There was no intercommunication between lines. Used to replace messengers between offices and warehouses or factories of commercial firms, at least 150 of these lines were in existence by 1878.[73]

With the invention of the switchboard, first set up in New Haven, Connecticut, in 1878, new vistas opened for local telephone users. Now if a switchboard were put into operation in the Crescent City, it would be possible to connect one local line with many others instead of merely with its own terminal point. Taking the initiative in this direction, Bofinger and his associates made the following proposition to the owners of telephone lines.[74] Bofinger's firm bought a switchboard for $9,000 to initiate a central telephone exchange. As their part of the project, the owners of lines who desired the service would pay the expense of connecting their lines to the central exchange. The charter of this new system, the New Orleans Telephonic Exchange, was granted to Bo-

72 The New Orleans Public Service, Incorporated, came into being in 1922. By the beginning of 1926 it completely controlled gas, streetcars, and electricity in the city. Blain, *A Near Century of Public Service in New Orleans*, 61–70.

73 *Telephone Conditions in New Orleans, Louisiana: Being a Report Presented by a Special Committee of the New Orleans Board of Trade Approved April 8th, 1908* (New Orleans, 1908) , 52–54.

74 For information on the switchboard see Roger Burlingame, *Engines of Democracy: Inventions and Society in Mature America* (New York, 1940) , 112–16.

finger and associates by the city council in 1879.[75] Of the approximate three hundred lines Bofinger had installed between 1878 and 1879, ninety-nine were listed as subscribers in the first directory of the new company in December, 1879.[76]

The following year the owners of this company expanded by turning over the local exchange to their newly-formed Louisiana Telephone Company, whose service they hoped to extend all over the state. Long distance to Baton Rouge was installed in 1883 or 1884. The charge was about sixty cents for five minutes. In addition to the local exchange, which had around 876 subscribers, the *Daily States* reported in 1883 that there were nineteen others in Louisiana serving an approximate 1,600 subscribers. Although service began to be extended to wealthy businessmen's homes in the Garden District in 1882, telephones, as a rule, were confined to business and industrial uses. The Louisiana Telephone Exchange sold out to the Great Southern Telephone and Telegraph Company in 1883. A truly fundamental change affected the New Orleans business world the next year when the telephone company hired about twenty women as telephone operators. The applications of five hundred women for these jobs proved that local women were ready and eager to work despite southern prejudices against their participation in business.[77]

Between 1884 and 1898, the year the Great Southern turned over their Louisiana and Mississippi exchanges to the Cumberland Telephone and Telegraph Company, the local exchange prospered, but not in proportion to the strides it had made during its first few years. When Cumberland assumed control in 1898 there were only 1,641 telephones in use. The area in which they were concentrated was bounded by Jackson Avenue, Claiborne Avenue, Iberville Street, and the river. Only one hundred phones could be found outside of this territory. Algiers had a mere eight.[78]

The local telephone system, as it existed up to 1898, was an open wire system whose service was on grounded or single lines with

[75] Flynn, *Flynn's Digest*, 1,124.
[76] Dabney, *One Hundred Great Years*, 332.
[77] *Telephone Conditions in New Orleans*, 52–56; *Daily States*, April 7, 1883; *Times-Democrat*, July 27, 1882; *Daily Picayune*, April 20, 1884.
[78] *Telephone Conditions in New Orleans*, 54–56.

less than three miles of cable in the entire operation. The wires were strung on poles owned jointly by the telephone, telegraph, electric light, and streetcar companies. Sometimes, wires were even attached to trees. Long distance lines were limited to connections with Baton Rouge, Donaldsonville, and St. Bernard and Plaquemines parishes. A survey of the facilities of the Cumberland Company in 1908 showed that this firm had installed much new equipment and had increased the number of telephone subscribers in the city to thirteen thousand. This, however, was considered a meager showing for a metropolis with a population of more than a third of a million persons.[79]

Like other phases of life in this period, sanitary services and public utilities tended to consolidate by the twentieth century. Services vital to health and the carrying on of everyday living in a large city—such as drainage, sewerage, and drinking water—were taken over by the city government. The major steps in this movement came between 1896 and 1900 when a reform administration influenced by the progressive ideas of the Municipal Reform League was in office. Such "natural" monopolies as electricity and streetcars were drawn together when streetcars were electrified. Gas was united to local electrical interests since both were street light illuminators, with electricity proving the most popular of the two by the turn of the century. None of these three—electricity, gas, and streetcars—primarily involved health or was absolutely necessary to sustain life. They were, therefore, allowed to remain under private control and eventually to consolidate.

[79] *Ibid.*, 54–56, 102.

7

PUBLIC HEALTH, CHARITY
AND EDUCATION

THE SWEDISH BARK *Excelsior* arrived at New Orleans on July 5, 1880, after taking on a cargo of coffee at Rio de Janeiro a month earlier. It had passed through the usual twelve days of detention and fumigation at the Mississippi River Quarantine Station below the city. Despite these precautions, however, two days after making port one of its crew members became ill. On July 10 he died at Touro Infirmary with symptoms of yellow fever. As soon as his illness had been discovered, the *Excelsior* had been inspected, its crew directed to remain on board, and the vessel ordered by the Board of Health to return to the quarantine station. Three other crew members contracted yellow fever and only one recovered.

The ship was detained at the quarantine station for over a month after the last case of fever was diagnosed. When it was allowed to leave, it was only permitted to tie up at a remote landing on the west bank of the city, and its crew kept on board while it took on a cargo of grain.[1] Quick acknowledgment of the *Excelsior's* contamination and stiff isolation of its crew by the Board of Health had prevented the fever from becoming a city-wide epidemic such as the one that cost over four thousand lives in 1878. New Orleans seemed to have learned a bitter lesson in early identification and prevention of the disease's spread.

[1] Virginia Parsons, "A Study of the Activities of the Louisiana Board of Health From 1855 to 1898 in Reference to Quarantine" (M.A. thesis, Tulane University, 1932) , 99–102.

But Crescent City health officials received no praise for their courage and quick action. Some local commercial elements thought of them as bungling extremists who had hurt trade with the rest of the Mississippi Valley. Furthermore, little confidence in their sincerity or ability to control the disease was shown by adjacent areas. Remembering past instances in which New Orleans doctors had hidden or minimized the number of yellow fever victims until it was too late to keep a full-scale epidemic from sweeping across state boundaries, Mississippi and Tennessee declared a quarantine against the entire state of Louisiana as a result of the *Excelsior* infection. Galveston, which sent a delegation to investigate, decided against quarantine when its committee found not a single case of yellow fever in the city.[2] For weeks after the ill-fated *Excelsior* sailed away, the memory of its grim cargo of death hindered New Orleans's normal contact with neighboring areas. This reputation as a harbor of pestilence whose officials could not be trusted to tell the truth about disease in the city was to stick to New Orleans until the end of the nineteenth century, although by that time it was not always justified.

The *Excelsior* affair illustrated that a new era had begun in local public health, even though nearby states were unaware of it. From 1880 on, the state Board of Health, which actually was almost exclusively concerned with New Orleans rather than the state as a whole, showed courage and unwavering determination in stiffening quarantine, perfecting methods of disinfection, and in facing the pressures of influential commercial groups who had their own way in relaxing quarantine in antebellum years and the mid-1870's. Under commercial pressure, the state legislature in 1876 had passed an act allowing the Board of Health to let any ship arriving from a tropical port avoid quarantine if it had no disease aboard and was fumigated with carbolic acid.[3] This loophole in the quarantine system was doubtless responsible for the terrible epidemic of 1878.

In 1880 when the Board of Health was reorganized, four of its

2 *Ibid.,* 98–99.
3 *Ibid.,* 25–26; Kendall, *History of New Orleans,* II, 763; G. Farrar Patton, *History and Work of the Louisiana State Board of Health* (New Orleans, 1904), 9–10.

members were chosen by the governor and five by the city council. This local control over the board's membership did not mean that it would be the pawn of privileged interests, for its new president, Dr. Joseph Jones, was a man in whom the business enemies of quarantine met their match. Dr. Jones continued the former policy of sulphur fumigation of ships at the Mississippi River Quarantine Station and boldly called for complete quarantine in 1883 to avoid importing yellow fever from Havana and Vera Cruz. Public sentiment was indignant over this action, but Dr. Jones's will prevailed and yellow fever did not reach the city.[4]

Harassed by public hostility, powerful business interests, and lack of funds, the Board of Health was naturally suspicious of any offers of help, which might turn out to be Trojan horses. The Auxiliary Sanitary Association (A.S.A.), organized in 1879 as a private volunteer sanitary corps, soon proved its sincerity and success in aiding the Department of Public Works and the Board of Health.[5] It also proved that not all businessmen were enemies of public health measures. It was founded by a group of businessmen who felt the health of the city was tied up with its commercial prosperity and deserved their attention. Its president was Charles A. Whitney, director of Charles Morgan's Louisiana Steamship and Railway Company, the Houston and Texas Central Railway Company, and founder of Whitney Iron Works. Edward Fenner, its vice-president, owned a saddlery store and was active in the Chamber of Commerce. The membership of this organization also included three insurance company presidents, a steamship company agent, and members of the cotton and stock exchanges.[6] One of its first projects called attention to the faulty construction of many privies

4 Patton, History and Works of the Louisiana State Board of Health, 20–21. A biographical sketch of Dr. Joseph Jones appears in John Duffy (ed.), The Rudolph Matas History of Medicine in Louisiana (Baton Rouge, 1962) II, 390–91.

5 Organization of the Auxiliary Sanitary Association is mentioned in Waring and Cable, "History and Present Condition of New Orleans," 286–87. The combined efforts of the Board of Health and the Auxiliary Sanitary Association definitely increased public interest in the sanitary welfare of the city by 1881. In an editorial on April 9, 1881, the Daily Picayune called the favorable reaction to their efforts "extraordinary."

6 Dennis East, II, "Health and Wealth: Goals of the New Orleans Public Health Movement, 1879–84," Louisiana History, IX, (Summer, 1968), 252–54.

in the city and their general unhealthy condition. In addition, the habit of emptying chamber slops along with laundry water into superficial drains which flowed into open street gutters was sternly criticized by the association.[7] In an attempt to clean out such foul-smelling gutters, it built a pumping station on the river to flush gutters and drainage canals. A campaign was launched by the A.S.A. at the same time to grade city lots. This culminated in an ordinance requiring such grading to aid drainage.[8] It advocated vaccination and supervised a number of volunteer workers to help Board of Health sanitarians in their health inspections of local residences.[9] When moral support was needed for an unpopular quarantine decree, the Auxiliary Sanitary Association could be counted on to back the Board of Health.

Another group, whose contact with the Louisiana board was not as profitable to local public health as that of the Auxiliary Sanitary Association, was the National Board of Health. Created in 1879, it had vague powers to investigate disease, make reports to Congress, and set up some quarantine outposts.[10] Since New Orleans was regarded as one of the major sources of disease influx, it was only natural that the national board took more than a passing interest in its condition. Bad feeling between the Louisiana and national boards grew up by the early 1880's over the latter's insistence that the state board agree to the establishment of a federal quarantine station on Ship Island. The local board argued for the continuation of its own station at the mouth of the Mississippi and felt that its ability to guard against disease was being questioned by this Ship Island suggestion. The state board also resented its national rival's request to send a health officer to Port Eads to work alongside state health officials at the quarantine

7 Duffy, Rudolph Matas History of Medicine, II, 466–67.

8 On the pumping station and flushing of ditches and canals, see Daily Picayune, January 16, 18, 20, March 15, 16, April 13, May 8, 1881; January 13, May 22, 1882; Waring and Cable, "History and Present Condition of New Orleans," 276. On the ordinance requiring the filling of lots, see Daily Picayune, July 13, 1881, and Flynn, Flynn's Digest, 391.

9 On Auxiliary Sanitary Association's sanitary corpsmen, see Daily States, March 28, 1883, and Daily Picayune, June 27, 1884.

10 Parsons, "Activities of the Louisiana Board of Health," 63–67; Duffy, Rudolph Matas History of Medicine, II, 470–71.

station and to have an observer at all state Board of Health meetings.[11]

The Auxiliary Sanitary Association endorsed the general aims of the national group and advised the state board to cooperate with it. One physician member of the Louisiana board resigned when his fellow members showed hostility to the National Board of Health.[12] At least one newspaper and some vocal elements of the public, however, entered the fray on the side of the local board. The *Picayune* engaged in a verbal feud with the Memphis *Avalanche* in 1881 over the latter's insinuation that New Orleans was the source of infection of the whole nation and should be supervised by a national health agency.[13] In retaliation the *Picayune* ran an editorial with statistics damaging to Memphis asking, "Is Memphis a Pest House?" [14] By summer one journalistic wag noted that "New Orleans is apt to have a comparatively healthy summer if the people are not driven to insanity by the opinions of doctors." [15]

The unfortunate hostility which had grown up between the Louisiana Board of Health and its federal counterpart came to an end by 1883 when the congressional appropriations for the national board ceased, and quarantine power reverted to the Marine Hospital Service. The national board continued to exist until 1893, but without any real influence.[16] Although some national supervision of quarantine was sorely needed, public opinion and state officialdom in the 1880's was not ready for such a service. The Louisiana Board of Health, sensitive to the nationwide belief in its inability to control the spread of disease from incoming ships, was naturally anxious to prove its competency and good faith. Convinced that it knew better how to cope with local quarantine than a national board, the Louisiana body was the national group's

11 Parsons, *"Activities of the Louisiana Board of Health,"* 69–91; *Daily Picayune,* March 16, 1881.

12 *Daily Picayune,* January 30, March 16, April 3, 1881.

13 *Ibid.,* January 7, 1881.

14 *Ibid.,* May 3, 1881.

15 *Ibid.,* June 20, 1881.

16 Parsons, "Activities of the Louisiana Board of Health," 67–68. For a detailed account of the acrimony between members of the two rival boards, see Duffy, *Rudolph Matas History of Medicine,* II, 471–76.

bitterest enemy up until the latter's untimely demise. This provincial attitude was to be softened over the years as the local board gained in respect and self-confidence. By 1897 outstanding members of the Orleans Parish Medical Society were vigorous in their urging of the formation of a national public health service.[17] When quarantine finally passed over into federal hands in 1907 under the recently created United States Public Health Service, the changeover was cordial, unlike the atmosphere of jealousy and bickering that had surrounded the national and state boards of the 1880's.

The great desire of the Board of Health to prove it could check the maritime entry of yellow fever into New Orleans was realized mainly through the improved system of fumigation devised by Dr. Joseph Holt, the successor of Dr. Jones as head of the board from 1884 to 1888. Dr. Holt substituted bichloride of mercury for the carbolic acid formerly used in disinfecting ships. He constructed a furnace to vaporize the solution and directed it into the holds of vessels by means of a steam-propelled fan which blew the fumes through a galvanized conductor. He also built a heating chamber to fumigate clothes, bedding, and other personal articles of crew members and passengers.[18]

Dr. Holt's system was based on his belief that yellow fever was caused by a germ which could be annihilated by the bichloride of mercury. The fact that this substance was fatal to mosquitoes, the carriers of the infection, doubtless accounts for the relatively clean bill of health the city enjoyed in regard to yellow fever between the 1880's and 1897. When a mild epidemic did break out in 1897, it was introduced into the city by rail from Ocean Springs, Mississippi, not by maritime traffic. Dr. Holt's success was due as much to his ability as a diplomat as it was to his skill as a doctor. He successfully won over to his maritime plan of disinfection antagonistic commercial elements and state legislators who were at first

17 *Proceedings of the Orleans Parish Medical Society, New Orleans, 1897* (New Orleans, 1898) , 232–45.

18 Kendall, *New Orleans,* II, 764–65; Rightor, *Standard History of New Orleans,* 212; Dabney, *The Indestructible City,* 11; Parsons, "Activities of the Louisiana Board of Health," 44–46; Patton, *History and Work of the Louisiana Board of Health,* 25–26.

frankly skeptical. This enabled him to get an appropriation of thirty thousand dollars from the legislature with which to carry out his plan.[19]

During Dr. Holt's presidency of the board, one of the most important legal cases involving public health in the United States was settled. Litigation had been instigated in 1874 by the Morgan shipping and railroad interests to prevent the collection of quarantine inspection fees by the Board of Health. Facing such a formidable adversary, the board in the 1870's did not attempt to lift the injunction secured against it. In 1882 the case began anew when the legislature passed a new series of inspection fees. Reaching the United States Supreme Court in 1886, this involved the fate of quarantine stations all over the country. If Louisiana's right to collect such fees were judged unconstitutional, other states would also be deprived of this revenue which was the financial bulwark of most of their budding quarantine systems. Fortunately, the Supreme Court rejected the Morgan company's argument that such fees were an impost on commerce, and accepted the board's interpretation of them as just compensation for a necessary sanitary service to maritime commerce without which it could not survive. A compromise on back fees owed by those companies that had refused to pay between 1874 and 1886 yielded $36,000 for the coffers of the Board of Health by 1888.[20]

Through this added revenue and the assurance of inspection fees in the future, subsequent Board of Health presidents were able to add to Dr. Holt's disinfecting system. His successor, Dr. Clement P. Wilkinson, improved the heating chamber and put up an entirely new plant further down the river in 1889. Dr. Samuel R. Olliphant, president of the board in the 1890's, further im-

19 Patton, *History and Work of the Louisiana Board of Health*, 24–25. Dr. Holt's appearance before the leaders of the commercial world at the Produce Exchange was one of the most crucial conferences on the city's health ever held. This important meeting is reported in detail in the *Daily Picayune*, June 21, 1884.

20 *Cases Argued and Decided In the Supreme Court of the United States* (October Terms, 1885, 1886, In 118, 119, 120, 121, 122 U.S.) (Rochester, 1958), XXX, 237–43; Parsons, "Activities of the Louisiana Board of Health," 102–13; *Louisiana Annual Reports* (Baton Rouge, 1884), XXXVI, 666–73; *Louisiana Board of Health Report for the Year 1884–1885* (New Orleans, 1885), 45.

proved the disinfecting apparatus.[21] Although the yellow fever outbreak of 1897 was in no way a reflection on the quarantine restrictions at the mouth of the river, the Board of Health was severely criticized for failing to quell it before 298 persons died. Under a storm of criticism, the Olliphant board resigned, and Dr. Edmond Souchon headed a new state board. The following year a long overdue step was taken when the state legislature created a separate Board of Health for the city of New Orleans, separating the city's multifarious health problems from those of the state in general.[22]

Yellow fever returned again in 1898 in a mild form to chalk up fifty-seven fatalities. But the treatment accorded New Orleans in 1898 differed sharply from the hysterical rejection and abuse it had received from other areas in 1880 during the *Excelsior* crisis. Dr. Souchon, in collaboration with other leading southern medical men and Dr. Henry R. Carter of the United States Marine Hospital Service, had drafted a set of rules for the movement of persons and freight during the existence of land quarantine which were ratified by southern health officials at a convention in Atlanta, Georgia, in April, 1898. Known as the "Atlanta Regulations," these rules made it possible for commerce to continue at almost normal capacity during the slight epidemic in New Orleans that fall.[23]

The part played by mosquitoes in transmitting yellow fever was finally proven by the turn of the century, and Dr. Quitman Kohnke of the city Board of Health tried vigorously but in vain to get an ordinance passed empowering him to attack the breeding places of *Stegomyia* mosquitoes. If his pleas for a mosquito campaign had been heeded, the city might have been spared its last yellow fever outbreak of 1905. Unlike much sentiment of the 1880's which had looked upon the National Board of Health as a meddler in their affairs, the public and the medical authorities in New Orleans in 1905 quickly sought the aid of the United States Public Health

21 Righter, *Standard History of New Orleans*, 212; Patton, *History and Work of the Louisiana Board of Health*, 27–29.

22 *Acts Passed by the General Assembly, State of Louisiana, Regular Session, 1898* (Baton Rouge, 1898), Act No. 192, pp. 437–45; Kendall, *History of New Orleans*, II, 767–68; Patton, *History and Work of the Louisiana Board of Health*, 32–38, 42–48.

23 Kendall, *History of New Orleans*, II, 768–69; Patton, *History and Work of the Louisiana Board of Health*, 38–41.

Service and gave federal officials full control of the situation. The metropolis raised $150,000 in private contributions, and the state pledged $100,000 to clean up the Crescent City as the United States government had done in Havana, Cuba.[24] The result was an unqualified success, ending the epidemic in record time and slaying at last what a British visitor had poetically called the "dragon hight Yellow Jack." [25]

While quarantine operations took the major share of the Board of Health's time and money and received the most publicity during this period, the general health of the city required the board to perform other sanitary services such as the recording of vital statistics, the inspection of private residences, public markets, and dairies through its corps of sanitarians, and the granting of permits for the construction of buildings and privies. By the 1890's it had established chemical and bacteriological laboratories and expanded its activities to include the dispensing of free antitoxin and smallpox vaccine.[26] Beginning with 1879, the year after the epidemic, the city council passed quite a number of ordinances enlarging the scope of the board's work and attempting to improve the sanitary condition of the city.

In regard to infectious diseases, city ordinances gave the Board of Health the right to take over infected residences and fumigate clothing and household effects.[27] Carbolic acid, used in this work, was called *acid diabolique* by the Creoles, some of whom armed themselves with shotguns and resisted the sprinkling of it on their property.[28] The visiting of persons known to have contagious diseases, the deliberate exposure of children to such sickness, and

[24] Kendall, *History of New Orleans,* II, 769–70; Duffy, *Rudolph Matas History of Medicine,* II, 433–36.

[25] "America Revisited," London *Daily Telegraph,* February 23, 1880 (clipping in scrapbook, Howard-Tilton Memorial Library) ; Sala, *America Revisited,* 42.

[26] Information on the Board of Health's duties may be found in Flynn, *Flynn's Digest,* 390–406; Parsons, "Activities of the Board of Health," 22–26; Waring and Cable, "History and Present Condition of New Orleans," 281; *Daily Picayune,* April 14, 1882. On the laboratories see Patton, *History and Work of the Louisiana Board of Health,* 32.

[27] Flynn, *Flynn's Digest,* 402.

[28] Cable, *The Creoles of Louisiana,* 307–308.

the allowing of any infected child to go from one building to another were prohibited. All city physicians, steamboat captains, operators of hotels, and boardinghouse proprietors were bound by law to report any persons with signs of infectious disease within twenty-four hours. Public funerals for victims of communicable maladies were forbidden, and quick burial was demanded.[29]

In criticizing health nuisances, the Board of Health and prominent doctors in the community all agreed that the improper drainage and garbage collection, the lack of sewerage, and the impure drinking water supply of New Orleans were its chief sources of contamination.[30] Other health menaces the board and city fathers had to combat included impure milk, adulterated foods and drugs, and such unhealthy habits of local citizens as the grading of empty lots with manure (which was finally made illegal), and the throwing of uncollected garbage into privies.

Filthy dairies and tubercular cows were a nagging source of infection throughout the Gilded Age and the early twentieth century. An 1879 investigation by members of the New Orleans Medical and Surgical Association pointed out that in dairies within the densely populated sections of the city, cows spent their entire lives in stalls that were never cleaned out or disinfected. Covered with filth the animals were milked without ever being cleaned or given a breath of fresh air or sunshine. The water they drank came from shallow contaminated wells. Dairies on the outskirts of the city were little better. Cows were allowed to graze on swampy land surrounding the dairies, but received water taken from the drainage canals, a source also used to wash out milk cans (and to adulterate the milk, the committee suspected).[31] This investigation was undertaken to prove the urgency for ordinances to regulate

29 Flynn, *Flynn's Digest*, 395, 396, 400.

30 For examples of the innumerable statements made on this subject see Joseph Holt, *The Sanitary Relief of New Orleans: A Paper Read Before the New Orleans Medical and Surgical Association, October 31, 1885* (New Orleans, 1886), and Holt, *The Sanitary Protection of New Orleans, Municipal and Maritime,* reprint from *The Sanitarian* (January, 1886).

31 Thomas Layton, W. P. Brewster, E. T. Shepard, and Joseph Holt, *Report on Milk and Dairies in the City of New Orleans, Presented to the New Orleans Medical and Surgical Association . . . July 5, 1879* (New Orleans, 1879), 1–16.

dairies currently being considered by the city council. The ordinances were passed, but the herculean task of enforcing them proved too much for local authorities.[32]

The 1891 report of the Board of Health condemned the unsanitary condition of dairies and acknowledged that the laws regulating them were difficult to enforce. In 1895 out of sixty-four cows tested for tuberculosis from twelve local herds, forty-eight showed a positive reaction. As late as 1902, 10 percent of the city's milk supply was still being adulterated, mostly by adding water, although the Board of Health noted this was an improvement over conditions in former years. Standards for milk content had been set up in a city ordinance as early as 1879, but it was 1907 before any far-reaching enforcement of such regulations could be established. The struggle for hygienic conditions in local dairies was a long one which extended up to the end of the 1920's.[33]

Ordinances forbidding the sale of impure or adulterated foods and drugs were passed every few years. The peddling of fresh seafood on the street and its sale within a building used as a residence were both outlawed.[34] Diseased cattle were restrained from traveling through or being discharged at New Orleans by river or rail, and meat inspection was made compulsory in 1880.[35] The unauthorized sale of drugs and of dangerous patent medicines was one evil that stubbornly resisted efforts to abate it. Druggists protested the sale of drugs by grocers in 1882. How often such grocers were fronts for the sale of narcotic drugs can only be surmised. They did have the right to sell patent medicines, as Mayor Shakspeare informed Algiers druggists who asked him to investigate the situation.[36] Only drugs requiring a prescription were the exclusive preserve of pharmacists, and any violation of this law could be

[32] See these ordinances in Flynn, *Flynn's Digest,* 386, 387, 390.

[33] For conditions of dairies and the struggle to improve them in the 1890's see *Louisiana Board of Health Biennial Report, 1890–91* (New Orleans, 1891), 111–12, and Paul Stock, "Historical Background to the Present Activities of the Board of Health of the City of New Orleans" (M.A. thesis, Tulane University, 1932), 79–81.

[34] Flynn, *Flynn's Digest,* 394–95.

[35] *Ibid.,* 393.

[36] *Daily Picayune,* May 16, 1882.

punished. The fact that druggists felt this right was being threatened may be drawn from their petition to the 1882 state legislature to set up standard regulation for the sale of drugs.[37] The resulting state pure food and drug law of 1882 was largely ineffective. It was strengthened in 1888 with a state pharmacy law which set up a board of pharmacy and required all future operators of drug stores to be qualified pharmacists. It also called for correct labeling of drugs and poisons.[38] This act improved the handling of prescription drugs, but patent medicines continued to do a flourishing business largely unsupervised. The *Picayune* almost daily ran an ad which read: "Dandruff is Removed by the Use of Cocaine, and it stimulates and promotes the growth of the hair. Burnett's Flavoring Extracts are the best." [39] The *Mascot* ran a parody on a patent medicine ad and called it "Slop Bitters" which was "guaranteed to galvanize a corpse, make Mare Shakspeare see the error of his ways, or straighten the curved propellers of that eminent statesman Mr. B. L. [Bow-Legged] Donovan . . ." ("Bow-Legged" Donovan was a city employee who frequently made the police news for fighting, stealing, or causing public disturbances).[40]

In their inspections of the living quarters of private residences, the Board of Health had the right to order citizens to provide themselves or their tenants with better cisterns or sanitary facilities, and it could condemn an entire structure which it considered uninhabitable. Some undesirable tenement dwellings did exist in the city, as a report of the city surveyor in 1879 noted with regret. The city surveyor felt such buildings, sometimes only twelve and a half feet wide and built side by side on a three-hundred-foot block, crowded the population too drastically and invited diseases of all kinds to strike.[41] In comparison with other big cities on this point in 1890, however, New Orleans had less tenement dwellers

37 On such petitions see *Daily Picayune*, May 16, 17, 1882, and *Petition in Behalf of State Medicine to the General Assembly of the State of Louisiana* (by the Louisiana State Medical Society, Orleans Parish Medical Society, New Orleans Medical and Surgical Association) (New Orleans, 1883) .

38 Duffy, *Rudolph Matas History of Medicine*, II, 416–18.

39 *Daily Picayune*, May 4, 1882.

40 *Mascot*, August 12, 1882.

41 Henry C. Brown (city surveyor) , *Report on the Drainage, Sewerage and Health of the City of New Orleans* (New Orleans, 1879) , 11.

than New York, Chicago, and Boston, but slightly more than Philadelphia. In density of population it ranked low, with only 10.20
persons per acre as compared to New York's 58.7 persons per acre.
(See Table 7 for full statistics.)

Contrary to its reputation earned during antebellum days as a
yellow fever graveyard, New Orleans counted most of its fatalities
between 1869 and 1900 from dysentery, malarial diseases, pneu-
monia, and tuberculosis.[42] Smallpox and typhoid were erratic,
hitting the city severely one year and barely touching it another

---

[Table 7]

*Population Living in Tenements and Common Lodging
Houses and Density of Population in Five Cities in 1890*[a]

Population living in tenements and common lodging houses including hotels in 1890 (%)		Density of Population per Acre in 1890	
New Orleans	5.63	New Orleans	10.20
New York	18.52	New York	58.87
Chicago	8.60	Chicago	10.70
Philadelphia	5.60	Philadelphia	12.64
Boston	8.52	Boston	18.51

[a] *Eleventh Census, Vital Statistics, Cities of 100,000 Population and Upward:*
Pt. 2, p. 4.

---

season. In 1883 smallpox deaths reached 1,266, and in 1884, 292.[43]
Vaccination, offered free of charge by the Board of Health, still
met with unyielding opposition from some influential sources as
well as from the most ignorant element of the population.[44]
The smallpox hospital, leased to a private physician by the city,

---

42 Annual report of president of Board of Health in *Daily Picayune*, April 6,
1881; Chaillé, *Life and Death-Rates*, 12–13; *Compendium of the Eleventh Census* (Washington, 1894), Pt. 2, p. 59; *Abstract of the Twelfth Census* (Washington, 1904) , 205.

43 Chaillé, *Life and Death-Rates*, 16.

44 *Daily Picayune*, April 13, 14, 1882. Some doctors opposed vaccination; see
Duffy, *Rudolph Matas History of Medicine*, II, 439–40.

was periodically investigated and usually found to be inadequate. This situation did not change until the construction of the Isolation Hospital in 1916.[45] Despite the existence of compulsory vaccination by 1900, 924 cases were reported that year, with 252 deaths.[46]

Typhoid fatalities in 1889 were so negligible that New Orleans' death rate for this disease was lower than that of the twenty-seven other cities listed in the 1890 census. It had a mere 18.59 deaths per 100,000 population.[47] But a decade later this disease sharply increased, to such an extent that the Board of Health began reporting on it for the first time. In the last years before the new drainage and sewerage system helped lower the rates of all local disease, typhoid claimed 141 victims in 1901, 333 in 1902, and 412 in 1903.[48]

In general the death rate of Negroes was higher than that of whites, and that of males higher than that of females. In 1890 New Orleans' white death rate was 25.41 per 1,000 persons, the Negro death rate, 36.61. A decade later, the 1900 census showed the white death rate had fallen to 23.8, but the Negro had risen to 42.4.[49] Dr. Stanford Chaillé, a leading physician and local representative of the short-lived National Board of Health, pointed out in an article in 1888 that while the Crescent City's total death rate was high when compared to that of other American cities, it was quite favorable when contrasted to southern European cities with the same climatic conditions that existed in Louisiana. (See Table 8.)

To Dr. Chaillé, the most significant fact revealed by statistics compiled by state and national agencies by 1888 was the enormous gains made in lowering the disease and death rate in the city since

45 *Daily Picayune*, March 15, 21, April 2, 1882; May 30, August 7, 29, September 5, 1883; Stock, "Historical Background to the Present Activities of the Board of Health," 42–43; Duffy, *Rudolph Matas History of Medicine*, II, 517–20.
46 Stock, "Historical Background to the Present Activities of the Board of Health," 42.
47 *Eleventh Census, Vital Statistics, Cities of 100,000 Population and Upward:* Part 2 (Washington, 1896), 78.
48 Stock, "Historical Background to the Present Activities of the Board of Health," 44.
49 *Eleventh Census, Vital Statistics*, Pt. 2, p. 5; *Abstract of the Twelfth Census* (Washington, 1894), 189.

[Table 8]

*Death Rates per 1,000 Population in
Eight United States Cities and Eighteen Foreign Cities*[a]

8 United States Cities	5 Years 1880–84	1 Year 1880	Remarks
New Orleans	29.11	*25.98	*26.02 by Louisi-
New York	27.76	26.47	ana State Board of
Baltimore	25.03	24.20	Health
Brooklyn	23.39	23.33	
Boston	22.67	23.53	
Cincinnati	22.52	20.29	
Chicago	21.83	20.79	
St. Louis	20.56	18.93	

18 Foreign Cities	5 Years 1880–84	1 Year 1880	Remarks
St. Petersburg	*41.40	46.10	*4 years, 1878–83
Budapest	32.24	33.60	
Munich	31.67	34.74	
Naples	32.84		7 years, 1878–84
Breslau	31.86	32.60	
Marseilles	31.05		
Berlin	27.75	29.67	
Vienna	28.26	28.22	
Rome	29.02		7 years, 1878–84
Brussels	25.22	25.10	
Hamburg	24.79	24.95	
Turin	27.99	23.99	
Dresden	25.35	24.81	
Leipsig	25.21	26.24	
Paris	23.49	24.27	
London	21.20	21.70	
Frankfort am Main	20.04	20.50	
Stockholm	24.89	28.79	

[a] These statistics originally compiled by the Michigan State Board of Health appear in Chaillé, *Life and Death-Rates*, 15.

the 1830's. From an average rate of 63.55 deaths per 1,000 population in that decade, the death rate fell to an approximate 28.36 during the eight-year period, 1880 through 1887. Also, every decade between 1830 and 1860 had at least four severe epidemics, each totalling thousands of fatalities. The 1860's had at least two severe ones, and the 1870's, one final great outbreak in 1878, which took over 4,000 lives. The 1880's saw no such wholesale attacks of yellow fever or cholera. The period between 1880 and 1887 recorded only nine such deaths.[50]

Granted that New Orleans's general health level was below national par, it was better in the 1880's than in previous decades. More vigilant maritime quarantine and disinfection after 1880 could take credit for holding back the tide of plague. But the death rate could not be lowered further until sanitary services in the city were improved. It remained approximately 28 deaths per 1,000 population through the Twelfth Census in 1900. The toll taken by dysentery, malaria, and consumption—the silent killers whose yearly harvest was greater than the much publicized yellow fever—was not lessened until drainage, sewerage, pure drinking water, and pasteurized milk became everyday facts of life in the twentieth century.

Hospitals serving New Orleans in 1880 included the state-controlled Charity Hospital, with a capacity of 1,000 beds; Louisiana Retreat for the Insane, 40 beds; Touro Infirmary, 40 beds; and the smallpox hospital, the Luzenberg Hospital for Contagious Diseases, which had a private contract with the city to handle all cases of this disease. Its capacity was 50 beds.[51]

[50] Chaillé, *Life and Death-Rates*, 12–16.

[51] Duffy, *Rudolph Matas History of Medicine*, II, 524. These bed capacities come originally from Waring and Cable's article on New Orleans in the 1880 Tenth Census. The figure of 1,000 beds for Charity in 1880 seems high and may be taken as the estimate of its capacity in times of emergency rather than under normal conditions. Also included between 100 and 200 elderly invalids later removed to the almshouse. By 1900 the board report of Charity listed its capacity at 600 beds. On this last estimate of bed capacity, see Stella O'Connor, "The Charity Hospital of Louisiana at New Orleans: An Administrative and Financial History, 1736–1941," *Louisiana Historical Quarterly*, XXXI (January, 1948), 80.

The publicly operated Charity Hospital at New Orleans was one of the largest public institutions of its kind in the United States. The physical plant of the hospital in the last half of the nineteenth century dated back to the 1830's and was the third such structure since the hospital's inception in the 1780's. The massive brick building to which wings had been added in the intervening years, by the 1880's formed a square with an inner courtyard laid out in about an acre of flowerbeds, trees, and walks.[52] The hospital had suffered severe financial deprivation during Reconstruction. The official reports of this institution reveal that by the end of the 1870's there was a lack of bedding, mattresses were almost unusable, and supplies of medicine were depleted. Stairways and galleries were rotten and unsafe. With the administration of Governor Nicholls in 1877, these conditions began to get some attention from the state government. Seventy-one thousand dollars was appropriated by the legislature in 1879 for repairing the dilapidated buildings and for purchasing new equipment such as steam radiators, an elevator, a telephone, microscopes, and surgical instruments.[53] The year 1877 was eventful for Charity not only in its physical renovation, but in the introduction of competitive examinations for student interns. A successful applicants for one of these first internships was Rudolph Matas, who was to become world famous for his pioneering in surgery and anesthesia, and remained connected with Charity Hospital in various capacities for sixty-three years.[54]

The 1880's saw advances and attempts at new departures in medical care at Charity Hospital. Interns were required to have one year's medical study and to pass a competitive examination before being admitted as student interns by 1880. In 1882 an attempt was made to set up a nursing school by the vice-president of the board of administrators, Dr. Daniel C. Halliday. Unfortunately, this proposal raised a storm of controversy in which everyone from newspaper editors to the governor were embroiled. The controversy centered around the fear that this was a plot to

52 Coleman, *Historical Sketch Book*, 130–31.
53 Duffy, *Rudolph Matas History of Medicine*, II, 497–502; O'Connor, "The Charity Hospital of Louisiana at New Orleans," 65–69.
54 Duffy, *Rudolph Matas History of Medicine*, II, 502.

usurp the place of the Sisters of Charity at the hospital. The affair ended with the removal of the board of administrators and the house surgeon by Governor Samuel D. McEnery and the abandonment of the nursing school plans. It was not until 1893 that such a school was initiated at Charity. Ambulance service was first put into operation at Charity in 1885, and by 1886 the hospital opened its first dental clinic.[55]

In addition to the patients confined to beds in the hospital's wards, out patients were treated. In 1885 they numbered about thirty-five to forty daily and were examined and treated in the wards along with the bed patients.[56] Separate clinics for such patients were not set up until 1892.[57] Anyone desiring to visit the hospital could pay an admittance fee of ten cents. Visiting hours were 8 A.M. to 5 P.M.[58]

Of the many postwar problems which the Charity Hospital faced in the 1870's and 1880's, the most pressing were the increase in the number of Negroes who were admitted since emancipation, the burden of caring for chronically ill or elderly persons who had no adequate haven prior to the opening of the new almshouse in 1883, and a rise in the number of indigent strangers it received. Even up to 1890 almost two-thirds of the patients were either natives of other states or foreign countries.[59] Often they died without leaving any trace of survivors. Coleman's *Historical Sketch Book* noted that by 1885 over 38,000 persons without known friends or relatives had died at Charity Hospital since it opened its doors. Such persons were buried at the hospital's expense in the rear of St. Patrick's Cemetery in the decade of the 1880's. Plain wooden boards with their hospital numbers were placed over the burial plots of these unfortunates in case someone might come to claim their remains.[60]

[55] Duffy, *Rudolph Matas History of Medicine*, II, 502–506; O'Connor, "The Charity Hospital of Louisiana at New Orleans," 70–75; *Daily Picayune*, February 26, March 21, 1882; *Mascot*, March 4, 1882.
[56] Coleman, *Historical Sketch Book*, 131.
[57] Duffy, *Rudolph Matas History of Medicine*, II, 506.
[58] Coleman, *Historical Sketch Book*, 131.
[59] Duffy, *Rudolph Matas History of Medicine*, II, 498–500; O'Connor, "The Charity Hospital of Louisiana at New Orleans," 65.
[60] Coleman, *Historical Sketch Book*, 131.

Closely allied to the improving of health and of public hospital facilities was the care of the city's poor, aged, orphaned and insane in public and private institutions. Following every large-scale, antebellum epidemic new orphan asylums had sprung up, operated usually by private nondenominational or religious groups. The municipal grants made to such institutions before 1852 had been haphazard, depending on the necessity of the moment. But in that year an ordinance gave the mayor power to pay out of tax funds $14 per annum for each orphan he placed in city institution, a power which he exercised to the fullest the following year as a result of the 1853 yellow fever epidemic. City grants to private charitable institutions in 1853 totalled $9,627.97. By 1860 this sum had risen to $14,453.50, and by 1870 to $26,995.43. But a decade later the impecunious city could not afford the subsidy earlier granted by carpetbag officials. The city appropriation to private charitable institutions in 1880 was only $15,919.93. Twenty-one institutions shared this sum, an increase of nine over the number that had received aid in 1870. In 1890 the municipal subsidy to private charity was $22,500 and this was increased to $30,110 by 1900. The institutions which were recipients of this charity had also increased, to thirty-four.[61]

Supervision of private institutions was left strictly in the hands of their boards. The few municipal-operated institutions in existence by 1870 were also left largely to shift for themselves. Officially under the supervision of the administrator of waterworks and public buildings, they received so little attention that an investigation of the city's Home for the Aged and Infirm revealed thirty-one inmates living in the deepest privation without any matron or supervisor in charge or even the care of a visiting physician.[62]

Such a lack of cohesion in operating the three public institutions, the Home for the Aged and Infirm, the Boys' House of Refuge, and the City Insane Asylum, led in the early 1880's to attempts at reform. George Washington Cable, the small, quiet Cotton Ex-

[61] Evelyn C. Beven, *City Subsidies to Private Charitable Agencies in New Orleans: The History and Present Status, 1824–1933* (New Orleans, 1934), 12, 13, 24, 26.

[62] *Ibid.*, 30–31.

change clerk-turned-author, whose searing vision pierced so many dark corners of the city's conscience in this period, was mainly responsible for inaugurating this movement. In 1881, when Cable's literary efforts, *Madame Delphine, Old Creole Days,* and *The Grandissimes,* began to make his career as a writer seem secure, he gave up his job at the Cotton Exchange to concentrate on his writing. But reform work claimed a large share of his time during the next two years.[63]

A scandal in the City Insane Asylum in the summer of 1881 was the event that forced the public spotlight upon conditions in municipal institutions. Cable happened to be serving on the grand jury which investigated this scandal involving an attack on a woman mental patient by one of the asylum orderlies. He offered to investigate the procedure followed in model public asylums and prisons on an eastern trip he planned to make. Mayor Shakspeare agreed. Upon his return, Cable suggested to the city council that they create a Board of Prisons and Asylums as an inspection committee and data-collecting board. This was done in November, 1881.[64] By December, Cable was calling for the organization of an aid association which would work with the board in inspection and perform any committee work the Board of Prisons and Asylums might require. This association was formed in March, 1882, and began its attempts to aid the board through inspection and publicizing of conditions in public institutions.[65] Women and church offiicials took an active part in this work. The president of the board itself was Hugh Miller Thompson, pastor of Trinity Episcopal Church. Thompson and the other fourteen commissioners on the board were required to visit each public institution quarterly and report annually to the city council.[66]

[63] Arlin Turner, *George W. Cable, A Biography,* Chapter 8 and Chapter 9. Turner, "George W. Cable's Beginnings as a Reformer," *Journal of Southern History,* XVII (May, 1951), 150–52.

[64] Joseph A. Shakspeare to George W. Cable, May 17, 1881, in George Washington Cable Collection, Special Collections Divisions, Howard-Tilton Memorial Library, Tulane University; Turner, "George W. Cable's Beginnings as a Reformer," 150; *Daily Picayune,* November 1, 3, 8, 1881; *Democrat,* November 17, 1881.

[65] Turner, "George W. Cable's Beginnings as a Reformer," 150.
[66] *Ibid.*

The first problem to attract attention, the City Insane Asylum was also the first to be settled. The asylum was located in the former United States Marine Hospital building, a dank, gloomy establishment with no yard space.[67] Consequently mental patients could never be allowed outside for exercise or sunshine. The asylum was kept reasonably clean, but many of the inmates wore threadbare clothing and slept under meager covering. There were no women orderlies and no regular physician on the premises. As one orderly put it—a doctor was summoned only "if someone took sick." No attempts at treating patients' disorders and helping them to recover were ever made, and feeble-minded and insane persons were incarcerated together in this grim "jail." One woman patient who proved violent was tied on an outside balcony all night to keep her from disturbing the others.[68]

On one occasion when several commissioners of the prison and asylum board visited the Insane Asylum incognito, they were dumbfounded at the "show" that orderlies were putting on, making patients dance and sing. The shocked commissioners reported this incident to the papers and pointed out that there were no restrictions on asylum visitors. Anyone who wished to satisfy his curiosity by staring at the unfortunate inmates could gain admittance, and many did.[69]

The most startling revelation about the Insane Asylum that the board unearthed was the institution's death rate—41 percent in 1881. Most of the deaths had probably been caused by extreme malnutrition. This moved the *Mascot* to exclaim, "Great God, has it come to this, that right here in New Orleans sick persons have regularly for a long time been tortured to death by hunger and bad treatment without attracting public notice?" The accuracy of this charge was proved when the death rate dropped to 24 percent in 1882 after the patients were given a better diet.

67 Joseph Jones, *Quarantine and Sanitary Operations of the Board of Health of the State of Louisiana during 1880, 1881, 1882, and 1883 (Introduction to the Annual Report of the Board of Health to the General Assembly of the State of Louisiana, 1883–1884)* (Baton Rouge, 1884), cxviii.

68 Grand jury report in *Daily Picayune,* July 8, 1881. See also *Daily Picayune,* May 24, 30, 1882; *Mascot,* May 6, 1882; Turner, "George W. Cable's Beginnings as a Reformer," 153–55.

69 *Mascot,* May 6, *Daily Picayune,* May 30, 1882.

Another improvement was the hiring of matrons to care for the women's section of the asylum.[70]

In probing the insane asylum's history it was found that the place actually had no legal existence. It had been opened during the Civil War when patients could not be sent to the state institution at Jackson. What had begun as a temporary measure continued after the war on a permanent basis. In 1882 the Board of Prisons and Asylums recommended that the city close its asylum and send its patients to Jackson where they could have better care and outdoor exercises. When the inmates moved, the courts discovered that many of the patients were too rational to be transported under court warrants, and these persons were released.[71]

One other institution on which the board had an influence was the Boys' House of Refuge, for orphans, delinquents, and abandoned boys. Although the city contributed funds to other juvenile institutions, this was the only one completely under city direction. Because of its location in a swamp adjacent to Metairie Ridge, most of its occupants suffered from malarial chills and fever. Although the boys were fed plain, but filling meals, their sleeping quarters were pathetically inadequate. More than a hundred of them had to share a single dormitory room, because the only other room was uninhabitable due to the rotten floors, leaky ceiling, and broken windows. No blankets were available, sheets being the only covering. In the morning the boys washed their faces and hands in the yard in a wooden trough which could accommodate eight at a time. They attended school four hours a day and took part in military drilling for two hours.[72]

During Shakspeare's first term, a shoemaking establishment had been opened at the home. The shoemaker received the boys' service for a period, after which he paid the city a small fee for each

[70] *Mascot,* May 6, 1882; Turner, "George W. Cable's Beginnings as a Reformer," 156; *Times-Democrat,* July 18, 1882.

[71] Turner, "George W. Cable's Beginnings as a Reformer," 156; *Times-Democrat,* September 28, 29, 1882. For information on number of persons in asylum and length of their detention, see the entries in Record of Entries and Releases, City Insane Asylum, September 1, 1872–September 1, 1882, 2 vols. (MS in the Archives of the City of New Orleans, New Orleans Public Library.)

[72] Grand jury report in *Daily Picayune,* April 1, 1881, and August 14, 1881 of the same paper.

one employed. This shop and a broom factory at the home kept them occupied. The revenue from the shoemaking was meager, and the broom-makers had a difficult time finding buyers for their products. The chief problem of the Boys' House of Refuge, however, was its unhealthy location. This, the Board of Prisons and Asylums suggested, should be changed. After the City Insane Asylum was abandoned, Shakspeare at the end of his term received permission from the federal government to use the asylum's former quarters for the boys' home. While this building was not ideally built to serve institutional purposes and had little yard space, it was an improvement over the old location. The boys moved into this structure about a month after Mayor Behan took office.[73]

Securing a new almshouse was one reform initiated by Shakspeare and carried through by Behan, rather than by the Board of Prisons and Asylums. The need for such an institution was made clear to Shakspeare during his first year in office when destitute old people appeared at City Hall and pleaded to be placed in the Home for the Aged and Infirm, an overcrowded building practically falling in on its elderly occupants. It employed one matron, and the aged inmates themselves had to do the cooking, scrubbing, and cleaning up of the quarters.[74] One old blind man slept in the corridor of City Hall for several nights when told that the home was too crowded to receive him. He was finally sent to an institution for the blind in Baton Rouge. An old soldier requested permission from the City Hall to sing martial songs of the Civil War on the streets for a living.[75]

Such cases made Shakspeare decide to use the proceeds of the gamblers' fund to construct a new almshouse. In this institution would also be placed the incurable charity cases which were currently cared for at Charity Hospital. Work on the new almshouse began in 1882; it was discontinued when the financial condition of the city caused the gamblers' fund to be directed to other expenses, and was finally completed by Mayor Behan. The city's poor

73 *Daily Picayune*, December 28, 1880; January 5, March 8, 9, 10, August 14, 1881; November 17, December 12, 28, 1882.

74 Annual report of the Board of Prisons and Asylums in *Daily Picayune*, May 30, 1882.

75 *Daily Picayune*, July 19, 1881; April 12, 1882.

and elderly wards moved into the new almshouse on August 13, 1883. Located on ten squares of ground fronting on Cornelius Street and bounded by Joseph Street and Nashville Avenue, the two-story, brick home, in the Tudor style of architecture, cost approximately $30,000 and had about forty rooms. It could accommodate over a hundred persons.[76]

In the years that followed the reforms of the early 1880's little else of importance was done to improve the city's public charitable institutions, largely because of the lack of funds. The almshouse, which was supposed to receive the revenue from the gamblers' fund, probably never received the full yearly collection, averaging around $20,000. In 1885 it got only $4,000, and after 1887 this source of income ceased entirely when the Shakspeare Plan was declared illegal by the courts. By 1900 the almshouse's income had been cut to $7,500, and the next year the maintenance of the home, in desperate need of repair, was $984.60 in excess of alimony. Aid was found in the remains of the long-dormant Touro Fund, which equalled $14,610.85 in 1901. This was turned over to the needy almshouse together with the income from property connected with the fund. Renamed the Touro-Shakspeare Almshouse, the institution was extensively repaired and entered a more solvent decade than it had ever known.[77]

By the end of the century the Boys' House of Refuge became essentially a home for delinquents. Its management was especially subject to political pressure, and in 1889 the grand jury succeeded in getting an ordinance passed placing it under the control of a board of nonoffice holders. (This had been done with the almshouse in 1884.) The superintendent of the home, nevertheless, remained the "boss." In 1891 the *Mascot* complained that he was

[76] *Ibid.*, September 7, 1881; January 12, April 12, December 27, 1882; July 31, August 14, September 4, 1882; *Times-Democrat*, August 10, 1882; Beven, *City Subsidies to Private Charitable Agencies*, 20; *Report of Board of Managers, Touro-Shakspeare Almshouse, Being a Report and Inventory of Improvements made during the Period 1901–1908* (New Orleans, 1908), 7; Jewell, *Jewell's Digest*, 381.

[77] For the end of the Shakspeare Plan see Chapter 4 of this study. For the history of the Touro Fund and its connection with the almshouse, see Beven, *City Subsidies to Private Charitable Agencies*, 20, and *Report of Board of Managers, Touro-Shakspeare Almshouse, . . . 1901–1908*, 7–9.

housing his family at the House of Refuge, using its funds for their support, and interfering to the point of anarchy in the operation of the shoe shop.[78]

Care of the insane was the one charitable service that showed drastic deterioration. Although the inmates of the old City Insane Asylum had probably benefited from removal to Jackson, the abandonment of this structure left no temporary haven for the mentally ill. Persons judged insane were placed in the Parish Prison or House of Detention. Their incarceration in these humiliating surroundings lasted until city officials felt that there was a sufficient number of them to merit paying for their transfer to the state hospital at Jackson.[79] This condition continued to exist into the twentieth century.

A few ordinances embracing general improvements in the field of charity were passed by the city council. After 1889 all charitable institutions connected with the municipality had to keep record books and submit monthly statements to the mayor. An attempt to regulate private institutions was made in 1893 when it became unlawful to open any rest home or hospital without permission from the mayor and city council. Furthermore, the powers of the Board of Prisons and Asylums were broadened in 1897. The board was reorganized with authority to exercise jurisdiction over all charitable institutions, private as well as public. In that year also, the Mayor's Charity Fund was created. It came from fees collected by the mayor for issuing permits.[80]

Rounding out benevolence in vital areas which the city failed to consider were private groups whose work paralleled that being inaugurated in other American cities. A New Orleans Conference of Charities was formed in 1883 to act as a clearing house for charitable agencies and to prevent them from being exploited by mendicants. A similar body, the Charity Organization Society, began operations in 1896. It also offered diversified help to needy cases— providing clothes, rent, transportation, admittance to private

[78] Flynn, *Flynn's Digest,* 68; *Mascot,* January 3, 1891.

[79] *Annual Report of the Board of Commissioners of Prisons and Asylums of New Orleans, Louisiana, November 1, 1898* (New Orleans, 1898) , 6.

[80] Flynn, *Flynn's Digest,* 67; Beven, *City Subsidies to Private Charitable Agencies,* 53–55.

charitable institutions, and home nursing care. The Christian Woman's Exchange, begun in 1881, based its work upon a premise dear to the Gilded Age philanthropists, "Help the needy to help themselves." Among the exchange's activities were the renting of rooms to needy women, the sale of valuable possessions of indigent women to bolster their income, and the opening of an employment bureau for them in 1883. By the late 1890's one of the private charities receiving funds from the city was the local Society for the Prevention of Cruelty to Children, an organization that opened a new field in child welfare by reaching needy or abused children who were not orphans.[81]

While public health matters and charities made headlines frequently and received sympathetic consideration from private official sources, another responsibility, the city's public schools, received little notice. No other public service was more deprived in the Gilded Age than the educational system. Not only a pitiful shortage of funds but a lack of public belief in the value of education was responsible. Public schools were under the supervision of the Orleans Parish School Board. When it was reorganized in 1888, eight of its members were appointed by the State Board of Education and twelve were chosen by city officials.[82]

The major portion of school funds came from the city. State expenditures on local education were minor and sometimes doled out tardily. One private endowment to the city's public schools which was of invaluable service during these lean years was the McDonogh Fund. John McDonogh, a native of Maryland who had settled in New Orleans and become a wealthy merchant, had left upon his death in 1850 an estate valued at $1,408,880 to be divided between the public school systems of New Orleans and Baltimore. In 1855 the New Orleans city government appoint-

81 *Daily Picayune,* May 3, 16, 17, 1883; *First Annual Report of the Charity Organization Society of New Orleans, Louisiana, From December 1st, 1896 to December 31st, 1897* (New Orleans, 1896), 22–23; [Joy Jackson], "Help to Help Themselves," *Dixie Roto Magazine,* New Orleans *Times Picayune,* November 11, 1956 (This article was a history of the Christian Women's Exchange written to commemorate its seventy-fifth anniversary.) ; Beven, *City Subsidies to Private Charitable Agencies,* 26; King, "The Higher Life in New Orleans," 756–57.

82 Albert P. Subat, "The Superintendency of the Public Schools of Orleans Parish, 1862–1910" (M.A. thesis, Tulane University, 1947), 41–42.

ed a commission to administer its share of the property from the McDonogh estate, and by 1860 an ordinance was passed creating the Board of Commissioners of the McDonogh Fund. By the end of the 1890's, thirty schools with a total of 366 classrooms had been constructed with this fund. Nineteen were brick; eleven were of frame construction. A total of 16,660 children attended the Mc-Donogh schools. Money from this fund was used primarily to build new schools and keep them in repair. (In the period from 1860 to 1893 no schools were built with city funds.) Sometimes, the Mc-Donogh Fund commissioners would pay the cost of repairs to public schools other than the ones they had constructed. But in 1899 this practice was discontinued after legal opinions rendered this outside of the original McDonogh bequest.[83]

Some federal aid to local education seemed a possibility and was considered by Congress between 1881 and 1890 through the various versions of the Blair bill, which would have distributed part of the surplus in the United States Treasury to individual states on the basis of their illiteracy rates. This bill was sponsored by Henry W. Blair of New Hampshire. But while its author was from New England, it found many of its most avid champions among southern congressmen and in the southern states. Louisiana and particularly New Orleans were enthusiastic about the Blair bill. Louisiana Senator Randall L. Gibson and Congressman John F. King worked vigorously but in vain to aid its passage. The *Daily Picayune* was one of its strongest boosters, and the Louisiana legislature three times passed petitions addressed to the Louisiana representatives in Congress urging them to support this measure. Finally, George Washington Cable, aware of the dire illiteracy

[83] Minute Book, Commissioners of the John McDonogh School Fund (Typescript in the Archives of the City of New Orleans, New Orleans Public Library); Francis P. Burns to the Commissioners of the McDonogh Fund, June 24, 1925, in Archives of the City of New Orleans, New Orleans Public Library; *Report of the Board of Commissioners of the McDonogh School Fund, from January 1, 1881 to December 31, 1881* (New Orleans, 1882), 18–23; *Report of the Board of Commissioners of McDonogh School Fund, from January 1, 1892 to December 31, 1895* (New Orleans, 1896), 66; *Report of the Board of Commissioners of the McDonogh School Fund, from January 1, 1896 to December 31, 1899* (New Orleans, 1900), 13; Malcolm Francis Rosenberg, "The Orleans Parish Public Schools under the Superintendency of Nicholas Bauer" (Ph.D. dissertation, Louisiana State University, 1963), 10–11.

rate among local Negroes, wrote articles in national journals advocating the Blair bill's passage. Despite the hopes of local persons interested in additional funds for education, the Blair bill was defeated by the Senate in 1890.[84]

Teachers' salaries were the prime target of retrenchment by both state and city governments. City superintendents of the schools in this period were vigorous in their efforts to retain good teachers, but had a slim budget to combat as well as the vicious custom of paying teachers in city certificates rather than cash. Several members of the School Board were brokers who bought up these certificates at a discount and held them until the city could redeem them in full. Naturally they did not exert themselves to demand that teachers receive prompt monthly pay. With their monthly salaries in the 1880's ranging from $35, about the lowest paid to women teachers, to $96, the highest paid to white men, most teachers struggled to keep their positions since the School Board had on file the names of hundreds of substitutes eager to fill any vacancy that occurred. The number of teachers employed by the system in 1880 was 432. This fell to 395 in 1883, rose to 406 by 1889, to 422 in 1890, and 583 by 1895. The three men who headed the Orleans school system as superintendents during this era were William O. Rogers, 1877–84, Ulric Bettison, 1884–88, and Warren Easton, 1888–1910.[85]

Politics played far too important a part in getting and holding a teaching position in the Orleans Parish school system. A war of nerves kept the teachers on edge every time the School Board began discussion of "reorganizing" its staff. Demoralization of the schoolteachers probably was most acute in 1883, when lack of funds

84 Allen J. Going, "The South and the Blair Education Bill," *Mississippi Valley Historical Review*, XLIV, (September, 1957) , 267–90.

85 On school board members who were brokers, see scattered references in Chapters 2 and 3 of Margaret M. Williams, "An Outline of Public School Politics in Louisiana Since the Civil War" (M.A. Thesis, Tulane University, 1939) 19–57; *Daily Picayune* September 30, 1883; Subat, "The Superintendency of the Public Schools of Orleans Parish," 43; Waring and Cable, "History and Present Condition of New Orleans," 290. *Daily Picayune*, June 24, 1883; *Report of the Commissioners of Education, 1888–1889* (Washington, 1891) , 816; *Compendium of the Eleventh Census: 1890*, Pt. 2, 254; *Annual Report of the Board of Directors of Public Schools for the Parish of Orleans*, December, 1895 (New Orleans, 1895) , 3–4.

prevented the opening of schools for the fall semester. Some got permission to hold private classes in public school buildings. When the public schools reopened the next semester, this caused confusion because instructors wanted to continue their private classes in the public classrooms.[86]

One of the most graphic pictures of the teachers' plight during this period was presented by the *Picayune's* woman feature writer, Mrs. Martha R. Field, who wrote under the pen name of Catherine Cole. Written in the baroque, melodramatic style of the Gilded Age sob sister, it still manages to be both touching and sincere in its presentation of a real-life personality. Entitled "Our Poorly-Paid School Teachers," this article included this passage:

During the past year a public school teacher, a young lady who had both mother and sister to support had the ill fortune to live a long distance from the school. In fact, the distance was over forty blocks. Come rain or shine, whether the winds blew hot or cold the early passenger on the car route used to see the patient, shabby little woman trudging along to her daily task. Carfare? On $35 a month with a mother and sister to keep and care for? . . . Forty blocks is a long walk . . . when one had staid up half the night pouring over a piece of Kensington embroidery, or making chemises for the ready-made underwear store, and had only baker's bread and coffee for breakfast. . . . Want, privation, anxiety braided fine lines about the tired eyes and drooping mouth. The shabby dress wore shabbier; the sharp, thin fingers pierced through the patches in the black gloves. . . . The tax-paying parents rode by in the car and looked out with mute pity on the bent, plodding figure, and those who knew her story thought of demanding that her wrongs and their wrongs be righted but nothing ever came of it. She kept on, faithful and patient . . . taught all day and washed, sewed, embroidered of a night, and when Sunday came she went around and sold her poor, ungraceful, pathetic little bits of Kensington.[87]

86 *Daily Picayune*, September 30, 1883; *Mascot*, August through December, 1882; Williams, "An Outline of Public School Politics in Louisiana Since the Civil War," 53–56; Elsa L. Behrend, "The New Orleans Public School System Since the Civil War," (M.A. thesis, Tulane University, 1931) 53–54. William C. Rogers, *Report of the Chief Superintendent of the Public Schools of New Orleans, Louisiana, to the Board of School Directors* (New Orleans, 1884) , 10.

87 *Daily Picayune*, September 30, 1883.

The story of insufficient funds and inadequate schools was mirrored in official reports throughout the last two decades of the century. The annual report of the School Board directors to the city council in 1882 pointed out that the antebellum expenditure on education in local public schools had been $20 per pupil, the 1882 cost was $16 per pupil. Before the war the estimated annual expenses for schools had reached $480,000. This had been reduced to $300,000 after the war by a 40 percent cut in teachers' salaries and a vacation of three and a half months. The school appropriation from both state and city sources for 1883 would reach $220,000, the report noted, but expenditures would exceed this figure. This discrepancy caused the closing of the schools from September through December, 1883. By 1885 teachers' salaries were reduced 25 percent by discontinuing compensation to them during the school vacation.[88]

When the 1880 census was compiled, New Orleans had 61,456 children of school age. But in 1882–83 only about 23,000 children attended school. Private schools accounted for 6,000 of this number. One sixth of the total school population were Negroes, although one fourth of the total population was Negro. Altogether only about 37 percent of the city's total school-age population were actually in school. This meant that 20,000 children between the ages of 6 and 18 did not attend at all. Of those who did attend, about 2,000 were under 8 years old, 3,000 over 11 years old, and the majority between 8 and 11. The average student went to school for only three or four years and then was removed by his parents to work in shops or factories. No statute for compulsory education and no child labor law existed to protect minors. In 1881 there were only 271 candidates for admission to the two city high schools out of a total public school enrollment of 24,000. Most children never completed grammar school.[89]

88 *Daily Picayune*, December 13, 15, 1882; February 16, August 29, October 4, 1883; Williams, "An Outline of Public School Politics in Louisiana," 44; *Biennial Report of the State Superintendent of Public Education, 1886–1887, To the General Assembly* (Baton Rouge, 1888), 240.

89 Waring and Cable, "History and Present Condition of New Orleans," 290; *Daily Picayune*, June 24, 1883. A compulsory education act was finally passed by the state legislature in 1910. Rosenberg, "The Orleans Parish Schools Under the Superintendency of Nicholas Bauer," 23.

The report of the school superintendent to the School Board in 1886 showed a few improvements over 1883. It stated that the enrollment for 1885 of 24,332 students had been the largest since 1882. But it admitted at the same time that approximately 12,000 children of school age were employed in shops or offices and over 14,000 were either at home or running the streets. It called attention to the increased number of students who took the entrance examination for high school, and to the fact that only 207 of the 355 applicants passed. The opening of a local state normal school in December, 1885, to train white teachers was also mentioned. Southern University in New Orleans served this purpose for Negroes; and its first graduating class of seven members received their diplomas in 1887.[90]

By 1889 the annual report of the United States Commissioner of Education listed the New Orleans public school enrollment as 25,649 out of a potential 69,131 of school age. The average daily attendance was 15,761 and the school year lasted only six months. Total expenditures for schools in 1888–89 were $214,236, showing that grants to education had not increased in the decade of the 1880's. School enrollment, furthermore, had gained only a slim 2,000 over its 1882 figure. The School Board's report in 1895 revealed that the enrollment had reached 28,000 and the school budget increased to $379,700. The enrollment in both public and private schools by 1900 reached 37,189, which was still only 39 percent of the total school age population in the city, an increase of a scant 2 percent since 1882.[91]

The result of a generation of neglect of its educational institutions was revealed in 1900 to New Orleans by the illiteracy statistics in the Twelfth Census. New Orleans with 13.6 percent of its population illiterate compared unfavorably with the national av-

[90] *Report of the Chief Superintendent of Public Schools to the Board of Directors of the Public Schools, January, 1886* (New Orleans, 1886), 1–8. A thorough study of New Orleans high schools is in Steve J. Ozenovich, "The Development of Public Secondary Education in New Orleans, 1877–1914" (M.A. thesis, Tulane University, 1940); *Daily Picayune,* June 25, 1887.

[91] *Report of the Commissioner of Education, 1888–1889,* II, 794, 894–95; *Annual Report of the Board of Directors of Public Schools for the Parish of Orleans, December, 1895* (New Orleans, 1895), 3–5; *Abstract of the Twelfth Census,* 1900, p. 113.

erage of 5.7 percent for 160 cities with 25,000 population or over. The local Negro population alone was 36.1 percent illiterate. Out of a school-age Negro population of 25,282 in 1900, only 8,342 attended school. Institutions of higher learning for Negroes included Leland University, Straight University, the state-operated Southern University, and New Orleans University, an outgrowth

[Table 9]

Illiteracy Rates in Population
At Least Ten Years of Age in Twenty-three Cities in 1900[a]

Seven Major Cities	Percentage of Illiterates
New Orleans	13.6
New York	6.8
Philadelphia	4.4
Boston	5.1
St. Louis	4.4
Baltimore	7.2
Chicago	3.9

Sixteen Southern Cities	Percentage of Illiterates
Atlanta	15.8
Augusta	21.7
Birmingham	19.1
Charleston	17.4
Chattanooga	15.5
Dallas	7.2
Houston	11.4
Jacksonville	14.1
Knoxville	11.6
Memphis	18.3
Mobile	20.8
Montgomery	26.7
Nashville	14.4
Norfolk	18.4
Richmond	13.7
Savannah	19.0

[a] *Abstract of the Twelfth Census* (Washington, 1904), 115–17.

of the Union Normal School established by the Freedmen's Bureau in 1869. None of these schools, however, offered studies of true university caliber, and their turnout of graduates was not large.[92] As Table 9 reveals, southern localities with sizeable Negro populations showed high illiteracy rates. Compared to most southern communities, New Orleans's rate was favorable.

Private higher education for white students received stimulus in the 1880's and 1890's, a trend common to the nation as a whole. Soule Commercial and Literary Institution, which had been established in 1856, became coeducational in 1884. Spencer's Business College opened in 1897, and in 1899 the first dental school of its kind in the Gulf states, the New Orleans College of Dentistry, was founded. Home Institute, operated by Sophie B. Wright, inaugurated a free night school for workingmen and boys in 1887 and attracted 1,200 who were taught in shifts. Tulane University was incorporated in 1884, followed by the establishment of Newcomb College for women in 1886. By the beginning of the twentieth century, Tulane was well on its way to becoming one of the outstanding new universities in the South. In addition, the public library movement received a definite boost in 1896 when the Fisk Free Library was merged with the Lyceum Library, which until then had circulated among life members and public school teachers. This combined City Library was set up in St. Patrick's Hall, the former criminal courts building on Camp Street facing Lafayette Square, and may be considered the beginning of the present New Orleans library system.[93]

In summarizing the problems of public health, charity, and education in New Orleans in the Gilded Age, several facts stand in bold relief. Centralization of governmental functions was evi-

[92] *Abstract of the Twelfth Census*, 1900, p. 115–16, 269; Negro education is discussed in Rightor, *Standard History of New Orleans*, 246–49, and in Betty Porter, "The History of Negro Education in Louisiana," *Louisiana Historical Quarterly*, XXV (July, 1942), 728–821.

[93] On educational institutions see Rightor, *Standard History of New Orleans*, 243–54; on Tulane University, see John P. Dyer, *Tulane: The Biography of a University, 1834–1965* (New York, 1966); on the public library see Rightor, *Standard History of New Orleans*, 435–39, Kendall, *History of New Orleans*, II, 508–509, and Helen A. Manint, "A History of the New Orleans Public Library and Howard Memorial Library," (M.A. thesis, Tulane University, 1942).

dent in the final federal takeover of the quarantine station guard-
ing the city and on a municipal level in the merging of the city's
district school systems (which were divided before the Civil War)
into one department in the postwar period. Great faith was shown
in the ability of nonpartisan boards to operate the city's charitable
institutions. By 1897 the range of the functions of the Board of
Prisons and Asylums had been widened to include the supervision
of private as well as public institutions, proving the municipal
government realized it had a duty to regulate all such charitable
agencies.

The biggest drawback to bettering public health, welfare services, and educational facilities was municipal poverty. This was
not the whole story; hostile or apathetic public opinion also complicated their improvement. The poor Creole pointed his shotgun
at the Board of Health officer who tried to sprinkle disinfectant
inside his house. The steamship tycoon refused to pay quarantine fees, branding them as illegal imposts on commerce. Equal
portions of public poverty and apathy allowed the almshouse to
be supported by the gamblers' fund and the teachers to be paid
in certificates which had to be redeemed by brokers. Doubtless the
New Orleans public of this generation was no more heartless or
disinterested than citizens of any other day and age in furthering
progress. But, weaned in the corrupt, hopeless atmosphere of the
1870's, it was extremely suspicious and was loathe to place increased power in the hands of its governing officials.

8

THE CORNUCOPIA
OF WEALTH

THE WORLD'S INDUSTRIAL and Cotton Centennial Exposition, which opened at New Orleans' Upper City Park in the inhospitable month of December, 1884, was a manifestation of the city's commercial renaissance in the early 1880's. Technically it was held to commemorate the appearance of cotton in international trade— the shipment of one bale from Charleston, South Carolina, to a foreign port in 1784.[1] In reality, it had much deeper significance for New Orleanians, representing their emergence into active competition again with other American cities for more business, industry, and capital.

The exposition itself was destined to be a financial failure. It closed with a deficit in June, 1885, after running for only six months. Reopened under new management and the title of the American Exposition, it shut down finally in March, 1886, and was sold at auction to liquidate its debts.[2] Although New Orleans had about a half dozen railroads connecting it with the East, North, and West, and numerous river boats plying the Mississippi and its tributaries below Memphis, travelers did not flock to the exhibit. The Crescent City was far from the teeming populations of the East and Middle West, and travel over long distances for pure pleasure was, as yet, not a universal habit of the common man. New Orleans' reputation as a fever spot also did not aid its attempts to attract tourists. Furthermore, the act of Congress which

1 Kendall, *History of New Orleans,* I, 457–67.
2 *Ibid.*

204

had provided federal support to the enterprise stipulated it must begin in 1884. As a result, the cotton exposition was forced to open on December 17 of that year, although it was still incomplete, and the sound of hammers could be heard reverberating through its exhibit halls up to an hour before it was dedicated. The middle of the winter was not the most advantageous time for its inauguration in a remote section of the city. Steamboat service to the grounds was erratic and carriage fare exorbitant; streetcar service was interrupted during its first two weeks by strike violence.[3] Since newspaper correspondents were on hand from other cities and foreign countries, these facts did not go unpublished.

Securing the city's $500,000-share of the exposition funds (of which the municipal government pledged $100,000 and $400,000 had to be privately raised) was no easy task. Construction hit snags when workers went on strike. Deciding where and how individual exhibits should be set up was a job which would have taxed Solomon. When it finally opened, the exposition featured five main buildings surrounded by other smaller ones set in 245 acres of oak-shaded land only recently converted from cow pastures. The Main Building, covering thirty-three acres, was the largest such exhibition hall up to that time. The Music Hall, a part of this structure, seated eleven thousand persons. Other buildings included the Government Building, the Horticultural Hall, built by the city and intended as a permanent structure, the Art Building, and the Mexican Building.[4] The most elaborate state and territorial exhibits were those from the South and West, the Northeast almost ignoring the exposition. Cotton displays were scattered among the states and unfortunately tended to be overshadowed by other products. Western exhibits were naturally the most flamboyant— Nebraska reproduced out of hay and corn cobs Bartholdi's Statue

3 *Congressional Record,* 48 Cong., 1 Sess., 3981–83; London *Daily Telegraph,* February 14, 1885 (from a clipping in a scrapbook in Howard-Tilton Memorial Library) ; *Daily Picayune,* December 28–30, 1884.

4 For a full description of the exposition, see D. Clive Hardy, "World's Industrial and Cotton Centennial Exposition and the New South, 1884–85" (M.A. thesis, Tulane University, 1964) ; Herbert S. Fairall, *The World's Industrial and Cotton Centennial Exposition, New Orleans, 1884–1885* (Iowa City, 1885) ; *Visitors' Guide to the World's Industrial and Cotton Centennial* (New Orleans, 1884) ; Kendall, *History of New Orleans,* I, 457–67.

of Liberty; and the Dakota display (a favorite with the public) featured a live Indian, who sat at the door of his tent and sold photographs of himself with "the imperturbable face of a croupier at Monaco." [5]

One comic opera touch was the controversy over the exhibiting of the Liberty Bell at the cotton exposition in 1885. New Orleans asked Philadelphia to lend the historic bell for a brief period. In the Crescent City a storm of protest arose over the large sum of money spent by councilmen to visit Philadelphia and negotiate for the bell. In Philadelphia all sorts of wild rumors floated about— that southerners would melt it down and cast a statue of Jefferson Davis, or that it would become a prize in the Louisiana Lottery. The Philadelphia Colored Kalsominers' Union No. 6 even went on record as resolved to prevent the bell from leaving. But Philadelphia councilmen were more cordial. They sped the bell on its way with speeches, a procession, brass bands, and an honor guard consisting of a police unit and thirty-two reserve constables.[6]

One English visitor found the displays of farm machinery and of the federal departments the most satisfying. He was especially impressed by the hundreds of patent models set up by the Patent Office.[7] The foreign exhibits of Central American nations, of Russia, France, and England were likewise well chosen, but many foreign booths were merely fronts for cheap bazaars, those of Italy and Jerusalem being the worst offenders.[8] A dash of authentic color was the presence of the Mexican military band which serenaded visitors and lived on the premises at the Mexican Building. At night fireworks and electric lights, still comparatively new in the Crescent City, illuminated the polyglot assemblage of people, machines and exhibition farm animals.

Through all this color and confusion, the exposition's director-general, E. A. Burke, moved with ease and assurance. His appointment to the position of manager of the exposition was the height of his extraordinary career. Like an elegant chameleon, he darted back and forth between a variety of roles—as *Times-Demo-*

5 London *Daily Telegraph,* February 14, 1885.
6 *Ibid.,* February 19, 1885.
7 *Ibid.,* February 14, 1885.
8 *Ibid.*

crat editor, railroad authority, state machine politician, and suave
director-general. In getting the act of Congress passed which authorized a federal loan of $1,000,000 to the exposition, Burke
had had to swallow his pride and make overtures to Congressman
Ellis to enlist his aid. Burke had tried to keep Ellis from getting
renominated in 1882 as the Democratic candidate for Congress in
the Second Congressional District. Now Ellis had the satisfaction
of Burke's solicitation. Writing of the incident later to his brother,
Thomas, Ellis asked humorously, "Well, I suppose you know I
made friends with Burke?"

He explained how Burke had contacted him through Senator
Benjamin F. Jonas and arranged for a reconciliation. When they
met, Burke blamed their political estrangement on "misunder-
standing" and added "We fought—you won. Let us be friends
again." Ellis extended his hand to Burke and answered "I have
forgotten all that was unpleasant." Ellis then promised full support of the exposition bill and felt it never would have been passed
without his effort.[9] When President Chester A. Arthur officially
opened the exposition by pressing a button in his office that turned
on the electric lights at the New Orleans exposition grounds,
Congressman Ellis had the satisfaction of being a member of the
special committee who attended the White House ceremony.
Burke, however, was the one who got most of the praise and
credit for the exposition in Louisiana. One political opponent
willingly admitted that Burke, in his handling of the exhibit, was
an Aladdin whose magic lamp would conjure up good fortune for
the city.[10] Such faith in his ability as a promoter and in the power
of the exposition to add substantially to the local prosperity was,
of course, mistaken optimism. But the mere fact that such an exposition was taking place at all was the cause for rejoicing.

For almost a generation prior to the exposition, New Orleans
commerce had been hindered by the war's ruin in its trading area,
the depression which followed the Panic of 1873, and the depreda-
tions of Reconstruction. With the completion of the jetties at the
mouth of the Mississippi in 1879 and the junction of the Southern

9 E. John Ellis to Thomas C. W. Ellis, May 15, 1884, in E. John Ellis Collection, Department of Archives and Manuscripts of Louisiana State University.
10 *Daily Picayune,* June 3, 1884.

Pacific railroad with eastern lines in 1883, linking its harbor with the grain fields of the Far West, the local economy was vigorously stimulated. The exposition was both a result of this revitalized commerce and a further stimulus to Crescent City businessmen and merchants. Although a financial failure, it still had a measure of success as a morale booster to a reawakening economy imbued with the philosophy of the New South.

Actually the troubles against which New Orleans commerce struggled in the 1880's and 1890's had their roots in antebellum times. Her supremacy as the trade mart of the Mississippi Valley had been challenged early in the century by the building of canals and in the 1850's by railroads. In the three decades between 1830 and 1860, local businessmen and city officials were involved in numerous schemes to increase the railroad mileage linking the Crescent City with other points in the Mississippi Valley and the Southwest. The Panic of 1837 and the depression years which followed ended the first railroad boom. By the close of the 1850's, promotion of railroads was again a popular investment. The municipality of New Orleans itself contributed $4,113,126 in stock subscriptions toward the building of railroads in the Louisiana-Mississippi area. Although this amounted to over half the entire railroad stock in these two states, by 1860 New Orleans had little to show for its faith and financial stake in railroad building. Rail lines reached from the city only as far as Jackson, Mississippi, and westward to the Atchafalaya River. The Civil War ended what railroad construction was in progress in the lower South and devastated the lines already in existence.[11]

11 Merl E. Reed, "Government Investment and Economic Growth: Louisiana's Ante Bellum Railroads," *Journal of Southern History,* XXVIII (May, 1962) , 183–201. Reed's article gives a thorough account of the attempts of the state government and the city of New Orleans to sponsor railroad building through loans, tax subscription plans and public bond issues. Another study of antebellum railroads and government aid is Edwin Dale Odum, "Louisiana Railroads, 1830–1880: A Study of State and Local Aid" (Ph.D. dissertation, Tulane University, 1961) . A discussion of the antebellum competition of rail to water transportation in the Southwest and of how Charles Morgan met this competition by the 1870's with the beginning of consolidation of rail-water systems is thoroughly covered in James P. Baughman, "The Evolution of Rail-Water Systems of Transportation in the Gulf Southwest, 1836–1890," *Journal of Southern History,* XXXIV (August, 1968) , 357–81.

In regard to Mississippi River trade, even during the most prosperous years only half as much merchandise was shipped upriver from New Orleans' wharves as floated downstream. Aside from some machinery and such products as coffee and sugar, most upriver shipments from this port in the late antebellum period were made to Louisiana and Mississippi plantations. The city suffered at the same time from a dearth of manufacturing establishments; concentration upon the one staple, cotton; high port charges; and the inability of new, larger ships to pass easily over the bars at the Mississippi's mouth. The Civil War compounded all these problems and added numerous others. While the city suffered little physical harm, the war's ruination of cotton plantations in its trading area presaged a long, hard struggle to recover.[12] It was 1889 before the cotton receipts at the port of New Orleans equalled the all-time high they had reached in 1859–60.[13] The value of all commerce passing through the port had also set a record of $473,-290,000 in that last season before the war. This was topped in 1889 by a total commerce of $521,484,618, which fell, however, to $419,-580,708 by 1896.[14]

The Panic of 1873 probably hit New Orleans harder than any other city.[15] The yellow fever epidemic of 1878 administered another blow to commerce just as it was recovering from the depression. It was probably no accident that James B. Eads was given authority by the federal government to go ahead with his scheme to deepen the channel at the mouth of the river and enable larger

[12] Harry A. Mitchell, "The Development of New Orleans as a Wholesale Center," *Louisiana Historical Quarterly*, XXVII (October, 1944), 941–58. See also Alice T. Porter, "An Economic View of Ante-Bellum New Orleans, 1845–1860" (M.A. thesis, Tulane University, 1942); Claude Babin, "The Economic Expansion of New Orleans Before the Civil War" (Ph.D. dissertation, Tulane University, 1954); David Allan Walker, "A History of Commerce and Navigation on the Lower Mississippi River, 1803–1840" (M.A. thesis, Louisiana State University, 1965); John G. Clark, "The Antebellum Grain Trade of New Orleans: Changing Patterns in the Relation of New Orleans with the Old Northwest," *Agricultural History* (July, 1964).

[13] *Times-Democrat Almanac for 1896* (New Orleans, 1896), 17.

[14] Rightor, *Standard History of New Orleans,* 566, 576.

[15] Janey Marks, "The Industrial Development of New Orleans Since 1865" (M.A. thesis, Tulane University, 1924), 379–80. For discussion of hard times following the Panic of 1873, see also Shugg, *Origins of Class Struggle in Louisiana,* 296–97.

vessels to enter without running aground. By the end of the 1870's southerners were desperate for internal improvements and were not hesitant in badgering the United States Congress for such aid. Since Eads undertook the work at his own risk (he was not to be reimbursed if he failed) the federal authorities had little to lose. His brilliant system of jetties was a reality by 1879.[16] Another improvement dear to the hearts of local businessmen was the completion of a railroad to the Pacific along the southern route to tap the grain harvests of the West. The rivalry of the Texas and Pacific, building westward and strongly favored in the South, and the Southern Pacific, extending eastward, is a complicated story.[17] By 1883 the two roads had settled their differences through negotiation, and the Southern Pacific was linked with New Orleans by several different lines. The first freight car of wines from San Francisco via the southern route arrived on February 27, 1882.[18] By the beginning of the next year the Southern Pacific had inaugurated regular shipments to the Crescent City, making use of the rail facilities of the Texas and New Orleans, the Louisiana Western, and other Morgan lines to connect with its own across the Southwest.[19]

Railroad building and consolidation in the next twenty years was to put New Orleans in touch with a more vast territory than that reached by the direct rail connections of any other American city.[20] Railroad tonnage at the port of New Orleans increased

[16] For a description of the struggle to clear the mouth of the Mississippi and the execution of Eads's plan for the jetties see Walter M. Lowrey, "The Engineers and the Mississippi," *Louisiana History*, V (Summer, 1964), 233–55.

[17] Woodward's *Reunion and Reaction* relates in detail the Congressional lobbying connected with this rivalry.

[18] *Daily Picayune*, February 28, 1882.

[19] Rightor, *Standard History of New Orleans*, 304.

[20] Stuyvesant Fish, *Statement to the United States Industrial Commission (Relative to the Great Central Basin Drained by the Mississippi River and New Orleans the Seaport of that Basin), October, 1899* (New Orleans, 1899), 10. On the development of individual lines in the city see John Land, *Pen Illustrations of New Orleans, 1881–1882* (New Orleans, 1882), 27–29, and A. J. R. Landauer, *Resources and Industries of the State of Louisiana Together with a General Review of the trade of New Orleans* (New Orleans, 1883), 76–94. On the combination steamship-railroad lines of Charles Morgan, see James P. Baughman, *Charles Morgan and the Development of Southern Transportation* (Nashville, 1968).

691.9 percent between 1880 and 1896, and the value of products handled by rail rose 119.8 percent.[21] By 1899 the railroads serving the Louisiana metropolis were the Southern Pacific, the Queen and Crescent, the Louisville and Nashville, the Texas and Pacific, the Yazoo and Mississippi Valley, and the Illinois Central. Their total mileage tributary to New Orleans was 19,086 miles. Despite this vast expanse of territory, Stuyvesant Fish, the president of the Illinois Central, in 1899 admitted that the railroads entering the city did not bring nearly as much freight into the port as they could.[22] In an address to the city council in 1888, another Illinois Central official blamed the inadequate port facilities for the railroads' failure to increase their Crescent City business.[23] Other Gulf ports were advancing their rail connections, however, along with New Orleans. As a whole, the Gulf ports increased the value of their exports 142.7 percent between 1880 and 1900.[24] New Orleans alone showed a gain in value of only 72.6 percent in 1898–99 over its exports.[25] While it was therefore losing business to rapidly developing outlets on the Gulf, it still managed to stay ahead of South Atlantic ports which increased the value of their exports only 56.9 percent in this twenty-year period.[26] It also ranked second in overall commerce, second in foreign exports, and fifth in imports in the United States by 1892. (Table 10 gives a statistical review of New Orleans commerce.) In cotton, its largest single export, it led all other seaports in the nation and was probably surpassed worldwide as a cotton port by Liverpool.[27]

Despite this apparent good record, New Orleans' share of the total commerce of the United States was much lower than it had been before the Civil War. Comparing the showing of New Or-

21 *Times-Democrat Almanac for 1896* (New Orleans, 1896) , 16.

22 Fish, *Statement to the United States Industrial Commission,* 9–10.

23 Edward T. Jeffrey, *Remarks of E. T. Jeffrey before the City Council of New Orleans on Extent of Illinois Central and its Bearing on the Prosperity and Commerce of New Orleans* (New Orleans, 1889) , 1–9.

24 Woodward, *Origins of the New South,* 125.

25 For New Orleans export statistics see customs receipts as quoted in *Times-Democrat Almanac for 1896,* p. 14, and Rightor, *Standard History of New Orleans,* 575.

26 Woodward, *Origins of the New South,* 126.

27 George Engelhardt, *The City of New Orleans* (New Orleans, 1894) , 6; *Biographical and Historical Memoirs of Louisiana,* I (Chicago, 1892) , 218.

leans and New York in the five-year period 1856–60, President Fish of the Illinois Central Found that New Orleans handled 28.38 percent of the country's domestic exports and New York handled 30.-95 percent. During the five-year period 1894–98, however, New York's tremendous growth gave it 43.52 percent of the domestic exports, while New Orleans handled a mere 8.37 percent. This was a little more than a 20 percent drop in domestic exports for the

[Table 10]

*Total Commerce and Cotton
Receipts at the Port of New Orleans*[a]

TOTAL COMMERCE OF THE CITY	
Seasons	Value
1876	$371,664,126
1886	456,062,948
1889	521,484,618
1890–91	531,764,118
1891–92	496,465,741
1892–93	527,830,632
1893–94	483,507,065
1894–95	455,659,431
1895–96	419,580,908
1896–97	479,751,019
1897–98	486,131,712
1898–99	439,724,621

COTTON RECEIPTS		
Seasons	Total Cotton Crop in Bales	Bales received at New Orleans
1858–59	3,851,481	1,669,279
1859–60	4,675,770	2,139,425
1882–83	6,949,756	1,690,709
1889–90	7,313,726	2,149,370
1892–93	6,717,142	1,374,860
1894–95	9,901,251	2,702,931

[a] *Times-Democrat Almanac for 1896* (New Orleans, 1896), 17: Rightor, *Standard History of New Orleans,* 576.

southern port. No other major port showed such a radical change in trade patterns.[28] The railroads, which helped the city to make some progress, also were responsible for creating many inland trade centers and cotton mills, booming smaller Gulf ports, and diffusing much freight that in earlier days would have had no other choice but to come through the port of New Orleans.

In regard to imports, the Crescent City handled 7 percent of the total entering the United States in 1848. Forty years later its share of the total imports was 1.6 percent.[29] Furthermore, while the value of the cotton handled at New Orleans grew each year and kept this cotton mart well ahead of all others, the percentage of the entire crop controlled by the city dwindled. In 1858 it had controlled 50 percent; in 1870, a little over 36 percent, and in 1896, only 8 percent. This did not mean that other major ports were increasing at its expense, since New York's share of the entire crop fell from 41 percent in 1868 to 2.5 percent in 1894, and Charleston's share went from 8 percent in 1883 to 2 percent in 1894. The rise of domestic mills and of rail overland travel in lieu of water connections accounted for this phenomenon.[30]

Between the end of Reconstruction and the 1890's the major achievements of the New Orleans port were its steady increase in shipment abroad of the staples, cotton, cottonseed oil and oil cake, the growth of its coffee and sugar trade, and a tremendous increase in exports of grain and imports of tropical fruit. According to customs receipts, its chief exports by 1893 were cotton, cottonseed meal and cake, cotton oil, grain and flour, staves and lumber. The chief imports consisted of sugar, coffee, and tropical fruit.[31] The by-products of cottonseed and tropical fruit were items of commerce which came to prominence in the Gilded Age. Lumber and grain, important articles of trade in antebellum days, never figured in the local economy to the extent that they did in the 1890's. In

[28] Stuyvesant Fish, *Statement to the Committee of the House of Representatives on Rivers and Harbors Relating to the Foreign Commerce of the United States Before and After The Civil War Through the Port of New Orleans, March 6, 1900* (New Orleans, 1900), 3–5.

[29] Jeffrey, *Remarks of E. T. Jeffrey before the City Council of New Orleans*, 9.

[30] Henry Hester, "Cotton," *Manufacturer's Record*, XXIX (July 17, 1896), 3–5.

[31] Engelhardt, *The City of New Orleans*, 74.

recognition of the rise of southern lumber mills the *Lumber Trade Journal,* the authoritative magazine in this field, moved from Chicago to New Orleans in the last decade of the century.[32] The railroads were mainly responsible for building up the city's grain trade and making it possible to deliver bananas and other tropical fruits to points hundreds of miles into the interior in the shortest possible time. Around fifty thousand bunches of bananas entered the Crescent City in 1880. This number grew to 1,867,011 in 1887, and the local port by the 1890's was second to New York in tropical fruit imports.[33] General trade with Latin America naturally increased as a result, and local businessmen became acutely aware of its future potentialities. The movement to build an isthmian canal found some of its most ardent backers in the local Board of Trade.

The completion of the Southern Pacific connection between California and New Orleans in 1883 had come at a highly opportune time for New Orleans participation on the world market. Between 1879 and 1881, the failure of grain harvests in Britain and Europe, forced these areas to turn to the wheat fields of the United States. Wheat acreage in the United States had shown remarkable growth between 1873 and 1882, rising from 29 to 41 million acres. Bushels of wheat exported from this country in this same span of time rose from 40 to 150 million bushels.[34] On the Pacific coast the 1881–82 season saw 550 ships sail from San Francisco for Liverpool laden with wheat and flour.[35] While New York ranked first and San Francisco, second, New Orleans in 1880 was fifth in the nation in wheat exports. It ranked fourth in rye exports. The quantity of other types of cereals exported was negligible. Grain and rye exports totaled $5,045,882. By 1892 the value

32 *New Orleans of 1894* (New Orleans, 1894) , 18. Taken from the annual commercial edition of the *Daily Picayune,* September 1, 1894, and published by the Young Men's Business League.

33 Jeffrey, *Remarks of E. T. Jeffrey before the City Council of New Orleans,* 12; Engelhardt, *The City of New Orleans,* 6.

34 Morton Rothstein, "America in the International Rivalry for the British Wheat Market, 1860–1914," *Mississippi Valley Historical Review,* XLVII (December, 1960) , 404.

35 Rodman W. Paul, "The Wheat Trade between California and the United Kingdom," *Mississippi Valley Historical Review,* XLV (December, 1958) , 403.

of the total exports of grain and breadstuffs from New Orleans had risen to $22,195,700. In 1896 New Orleans had climbed to third rank among American ports in grain exports.[36]

Aside from developing new lines of imports and exports, New Orleans merchants adopted new methods of business which virtually amounted to a commercial revolution. By the 1880's almost all merchants dealing in major staples did business through exchanges, instead of individually in saloons, on the levees, or at some street corner as in antebellum days. The Cotton Exchange was founded in 1871 and by the 1880's had regular calls for those dealing in futures, a great innovation in the cotton trade. According to its charter, this exchange was formed for a variety of reasons: to provide suitable rooms where cotton men could meet to adjust controversies, to establish uniform rules and regulations for cotton trading and standards for classification of cotton samples, to disseminate information on the cotton crop and thus cut down on the risks involved in cotton marketing, and in general to increase the cotton business of New Orleans.[37]

To help this fledgling organization achieve these goals, its officers fortunately appointed as its superintendent a young but unusually well-informed journalist, Henry G. Hester, who had written for the *Price Current* since he was sixteen. Hester was twenty-four in 1871 when he assumed the job of superintendent. To this was soon added the duties of secretary. He was to remain in that latter capacity for sixty-two years, retiring in 1933 with the title secretary emeritus and a world-wide reputation as a cotton authority.[38] No man in the last century has made a greater contribution to the cotton trade than Hester through his pioneering in cotton statistics.

When Hester went to work for the Cotton Exchange, French

[36] *House Executive Documents*, 46th Cong., 3rd Sess., XVI, No. 7 (Washington, 1881), 214–15; Engelhardt, *The City of New Orleans*, 6; Rightor, *Standard History of New Orleans*, 577; Rothstein, "America in the International Rivalry for the British Wheat Market, 1860–1914," 402–404; James P. Baughman, "Gateway To the Americas," in Hodding Carter (ed.), *The Past as Prelude: New Orleans, 1718–1968* (New Orleans, 1968), 286.

[37] James E. Boyle, *Cotton and the New Orleans Cotton Exchange: A Century of Commercial Evolution* (Garden City, 1934), 70–72.

[38] *Ibid.*, 98–99. A biographical sketch of Hester is given in Kendall, *New Orleans*, II, 208–10.

and English papers and trade journals, mainly in Liverpool, were the chief sources of the South's information on its own cotton crops. Hester's extraordinary job of collecting cotton information and disseminating it, first to the New Orleans exchange and later throughout the world, was to change this. He invented new methods of reporting more accurately on the cotton crop, and his techniques were copied by exchanges set up throughout the South. By the 1930's the Hester Reports appeared in papers of the leading cotton ports of the world—*Financial Times* of London, the *Manchester Guardian*, the *Liverpool Post*, the *Bergerkszeitung* of Düsseldorf, and the *Commerce* of Calcutta—to mention only a few.[39] Through his patient and exacting life's work as a statistician, Hester made the South its own authority on its leading staple.

His program for the local exchange in the 1870's and 1880's included furnishing as much information as he could, even though members at first wrung their hands over the cost of the telegraph bills. Soon they realized it was a worthwhile investment. He also believed that a spot market and future market could grow up simultaneously in the city, the futures acting as insurance for the spot cotton. It was largely through his perseverance that the sale of futures in cotton finally was accepted locally in the 1880's. Closely allied to this was his determination to improve the grading and handling of cotton, so that the highest possible uniformity and lowest possible loss might be achieved. He was so successful in this endeavor that in 1895, when the Liverpool Cotton Exchange warned American shippers it would place a penalty upon tattered bales arriving the next season, this warning did not apply to New Orleans cotton, because it was usually shipped in proper condition.[40]

Following the example of the cotton men, the produce merchants, after several unsuccessful attempts, founded the Produce Exchange in 1880. Its members were active in politics and quarantine matters as well as in commerce. Realizing that a broader consolidation was needed, this exchange united in 1889 with the Chamber of Commerce and the Merchants and Manufacturers'

[39] Boyle, *Cotton and the New Orleans Cotton Exchange,* 96–97.
[40] *Ibid.,* 87, 94, 97, 101.

Association to form the Board of Trade. Members of the Cotton Exchange also joined and by 1898 the Maritime Association was merged into this organization, making it a true cross section of interests.

It became the unofficial voice of the merchant community and played a vital part in every commercial improvement of this period. It was instrumental in bringing a Navy yard and dry dock to the city, in securing public ownership of the wharves by the end of the 1890's after years of leasing them to private interests, and in the creation of the Louisiana State Railroad Commission in 1898. The Board also consistently advocated a public belt railroad, a Mississippi river bridge, and a railroad union terminal, although these improvements were not to come until the twentieth century.[41] Other commercial combinations included the Sugar Exchange, founded in 1883 to disseminate information on the crop and offer a meeting place for sugar merchants, the South American and Mexican Exchange, formed to promote Latin American trade, and the Merchanics', Dealers', and Lumbermen's Exchange, reorganized in 1881 from a group originated in 1806.[42]

Progress in the financial world kept pace with commercial advances. In 1880 New Orleans had eleven banks, national and state, with a total capital and surplus of $5,327,600. Sixteen years later, the city could boast nineteen banks; nine national, six state, and the addition of a new type, the savings banks, of which there were four local examples. In 1895 the nineteen banks had a capital and surplus of $8,421,742 and deposits of $23,535,172. The four savings banks had 9,462 depositors and deposits totalling $2,862,346. These statistics represented a 72.7 percent increase in the number of banks between 1880 and 1895 and a 58.4 percent increase in their capital and surplus.[43]

One feature of Gilded Age banking which had not existed formerly was the New Orleans Clearing House Association formed in

[41] The formation and activities of both the Produce Exchange and the Board of Trade are discussed in H. S. Herring, *History of the New Orleans Board of Trade, Limited, 1880–1930* (New Orleans, 1930), 31–104.

[42] *Progressive New Orleans*, 100; Zacharie, *New Orleans Guide*, 124; *The Mechanics, Dealers, and Lumbermen's Exchange, Its Imprint and Purposes, New Orleans Souvenir* (New Orleans, 1895).

[43] *Times-Democrat Almanac for 1896*, 16.

1872. By the 1890's this group was serving sixteen banks. Aside from the time saved and the elimination of danger involved in transferring actual funds from one bank to another, the Clearing House acted as a stabilizer upon finance in times of panic. It required member banks to keep a reserve fund on hand in case emergencies arose.[44] In the financing of real estate a great innovation was the rise of homestead associations. In 1880 there were none in the city; by 1896, twenty-four had been established. Real estate sales increased 111.5 percent between 1880 and 1896, one illustration of what a boon these associations were to local land and property.[45]

While such strides were made in private commerce and finance, the physical facilities of the port itself displayed an obsolete and shabby appearance. Since the late 1870's the wharves located on the east bank had been let out by the city to private lessees. The dilapidated condition of the wharves and the high wharfage fees charged steamboats and ships were a constant source of discussion among local businessmen and of criticism in the daily newspapers. In addition, the docks were overcrowded and offered inadequate facilities. Many ships sought berths on the west side of the river as a result. The west, or Algiers, bank was devoted mainly to dry docks and the private landings of various railroad lines. The encroachment of railroad tracks upon the levees of the main, or east, bank evoked the enmity of steamboat companies, who realized that the trains were usurping their traditional place. Steamboat traffic was steady through the 1880's but began to fade rapidly by the end of the century. Such magical names as the *Robert E. Lee* and the *Natchez* could be read occasionally in the shipping news in the early 1880's, but the activities of the railroads merited entire editorial columns.

River trade by the 1890's had become more localized than in former years. It served mainly bayous and tributary rivers in Lou-

44 Engelhardt, *The City of New Orleans,* 45–46.

45 *Times-Democrat Almanac for 1896,* 16. On background of the homestead association, see William J. Phillips, "Study of Building and Loan Associations in New Orleans: Early History and Development and their Present Financial Condition" (M.A. thesis, Tulane University, 1933).

isiana, Mississippi, and Arkansas, though there were still such elegant packets as those of the Anchor Line running to Memphis and St. Louis. River traffic included regularly established freight and passenger lines, independent steamboats operated only in boom seasons, barge lines which towed coal, grain, iron, cottonseed, and other freights (increasing as the steamboats decreased), and luggers plying Lake Pontchartrain and the city canals.[46] The New Basin Canal, owned by the state, offered an outlet to trade across the lake. Its receipts for 1893–94 show how considerable this trade was: 3,367 vessels arrived via the canal, carrying 14,300,000 feet of logs, 47,335 feet of lumber, 6,850,000 bricks, 8,884 bales of cotton, 339,700 barrels of charcoal, 13,539 barrels of resin, 409,460 barrels of sand, 7,689 sacks of rice, and 10,078 cords of wood.[47] The Old Basin, also a navigable waterway, was operated by private owners. Its facilities and traffic, however, were not as extensive as those of the New Basin.

With a river and canal trade of importance and a seagoing traffic of constantly growing proportions, New Orleans as the second port in the nation sorely needed improvements in its accommodations. Attempts had been made by Mayor Shakspeare and the exchanges and commercial interests in 1881 to draft a wharf lease lowering port fees and requiring the lessees to put up electric lights on the wharves. As a result of the contract finally agreed upon, electric lights were installed along the river front, but the fees were not lowered.[48] It was 1896 before attempts to return the wharves to public management were successful. During the closing months of Fitzpatrick's term, through the prodding of the Board of Trade and other commercial groups, the city council passed an ordinance directed at securing public control of the wharves. This was immediately repealed by the incoming Flower administration and replaced with a similar ordinance of its own. With the assent of the Flower government, a joint committee of commercial interests drew up a state law creating the Board of Commissioners of the Port of New Orleans which was passed by the legislature in

[46] Engelhardt, *The City of New Orleans,* 69–73.
[47] *Ibid.,* 70.
[48] *Daily Picayune,* March 10, April 15, 16, 21, May 17, 28, and scattered references for November and December, 1881.

1896.[49] This was amended in 1900 to give the Dock Board (as it was and is called) complete control of the wharves.[50] When the contract of the lessee, the Louisiana Construction and Improvement Company, ended in 1901, the Dock Board took charge.[51]

This board immediately reduced wharfage fees. Originally it hoped to make New Orleans a free port, but wharf improvements meant that some source of revenue had to be kept in operation. Through bank loans and loans from shipping and railroad companies to improve their wharves, the board constructed new docks and sheds along the river by 1904. In that year the legislature authorized the Dock Board's issuance of bonds for further improvements. In later years subsequent bond issues were to make possible the construction of the publicly operated Cotton Terminals and the Public Grain Elevator.[52]

The issue of a belt railroad to serve the frightfully congested levees was often discussed and several times acted upon by the city council, granting rights for such a railroad to private interests. But it was never settled in this period. The only feature of this sorely needed rail connection agreed upon was that it should be publicly owned. The episode of the Fischer franchise in 1894 convinced all elements of the business world of this fact. As a result of the municipal solvency and prosperity of the early twentieth century in New Orleans, the Public Belt Railroad finally became a reality in 1908.[53]

Compared to its commercial record, the city's manufacturing seemed puny. No matter how glowingly the local industrial bro-

[49] Campbell, *Manual of the City of New Orleans*, 41–42; Kendall, *History of New Orleans*, II, 508; Herring, *History of the New Orleans Board of Trade*, 56–57; *Acts Passed by the General Assembly, State of Louisiana, Regular Session, 1896* (Baton Rouge, 1896) , Act No. 70, p. 102.

[50] *Acts Passed by the General Assembly, State of Louisiana, Regular Session, 1900* (Baton Rouge, 1900) , Act No. 36, p. 44.

[51] Herring, *History of the New Orleans Board of Trade,* 57.

[52] *Ibid.,* 57–58. The Stuyvesant Docks were also constructed by the Illinois Central Railroad which was granted the privilege of building this extensive wharf in return for keeping several miles of levee in repair. Kendall, *History of New Orleans,* II, 508.

[53] In this year the first section of the belt line was opened to traffic and a two-million-dollar bond issue authorized by the state legislature to complete the rest of the railroad. Herring, *The History of the New Orleans Board of Trade,* 61.

chures or the *Manufacturers' Record* painted the future of manufacturing in the Crescent City, the fact remains that it was always secondary to commerce. Northern critics like to point to the excessive violence in the South, the legacy of Reconstruction, as a deterrent to outside capital to enter and develop its industrial potential.[54] But this was not a valid reason in connection with the Crescent City. In 1879 at the end of two decades of violence, out of forty-eight prominent merchants, industrialists, and professional men mentioned in Waldo's *Visitors' Guide to New Orleans*, thirty-seven were not natives of the city or state.[55] Twelve were originally from European countries, and twenty-five from other states, mainly from New York, Kentucky, and Ohio. A more logical explanation for the relative small number of industries in the city was its location at the lower end of the Mississippi Valley. Ideal for commercial reasons, it was too remote to make large-scale manufacturing practical.

Most of the major industries in the city were adjuncts of some commercial interest. The most obvious examples were the cotton presses, cottonseed oil factories, rice cleaning mills, sugar refineries, and foundry and cooperage establishments serving mainly the sugar and molasses trade. New Orleans by the 1890's had in addition at least a half dozen breweries, a large cordial works and a packery of oysters, and numerous lumberyards and planing mills. The men's ready-to-wear clothing industry became important by 1900, employing a large number of pieceworkers whose labor was performed in the dingy quarters of their homes. Another industry of

54 For an example of this type of criticism, see E. L. Godkin, "Why Capital Does Not Flow into the South," *The Nation*, XXXV (December, 1882), 501. Numerous brochures were prepared by hometown statisticians praising the virtues of New Orleans to prospective manufacturers. Two excellent examples by Andrew Morrison are *The Industries of New Orleans* (New Orleans, 1885), and *New Orleans, Her Relation to the New South* (New Orleans, n.d., but probably 1888).

55 See scattered biographies in Waldo, *Visitors' Guide to New Orleans*. Outsiders from the East and Midwest and from Europe had played a significant role in the city's business and commercial life throughout the nineteenth century. See Tregle, "Early New Orleans Society: A Reappraisal," 20–36; William W. Chenault and Robert C. Reinders, "The Northern-Born Community of New Orleans in the 1850's," *Journal of American History*, LI (September, 1964), 232–47; Joe Gray Taylor, "New Orleans and Reconstruction," *Louisiana History*, IX (Summer, 1968), 189–208.

significance was the manufacture of cigars and other tobacco products.[56] (See Table 11 for statistics on the leading local industries in 1894).

Between 1880 and 1900 manufacturing showed an encouraging increase in overall value of products. In 1880 the total manufac-

[Table 11]

Major Industries of New Orleans in 1894[a]

Type of Industry	Number of Concerns	Estimated Value of Products
Cotton oil and other cotton seed products	4	$4,000,000
Rice cleaning and polishing	7	4,000,000
Sugar Industry:		2,500,000
Sugar refining	3	
Molasses reboiling	12	
Tobacco and cigars	80	2,000,000
Breweries	7	2,000,000
Foundries	33	2,000,000
Clothing	25	2,000,000
Lumber and building material	22	2,000,000
Crackers and confectionery	....	1,500,000
Cotton goods	4	1,500,000
Boots and shoes	25	1,000,000
Cotton compressing	19	1,000,000
Printing	80	1,000,000

These industries turned out about a third of the entire factory product of the city; other sizeable manufacturing lines included the following:

Saddlery	$500,000
Ship building	500,000
Carriage making	500,000

[a] Engelhardt, *The City of New Orleans,* 136.

---

56 Marks, "The Industrial Development of New Orleans Since 1865," 386–409; Engelhardt, *The City of New Orleans,* 136–37.

tured goods of the city were worth $18,808,096, while in 1900 this category had climbed to $63,514,505. The cost of materials used to produce the 1900 manufactures was four times greater than that of 1880. But while the total number of manufacturing establishments in 1880 was 915; and in 1890, 1,961; in 1900 it had fallen to 1,524—showing a trend to consolidation into larger units. With consolidation came more mechanization and efficiency in operation which in turn cut down the number of workers in manufacturing establishments. In 1880 only 9,504 persons were employed in such work. This rose to 22,342 persons by 1890, then fell to 19,-435 by 1900.[57]

In addition to manufacturing, New Orleans had a large jobbing trade in supplying plantations in Mississippi, Louisiana, East Texas, Arkansas, and for a while even Florida. Competition with St. Louis, Memphis, Cincinnati, and rising towns in Texas kept this business highly competitive. New Orleans was, however, the Deep South distributor of California wines and did well in the grocery and provision trade, dry goods, boots and shoes, machinery and hardware. It was also the purchasing center for mules so necessary to the operation of Gulf state plantations.[58]

The combination of businessmen in exchanges and other business groups was not the only sign of economic concentration in Gilded Age New Orleans. Labor organizations enjoyed a rise in power that reached its peak in the general strike of 1892. Only two unions, the Screwmen's Beneficial Association and the Typographical Society, existed before the Civil War. (A screwman was the last individual to work with a bale of cotton in the hold of a seabound vessel. With the aid of a jackscrew, a large hook, he literally screwed or packed the bales together into the smallest possible space.) During the 1870's the number of unions grew to eighteen. In 1881 a confederation of almost all unions in the city was affected in the Central Trades and Labor Assembly, largely through the leadership of the Typographical Union. This confederation numbered thirty unions with about 15,000 members by 1884. Its policies were guided by a council of three delegates from

57 *Abstract of the Twelfth Census*, 357.
58 Engelhardt, *The City of New Orleans*, 101–03.

each of the member associations, which included both white and Negro unions.[59]

Some idea of its membership may be given by a glance at the groups marching in its third annual parade in 1884: Screwmen's Benevolent Association, over 1,000 members, founded in 1850; Cotton Yardmen's Association, around 1,100 men, founded in 1879; Cotton Yardmen's Association, No. 2, Negro union founded in 1880, around 6,000 members; Teamsters' and Loaders' Benevolent Association, 400 members, organized in 1880; Longshoremen's Protective Union, 250 Negro members, founded in 1872; Screwmen's Benevolent Association, No. 2, 350 Negro screwmen, founded 1870; the Typographical Union, founded before the Civil War, with 200 members; the Coopers' Benevolent Association, 450 members, organized in 1880; and the Street Railroad Employees' Benevolent Association organized in 1882 with 2,280 members.[60] Other newly formed unions in the 1884 parade were the Lumberyard Teamsters' Association, the Boss Draymen's Benevolent and Charitable Association, the Retail Dry Goods Clerks' Protective Association, the Round Freight Handlers' Association, the Cotton Weighers' and Reweighers' Association, and the Cotton Classes' and Employees' Association. Trade unionism had become so popular by this time that even the shoeshiners and horseshoers organized.[61] Strongest of all the unions and the most respected were the screwmen's associations, the Typographical Union, and the Street Railroad Employees' Benevolent Association.

During the 1880's the Knights of Labor were active in the state, numbering, by 1887, twelve groups in New Orleans and thirty in the rest of Louisiana. Their influence, hurt nationally by the Haymarket Affair, was weakened in Louisiana in 1887 by a strike of Negro sugarcane workers in the Teche country, whose demands of higher wages were interpreted as a racial insurrection and were

[59] The Screwmen's Beneficial Association and the Typographical Society were known after the Civil War as the Screwmen's Benevolent Association and the Typographical Union. On their early history see Arthur Raymond Pearce, "The Rise and Decline of Labor in New Orleans" (M.A. thesis, Tulane University, 1938) , 4–17. The Central Trades and Labor Assembly is discussed in the *Daily Picayune*, November 26, 1884.

[60] *Daily Picayune*, November 26, 1884.

[61] *Ibid.*, September 13, October 6, 30, 1884.

met with strikebreakers and the militia.[62] The other national organization, the American Federation of Labor, came to prominence locally in the 1890's and its unions were responsible for the 1892 general strike.[63]

In politics organized labor was active, as it had been before the Civil War. By 1860 labor leaders had become prominent in the counsels of the local Democratic Party. During the 1860's many workers joined the Free State Party, influenced by the sympathy of General Nathaniel Banks and the wage scale he imposed upon employers. Such laborers participated in the constitutional convention of 1864 and wrote into the new constitution clauses on minimum wages and hours on public works as well as the abolition of slavery.[64] The abuses of carpetbag government, however, turned the overwhelming majority of white labor back to the ranks of the Democratic-Conservative Party. In the 1880's and 1890's the ward leaders of the Ring were either labor leaders like Patrick Mealey, or were intimately connected with labor, like John Fitzpatrick. The latter's sympathy with the strikers in 1892 was deeply resented by the business classes, and the *Mascot* accused the mercantile reformers of marking him for impeachment because of their personal animosity against him.

Because of its close association with the Democratic machine, New Orleans labor was not in a position to cooperate fully with the Populists.[65] Labor journals in the city did praise the third party and take note of the mutual aims of workingmen and farmers, but in 1896 the Populists, in their efforts to gain some foothold in the city, were forced to join the reformer forces who as businessmen were essentially hostile to their program. This unnatural alliance only lasted through the election. In recognition of their support of the Ring, labor leaders secured a measure of patronage, mainly on the police force. This was the reason why the police were usually sympathetic to strikers.

[62] Roger W. Shugg, "The General Strike of 1892," *Louisiana Historical Quarterly*, XXI (April, 1938), 547–60.

[63] Woodward, *Origins of the New South*, 231.

[64] Shugg, *Origins of Class Struggle in Louisiana*, 196–210.

[65] On labor and the Populists see Vera M. Vegas, "The Populist Party in Louisiana" (M.A. thesis, Tulane University, 1942), 72–76.

Since New Orleans was the largest southern city during this period, with the second largest commerce in the nation, it was understandable that its labor should organize and become prominent in politics, despite the Old South notions still prevailing that southern labor was docile and would not effectively organize. In the 1880's New Orleans, although far advanced over other southern cities in the scope of its union movement, was not the only city south of the Mason and Dixon line in which labor elements organized and entered politics. The Knights of Labor claimed political successes in Richmond, Lynchburg, Mobile, Macon, Vicksburg, Anniston, and Jacksonville between 1886 and 1888.[66]

The relation of white and Negro laborers was a delicate issue which management did not fail to capitalize on when they had the opportunity. Realizing that they had common economic problems, however, unions of both races attempted to cooperate with each other. On the cotton docks the white and colored screwmen had an agreement for dividing the work between them. Frequently the two races participated jointly in strikes. In 1881 two thousand white and Negro union members marched together in the funeral procession of a Negro laborer killed during an outbreak of strike violence.[67] The Central Trades and Labor Assembly was composed of white and Negro unions, and its vice-president was a Negro.[68] This confederation of workers was credited with doing more "to break the color line in New Orleans than any other thing . . . since emancipation of the slaves." [69] If this was so, it was unintentional, since the confederation's aims were purely economic. The white men's wages could not be raised if Negroes were available to work for less. As competition became fierce for the few jobs open in times of economic panic and depression, racial antipathy tended to flare up. Usually employment went to the Negroes, whose standard of living allowed them to accept less than white workers. Following the Panic of 1873 and again in the year after the Panic of 1893, racial clashes occurred between laborers.

[66] Woodward, *Origins of the New South,* 230–31.
[67] *Daily Picayune,* September 12, 1881.
[68] *Ibid.,* November 26, 1884.
[69] George E. McNeill (ed.) , *The Labor Movement: The Problem of Today* (Boston, 1886) , 168.

Advances were made in raising wages and shortening working hours in a few cases, but the depression of the nineties plunged labor into a period of hard times once more. A nine-hour day was established for city workers and was also the average working day for most dock laborers and carpenters.[70] The mule drivers on streetcars, who worked sixteen hours a day, were a prominent exception. They finally got a cut in hours in 1892 as well as an agreement by management to the closed shop.[71] Skilled and unionized dock workers were the highest paid workers in the city. As a result of an 1866 strike, screwmen secured $6 a day, with $7 for a foreman. Since their work was seasonal, this was not as high a salary as it appeared. Teamsters in 1880 secured a raise in their minimum weekly wages from $12 to around $18.[72]

Colored waiters at the St. Charles and St. James hotels were drawing $15 a month; when they struck for higher pay in 1880 they were replaced by young white girls willing to work for $12 a month. The Cigar Makers Union, likewise, found competition from low-paid female help a deterrent to wage increases. Some women employees in this trade worked for as little as $1.50 a week.[73] Women and children in industry were increasing steadily by the end of the century. They often worked part time or did piecework at home, mainly for the clothing industry. More than a fifth of those employed locally in manufacturing establishments by 1894 were women, half of whom did piecework. They averaged a little over $167 each for a year's work.[74] Wage raises were meager, since any profits realized by management were not utilized in this direction.

In the ten years from 1885 to 1895, cigar makers were raised from a maximum of $5.32 to $6.55 a week, and press compositors from $12.95 to $13.31. Bricklayers made the most significant gains, going from 40 to 45 cents an hour. In many lines of work, however, wages fell and the *Times-Democrat* noted in 1888 that the average daily wage in New Orleans had fallen from $1.50 in 1883 to $1.00.

70 On the municipal nine-hour day see Flynn, *Flynn's Digest,* 294.
71 Shugg, "The General Strike of 1892," 547–60.
72 Pearce, "The Rise and Decline of Labor in New Orleans," 17, 19–20.
73 *Ibid.,* 23.
74 Engelhardt, *The City of New Orleans,* 137.

Furthermore, the remuneration of skilled workers such as carpenters was only a half to two thirds as great for a nine-hour day locally as that earned in New York and Philadelphia in eight hours. In order to survive, at least two out of the average family of five had to work. While men earned an average of $10 a week, women and children seldom received more than $5.[75]

With the rapid union organization of the 1880's came strikes to protest the depressed condition of workers. In 1880 and again in 1887 there were epidemics of strikes, but no year passed without at least a few. The most bitter and sometimes violent strikes occurred on the docks and in connection with streetcar lines. The climax of labor's struggle to secure its rights through the strike came in 1892 with a general walkout involving over 20,000 workers. It has been called the first "in American history to enlist both skilled and unskilled labor, black and whites, and to paralyze the life of a great city." [76] In 1892 union organization received stimulation from the American Federation of Labor's drive to charter new affiliates. Thirty new associations were created locally, giving the city a total of ninety-five unions. The AFL unions numbering forty-nine were joined together that year under the Workingmen's Amalgamated Council. The labor struggle of 1892 was to revolve around this council pitted against the Board of Trade, representing the business community.[77]

The strike was called to back up the demands of the Triple Alliance (unions of teamsters, screwmen, and packers) for a ten-hour day, overtime pay, and the preferential closed shop. This last demand was the most crucial and the one upon which the strikers felt their victory or defeat depended. After the Board of Trade at first refused to recognize the representatives of the Workingmen's Amalgamated Council and later to accede to its demands, the threatened general walkout became a reality on November 8. The forty-two AFL unions with about 20,000 workers left their jobs. This number included various types of dock workers, employees

75 Shugg, *Origins of Class Struggle in Louisiana*, 293–95.

76 Shugg, "The General Strike of 1892," 547.

77 *Ibid.*, 547–55. The discussion of the general strike is taken from Shugg, "The General Strike of 1892," 547–60; Woodward, *Origins of the New South*, 231–32; *Daily Picayune*, November 3–11, 1892, and *Times-Democrat*, November 3–11, 1892.

of the gas and electric light plants, and typesetters. As a result, traffic on the wharves and city streets came to a standstill, the city was plunged into darkness at night, and newspapers were hard pressed to find volunteer replacements for their backshop workers and get out daily editions. With numerous other activities of the metropolis also curtailed, the Board of Trade vowed to offer no quarter in the fight and to import outside laborers.

Mayor Fitzpatrick was openly sympathetic to the strikers and refused to let the police act as strikebreakers by operating the utilities. But Governor Murphy J. Foster, who had been backed by the commercial classes in the 1892 election, threw his support to the businessmen on the third day of the strike by issuing a proclamation calling for a return to normalcy and threatening the use of the militia. This effectively broke the laborers' resistance. Although it had been a city-wide movement marked by much bitterness, the general strike was handled by labor without resort to violence. The result of the incident was a compromise—the Triple Alliance gained its original demands on hours and wages. But the principles of collective bargaining and the closed shop, the most important issues at stake, were effectively ignored by the Board of Trade.

One interesting legal sidelight followed the settlement of this strike. A suit was entered in Federal District Court against forty-four labor leaders for violation of the Sherman Anti-Trust Act by conspiring to restrain trade through a general strike. This case, the first application of the Sherman law against labor, was eventually quashed and few, if any, realized how effective this legal argument was to become in the future.[78]

Between the culmination of the general strike and the local dock riots of 1894, the economic condition of the working classes suffered a setback. Although the conservative-minded newspapers and trade brochures claimed that New Orleans was not as adversely affected by the panic of 1893 as northern cities, it did suffer to some extent. Exports decreased over $1,300,000 and imports over $9,400,000 as a result of the panic. Bank clearings fell off 16 percent. Grain shipments to the city were severely curtailed and the lack of demand for luxury items cut deep into the port's foreign

[78] Shugg, "The General Strike of 1892," 558–60.

trade. Only the railroads showed an increase of tonnage into the city in the year following the panic.[79]

This, however, meant little alleviation for the laboring classes, because the railroads' policy of through shipments of the major staple cotton from interior presses actually took work away from cotton-affiliated trades as well as cutting out many cotton factors in the city. In former years all cotton which arrived at New Orleans came to seek a market and was pressed and stored in this city. But by the late 1880's and 1890's more and more cotton was bought at interior ports by British steamship lines, shipped to New Orleans at special through rail rates, and promptly placed on board ship. Independent cotton shipped to factors in the city did not receive the cheap rail or storage rates of through cotton. As a result the cotton trades of New Orleans struggled in vain to compete against through cotton and still make a profit. Along with the factors, cotton laborers of all types, a large segment of the city's employed, were the natural victims in this grim economic battle.[80] The Panic of 1893 only added another dark cloud to the already gloomy horizon.

The dock riots of 1894 were the result of desperation on the part of white screwmen, the aristocrats of the wharves, when British cotton shippers attempted to replace them with Negro screwmen at lower wages, thus upsetting the division of work between these two groups which had been traditional for decades. As always happened under economic stress, racial animosity erupted on the wharves. White screwmen boarded vessels, threw the tools of Negroes overboard, and several Negroes were drowned after jumping into the river to avoid being beaten. Violence, killings, and the burning of sheds on the dock occurred in October and November of 1894 and the spring of 1895. Governor Foster had to call out the militia in March to protect Negro screwmen recently hired by an English shipping firm.[81]

[79] New Orleans of 1894, pp. 21–22.

[80] For a discussion of the through cotton problem in New Orleans see Hester, "Cotton," 3–5, and the Mascot, May 25, 1889.

[81] Pearce, "The Rise and Decline of Labor in New Orleans," 31–37; Woodward, Origins of the New South, 267; Daily Picayune, October 27, 28, 30, November 5, 6, 7, 1894; March 15, 1895.

But as prosperity returned to the country by the late 1890's the unrest along the riverfront subsided. By the end of the century both capital and labor had substantially changed from the days of Reconstruction. Both had organized and centralized their efforts. Commerce had increased, not at its antebellum rate, but still rapidly enough to keep New Orleans the second port in the 1890's. Railroads had replaced steamboats as the common carriers of freight and passengers for the Crescent City by 1900, and scientific studies of crops and their movements, such as the famous Hester Reports on cotton, made fluctuations in the market much less likely. Meanwhile, throughout its development in the 1880's and 1890's, labor was always conservative. Socialist doctrines largely fell on unsympathetic ears.[82] Practical goals and mutual cooperation to reach them was local labor's credo. For a city as fraught with racial tension as New Orleans had been in the 1860's and 1870's, the collaboration of white and Negro unions in the last two decades of the century was an admirable accomplishment. That this good feeling was broken down in times of economic distress is understandable, since racial difference among their employees were exploited by capitalists whenever feasible.

In the great general strike of 1892, the commercial classes hoped to halt the advance of unionism. The Board of Trade's refusal to recognize the labor committee running the strike and to accede to its demands for the closed shop were hailed by the conservative elements of the city as a sweeping victory of management over labor. In reality it was simply a setback. The Workingmen's Amalgamated Council continued to exist and the AFL unions to grow. Organized labor, like the commercial exchanges, was a reality of the New South and of the new century about to begin.

---

[82] Pearce, "The Rise and Decline of Labor in New Orleans," 23–24; Shugg, *Origins of Class Struggle in Louisiana,* 305.

9

CRIME AND THE CONSCIENCE
OF A CITY

A GENERAL ATMOSPHERE of lawlessness plagued New Orleans in the last twenty years of the century. It was in part a social malady shared by other metropolitan centers in the United States. But its local causes differed in some respects from those responsible for crime and vice in northern cities. The major difference was the coarsening of the moral fiber of the Crescent City population that had resulted from military occupation during the Civil War and the struggle to overthrow Reconstruction carpetbaggers in the 1870's. Spontaneous disorders, contempt for constituted authority, the carrying of concealed weapons, and the employment of any means (including bribery and violence) to gain political ascendancy had been the order of the day between 1862 and 1877.

Extraordinary violence had included the race rioting of 1866 and the armed overthrow of the carpetbag state government in 1874.[1] Even upper-class women, usually the defenders of law and order, had turned in fury against the hated federal rule of General Benjamin "Beast" Butler.[2] Ladies made it fashionable to defy authority by taunts, jeers, and other minor infractions of the peace. When New Orleanians recovered control of their city government, respect for the law as the arbiter of justice was at an all-

[1] Donald E. Reynolds, "The New Orleans Riot of 1866, Reconsidered," *Louisiana History,* V (Winter, 1964) , 5–27; Shugg, *Origins of Class Struggle,* 216–17; Warmoth, *War, Politics and Reconstruction,* 46–49.

[2] See the discussion of Butler's Woman Order in Gerald M. Capers, Jr. *Occupied City: New Orleans Under the Federals, 1862–1865* (Lexington, 1965), 66–76.

time low. This was truly unfortunate since the Crescent City had never been a model, law-abiding town, even in its palmiest ante-bellum days. As a port it had received the flotsam and jetsam of European society to swell the ranks of native criminals. Moreover, its position as the entrepot for western produce had kept it in touch with the frontier and its brawling culture. Fighting and carousing flatboatmen from upriver had been a commonplace in old New Orleans.[3]

What Reconstruction added, however, was the defiance of law by persons from all walks of life, with their leaders being members of the upper classes. No matter how repressive and repugnant the Radical Republican government may have seemed and no matter how the New Orleans Redeemers might be lauded for their revolutionary activities in the September 14 coup, they still had set a precedent for letting people, rather than the law, administer justice. This tendency to take the law into one's own hands was furthered during the 1880's by the weakness and corruptibility of the law enforcement agencies in the city.

The hated Metropolitan police of Reconstruction days had been under state carpetbag control and had ruled with the brutal might of an army.[4] When they finally were disbanded in 1877 and control of the force returned to Redeemer city officials, a loathing of strong-arm officers kept the police from receiving the proper personnel and equipment that they needed to patrol the city. In addition, the empty city treasury was further cause for not strengthening the force. As a result, citizens were more or less thrown upon their own resources for protection from criminals and lived in fear similar to the state of mind existing locally in the early 1860's. During the federal occupation one woman, fearful of the local brigands and newly-freed Negroes in the city, had kept a hatchet, a tomahawk, and a vial of acid handy to repel housebreakers.[5] Such precautions again became common in the

[3] Flatboatmen are discussed in Ray Samuel, Leonard V. Huber, and Warren Ogden, *Tales of the Mississippi* (New York, 1955), 11–23, and Asbury, *The French Quarter*, 73–105.

[4] Rightor, *Standard History of New Orleans*, 113–15.

[5] Julia LeGrand, *The Journal of Julia LeGrand, New Orleans, 1862–1863*, edited by Kate Mason Rowland and Mrs. Morris L. Croxall (Richmond, 1911), 59. Such precautions as that taken by the woman mentioned here were prompted by fear and uncertainty of what Federal occupation might bring dur-

1880's when the police force was too small to offer adequate service. Several groups of vigilantes sprung into being in response to local crime waves, and then faded away. Many persons carried weapons of defense on the streets, and thousands kept weapons in their homes. In such an atmosphere where the police were weak and the populace was forced to defend itself, the community at times came close to reverting to a frontier level of law enforcement. But the Hennessy murder and the lynching that followed was to be the climax of an age of deteriorating law and order. The terrible cathartic effect of this incident scoured the conscience of the city and set it back upon a path of more civilized justice.

Like other American cities New Orleans had its share of minor criminals. Juvenile delinquents stoned streetcars, snatched purses, wrecked grocery stores, broke gas lights, carried off park benches, and stole merchandise from the levees and local lumberyards. It also was invaded during the mild winter months, particularly during the Carnival season, by tramps, pickpockets, and confidence men. Since Mardi Gras on even its calmest occasions was a violent day, the mayor sometimes ordered all vagrants picked up and detained in jail several days before this hectic celebration. Confidence men were likewise subjected to periodic roundups by the police. Under Mayor Behan such bunko artists as gold brick salesmen and operators of tambola wheels, or wheels of fortune, in the public markets were frequently arrested. The tambola men were treated as confidence operators rather than gamblers because there was no element of chance in their game—it was a strictly controlled, crooked swindle.[6]

Gambling, fair and crooked, was a universal vice which the police only halfheartedly attempted to suppress. For a few years

---

ing its early days rather than by lack of proper law enforcement. Actually the Federal command saw that the city was reasonably well patrolled against criminals.

[6] On tramps, see *Daily Picayune*, January 29, February 19, 1881, and on confidence men, see *ibid.*, February 6, 27, 1883, and *Daily States*, April 16, 1883. Juvenile delinquency is chronicled in almost every issue of the local papers during the early 1880's. For example, see *Daily Picayune*, January 13, 16, 1881; June 18, 1883.

the Shakspeare Plan upgraded the caliber of gambling establish-ments. But after 1887, when the arrangement was condemned by the grand jury and abandoned by city officials, gambling resumed its disreputable character. Strangers who allowed flashy and out-wardly friendly individuals along Royal Street to entice them into the back rooms of saloons for games of faro were almost sure to be cheated.

A year after the Shakspeare Plan had been inaugurated, the problem of dope addiction was brought to the attention of the mayor in an incongruous way. Shakspeare received a letter from a Chinese citizen requesting that he devise an understanding about the operation of opium dens similar to the arrangement he had with the gamblers. Signed "Hing Loong," the letter requested that houses for smoking opium be licensed under any restrictions the mayor wished to impose. It pointed out that native Americans, both men and women, frequented local opium dens along with Chinese.[7] Another letter from "W. Gorge," a Chinese of different views castigated opium dens as the ruination of otherwise hard-working, law-abiding Chinese and concluded that "in behalf of those of my countrymen in this city who desire to become honest, useful and intelligent citizens, I respectfully petition that no such places be licensed." [8] The result of this controversy was to in-tensify police surveillance of suspected drug hangouts. On the day Gorge's letter was published in the papers, an opium den was raided on Common Street between Rampart and Basin, the loca-tion of numerous Chinese shops and the probable center of the illicit drug trade.[9] Such dens, while not a major threat to the general public, continued to exist through the 1890's. The *Mascot* occasionally called attention to their evil influence by publishing sensational cartoons depicting opium users in a comatose state within such drug hideaways.[10]

Far more alarming problems than opium dens were the gangs of thieves and cutthroats that infested the city and the often-erupting violence between petty politicians, whose blood stained

7 *Daily Picayune,* April 26, 1882.
8 *Ibid.,* May 2, 1882.
9 *Ibid.,* May 3, 1882.
10 *Mascot,* August 3, 1889.

the sidewalks with alarming frequency. Like New York's notorious Whyos, New Orleans' Shot Tower gang, the Yellow Harry mob, the Spiders, and the gang that hung around St. Mary's Market terrorized local citizens, extorted money from gambling houses and barrooms, and even intimidated the police. When a patrolman was beaten up by thugs while walking through St. Mary's Market, he refused to divulge the identity of his attackers who were obviously known to him.[11] Underworld derelicts of the lowest order also hid in the shadows of the wharves as they waited to rob unsuspecting strangers walking alone at night along the river. These "wharf rats" actually lived in shanties they built under the wharves and entered through loose boards or by makeshift ladders. A large number of bodies found floating in the river were victims of these criminals, believed the *Picayune*. But this was never proven and the culprits went free. If one such "nest" of "wharf rats" was broken up, another would take up residence under a wharf at a new location.[12]

Violence caused by petty politicians or their hangers-on was the open, much criticized scandal of Gilded Age New Orleans. Numerous murders of and by political figures occurred—two of the most famous being the fatal shootings of Cap Murphy in 1884 and of Commissioner of Police and Public Buildings Patrick Mealey on New Year's day in 1888. Mealey's murderer, Louis Clare, was one of Guillotte's special appointees to the police force. At the time of his appointment as a patrolman six months before the murder, he had a lengthy police record including thirty arrests in one year for everything from disorderly conduct to stealing.

In addition to lesser altercations engaged in by such prominent men as Treasurer Walshe and Commissioner Fitzpatrick, local papers in the 1880's chronicled the stories of a coroner who bit off the tip of his opponent's nose in a street fight, a deputy sheriff who fatally gouged out the eye of an enemy with an umbrella, and a keeper of the Parish Prison arrested for petty larceny and for attempted murder.[13] The city employee whose exploits appeared most frequently in the police reports and in the columns of the

---

11 *Daily Picayune,* December 18, 1880; Asbury, *The French Quarter,* 402–404.
12 *Daily Picayune,* July 29, 1881; December 23, 1884.
13 *Ibid.,* January 6, 13, July 7, 8, 1881; January 10, March 7, 1882.

Mascot was John "Bowlegged" Donovan, a city pound keeper who was often arrested for picking both fights and pockets without discrimination. Donovan was described by the *Mascot* as the strong-arm flunkey of Ring bosses Fitzpatrick and Mealey.[14] Addicted to heavy drinking, Donovan met his end with delirium tremens brought on by alcohol. His last days were spent chained to a bed in Charity Hospital to restrain his violent outbreaks. In addition to the infamous Donovan, numerous other city employees were arrested for fighting on streetcars and in saloons, or for committing minor misdemeanors.

Labor disturbances were also frequently violent, and fatalities resulting from strike clashes were not uncommon. Preserving order during such emergencies was a difficult task for the mayor and police chief since many policemen were former union members themselves who were openly sympathetic to the cause. Strikers did not hesitate to set fire to cargo or ships, to stop streetcars and turn out the passengers, and beat up strikebreakers unmercifully even though police were stationed nearby. In 1881 the wives and children of Negro cotton press draymen wielded frying pans and threw rocks at policemen attempting to pick up a striker for questioning.[15] As late as 1902, a private detective imported from Chicago by a streetcar company to protect its scabs was himself beaten black and blue by irate striking drivers. He later admitted that the trouble he encountered in New Orleans was worse than anything he had ever experienced in northern cities.[16]

A variety of circumstances kept the police on the defensive rather than the offensive in coping with crime and violence. The skimpy budget of the police department, the payment of salaries in certificates which had to be sold to brokers, and the pitifully small number of active patrolmen stood out as three of its major weaknesses. Reviewing the police situation in November, 1882, the *Picayune* noted:

Before the war the city employed some five hundred policemen, and paid them promptly in cash. The salary of a patrolman at that time was $58 per month. The number of the old metropolitan police varied from

14 *Mascot,* June 6, 1882.
15 *Daily Picayune,* September 11, 1881.
16 Pearce, *The Rise and Decline of Labor in New Orleans,* 57–58.

five to six hundred men, and more than a half million dollars was annually appropriated to its maintenance. During Mayor Pilsbury's administration under act no. 35, the Crescent City police was organized to replace the metropolitans. Its number was at first limited to 315 men, all told, and the amount appropriated to its support was $325,000. The salary of a patrolman was then fixed at $60 per month, and the force was reduced to a little over 200 men, and $285,000 was the annual appropriation to that service. Under Mayor Shakspeare the appropriation was $185,000 and the force was still further reduced until now it numbers in all less than 100 men for active duty. In the meantime the territory to be guarded has increased to about 150 square miles, or three times what it was immediately before the outbreak of the late war.[17]

This dark picture was somewhat brightened under Mayor Behan between 1882 and 1884. Through careful personal management of the $185,000 police appropriation, the mayor managed to add 100 men to the force, bringing the number of active patrolmen up to around 239.[18] But sufficient patrolmen to cover the entire city was a goal never reached in the nineteenth century. In 1899 the Police Board regretted in its annual report that the force had an inadequate number of officers and totaled only 315 men to serve a city of almost 280,000 population.[19]

Other demoralizing factors contributing to the inefficiency of the police were the sharp power struggle for its control waged by the various mayors against the Police Board, and the political corruption that permeated the entire force and part of the municipal court system. Between 1880 and 1888 the Police Board consisted of four regular members appointed by the mayor, and two ex officio officers (the mayor himself and the commissioner of police and public buildings).[20] A mayor conscientious in disciplining the police, such as Shakspeare or Behan, might influence the board to deal stiffly with officers committing infractions of police rules. But often the board, if appointed by a previous administration, was at

17 *Daily Picayune,* November 21, 1882.

18 *Ibid.,* June 6, 12, 13, 14, 18, July 12, 1883.

19 *Annual Report of the Board of Police Commissioners of the City of New Orleans* (New Orleans, 1899) , 5–6.

20 Waring and Cable, "History and Present Condition of New Orleans, Louisiana," 291.

odds with the mayor. During one meeting of the board at which Mayor Shakspeare was absent, its other members dismissed the case of an officer who had allowed a man charged with rape of a minor to go free without posting bail. Naturally the alleged rapist had never showed up to stand trial.[21] Frequent cases came before the board of patrolmen who got drunk on their beats or neglected their duty in other ways. Perjured testimony was a commonplace at such investigations.[22]

Appointed usually for political reasons without regard to their fitness for police work, the individuals on the force had little *esprit de corps* as law officers. Their appearance was likely to be casual and their uniforms haphazard. Sometimes officers did not even bother to wear the regulation uniforms. One visitor in the 1880's drew this word picture of them:

> In process of time and by dint of persistant observation you descry a policeman; but the New Orleans municipal has little in common either in stature or costume with his colossal brother in New York or Philadelphia. Still less does he resemble the stalwart 'peeler' of London streets, or the well-brushed, well-girthed, trim-moustached *sergent-de-ville* of Paris. The New Orleans policeman is apt to be young and slim, and to be attired on the 'go-as-you-please' principle. It is true that his clothes are blue and his buttons metallic, and that he wears a black felt hat with a slouched brim, somewhat similar to the head-gear affected by brigadier-generals during the Civil War. Still it is the business of a policeman to inspire awe; and how can you expect to be awe-stricken by a personage who wears a turn-down collar and a Byron tie, who carries a gold watch and chain at his fob, and who smokes a cigar on duty? [23]

Since petty political lawbreakers were usually set free by corrupt juries, policemen shied away from arresting them. Furthermore, some minor court officers readily took bribes, and every few years a city judge, or recorder, was investigated for such malprac-

---

21 *Daily Picayune,* February 16, 1881.

22 *Ibid.,* January 10, 11, 22, 1881.

23 "On Canal Street," from "America Revisited," XXIV, in London *Daily Telegraph,* February 19, 1880 (from a clipping in a scrapbook in Howard-Tilton Memorial Library). Sala, *America Revisited,* 15–16.

tices as putting up bail for persons appearing before his own court. Criminals felt so confident that one gambler even threatened a recorder in his chambers after the judge had sentenced the gambler's friend.[24] Because the district attorney did not have a staff large enough to aid him in gathering evidence, securing witnesses to testify against hoodlums under political protection was close to impossible. Jury duty could be avoided in any of the courts by merely paying a fee of fifty dollars into the militia fund. The respectable elements of the population dodged such service, leaving it entirely in the hands of courthouse loafers and mercenary politicians who made a travesty of the jury system.[25] Under these circumstances, rowdies felt free to carry concealed weapons, to fight, and to annoy complete strangers without fear of effective prosecution. Demoralized by low pay and the futility of arresting thugs who could not be convicted, the police sometimes refused to answer calls to break up fights between city employees in saloons.

Vigilante groups in protest against such conditions sprang up every few years just as they did in other cities or frontier communities when law enforcement seemed to be too big a job for the local peace officers. The Committee of Public Safety, which existed in 1881–82, was such a group, probably patterned after the famous Committee of Seventy in New York. It differed from that organization in being a secret society whose communications in the newspapers were issued through its attorney. At least eight branches of this committee operated on a city-wide basis, sometime even patrolling their districts with shotguns. Their main concern, however, was the securing of evidence and witnesses willing to testify against hoodlums arrested by the police, who cooperated gladly with these volunteer helpers of the law.[26] After the committee had faded away, the grand jury in 1883 suggested that com-

---

24 On court officers taking bribes, see *Daily Picayune*, February 23, 1881. On investigations of recorders, see the same paper, August 3, October 29, 1881; March 16, 1882; May 8, June 29, 30, 1894. The gambler's threatening of a recorder is also in the *Daily Picayune*, June 14, 1883.

25 Such conditions were brought out in stories on the Committee of Public Safety in *Daily Picayune*, August 4, September 4, 1881.

26 *Democrat*, September 1, 1881; *Daily Picayune*, July 23, August 3, 10, 11, September 4, October 30, November 6, 1881; January 17, 27, March 16, April 2, 1882.

missions be issued to five property holders in each ward to organize an auxiliary police force to aid the police in the same manner
that the Auxiliary Sanitary Association helped the Department of
Public Works.[27] Although this suggestion was seriously considered, it was not put into permanent operation.

During Mayor Guillotte's administration, between 1884 and
1888, several groups aimed at curbing political corruption were
formed, including the Committee of One Hundred, the Law and
Order League, and finally the political faction called the Young
Men's Democratic Association.[28] The first two groups were not
vigilante groups in the strictest sense of the term. Their chief
concern was unearthing skullduggery by the city council. But they
were fully aware of the ineptness of law enforcement in the city
and deplored its deterioration. The Young Men's Democratic Association, formed to oppose the Ring in the municipal election
of 1888, actually performed vigilante duty on election day. They
placed armed guards at the polls to make sure that no ballot box
tampering took place. With the election of the Y.M.D.A.'s ticket
in 1888, a major reform was initiated by adherents of this group
in the state legislature with the passage of a bill reorganizing the
Police Board and creating civil service tests for policemen. Although both Mayor Shakspeare and Mayor Fitzpatrick were to
argue with the new board in the 1890's over control of the force,
this reorganization marked the beginning of a brighter chapter in
the history of the police.[29]

Conditions in the city's police stations and prisons were aired in
the press when the Board of Prisons and Asylums began its inspection of these facilities in the early 1880's. All of the police stations were old, run-down buildings. Women arrested on theft
charges were searched by male officers since there were no police
matrons.[30] After this situation was criticized by the board, two
matrons were hired. The condition of Parish Prison itself was the

27 *Daily Picayune,* June 12, August 12, 1883.

28 See Chapter 4 of this study for information on these three organizations.

29 For a full discussion of the Police Board conflict between the mayor and
the commissioners, see Chapter 4 of this book.

30 Turner, "George W. Cable's Beginnings as a Reformer," 155; annual report
of the Board of Prisons and Asylums in *Daily Picayune,* May 30, 1882.

most pressing problem that the board faced. It was a dilapidated, ancient structure whose stairways were rotting away, and whose eaves were infested with bats that were allowed to remain because of the contemporary belief that they were a protection against yellow fever.[31]

Prisoners of all types—those awaiting trial, serving time for first offenses, or in prison for murder or other capital crimes—were allowed to mingle together in the prison's courtyard.[32] Children arrested for stealing might come in contact with criminals of the most vicious character, since no special facilities existed for juveniles. A little girl arrested for removing flowers from a grave in one city cemetery was locked up pending trial as if she were an adult thief. In a raid on "The Blue House," a house of prostitution, the five-year-old son of one of the occupants was taken into custody. He was removed to the police station and allowed to sleep on a bench in the outdoor courtyard, since the police disliked to lock him up with adult prisoners.[33] However, by the 1890's care of juvenile offenders was improved. The House of Good Shepherd cared for wayward girls, and delinquent boys were placed in the Boys' House of Refuge.[34]

Within the walls of Parish Prison, a sharp difference existed between the living conditions of the poor and the well-to-do. Those prisoners who could pay for the privilege were allowed to live in a section of the prison that was comfortable, roomy, and far superior to the quarters of the other inmates. It was called the "Orleans Hotel" by the less fortunate prisoners who could not afford its luxuries. Occupants of the "Orleans Hotel" could have salesmen with clothing or other merchandise visit them in prison; sumptuous dinners could be brought in to supplement the watery soup and bread which was the ordinary prison fare.[35]

Parish Prison discipline varied from laxity to outright barbarism. A convicted murderer was allowed to handle the prison's

31 Jones, *Quarantine and Sanitary Operations of the Board of Health of the State of Louisiana during 1880, 1881, 1882, and 1883*, cccxiv.

32 Annual report of the Board of Prisons and Asylums, *Daily Picayune*, May 30, 1882.

33 *Daily Picayune*, July 10, 1881.

34 *Annual Report of the Board of Prisons and Asylums of New Orleans, Louisiana, November 1, 1898*. (New Orleans, 1898) , 3–5.

35 *Daily Picayune*, July 15, 1883.

drugs and poisons, and other serious offenders were often sent to carry messages outside of the prison.[36] This practice obviously resulted in the occasional disappearance of such trustees. In contrast to this leniency, any prisoner who misbehaved violently was placed in stocks with his face toward the floor and his ankles drawn together so tightly with rope that it cut his flesh. This punishment could be endured no longer than a few minutes.[37]

From the viewpoint of the reformers, idleness was one of the chief curses of the prison. Local newspapers frequently stated their belief that river roustabouts and other seasonal laborers deliberately caused disturbances so that they could be arrested and locked up during winter months. With work difficult to find, they could eat and sleep at city expense without performing any tasks in prison.[38] Shakspeare's first administration tried to remedy this situation by creating a separate House of Detention for vagrants, drunks, and other minor offenders who would be compelled to do street work. In a court case involving one of the inmates, however, the employment of such prisoners was declared illegal. The judge ruled that persons committed for minor offenses by recorder's courts (without a trial) could not be forced to work at hard labor.[39] This difficulty was overcome in 1884 by the passage of an ordinance making such work by prisoners voluntary. They received a day off their sentence for every eight hours of work they performed. To encourage volunteers for street work, barrels of whiskey were furnished the House of Detention to be rationed out to those who cooperated.[40]

Through a slow but steady campaign of heckling the city council and securing newspaper publicity, the Board of Prisons and Asylums secured some reform. In 1883 an ordinance was passed calling for the separation of prisoners in police vans.[41] Police matrons also became a permanent addition to the law enforcement

[36] Turner, "George W. Cable's Beginnings as a Reformer"; grand jury report in *Times-Democrat*, February 4, 1882.
[37] *Daily Picayune*, June 2, 1883.
[38] *Ibid.*, December 18, 1880; grand jury report in *ibid.*, February 4, 1882; annual report of Board of Prisons and Asylums in *ibid.*, May 30, 1882.
[39] *Ibid.*, January 28, February 2, September 8, October 20, 1881.
[40] *Ibid.*, June 20, 25, September 20, and annual report of Board of Prisons and Asylums in issue of November 20, 1884.
[41] Turner, "George W. Cable's Beginnings as a Reformer," 157.

setup.[42] Finally, in 1892, a new combination criminal courts building and jail was constructed.[43] But an ordinance abolishing confinement in the stocks and the unequal privileges granted occupants of the Parish Prison's "Orleans Hotel" had been defeated in 1883.[44] The council doubted its power to draft such legislation on prison regulations. Brutality by some policemen was still being complained of by the grand jury in 1889, and the cruel use of the sweatbox to force prisoners to talk or to punish them continued to be used throughout the 1880's.[45]

With the triumph of Shakspeare and the Young Men's Democratic Association, better law enforcement seemed to be an immediate prospect. In addition to the new Police Board's reorganization of the force through civil service tests and tests of physical fitness, provision was made for a police pension fund. Shakspeare also appointed the most brilliant lawman in the city, David C. Hennessy, to the office of chief of police. His choice was praised in a letter from William A. Pinkerton, head of the famous detective agency.[46] Hennessy's career as chief was to be too brief, unfortunately, for him to see the full beneficial results of police reforms inaugurated with the beginning of his tenure in 1888. His assassination in 1890 and the lynching of those accused of his murder in 1891 dramatically brought together all the old problems of law enforcement in the city and focused the attention of foreign countries as well as that of other American cities upon them.

Hennessy's whole life was marred with tragedy. His policeman father had been shot to death over a grudge when Dave was still a boy. Young Dave then went to work as a messenger for the police to support his mother. Unlike many of the political appointees

---

42 *Ibid.*

43 Kendall, *History of New Orleans,* II, 506–507.

44 *Daily Picayune,* July 26, 1883. This ordinance was discussed in council meetings from August through December. See scattered references particularly in December, 1883 issues of *Daily Picayune.*

45 *Daily Picayune,* grand jury report on June 1, 1889; *Mascot,* September 29, 1888.

46 *Daily Picayune,* April 24, 1888. William A. Pinkerton was the son of Allan Pinkerton, the famous detective and founder of the Pinkerton Agency. When his father died in 1884, William assumed control of the worldwide activities of the Pinkerton firm. *Who Was Who in America, 1897–1942,* I, 975.

on the force, he was trained from youth in police work and showed a dedication and aptitude for criminal detection unmatched by any others on the local squad. By the time he reached his twenties, he had worked his way up to the rank of detective, or aid, and special assistant to the chief of police. In 1881 his capture of the Italian mountain bandit Giuseppi Esposito made him nationally famous among law officers. Esposito had fled from Italy where he was being vigorously sought for numerous deeds of theft, murder, and arson, and had taken up a shadowy residence in New Orleans as an oyster fisherman and dealer under an assumed name. Bringing about six associates with him, he had formed a local underworld group which he called the Mafia. But it does not appear to have been directly connected with the Sicilian secret society of that name. An admirer of the Sicilian Mafia leader Leone, Esposito named his oyster lugger after him, and on some occasions flew the Mafia flag from its mast. After his arrest by Hennessy, Esposito's minions offered sums up to $50,000 in an attempt to bribe the young aid to release his prisoner. But Hennessy spurned such offers and personally escorted the bandit king to New York to face an extradition hearing. As a result, this criminal was deported and stiffly punished by the Italian government.[47]

Hennessy's fanatical devotion to duty and his superior ability in tracking down criminals made him the obvious choice to succeed Chief Thomas Boylan when the officer retired. But a dark fate was to decree otherwise. In 1881, shortly after his capture of Esposito, Hennessy and his friends on the force were irritated by the political appointment of Thomas Devereaux to the newly created post of chief of aids. Devereaux had never served as a policeman before he took over the job of heading its detective squad. Furthermore, his authority over it conflicted with that of Boylan, who deeply resented what he considered an inexperienced outsider. Hennessy's chances to become chief were now much slimmer, since Devereaux was the intimate of several administrators, some of whom owed him favors. Friction immediately arose be-

47 Hennessy's early life is discussed in John S. Kendall, "Who Killa de Chief?" *Louisiana Historical Quarterly*, XXII (April, 1939), 492–530, and in Kendall, *History of New Orleans*, I, 478–79. For an account of Hennessy's capture of Esposito, see *Daily Picayune*, July 8, 1881.

tween Devereaux and his staff, particularly with aid Mike Hennessy, Dave's cousin. The chief of aids attempted to have Mike removed from the force by the Police Board. In his anger over the board's refusal to accept his charges against Mike, he became so insolent that he himself was charged with insubordination and commanded to stand trial. Mike Hennessy was to be a witness at this board investigation.

Before it could be held, a wild gun battle broke out between Devereaux and Mike Hennessy that proved fatal to the chief of aids. Devereaux was discussing some investments in a brokerage firm when Mike Hennessy entered and challenged him over accusations he had made that Mike was a thief. Within seconds both men drew their guns and began firing. Dave Hennessy's part in this drama was clouded by conflicting testimony. One witness claimed that he saw Dave enter the office and come to Mike's aid by shooting Devereaux. Other eyewitnesses claimed that Dave was nowhere in sight during the shooting. He arrived, however, by the end of the shooting and helped his wounded cousin into a carriage and took him to Charity Hospital. Devereaux had been shot dead on the spot. Both Mike and Dave Hennessy stood trial and were acquitted of the charge of murder. But as a result of this incident, they were dismissed from the force.[48]

Tempestuous Mike moved to Houston, where he met a violent death some years later, his assailant never being apprehended. Dave became a bank detective and served as chief of the special police hired to patrol the Cotton Centennial Exposition in 1884 and 1885. Thereafter, he went into partnership with his old friend and former chief, Thomas Boylan, in a detective agency. He had settled down to the life of a successful executive in this flourishing firm when Shakspeare asked him to return to the police force as its chief in 1888.[49] Faced with the realization of his boyhood dream which the Devereaux scandal had almost snatched from him forever, Hennessy gave up a profitable, routine existence to take on

[48] On the entire Devereaux incident, see *Daily Picayune*, April 1, 6, 8, July 2, October 4, 14, April 28. The actual shooting of Devereaux took place on October 13, 1881, and the acquital of the Hennessys on April 27, 1882.

[49] On the activities of Mike and Dave Hennessy after the Devereaux affair, see Kendall, "Who Killa de Chief?" 492–530.

one of the toughest jobs in the city. His love of police work and the possibility of effecting real reforms in the work of the force, now that civil service tests insured a better caliber of officers, convinced Hennessy that he should become police chief.

Knowing that local secret societies, similar to that headed by Esposito in 1881, were in existence, Chief Hennessy decided the time had come to crack down fearlessly on them when two brothers, Joseph and Peter Provenzano, convinced him that they had been sent to prison on perjured testimony by such an order of desperadoes. The Provenzanos were fruit dealers who had formerly controlled the unloading of fruit shipments from Latin America. But a rival fruit-handling faction organized by Charles and Tony Matranga had terrorized them into relinquishing their contracts with shipping firms and retiring from the riverfront to the grocery business. Tony Matranga was the operator of a concert saloon which was considered by the police to be one of the most unsavory hangouts in town. The Matrangas were also suspected by law officials of being the leaders of a local crime organization. In April, 1890, Tony Matranga and two of his men were ambushed with shotguns and seriously wounded. They identified seven men as their attackers, including the Provenzano brothers. The Provenzanos were found guilty by virtue of the testimony of the victims and their friends. Sent to prison, they continued, nevertheless, to protest their innocence, claiming that their names had been included in the roster of attackers through spite. Taking a personal interest in the case as a friend of the Provenzanos, Hennessy began a careful investigation of the testimony and of the backgrounds of the witnesses who had sworn to the brothers' guilt. He even sent to Italy to secure a dossier of their police records. The evidence he turned up convinced him not only that the Provenzanos had been framed, but also that a powerful clique of underworld characters existed in the city fashioned after the Mafia in Sicily. He secured a new trial for the Provenzanos and announced his intention of exposing any criminal secret societies he could uncover.[50]

Shortly before the date set for the new trial, one of the men who

---

[50] "Mafia and What Led to the Lynching," *Harper's Weekly*, XXXV (March 28, 1891), 226–27; Asbury, *The French Quarter*, 409–11.

had testified against the Provenzanos rented a shanty not fifty
yards from Hennessy's home and stationed in it a recent Sicilian
immigrant named Pietro Monasterio. Hennessy's movements
could be watched from this vantage point. On the night of October 15, 1890, almost nine years to the day since Devereaux's death
and four days before the second Provenzano trial was scheduled to
open, Hennessy was fatally cut down by several volleys from sawed-
off shotguns on Basin Street near Girod. He was returning home
from a Police Board meeting and was near his residence when a
boy ran by and whistled. Immediately the assassins opened fire
from the protection of nearby buildings. Three men, believed to
be the actual murderers, were seen running down Girod to Franklin Street where they disappeared. But not before several witnesses
attracted by the uproar had gotten a good look at them. Hennessy,
though mortally wounded, struggled to a nearby house from
which he was taken to Charity Hospital. Before his death the following day, he identified his killers as Italians.[51]

Hennessy's assassination shocked a stunned public supposedly
accustomed to sudden death in high places. Hennessy's reputation
as a fearless officer above corruption and the hope his appointment had held out to the community to insure the prosecution of
criminals caused the population to boil with indignation. If Hennessy could be destroyed by a mysterious band of alien terrorists,
what would become of ordinary citizens? Even the mayor reported
to a special meeting of city council members in his chambers on
October 18 that his life had been threatened.[52] An intensive
roundup of suspects began—nineteen men were eventually ar-
raigned, eleven on charges of murder or shooting with intent to
kill, and eight as their accomplices.[53] Several involved in the original Provenzano case and the immigrant Monasterio were among
this number. All were of Italian descent.

The trial of nine of these men opened on March 1, 1891. The
case against all but two was strong. The state abandoned the prosecution of one of these two and the judge ordered a verdict of ac-

51 "Mafia and What Led to the Lynching," Harper's Weekly, XXXV (March
28, 1891), 226–27; Asbury, The French Quarter, 409–11; Daily Picayune, October 16, 1890; Times-Democrat, October 16, 1890; Kendall, History of New Orleans, I, 477–78.
52 Times-Democrat, October 19, 1890.
53 Kendall, History of New Orleans, I, 480.

quittal for the other. But the courtroom crowd and the public at large confidently expected a verdict of guilty for the others. On March 13 the jury reached its decision—acquittal for six of the defendants and disagreement on the other three, who would, therefore, have to stand trial again. This verdict was greeted with popular anger; and rumors of jury-fixing were printed in the papers. Several groups of citizens met to discuss what they considered a miscarriage of justice, and a mass meeting was set for the next day, March 14, at the Clay Statue on Canal Street.[54]

A notice appeared in the newspapers on the morning of March 14 inviting the public to attend the vigilante meeting and join in the "steps to remedy the failure of justice in the HENNESSY CASE." Hundreds answered this call. Among those who issued this invitation and urged the crowd at the Clay Statue assembly to take justice into their own hands was William S. Parkerson, the man who had been campaign manager for Shakspeare in 1888. Walter Denegre and John C. Wickliffe, each made a brief speech backing up Parkerson's call for justice. They then led those who wished to follow them to a Canal Street gun store for arms and ammunition. Next they marched on Parish Prison with a list of eleven names of men they felt were guilty and whom they had marked for death. While Parkerson and a mob were demanding entrance to the main entrance of Parish Prison which was bolted against them, James D. Houston led a party around to another entrance and smashed in the wooden door. The angry men who poured into the prison swiftly rounded up the eleven on their list and killed them—five of the victims had not even come up for trial yet. Two were hanged and the rest shot to death.[55]

This lynching action immediately became an international incident since several of the victims of the mob had been Italian citizens. Newspapers in every major city in America discussed the case. A French language paper, the New York *Courrier des Etats Unis*, aptly described the tenor of the national interest in this event when it observed that "the details were read with avidity

54 "Mafia and What Led to the Lynching," 226; Kendall, *History of New Orleans*, I, 480; *Daily Picayune*, March 13, 1891.
55 Asbury, *The French Quarter*, 416–18; "Mafia and What Led to the Lynching," 226–27; Kendall, *History of New Orleans*, I, 480–81; *Daily Picayune*, March 14, 15, 1891; *Times-Democrat*, March 14, 15, 1891.

and the press make a sort of moral inquest on the subject that
might be called a self-examination of conscience on the part of
'Uncle Sam.' " [56] The press of New Orleans condoned the lynching in rhetorical terms. Out-of-town papers, on the other hand,
agreed that mob violence and lynching were dispicable. But most
of them pointed out that the grave conditions supposedly responsible for this incident—secret criminal bands and a corrupt jury
system—were evils common to all big cities. The Boston *Journal*
observed that the conservative commercial exchanges in New Orleans had condoned their action. For conservatives to be stirred to
such drastic action, they must have believed civilization itself
threatened, this paper concluded; it warned its northern readers:
"It does not behoove any body to point the finger of Pharisaical
scorn at New Orleans. The frightful tragedy really has an impressive lesson in its for every city in the land." [57]

The *Chicago News* likewise warned that

> It must not be assumed that this latest exhibition of mob vengeance is
> in any sense due to greater lawlessness in the South than in other sec-
> tions of the Union. Such an assumption is not borne out by facts. The
> frontier towns of the West have led in this form of lawlessness, and
> there are vengeance societies, regulating 'committees,' and 'white caps'
> scattered through many of the Northern States. It is not long since a
> Cincinnati mob destroyed the court-house in that city. Instances are
> numerous where the work of Northern mobs has been diabolical in its
> fiendishness. . . . The supreme lesson from this New Orleans traegdy is
> that the work of the jury-briber is responsible for the most dangerous
> lawlessness in this or any other country. If there is a National pest that
> the strong arm of the law must reach before American institutions can
> be considered safe it is the jury-tamperer." [58]

The Columbus (Ohio) *Dispatch* compared the Mafia incident
in New Orleans to troubles in other cities, citing the band of con-

[56] New York *Courrier des Etats-Unis*, March 16, 1891, as quoted in *Public
Opinion* (Washington and New York, March 21, 1891) , 564.

[57] Boston *Journal*, March 15, 1891, as quoted in *Public Opinion*, on March 21,
1891, p. 562.

[58] Chicago *News*, March 16, 1891, as quoted in *Public Opinion*, March 21,
1891, p. 562.

victs who caused trouble in San Francisco, and the burning of
the courthouse in Cincinnati in protest of crooked juries. It rea-
soned that violent action on the part of a long-suffering public was
bound to follow the breakdown of the processes of justice.[59] The
Cincinnati *Commercial Gazette,* which had seen what anarchy corrupt juries could bring, was particularly sympathetic to New Orleans. The Petersburg (Virginia) *Index-Appeal* noted that corrupt juries were the rule, rather than the exception in the United
States.[60] Northern metropolitan papers, on the whole, were perceptive in their editorials on the lynching. They understood the
problem of policing a big city. Southern newspapers, sensitive to
the fact that such an incident in their midst might bring national
criticism to their region as the lynching center of the country, were
more severe. The Mobile *Register, Florida Times-Union,* the Atlanta *Journal,* and Charleston *News and Courier* berated the Crescent City unmercifully. The Richmond *Time's* chief comment
was an expression of relief that northern dailies had shown mod-
eration in treating this "bloody and deplorable affair." [61]

Numerous newspapers implored the Italian-Americans who were
protesting the lynching and demanding retribution not to consider the affair as reflecting anti-Italian antagonism. The St.
Paul *Pioneer Press,* the Augusta *Chronicle,* the Providence *Journal,* the Philadelphia *Times* and the New York *Advertiser,* all
pointed out that the mob violence in New Orleans had been directed at the eleven Italians, not because of their nationality, but
because of the mob's conviction that they were agents of a criminal
underworld society.[62] This was well-founded advice since one of

59 Columbus (Ohio) *Dispatch,* March 16, 1891, as quoted in *Public Opinion,*
March 21, 1891, p. 562.

60 Cincinnati *Commercial Gazette,* March 17, 1891, and Petersburg (Virginia)
Index-Appeal, March 17, 1891 as quoted in *Public Opinion,* March 21, 1891,
pp. 563–64.

61 Undated excerpts from editorials in Mobile *Register,* Florida *Times-Union,*
Atlanta *Journal,* Charleston *News and Courier* as quoted in *Public Opinion,*
March 21, 1891, p. 564, and from the Richmond *Times,* March 17, 1891, as
quoted in the same issue of *Public Opinion,* 562.

62 St. Paul *Pioneer Press,* undated excerpt, Augusta *Chronicle,* March 17,
1891, Providence *Journal,* March 17, 1891, Philadelphia *Times,* March 17, 1891,
and New York, *Commercial Advertiser,* March 17, 1891, as quoted in *Public
Opinion,* March 21, 1891, pp. 563–64.

the figures in the plotting of Hennessy's murder and the man believed to have bribed the jury was an Irish private detective whose
criminal record the police chief was investigating at the time of
his death.[63] But such facts naturally did not keep Italians, both in
the United States and Italy, from resenting the lynching. One
Rome newspaper stated that the Italian government refrained
from sending a gunboat up the Mississippi to New Orleans only
because of reliance "on the foresight of the American authorities"
and on the friendship between the two countries.[64] Such statements did not ease the tension between the two governments.

The legal aspects of the case were discussed by James Bryce in
The Living Age and E. L. Godkin in *The Nation*.[65] Godkin
pointed out that bringing to trial the leaders of the lynching
group was a local matter which the federal government could not
handle. All that President Benjamin Harrison and Secretary of
State James G. Blaine could do was arrange for an indemnity payment to the Italian government. Godkin added—somewhat mali-
ciously—that in negotiations with the irate Italian diplomats,
"Secretary Blaine is now at last placed in a situation in which his
capacity in raising a cloud of words will stand him in good
stead." [66] Although the Italian ambassador was withdrawn from
Washington and the United States recalled its representative to

63 "Mafia and What Led to the Lynching," 226–27. The Irish detective was
Dominick C. O'Malley whose varied career included a term in an Ohio reforma-
tory and laborer work on the New Orleans' levees before he drifted into a shady
existence as a private detective. Accused at numerous times of everything from
perjury and bribery to attempted murder, O'Malley escaped the wrath of the
lynch mob by hiding in the office of Page Baker, editor of the *Times-Democrat*.
Although Baker detested O'Malley, he did not believe in vigilante justice.
O'Malley left town a few days later, but returned in a few months and resumed
his detective business. By 1894 he was able to pick up a bargain by purchasing
the New Orleans *Item* for $2704. Eight years later he is reputed to have sold it
for $100,000. The last decade of his life was spent respectably and uneventfully
in the wholesale fish business. Tinker, *Creole City*, 198–206; Asbury, *The French
Quarter*, 413.

64 *Romano Populo*, March 16, 1891, as quoted in *Public Opinion*, March 21,
1891, p. 565.

65 James B. Bryce, "Legal and Constitutional Aspects of the Lynching at New
Orleans," *The Living Age*, CLXXXIX (June 6, 1891), 579–85; E. L. Godkin,
"The Italian Trouble," *The Nation*, LII (April 9, 1891), 294.

66 E. L. Godkin, "The New Orleans Massacre," *The Nation*, I.II (March 19,
1891), 232.

Italy before the aftermath of this episode was concluded, Italian feelings were finally soothed through diplomatic channels. An indemnity payment of 125,000 francs was tendered to the Italian government by the United States in 1892.[67] In the meantime, a local grand jury had reviewed the events leading up to the lynching and decided to exonerate its perpetrators.[68] This closed the stormy saga of the Hennessy assassination, except that in subsequent years an aura of suspicion of Italian immigrants hung over the city. Although such prejudice had not caused the lynching, unfortunately it did result from the incident. For a decade or more street urchins were quick to taunt persons of Italian descent with the barb, "Who killa de chief?"

Dave Hennessy's murder was the last involving a prominent political figure in this period. The conduct of politicians and city employees in general improved in the 1880's. Furthermore, police morale and their effectiveness in dealing with hoodlums also slowly changed for the better in this decade. Under the encouragement of prompt salary payment and civil service protection the caliber of the force by 1900 was much higher than it had been in 1880. By the turn of the century all officers on duty wore regulation uniforms including derby-shaped helmets. They had achieved that awe-inspiring quality that the English visitor in the early 1880's had looked for in vain.

While wandering gangs of rowdies and housebreakers began to feel the sting of a revitalized law, organized crime in the form of gambling, lotteries, and prostitution defied all efforts at eradication. Indeed, it received a larger share of newspaper space in the last decade of the century than it had previously. This was probably due to the increased interest in reform societies manifested by the local populace. After the Louisiana State Lottery moved to Honduras in 1894, it continued to employ an underground network of vendors in New Orleans who were periodically hounded by the police, but who often managed to dodge detection. In the 1890's they sometimes used laundry shops as fronts for their business.[69] Gambling, after the collapse of the Shakspeare Plan, re-

[67] Kendall, *History of New Orleans*, I, 481–82.
[68] *Daily Picayune,* May 6, 1891.
[69] *Daily Picayune,* April 19, 1894.

turned to the status it had held before the 1880's. Gambling spots were left alone for months, then raided when their activities became too obnoxious.

Another vice, prostitution, received some regulation from the city fathers who were beset with protests from citizens over the nuisance created by boisterous parties and ragtime music in bordellos located in respectable neighborhoods.[70] In 1889 the city council made it illegal for prostitutes to reside on Canal Street. They were forbidden by an 1891 law to enter a public cabaret and drink with customers. Finally in 1895, to guard suburban neighborhoods from the disturbances of boisterous houses of ill fame, the council forbid the existence of such places in any part of the city outside of the area bounded by Poydras, Claiborne, St. Louis, and the river.[71]

Two years later, during the reform administration of Mayor Walter Flower, a new district—the famous Storyville—was created in an attempt to isolate and thus regulate prostitution. It was tolerated, although not legalized, within these limits: the south side of Customhouse (Iberville) Street, from Basin to Robertson streets, east side of Robertson from Customhouse to St. Louis streets, south side of St. Louis from Robertson to Basin. Named for Sidney Story, the councilman who introduced the original ordinance, it was to prove, through its concentration of vice, to be a far greater menace than had existed before its creation. Its wide-open barrooms, glittering palaces of sin such as those of Lulu White, Josie Arlington, and Countess Willie Piazza, and its pitiful backstreet crib hovels where red lights reflected the forms of pale-faced women behind the blinds—all were part of one of the most notorious sections in the country. A scandal to local citizens, it was a source of great curiosity to visiting tourists. The alderman who served the district, Tom Anderson, became its unofficial "mayor"; his barroom called "Arlington's Annex," at the corner of Customhouse and Basin Streets, was a "little city hall" for the demimonde. There one could secure a copy of the *Blue Book,* a list of names and addresses of the girls of Storyville. This raucous red-light dis-

70 *Mascot,* June 11, 1892.
71 Flynn, *Flynn's Digest,* 457–61.

trict existed until 1917 when it was broken up, after much local vice-crusading, by request of Josephus Daniels, Secretary of the Navy. A city ordinance officially closed Storyville on October 10, 1917.[72]

During Shakspeare's first term, the city council had passed an ordinance requiring all barrooms to close at midnight.[73] This restriction, which was designed to aid the police in reducing the number of barrooms brawls, was enforced only intermittently during subsequent administrations. Enforcement depended upon the pleasure of the current mayor; and numerous examples of its violation were frequently noted. In 1886, as the temperance movement gained momentum in Louisiana, the state legislature passed a Sunday closing law which was to be much more resented and ignored in New Orleans than the barroom midnight curfew. In 1888 an attempt was made to limit this closing law to cities under two thousand population. This failed, and so did another such attempt to kill the law in 1890. New Orleans Germans especially resented it since their annual *volksfest*—which featured all sorts of games, foods, and expertly brewed lager beer—was traditionally held on a Sunday. Violations of this law came to be the rule rather than the exception, and the police would have been hard pressed to crack down on the hundreds of violators. The *Mascot* ran a humorous cartoon showing one way in which the closing law was circumvented: "Fruit Stands" did a thriving business on Sunday, serving liquor under the guise of pineapple, orange, or other fruit juices.[74]

One activity on the borderline of legality that received much more critical attention in the 1890's than it had a decade earlier was the practice of voodoo, or hoodoo as it was locally called. Voodoo ceremonies marked by the beating of drums, burning of fires,

72 *New Orleans City Guide*, 216–19. The ordinance establishing the limits of Storyville was passed in 1897. The district opened in 1898.

73 *Daily Picayune*, May 24, 1881.

74 *Daily Picayune*, May 20, 1888; *Mascot*, November 17, 1888; July 19, 1890. An editorial on grand jury findings in the *Daily Picayune*, April 18, 1894, noted that the number of Sunday law violations awaiting prosecution was 14,425 and violations involving the unauthorized sale of lottery tickets numbered 916. Not one of these cases had been brought to trial or appeared likely to be heard in the immediate future.

and wails of participants were held on St. John's Eve along the un-inhabited stretches of the Lake Pontchartrain shore.[75] The in-tensification of hostility between whites and Negroes between 1894 and 1900 may have been the reason for the crackdown on this primitive superstitious cult. At some of the voodoo ceremonies broken up by the police, whites were arrested along with Negroes. Such emotional racial mixing was strongly disapproved of by the general white public, and the police did not miss any opportunity to put a stop to it.

Practitioners of voodoo, or hoodoo, were paradoxically both feared and patronized. Marie Laveau, the quadroon voodoo queen in the 1850's and 1860's, had combined voodoo with a perverted form of the Catholic religion. She had also capitalized on the curiosity of whites about voodoo by inviting them to her public (and therefore more orderly) ceremonies. The result of this was to gain for her a large following of white devotees who bought po-tions and charms and sometimes her services in helping them to escape a prison term or the hangman's noose. About ten years be-fore her death in the 1870's, she was replaced as voodoo queen by Malvina Latour who continued conducting the annual voodoo rites on St. John's Eve on the lake and attracted many tourists, journalists, and politicians as well as dedicated voodoos until 1890. By the last decade of the century, voodoo had degenerated into numerous small sects, and the word had been corrupted into "hoo-doo." [76]

In 1894 one Negro woman arrested at her residence on Monroe Street near Royal and the Barracks had bags full of letters from whites and Negroes all over the city requesting all sorts of amulets and potions for themselves or spells to be placed on others. Some of the letters were from well-to-do persons. Such trade brought this priestess an average of $14 a day from practice of her black magic. The front room of her dwelling had been turned into a shrine with an altar on which reposed a human skull, numerous human and animal bones, and bottles of snakes and toads. Hoodoo rites and dances were held here three times a week. At such times the

[75] Hunt, "New Orleans, Yesterday and Today," 646.
[76] Asbury, *The French Quarter*, 265–83.

priestess placed a piece of paper with the name of a person to be hoodooed under one of the bottles of toads and snakes in the center of the room. She lighted a circle of candles around it and then spoke her curse while dancing around this circle. After the police had taken her off to jail, neighbors admitted that they were glad to see her go but pleaded with the officers not to tell her they had said so.[77]

Public outbreaks of violence occurred in the Charles race riot of 1900, and again with lesser intensity in the streetcar strike of 1902. But no attempt to take over the execution of justice, as in the lynching of the hapless Italians, took place or was even considered by the local citizenry again. The Hennessy assassination had occurred at a time when law enforcement was about to take a turn for the better. The panic caused by the belief that a local version of the Mafia might feel free to strike down others if the acquittal were allowed to go unprotested triggered the lynchings. This event, however, was the last such premeditated mob action in the city, bringing to a close a little over two decades in which such tactics by vigilantes had taken place sporadically. The *Times-Democrat's* observation (made at the time of the Hennessy case) that the era of corrupt juries was over, became a reality by the early 1900's. Another thought voiced by the *Picayune* the day after the lynchings seemed destined to become the ruling spirit: "Popular justice is a desperate remedy. May many a generation of men pass away before it shall, if ever, become again necessary in this city." [78]

[77] *Daily Picayune,* September 20, 1894.
[78] *Ibid.,* March 15, 1891.

10

PATTERNS OF CULTURAL CHANGE
The Impact of Higher Education,
Organized Sports, and Popular Music

THE FIRST HALF-DECADE of the 1890's was a time of crisis and change in New Orleans. The murder of Chief Hennessy and the lynching of his alleged assassins, the crusade against the Louisiana Lottery culminating in the bitter election of 1892, the general strike later that same year, the scandals of the Boodle Council, and the attempt to impeach Mayor Fitzpatrick gave the impression that the city was on a downhill course into civic anarchy. Actually these years were critical, but constructive—they marked a turning point in the city's life beyond which better times lay ahead. Under civil service the police and the newly organized fire department showed more efficiency and less blatant political intervention than in previous decades. With the lottery gone after 1894, a great source of corruption which had played no favorites, but always tried to influence the political group or figure it felt had the best chance of winning, was removed from local and state politics.

One legacy of the lottery crusade to New Orleans in the 1890's was the popularity of "reform" as a social pastime which spawned a host of reform societies dedicated to introducing new techniques of government into the city, or to fighting vice and crime, or to stamping out drinking or smoking, or even to banning prizefighting. The founders of these societies were a new breed. Just fighting City Hall and capturing it like a chess piece was not enough for them—as it had been for the reformer businessmen element of the 1880's. They were aggressive, religiously dedicated to their "cause" whatever it might be, and usually imbued with new pro-

258

gressive ideas for positive changes in municipal government itself. The election of 1896 was to be their political triumph and the last four years of the 1890's was to see their program partially enacted into a new city charter and into other municipal reforms. Politically, then, the 1890's were to be fruitful years.

But the decade also saw some definite changes in the intellectual pursuits and cultural expressions of the local populace. Culturally the city was beginning to reveal by the 1890's the pattern which would set its character in the twentieth century. Intellectually it was to find sustenance from the rapidly expanding Tulane University and its affiliate for women, H. Sophie Newcomb College. On a popular level, the city's preoccupation with organized sports was more pronounced by the 1890's than ever before. The local passion for watching prizefighting made New Orleans the boxing capital of the United States for a brief period in this decade. Always a city which loved grand opera, brass bands, and dances, New Orleans by the end of the century was developing its own brand of indigenous music—jazz—which was to achieve worldwide fame in the next century. These three threads in the tapestry of Crescent City culture: the impetus of a budding university to community intellectual pursuits outside its ivy-clad walls, the rise of organized sports, and the beginnings of a popular music which was to win international acclaim stand out in bold relief by the 1890's.

Tulane, founded in 1884 on the nucleus of the old University of Louisiana, and Newcomb College, opened in 1886, became profound influences upon the intellectual life of New Orleans in the decade after their creation. Grace King, writing for a national magazine audience in 1896, summed up the university's contribution to the community.

Within the decade . . . since the University began its active work in the community, the whole framework of intellectual expression in society . . . has received a new and healthy impetus. Scientific, literary, and art circles have sprung into being where before existed only desultory efforts, or, more accurately speaking, longings; old, neglected libraries have been rehabilitated and started on a fresh career of usefulness, new ones have been created; extension lectures have been given, free drawing classes maintained. Four years ago there was no free reading-room for workingmen in the city; now there are four. The old State Historical Society, roused from a seven years' slumber, has gone to work again, with Professor Fortier as President, and Professor Ficklen (of History and Economics) as Secretary. Professor Fortier had already organized a local Folk-Lore Society. Professor Dillard is the President of a Lyceum Lecture Association. The University's free graduate courses in English and Latin for teachers, directed by Dr. Sharp and Professor Dillard, have led to the formation of English and Latin Clubs and given the inspiration to other associations among the teachers for improvement.[1]

In the fields of fine arts and physical education Newcomb College opened up new vistas for local women. From its campus in the Garden District, a square bounded by Washington Avenue, Sixth, Chestnut and Camp streets, the Newcomb faculty launched an art movement in the 1890's which gained a national reputation. Under the guidance of Ellsworth Woodward, director of the School of Art, the art program, particularly in ceramics, reached a high degree of excellence. Experimenting with St. Tammany clays and Mississippi River loam, Newcomb potters produced "Newcomb pottery" which won the bronze medal and international acclaim at the Paris Exposition of 1900.[2]

Although primarily a liberal arts institution, Newcomb pioneered in New Orleans in physical education for women. Miss Clara Baer, trained in the Swedish method of gymnastics, was hired to introduce Newcomb students to physical exercises.[3] She and her students even invented two indoor games, basquettes, a variant of basketball, and Newcomb, a type of volleyball played with a rope replacing the net between the two sides.[4] The year 1894 saw the introduction at Newcomb of blouses and bloomers as the gym costumes to replace the long, cumbersome dresses of the students. The bloomers were long and baggy, reaching almost to the ankles.

[1] King, "The Higher Life of New Orleans," 755.

[2] *Ibid.*, 756; Dyer, *Tulane: The Biography of a University,* 92, 96–97; Alberta Collier, "The Art Scene in New Orleans—Past and Present," in Carter, *The Past As Prelude: New Orleans, 1718–1968,* 162–63.

[3] Dyer, *Tulane: The Biography of a University,* 97.

[4] *Ibid.,* 98; Crozet J. Duplantier, "A Sportsman's Town," in Carter, *The Past As Prelude: New Orleans, 1718–1968,* pp. 200–201.

Black socks were worn with them. Naturally, the girls could not leave the gym in such daring costumes.[5] But the emphasis on physical exercise was not lost on other girls' schools in the city and they followed suit in adopting programs of gymnastics. Grace King, who heartily approved of the gym classes for young women and the varied athletic program followed by the men students at Tulane, observed that "the most popular recognition of Tulane's services comes from hearty appreciation of the great change it has wrought in students' lives outside the class-room; in the impetus it has given to open-air sports and athletic exercises as means of recreation. The wholesomeness of this change to general life can be appreciated fully only by those whose experience covers a time when the semi-tropical climate of the city was held sufficient warranty for a semi-languorous state of inactivity even in the young." [6]

This change in physical exercise and sports participation on the part of New Orleans students was one manifestation of an awakening interest in outdoor sports among the general public. This was a definite break with their past apathy. In the 1870's and 1880's, those few local citizens who had a taste for exercise and the facilities to indulge their whims, amused themselves with military drilling, gymnastics, and indoor team games. Exercise for health reasons was not stressed or considered worth promoting. Most men preferred to spend their hours after work or on Sunday afternoons at their social clubs, or at saloons and beer gardens. Often they engaged in card playing, always a popular pastime in gambling-prone New Orleans. Those who were too poor to belong to a club or to afford to imbibe at a local saloon, simply stood on street-corners or sat on the stoop of their front doorstep and talked. There was no incentive to go to Lower City Park, which was mainly a grazing place for cattle with no entertainment facilities or to Upper City Park (Audubon Park) which also was just a mass of weeds and semiswamp, prior to the Cotton Centennial Exposition in 1884–85. Also, the deplorable condition of the streets kept buggy riding down to a minimum and only a few citizens owned saddle horses. The mud and stagnant water standing in the city

5 Dyer, *Tulane: The Biography of a University*, 97–98.
6 King, "The Higher Life of New Orleans," 755.

thoroughfares even discouraged walking. Most citizens rode the streetcars instead. Women found even less opportunity than men for physical exercise. Dancing was the only strenuous activity they participated in with any degree of regularity.[7]

But by the 1890's this picture was definitely changing. A sports fever was sweeping the entire nation and New Orleans was no exception. Baseball, cycling, track and field events, tennis, rowing, yachting, and the introduction of football and golf offered a variety of organized sports to local enthusiasts. Baseball was undeniably the most popular sport in Gilded Age New Orleans. Amateurs played baseball on empty lots as early as the 1870's. Visiting teams from the North faced the best of local clubs at the Fair Grounds. In the early 1880's enough interest in baseball existed for a patent medicine company to sponsor a baseball league of just two teams, New Orleans and Mobile.[8] By 1886 the Southern League was formed, composed of six teams at first but later enlarged to eight in 1892. One of them was the local team that became known as the Pelicans. Abner Powell, the manager of the New Orleans Pelicans, was a promoter of baseball all over the South and was part-owner of several of the other teams in the Southern League. Powell's New Orleans team won the pennant in their league in 1887 and again in 1896. But professional baseball was plagued by the instability of the Southern League—it did not function in 1890, 1891, 1897, and 1900. In 1901 the Southern Association was organized and minor league baseball in the South entered a more stable era. The largest crowd that the Pelicans could command during the 1890's was usually around four to six thousand. But visiting major league teams from the North could sometimes pull in a gate as high as twelve thousand.[9]

The real strength of baseball in New Orleans by the end of the century lay in amateur and semiprofessional teams sponsored by businesses, clubs, churches, schools, military societies, or formed

7 Ann Maden, "Popular Sports in New Orleans, 1890–1900" (M.A. thesis, Tulane University, 1956) , 6–7.

8 New Orleans City Guide, 86.

9 Maden, "Popular Sports in New Orleans," 98, 103, 105, 181; Duplantier, "A Sportsman's Town," p. 202; New Orleans City Guide, 86.

on a joint stock company basis. By 1896 there were approximately 225 such baseball teams in the city. Three years later, the number had grown to 300.[10] These clubs had such provocative names as the Little Brown Jugs, the Women Haters, the None of Your Business Club, the Presbyterians, the Know-Nothings, the Treme Market Butchers, the Keller's Soap Workers, the Cotton Clerks, the Tulane Graduates, and the Hot Tamales.[11]

In the early 1890's there were both all-Negro baseball teams and racially integrated teams. But the practice of integration tended to disappear as the 1890's progressed and racial tension built up between whites and blacks in the depression years following the Panic of 1893. Women also appeared occasionally on a local baseball diamond. In 1886 Harry H. Freeman, manager of a traveling female baseball team, was arrested by New Orleans police for trying to lure a young local girl away from home to join his team. He had cut her hair and given her a blonde wig to wear. But the disguise was detected and the prospective baseball hopeful was returned to her family. Two of Freeman's players were found to be underage and were placed in the House of Good Shepherd until their relatives could be located. Several others were given tickets back to their hometown of Cincinnati. Freeman, himself, left town on a Louisville and Nashville train bound for Mobile.[12] In the decade following this episode, Newcomb women introduced bloomers as a gym costume, and numerous women cyclists adopted this mode of dress for outdoor riding by the late 1890's. The arrival in New Orleans, therefore, of baseball's famous Bloomer Girls in 1899 caused hardly a lifted eyebrow. They played a number of exhibition games and returned in 1900 when they beat a local male baseball team.[13]

The riding of bicycles ranked second to baseball as an overall favorite recreation in New Orleans. The first sign of enthusiasm for two-wheeled transportation came in 1869 when several wealthy young New Orleanians purchased velocipedes and set up a school to practice and give lessons and indoor exhibitions to their friends.

[10] Maden, "Popular Sports in New Orleans," 112.
[11] Ibid.
[12] Daily Picayune, May 5, 9, 1886.
[13] Maden, "Popular Sports in New Orleans," 97.

At evening exhibitions ladies attended to watch the fancy riding. After the velocipede shows, dances were held.[14] By the end of the 1870's the enthusiasm for the tricky and uncomfortable velocipede was dying out. But it still struck terror into the hearts of some timid pedestrians who encountered it on the city streets.

The author, Lafadio Hearn, who lived in New Orleans between 1877 and 1887 and worked on the *Item* and the *Times-Democrat*, wrote an amusing sketch about the peril of "The Unspeakable Velocipede" for the *Item*.

> "The velocipede is like a vicious dog, because it always attacks any one who runs away from it; but it is also like a lion which attacks any one who dares to face it boldly. It is like a fox in treachery, like a panther in agility, like a tiger in cruelty, like a gorilla in ferocity, like a greyhound in speed, like a badger in taking a good hold of the calf of your leg, and like the Devil for impudence. You cannot turn a corner so quickly that a velocipede cannot turn after you still quicker. There is but one possible means of escaping a velocipede. Velocipedes are like grizzly bears; they cannot climb trees. You must, therefore, climb a tree when you see a velocipede." [15]

Following the velocipede era, the next cyclist movement came to New Orleans in 1889, the year that the League of American Wheelmen (L.A.W.) was founded in the East. A group of socially elite gentlemen, merchants and professional men, formed the New Orleans Bicycle Club whose members rode high wheelers which they had to own personally in order to be eligible for membership.[16] Since these early bicycles were worth over a hundred dollars, cycling was limited at first to the well-to-do. The club members wore a uniform of blue jackets and blue knee breeches. One of their favorite rides on Sunday was from Commercial Alley and St. Charles out to Spanish Fort along the shell road beside Bayou St. John.[17]

During the 1880's the New Orleans Bicycle Club sponsored vis-

14 Dale A. Somers, "A City on Wheels: The Bicycle Era in New Orleans," *Louisiana History*, VIII (Summer, 1967) , 222.

15 Edward Larocque Tinker, *Lafcadio Hearn's American Days* (New York, 1924) , 373.

16 Somers, "A City on Wheels," 223.

17 *Daily Picayune*, June 9, 1881.

iting champion cyclists and long-distance cycling outings, and affiliated with the national League of American Wheelmen. A local magazine, *Bicycle South,* which was the Louisiana organ of this national group, made its appearance under the direction of N.O.B.C. members E. W. Hunter and Charles Genslinger in 1886. Another cycling group also sprang up in the city, the Louisiana Cycling Club.[18] In 1890 the Fifth District of the League of American Wheelmen sponsored a two-day program with nine races a day which they estimated drew about four to five thousand spectators.[19] The increasing popularity of cycling and the strength of the Louisiana division of the League of American Wheelmen received a setback in 1892 when the Louisiana members objected to the admission of Negroes to northern divisions of this group. Withdrawals from the group almost wiped out the local membership. But by 1894 the national constitution of the League of American Wheelmen was revised to include the word "white" as a prerequisite for admittance to this organization. Northerners, faced with a choice of a few Negro members or their large southern membership, had chosen to pacify the racial prejudice of their southern white brethren. This led to a revivial of the L.A.W. in New Orleans.[20] By this time also, the safety bicycle had been introduced which was much easier to ride and cost less than earlier models. Cycling now became a popular sport with all ages and classes, with women as well as men. Interest in competitive races, however, waned between 1892 and 1894. In the later year a new club, the Crescent Wheelmen, began to revive competitive racing.[21] Many smaller new clubs followed the lead of this group. A proper place for racing was lacking in the city with its poor streets and soft-surface roads leading out of town. An enterprising group, the Southern Wheelmen, decided therefore to build a quarter-mile concrete oval track for bicycle races. The track was built and operated under the name of the Young Men's Investment and Improvement Association. It proved to be a fast track on which several world's records were set by visiting champion riders.[22]

18 Somers, "A City on Wheels," 223–24.
19 Maden, "Popular Sports in New Orleans," 152.
20 *Ibid.,* 158; Somers, "A City on Wheels," 225–26.
21 Somers, "A City on Wheels," 229.
22 *Ibid.,* 230–31; Maden, "Popular Sports in New Orleans," 161; *Daily Picayune,* October 17, 18, 1895.

The year 1896 marked the apex of the bicycle madness in New Orleans. By this time there was a weekly periodical devoted to cycling, the *Southern Cyclist*; New Orleans was one stop on an 1896 cross-country series of L.A.W. races; and the first local cycle show was held in the Washington Artillery Hall, demonstrating all of the latest equipment in cycling.[23] For a second time the local L.A.W. members began to withdraw from the national group in 1896 following an edict against Sunday cycling by the national organization. New Orleans with its continental Sunday could not understand the puritanical Sabbath customs of the Northeast. By 1897 New Orleans cyclists had formed the Southern Cyclists' Association which dominated local bicycle circles until well into the next century.[24] One contribution of bicycle addicts to the welfare of the community was their campaigning for better streets. By the time the automobile began to appear on local streets in the early twentieth century, paving was beginning to become a common sight on the main thoroughfares of the city. Cycling groups had played a considerable part in advocating and achieving this improvement before the adult preoccupation with the bicycle gave way to the much greater fascination of the motor car.

Bicycle clubs were not the only examples of organized sports in the city by the 1890's. Rifle and gun enthusiasts founded thirty clubs dedicated to hunting and trapshooting. Tennis also became a popular sport featured by the New Orleans Lawn Tennis Club which claimed to be the oldest such group in the city dating back to 1876, the West End Tennis Club organized in 1890, the Elks Club and the Lindwood Club who were traditional rivals in matches, and two intracollegiate teams at Tulane. By the end of the century women were beginning to become interested in tennis and the New Orleans Lawn Tennis Club admitted distaff members by 1898.[25]

Golf got a slow start in New Orleans since it required a well-kept course, which did not exist in New Orleans. In 1895 a golf

23 Somers, "A City on Wheels," 230–31, 234; see scattered references in the *Daily Picayune* and *Times-Democrat* to the bicycle exhibit in Washington Artillery Hall the week before Mardi Gras, February 10–17, 1896.

24 Somers, "A City on Wheels," 231.

25 Maden, "Popular Sports in New Orleans," 63–64, 80.

devotee, John Tobin, attempted to form a country club for golf at the New Louisiana Jockey Club and used the Fair Grounds as a fairway to knock balls around. By 1898 Tobin was successful in interesting a number of New Orleanians in forming the Audubon Golf Club which had about thirty-eight members and used a section of Audubon Park for its golf links.[26] By the beginning of the twentieth century, golfing in New Orleans got a boost from the arrival of George Turpie, a native of Scotland and a golf professional, who spent several months a year as a teaching pro in New Orleans.[27] However, it remained a pastime of the wealthy, rather than a popular sport.

Other sports which attracted mainly the rich included rowing and yachting. Rowing clubs dated as early as the 1830's, but fell into decline during the Civil War and did not begin to revive until the 1870's. In 1893 they reorganized themselves into the Southern Amateur Rowing Association. Member clubs in the association included the St. John Rowing Club, the Louisiana Boat Club, the West End Rowing Club, the Tulane Rowing Club, the Crescent Rowing Club (later called the Young Men's Gymnastic Rowing Club), and a Pensacola-based group, the Southern Racing Club. The clubhouses of the New Orleans rowing clubs were mainly at West End or on Bayou St. John. Seasonal regattas were held on Lake Pontchartrain in which the clubs competed against each other.[28] The Southern Yacht Club, founded in 1849, was the second oldest in the United States and by the 1890's dominated the yachting scene, although there were several other yachting associations in the city. One of the most famous yachts associated with the Southern Yacht Club in the 1890's was Charles P. Richardson's *Nepenthe* which sustained a rivalry with a Mobile yacht, the *Annie*. Interest in their races was so keen that the Louisville and Nashville Railroad sponsored a special train to the Gulf Coast for New Orleanians who wished to see them race. By 1894 the *Nepenthe* had won the Brewster Cup of the Southern Yacht Club for the third time and got permanent possession of it. Throughout

[26] *Ibid.,* 58–61.
[27] Duplantier, "A Sportsman's Town," 207–208.
[28] Coleman, *Historical Sketch Book* 232–36; Rightor, *Standard History of New Orleans,* 621.

the summer season, regattas under the rules of the Southern Yacht Club were held along the Gulf Coast with yachting clubs from Mandeville, Biloxi, Pass Christian, Pascagoula, Bay St. Louis, and Point Clear taking part. In 1899, its fiftieth year of operation, the Southern Yacht Club decided to build a new club house at West End which was formally opened at the spring regatta in May, 1900. By that time the club boasted a membership of five hundred and a fleet of seventy-five boats, steam-powered as well as sailing vessels.[29]

On the Tulane campus, track was the major sport during the 1890's, with baseball also a popular pastime. In 1887 students had organized the Tulane Athletic Association which worked to promote the first track meet of the college in 1888. It was held each successive year until 1891 in Upper City Park on the former Cotton Centennial Exposition grounds. After 1891 it was shifted to the Fair Grounds. By 1894 Tulanian track men were engaged in intercollegiate competition with Alabama and Vanderbilt. Finally by 1895 Tulane got its own track laid out on the campus with stands to seat thirty-five hundred spectators. Baseball was played informally by Tulane students from the founding of the university. But in 1892 an intramural program definitely got under way. The next year a Tulane baseball team went to Baton Rouge to play a Louisiana State University team in their first intercollegiate baseball game. Football, which was destined to outshine the other two sports as the college sport par excellence, was first played in New Orleans in the 1880's by students returning from eastern colleges. They taught the rules to Tulanians and helped to organize two squads at the local university. These two Tulane teams played the first formal game of football in the city in 1888. By 1893, in addition to the Tulane team, the Southern Athletic Association had a football team. From then on football was part of college and city life in New Orleans.[30]

Two other sports which were popular spectator attractions and drew large crowds in the 1890's were horse racing and prizefighting. The city's Fair Grounds race track had been opened in

[29] Rightor, *Standard History of New Orleans*, 620–21; Maden, "Popular Sports in New Orleans," 72.

[30] Dyer, *Tulane: The Biography of a University*, 163–65.

1872 under the direction of the Louisiana Jockey Club. Both John A. Morris and Charles T. Howard of the Louisiana Lottery took an active part in this organization and the setting up of this racing course. By the end of the 1880's the ownership of the track was reorganized under the New Louisiana Jockey Club. The Fair Grounds by 1890 was offering a spring and a winter season of racing. As the race track prospered, its business and professional needs became more complicated and demanding. This led to an innovation. The New Louisiana Jockey Club, primarily a social club made up of business and professional men, decided to put their track under the supervision of professional racing experts. This was accomplished by 1892 when the Crescent City Jockey Club leased the Fair Grounds from the New Louisiana Jockey Club and put $600,000 worth of improvements into the track and its stables. A starting machine was installed by 1895 and opening day that year saw a crowd of seven thousand at the Fair Grounds.[31] Although the Fair Grounds did not hold the prominence in national racing circles that the defunct Metairie racing course of antebellum days had occupied, it did manage to bring top-rated horses and jockeys to the Crescent City for its racing seasons.

The beauty of the Fair Grounds with its green lawns, gardens, fountains and orchards of fruit trees made it a setting for other social and sporting events aside from racing. During the summer the New Louisiana Jockey Club held promenade concerts at the Fair Grounds which were attended by society's pace-setters. Under the illumination of Chinese lanterns and electric lights, several bands stationed at different points on the grounds entertained the members of the club and their fashionable guests late into the evening.[32]

In stark contrast to the aristocratic setting of the New Louisiana Jockey Club and its Fair Grounds was the other major spectator sport which attracted New Orleanians—prizefighting. Bouts might take place in back alleys, shabby gymnasiums, or even in the open on the edge of town behind the slaughterhouse to avoid the police. The national imagination was first captured by prize fight-

31 Maden, "Popular Sports in New Orleans," 13–14, 16, 19.
32 Rightor, *Standard History of New Orleans,* 473.

ing in 1882, the year that colorful John L. Sullivan, the Boston Strong Boy, defeated Paddy Ryan in a bare-knuckle contest to become United States heavyweight champion. Sullivan and Ryan trained in Mississippi for this fight but had to pack up and come to New Orleans to complete their workouts after the Mississippi legislature passed an act outlawing prizefighting. The *Daily Picayune* speculated that the bout would probably take place in Louisiana.[33] This proved to be incorrect since the fighters, followed by fans in special trains, slipped back into Mississippi where the fight took place in front of Barnes's Hotel in Mississippi City. Sullivan knocked Ryan senseless in the ninth round.[34] Among the spectators were most of the administrators of the New Orleans City Council. John Fitzpatrick, in particular, was to become one of the most avid fans and promoters that boxing would have in the New Orleans area.

In July, 1889, another milestone in prizefighting history occurred when John L. Sullivan defended his title against Jake Kilrain in a bloody two-hours-and-sixteen-minutes contest that went seventy-five rounds at Richburg, Mississippi, a lumbermill town of about three hundred residents which bulged with more than three thousand visitors for this fight. John Fitzpatrick served as referee for this historic bout. Once again the fighters had trained in New Orleans but fought in Mississippi, where authorities had tried in vain to prevent the match from taking place. Secrecy over the site of the contest was so tight that New Orleans fight fans had to purchase train tickets to an unknown location. The crowd was so great that three trains were put into service and reserved seat tickets ran as high as fifteen dollars apiece. The two fighters, Sullivan and Kilrain, and referee Fitzpatrick were later prosecuted and convicted in the Mississippi courts of breaking the law by staging this fight. They were let off eventually with fines. Their popularity with the general public, both in Mississippi and Louisiana, soared to heroic proportions, however.[35]

33 *Daily Picayune,* January 18, 19, 1882.
34 *Ibid.,* February 8, 1882.
35 Duplantier, "A Sportsman's Town," 194–96; William H. Adams, "New Orleans as the National Center of Boxing," *Louisiana Historical Quarterly,* XXXIX (January, 1956) , 93–96.

Prizefighting in the city of New Orleans had become a regular drawing card for sports fans by this time. Mayor Shakspeare, who disapproved of the growth of this bloody pastime, tried in 1890 to put a stop to local bouts through invoking a long-dormant city ordinance of 1885 which prohibited the fights. The popular outcry against his action forced the mayor to give up any attempt to stop the sport in the city. Instead the mayor and the City Council decided to follow the suggestion of the police department that boxing matches be allowed in New Orleans if leather gloves were worn, if the new Marquis of Queensbury rules were adhered to by the fighters, and a time limit was set for the rounds. A new city ordinance in March, 1890, legalized boxing under these terms.[36] In May of 1890 Governor Nicholls attempted to get a legislative act forbidding boxing contests, but the act was amended to read that the exhibitions would not be illegal when held within "the rooms of regularly chartered athletic clubs." [37]

This bill which became law without the governor's signature paved the way for the expansion of old athletic clubs and the creation of new ones to feature boxing exhibitions. By 1890 the most famous of these clubs was the Olympic Club. However, even exclusive groups like the West End Athletic Club and the Young Men's Gymnastic Club, which had formerly been devoted mainly to rowing, sponsored boxing matches. Some of the fighters who participated in boxing matches in the early 1890's included Louis Guillebeau, Tommie Miller, Tommie Morgan, Billy Myer, Andy Bowen, Bob Fitzsimmons, Jake Skelley, and Jack McAuliffe.

In 1891 the Olympic Club at 636 Royal Street, which could seat 3,500 persons, was the scene of a light-heavyweight championship fight between Jack Dempsey and Bob Fitzsimmons. After thirteen rounds, Fitzsimmons emerged the winner of the title and an $11,000 purse.[38] Boxing was of consuming interest to the local public in the early 1890's. The daily papers devoted almost entire pages to stories and drawings of the latest ring favorites. The ev-

[36] Adams, "New Orleans as the National Center of Boxing," 96–97; *Daily Picayune,* March 15, 1890.
[37] *Acts Passed by the General Assembly, State of Louisiana, Regular Session, 1890* (Baton Rouge, 1890) , 19.
[38] Adams, "New Orleans as the National Center of Boxing," 99–100.

eryday conversation on streetcars, in restaurants and saloons, or in offices always turned to the latest fighters and their merits. Small boys imitated the stances and punches of their ring heroes. Posters and printed cards with fighters' pictures flooded the city. The year 1892, when boxing's number one local fan John Fitzpatrick became mayor of New Orleans, saw boxing enthusiasm reach a high point in the city.

The Olympic Club sponsored a three-night "carnival of champions" in September, 1892, which featured Jack McAuliffe against Billy Myer for the lightweight title; Jack Skelley against George Dixon, a Negro, for the light-heavyweight crown; and the main event of the three, James Corbett pitted against heavyweight champion John L. Sullivan. The first night Myer defeated McAuliffe. The second night saw Dixon savagely whip his white opponent Skelley. This brought protests from the local papers which deplored the pitting of a white and a black man against each other—especially since the Negro had emerged with a smashing victory. Such integrated boxing was subsequently dropped in the Crescent City. The historic third bout, between Sullivan and Corbett, in which Sullivan, the greatest champion prizefighting had ever known was defeated by Gentleman Jim from San Francisco, took place on September 7, 1892. Former Mayor J. Valsin Guillotte appeared in the ring before the contest to announce the fighters' weights and request good behavior from the spectators. The fight lasted for twenty-one rounds and was followed over the wires of the press by almost every big city daily in the country.[39]

In the years following the defeat of the great John L. Sullivan, boxing suffered a number of setbacks in the Crescent City which eventually led to its virtual demise by the end of the century. The hightide of boxing fever had been reached with the Sullivan-Corbett bout and crowds began to fall off at matches held in 1893. The new governor, Murphy J. Foster, was also hostile to the sport and the state attorney general was instructed to file suit for an injunction against the Olympic Club to forbid further bouts. The

[39] *Daily Picayune,* September 1, 2, 4, 5, 6, 7, 8, 1892; *Times-Democrat,* September 2, 5, 6, 7, 8, 1892; Adams, "New Orleans As the National Center of Boxing," 101–105.

grounds on which the injunction was requested maintained that while boxing exhibitions were permissible under the law, the paying of prizes to the winners was illegal. Boxing, therefore, was suspended while this case was heard. Mayor John Fitzpatrick was one of the witnesses for the Olympic Club, while former mayor Joseph Shakspeare testified against the club and its boxing matches. The Olympic Club was successful in the lower court, but the state announced its intentions of appealing to the state supreme court. The state court's decision came in April, 1894 and favored the Olympic Club. The high court found, at the same time, that there had been irregularies in admission of testimony and allowed the state to resubmit the case. Until this rehearing by the state supreme court could take place, the Olympic Club and other boxing centers were free to return to staging bouts. Several fights were scheduled in the months between April and December, 1894.[40]

Then a fatal blow was struck to a local fighter Andy Bowen in a fight with George Lavigne at the Auditorium Club. Bowen lapsed into unconsciousness in the eighteenth round and died at a local hospital. The officials of the club which had sponsored this match were arrested, charged with manslaughter. Mayor Fitzpatrick, pressured by state officials to end such risky fights, revoked the permit for the next scheduled match in the city.[41] The rehearing before the state supreme court reversed the judgment of previous decisions, and fighting, whether with or without gloves, for a purse was pronounced illegal. The heyday of prizefighting in nineteenth-century New Orleans had come to an end.[42]

While organized sports had increased in variety and appeal greatly during the 1890's, the Crescent City's love of music, dancing, and brass bands which dated back to the beginning of the nineteenth century was also widening its scope to include a homegrown version of what contemporaries called "ragtime." By the World War I era it would be labeled "jazz." Before the Civil War New Orleans had been the first center of opera in the United States, the scene of the quadroon balls, and of numerous other

[40] Adams, "New Orleans As the National Center of Boxing," 106–10.
[41] Ibid., 110; Maden, "Popular Sports in New Orleans," 56.
[42] Adams, "New Orleans As the National Center of Boxing," 111.

balls both highbrow and lowbrow, a place addicted to dancing and parades with bands of martial music, and a center of singing societies.[43]

In its Circus Public Square, more commonly known as Congo Square (later named Beauregard Square), on the edge of the French Quarter, slaves held Sunday dances. To the beat of drums, both men and women swayed and gyrated to Afro-American calinda and bamboula rhythms. These Congo Square dance sessions continued after the Civil War until the mid-1870's when they were stopped by white Redeemer city authorities who feared the congregating of Negroes in such an emotional assembly.[44] With Reconstruction and its bitterness between white and black still hanging over the city, any minor incident might spark trouble between the races. The Congo Square dances were, therefore, a victim of the times. But they had served their purpose to local musical tradition.

In the 1880's and 1890's, as the humbler New Orleans Negro population turned to dancing in segregated dance halls and saloons, the dance steps and the rhythms of Congo Square were doubtless worked into their music and dancing. The reputation of such dance halls as "sights to see" was strong enough by the early 1890's to attract the mayor of New York during a New Orleans visit to stop by a Franklin Street cabaret to see Negro stevedores and their partners perform a local honky-tonk dance, "Hog Face." [45] The cafes along Franklin Street were the working spots of some of the earliest ragtime or jazz bands and of individual ragtime pianists and guitarists. The first great name in New Orleans jazz, Charles "Buddy" Bolden, and his band played the Twenty-Eight Club in the mid-1890's. Another Franklin Street cabaret, the "Big 25" became the musicians' hangout by the turn of the century. Other cafes on this street included Phillips Cafe, Pig Ankle Cabaret, Shoto Cabaret, Villa Cabaret, Spano's—where Willie Gary "Bunk" Johnson and Ferdinand "Jelly Roll" Morton per-

43 On music before the Civil War see Henry A. Kmen, *Music in New Orleans: The Formative Years, 1791–1841* (Baton Rouge, 1966) .

44 Martin Williams, *Jazz Masters of New Orleans* (New York and London, 1967) , I, 5–8.

45 *Mascot,* February 14, 1891.

formed in the early 1900's—and the Tuxedo Dance Hall, which was the place of origin for the Original Tuxedo Orchestra.[46] The musically hot-and-blue atmosphere of this notorious street was immortalized in "Franklin Street Blues" which Bunk Johnson loved to play on his cornet.[47]

Outside of New Orleans on nearby sugarcane plantations, the custom of Sunday dancing survived even after the Congo Square festivities had ceased. An itinerant French immigrant, Prosper Jacotot took a job cutting cane on a plantation along Bayou St. John on the outskirts of the city in the late 1870's. He worked alongside Negroes in the fields and on Sundays watched their dancing. Later he wrote of his fascination with the homemade drum, the wailing songs of the dancers, their supple movements in which their feet hardly left the ground, and the energy and good-humored abandon that seemed to go into the dancing.[48]

Another source of Afro-American music and dancing were the voodoo ceremonies that persisted in New Orleans until the end of the nineteenth century. Coleman's *Historical Sketch Book* contains a vivid description (probably written by Lafcadio Hearn) of a voodoo festival held in a two-room shack on the shore of Lake Pontchartrain on St. John's eve in the early 1880's. The writer, a white reporter, went with a group of white men which included Chief of Police Zach Bachemin to see the ceremonies. They found groups of Negroes huddled around bonfires along the lake's edge with pots of coffee and several tables laden with bowls of rice and gumbo, waiting for the drums to signal the beginning of the ceremonies in the shack nearby. The police chief got the party of white

[46] Al Rose and Edmond Souchon, *New Orleans Jazz: A Family Album* (Baton Rouge, 1967), 203, 218, 220. Franklin Street was the first street west after Basin Street. North Franklin extended from Canal Street through what was Storyville between 1898 and 1917 to Carondelet Walk. Now called Crozat Street, this thoroughfare has been shortened to a two-block street. South Franklin ran from Canal to New Canal, then to Philip Street. Today this street has been changed to Saratoga Street. Location of original Franklin Street is in Coleman, *Historical Sketch Book,* 51.

[47] Williams, *Jazz Masters of New Orleans,* 234, 248.

[48] Prosper Jacotot, "Voyage d'un ouvrier dans la vallée du Mississippi de Saint Louis á la Nouvelle Orléans, 1877", translated from French by S. Fucich and Mrs. F. Peterson, (Typescript in Special Collections Division, Howard-Tilton Memorial Library, Tulane University.)

men admitted to the shack. In the center of the room was a table cloth held in place by lighted candles at the corners. On it were spread a basket of herbs, some feathers, bones, white beans, corn, and several saucers of cakes.[49]

The music and dancing began as soon as the white men had been seated against one wall. The music was supplied by "an old negro man whose wool was white with years [who] began scraping on a two-stringed sort of a fiddle. The instrument had a long neck, and its body was not more than three inches in diameter, being covered with brightly mottled snake skin. This was the sign to two young mulattoes beside him, who commenced to beat with their thumbs on little drums made of gourds and covered with sheepskin. These tam-tams gave forth a short, hollow note of peculiar sound, and were fit accompaniments of the primitive fiddle." Dancers stepped forward, first a young Negro man who danced and sang in French with occasional responses from the audience, building up to a climax that the observing reporter called "a sort of wild frenzy." Two young women joined the first dancer and finally a fourth, a young man picked up the candles and danced along with the others. The dancing with many twistings and contortions continued until the dancers fell exhausted to the floor.[50] How much voodoo music contributed to later jazz must remain conjectural. But certainly it must have had some impact on the general music and dancing of Negroes in the city.

Another deep musical influence for New Orleans Negroes was their work songs, many of which dated back to plantation days, and their sacred music. After emancipation Negro freedmen from the country migrated into the city of New Orleans to find work on the riverfront or in the cotton presses, as draymen or as street vendors. They brought their work songs with them and flocked into Protestant segregated churches in their new urban environment. Jelly Roll Morton, the great jazz pianist of colored Creole background, reminisced in *They All Played Ragtime* that at the turn of the century on the New Orleans levee, the river boat roustabouts used to lighten the loads they carried on their back up the gang-

49 Coleman, *Historical Sketch Book,* 229–30.
50 *Ibid.,* 231.

plank by singing and moving in rhythm.[51] In the atmosphere of all-Negro churches, gospel music and spirituals developed to a high degree and were to have a definite influence on jazz later. Every jazz lover is familiar with the tradition which grew up at Negro funerals in New Orleans for a brass band to play religious music straight on the way to the cemetery and then to spark it up with a jazz beat on the way home. This was not a completely Negro custom. White funerals had stressed band music before the Civil War, and local Irish wakes were sometimes anything but staid affairs.[52]

In addition to the Negro freedmen and their offspring in the city, there was another older and more sophisticated group, half-white, half-Negro, who were the descendants of free persons of color and who referred to themselves as colored Creoles. They were, as a whole, a prosperous, educated, French-oriented petit bourgeois faction of local society. From antebellum times they had been a close-knit group, holding themselves aloof from the darker-skinned slaves. Most were business and professional men. But some were poets and writers; some, musicians who studied classical European music in France.[53] As segregation laws began to multiply rapidly in the 1890's, this proud group found themselves classified with the majority of the black population. Martin Williams in *Jazz Masters of New Orleans* speculates on how these two disparate groups, the black descendants of slaves who lived in uptown slums, and the lighter-skinned descendants of free persons of color mainly located below Canal Street, contributed to the development of jazz. While the colored Creoles retained their separate social life, the musicians among them were forced increasingly to find work in bands and orchestras made up of "faces from light brown to near black." Williams points out: "It has been said New Orleans jazz resulted from the juxtaposition of the Creoles'

51 Rudi Blesh and Harriet Janis, *They All Played Ragtime* (New York, 1966), 39.

52 Henry A. Kmen, "The Music of New Orleans," in Carter (ed.), *The Past As Prelude: New Orleans, 1718–1968,* p. 231; Lyle Saxon, Robert Tallant, Edward Dreyer (comps.), *Gumbo Ya-Ya* (Cambridge, 1945), 65–66.

53 For a picture of the colored Creoles in New Orleans see Rousseve, *The Negro in Louisiana.* This book deals mainly with the educated free persons of color and their descendants.

musicianship and the freed slaves' passion and feeling. Downtown sophistication plus uptown blues. To the downtown sophistication belongs a transplanted European musical tradition, ranging from the opera house to the folk ditty. And to the uptown tradition belongs work song, spiritual, field holler—an already developed African-American idiom. Put them together and an old French quadrille becomes 'Tiger Rag'." [54]

Al Rose and Dr. Edmond Souchon in their *New Orleans Jazz: A Family Album* called the style of uptown musicians such as Buddy Bolden and Joseph "King" Oliver the "cornfield style," while the colored Creole downtown music they label "Creole." They point out that when a band, either white or colored, played in a specific neighborhood for a dance, a funeral, a picnic, or political rally, it played in the style that was preferred, either "cornfield" or "Creole." The major place where the two styles blended was at the Lake Pontchartrain resorts, Milneburg, Spanish Fort, and West End.[55] Milneburg, which was a lively, middle-class white resort by the 1890's, was a particularly favored spot for white bands. Hundreds of summer camps were built on stilts out over the lake and facing the lake along the trestle of the Pontchartrain Railroad's "Smoky Mary" train were dance halls, saloons, stores, and a jail. Bands played in the dance halls for pay and later held impromptu contests between each other by gathering on the galleries of the camps and engaging in blowing contests to see which group could outblow the other.[56]

White musicians and melodic tradition made a contribution to New Orleans jazz that combined with its Afro-American elements. Authors Rudi Blesh and Harriet Janis point out that it differed from the ragtime played in Missouri by such pianists as Scott Joplin in that it contained counterpoint—two melodies played at the same time against each other. This quality, they noted, is present in French classics and French folk rounds such as "Frere Jacques" as well as in the chorales sung in Africa.[57] Thus both white

[54] Williams, *Jazz Masters of New Orleans*, 10.

[55] Rose and Souchon, *New Orleans Jazz*, 199–200.

[56] Richard R. Dixon, "Milneburg Joys," New Orleans *Roosevelt Review*, XXV (October, 1962) , 11–12, 15–16.

[57] Blesh and Janis, *They All Played Ragtime*, 166–67.

and black musical traditions came together in Crescent City music when ragtime began to be popular by the end of the 1890's. Later Dixieland jazz was to display the characteristic of counterpoint also. Which band was the first local ragtime or jazz ensemble is certainly impossible to say. Music historian Henry A. Kmen points out that there were numerous brass bands in the 1870's and 1880's, among which the St. Bernard Brass Band and Kelly's Band were two of the best Negro groups. Another Negro band, the Excelsior Brass Band, played at the Cotton Centennial Exposition in 1885.[58] Rose and Souchon list a group led in 1889 by Negro guitarist Charlie "Sweet Lovin'" Galloway as the first known jazz band using conventional instruments to play for dances and other social events. They hasten to add, however, that this was probably not the first such group—that ragtime or jazz developed so subtly that any attempt to pinpoint its "birth" would be futile. Galloway was partially paralyzed by polio and for awhile played on streetcorners for money. He later played with the man who did become the first recognized jazz idol of the local Negro public—Charles "Buddy" Bolden.[59]

Buddy Bolden was an uptown resident with a Baptist background who had grown up with church spirituals, the underground voodoo music, the old work songs, and the new popular songs of the day all around him. He was the leader of his own band when in his twenties. In the mid-1890's his band played at Lincoln Park, an uptown amusement park for Negroes with a barnlike main building for dancing and fraternal gatherings. The band consisted of three horns and three rhythms. Buddy himself played the cornet. A powerful, moody, innovative musician, Bolden became an idol to his audiences who called him the "King." Too much whiskey and fast living frayed Bolden's already unstable personality. He became unreliable on the bandstand or behind the barber's chair, a trade he followed by day. Finally in 1907 he went berserk during a street parade and spent the rest of his life until 1931 in the mental hospital at Jackson.[60]

[58] Henry A. Kmen, "The Music of New Orleans," 230–31.
[59] Rose and Souchon, New Orleans Jazz, 47, 130.
[60] Williams, Jazz Masters of New Orleans, Chapter I, pp. 1–23.

Other bands and musicians of the 1890's worth mentioning must include the white band impresario, George Vitelle Laine, or Jack "Papa" Laine, who was born in New Orleans in 1873. He organized his first band in 1888 when he was fifteen and played the string bass and alto horn and later the drums. He had a special talent for organizing bands and became well known for his numerous Reliance Brass Bands which he recruited in Exchange Alley, a meeting place for white musicians looking for work. Another white youngster of the 1890's who organized a spasm band of youths to play on street corners or at the lake and in Storyville after that bawdy section was opened in 1898 was Emile "Stalebread" Lacoume. The instruments of Lecoume's group were homemade, but the music they produced won them acclaim and the acknowledgment of being one of the first true jazz bands.[61]

Small ensembles such as those of Bolden, Laine, Lacoume, and others were in great demand in the music-conscious Crescent City of the 1890's for fraternal picnics, boat outings, weddings, funerals, and carnival balls and parades. They were hired to play before prizefights, and for special dances held on St. Joseph's Day, St. Patrick's Day, Fireman's Day, Bastille Day and the Fourth of July, and even for the annual screwman's parade. During the 1892 political fight against the lottery, the Anti-Lottery League sent two wagons around the city every night. In one was a speaker, in the other tailgate wagon was a brass band to follow his speech. Whenever a new store opened or a place of amusement wished to advertise, it hired a band. The *Mascot* complained in 1892 of a museum operator Eugene Robinson who had come to town with a monkey and a blue parrot and opened a dime museum in which he featured miniature steamboats in a trough of water and a "picture gallery" with drawings and photographs cut from magazines. To advertise his place, he hired a three-piece Negro brass band which played on the balcony over his Canal Street place of business. The band music was loud enough to scare the dead out of the local cemeteries, the paper complained. Robinson, however, was prob-

61 *Ibid.,* 26–27; Rose and Souchon, *New Orleans Jazz,* 71, 198; Stephen Longstreet, *Sportin' House: A History of the New Orleans Sinners and the Birth of Jazz* (Los Angeles, 1965) , 190–91.

ably satisfied, because its robust playing had landed him free publicity in the *Mascot's* columns.[62]

The piano was not ordinarily used in dance bands in the 1890's. Since such bands doubled as marching brass bands and dance bands, they had learned to get along without a piano. But solo ragtime "professors" were popular in small cafes. After the opening of Storyville, the ragtime piano player became a fixture of the more commodious places. Probably the greatest of the ragtime pianists who played in Storyville in the 1890's was Tony Jackson, a Negro musician who also wrote many compositions including "Pretty Baby" and "Some Pretty Day." [63] By the early 1900's Jelly Roll Morton was also playing in the red-light district. Although Storyville did give employment to some jazz greats such as Jackson and Morton, its role in the creation of New Orleans jazz has been overestimated. Rose and Souchon point out that "The district never employed more than two score musicians on any given night. . . . By the time Storyville came into existence there were hundreds of musicians who had already been playing jazz music for more than a decade." More influential to jazz's continued evolution after 1898 was the "Tango Belt," an area of several blocks around the confines of Storyville, that was crowded with cafes, dance halls and saloons which featured some kind of music and gave a livelihood to early jazz musicians.[64]

The first instrumental ragtime sheet music arranged in the midwest style was published in the United States in 1897. It found ready acceptance among the piano-playing and listening American public. The cakewalk and the turkey trot in ragtime rhythm swept the nation and were readily welcomed in Europe. In 1900 when John Philip Sousa and his band played the ragtime cakewalk "Bunch O'Blackberries" on tour in Paris, they were a musical sensation. In New Orleans, ragtime or jazz continued to undergo local innovations—it was more romantic in a French-Spanish style than the midwestern ragtime and it tended to feature a powerful

62 Alwes, "The History of the Louisiana State Lottery Company," 1091; *Mascot,* November 15, 1890.

63 Rose and Souchon, *New Orleans Jazz,* 60; Williams, *Jazz Masters of New Orleans,* 48–50; Blesh and Janis, *They All Played Ragtime,* 159–64, 169–74.

64 Rose and Souchon, *New Orleans Jazz,* 200.

beat, a "stomp" which commanded the listener's attention. Its special style was heard occasionally in midwestern and northern cabarets as individuals or groups left home and sought playing dates in other cities. But it was not until the era of World War I that Dixieland jazz (or jass as it was first called) won national recognition. By that time the pure, piano type of ragtime was becoming passé.[65]

In 1915 Tom Brown and his New Orleans group of white musicians adopted the name of "Brown's Dixieland Jass Band." The name "jass" which was flung at them by union bands in Chicago who resented their rivalry had connotations of bawdy house music. But Brown and his band turned the title into an asset as the public came to hear what "jass" was. The next year another white ensemble from New Orleans which called itself the Dixie Jass Band played Chicago. By 1917 they moved on to New York and sudden fame as the Original Dixieland Jazz Band when their recordings became national hits. By 1919 they sailed for a booking in England, repeating the combination of delight and denunciation that Sousa and the cakewalk had received in Paris in 1900.[66]

The music they helped to establish as a new American art form was the culmination of over a century of musical life in their hometown—it was the product of classical music forms, French folk tunes, white quadrilles, and Afro-American dances such as the bamboula and the calinda, spirituals, the voodoo tradition, minstrel ditties, the style of brass bands and ragtime pianos, of jail house blues and church social jubilees. Negro musicians had played an overwhelming part in shaping its style. But white music and musicians were also an integral part of its makeup. Somewhere in all of this musical integration the soul of New Orleans was set to music.

[65] Blesh and Janis, *They All Played Ragtime*, 4, and pictorial pages following p. 80; 166–67.
[66] Williams, *Jazz Masters of New Orleans*, 27–31.

11

THE IMAGE OF ROMANTIC
OLD NEW ORLEANS
AND THE GROWTH
OF THE CARNIVAL TRADITION

"WHEN I FIRST viewed New Orleans from the deck of the great steamboat that had carried me from gray northwestern mists into the tepid, orange-scented air of the South," wrote Lafcadio Hearn in the 1880's, "my impressions of the city, drowsing under the violet and gold of a November morning, were oddly connected with memories of 'Jean-ah Poquelin.' " He continued, "That strange little tale had appeared previously in the *Century*; and its exotic picturesqueness had considerably influenced my anticipations of the Southern metropolis, and had prepared me to idealize everything peculiar and semi-tropical that I might see. Even before I had left the steamboat my imagination had already flown beyond the wilderness of cotton-bales, the sierra-shaped roofs of the sugar sheds, the massive fronts of refineries and store-houses, to wander in search of the old slave-trader's mansion, or at least of something resembling it." [1]

In this deft and delicate introduction to "The Scenes of Cable's Romances" which first appeared in *Century* in 1883 and was later reprinted in the *Historical Sketch Book* in 1885, Hearn admits that George Washington Cable's fiction had helped to color his first impression of New Orleans, even before he viewed it for himself. Cable's haunting and romantic tales of Madame Delphine, of the Café des Exilés, of the Grandissimes, of Zalli and 'Tite Poulette created a picture of New Orleans in the mind of the reader which he tried to recapture in reality when he visited the Crescent

1 Coleman, *Historical Sketch Book*, 293.

City. Like Hearn, searching for the plantation of Jean-ah Poquelin, he might discover that the object of his search had long since
been replaced by a hotel or a warehouse. But in the case of some
buildings such as the house that was Madame John's legacy or the
"shattered brick skeleton" at the corner of St. Ann and Royal
streets which was the model for the Café des Exilés, he would feel
a thrill of discovery upon catching sight of an old architectural
relic linked with Cable's romances.[2]

One Creole gentleman complained in the 1890's that tourists
walked up and down the streets of the Vieux Carré with copies of
Cable's books trying to identify the locales of certain stories and to
pick out the local types among the populace.[3] Such invasions of
the privacy of the Creole section of the city were resented by its inhabitants, who felt Cable had grossly misrepresented them anyway. But like it or not, they had to face the fact that most of the
Vieux Carré landmarks that were tourist attractions and subjects
of national magazine articles by the 1890's were the places George
Washington Cable had chosen as the scenes of his stories in the
early 1880's. His sensitive genius created the image of "romantic
old New Orleans" which was to captivate and draw visitors into
the city by the last decade of the nineteenth century. It was on the
base of this image that later writers have enlarged and embellished
the legends of Creoles, quadroons, pirates, and voodoo until the
"romance" of old New Orleans has become a robust tourist industry.

Cable was not a typical New Orleanian—if such a figure really
existed. His father was a Virginian; his mother, of New England
ancestry. Possibly from his New England heritage came a puritanical streak which played the dominant role in Cable's personality.
He was devoutly Presbyterian, taught Sunday school, and refused
to do any work or follow any frivolous amusement on Sunday. He
was also deeply imbued with a humanitarian zeal. It was largely
through his work on the grand jury in the first Shakspeare administration that reforms in the city insane asylum were forthcoming

2 *Ibid.*, 295.
3 Harris, "The Creoles of New Orleans," 210.

and that the Board of Prisons and Asylums was set up.[4] Despite his serious and indeed somewhat prudish outlook on life, Cable had a streak of romanticism which relished the Creole heritage of his native city and the patois of French-speaking Negroes—their folk songs and the cries of street vendors. In an age when local color and dialect stories were to be a dominant trend in American literature, Cable set out to collect examples of local French-patois songs and folk tales. During the 1870's and 1880's when he worked as a newspaperman and Cotton Exchange clerk, he delved into yellowed newspaper files to dig out incidents which he could set down in story form. On walks through the Vieux Carré, he carefully selected picturesque buildings to use as the settings for his stories. Hearn later speculated that the Rue Royale (or Royal Street) must have been Cable's favorite street since it is almost always mentioned in his Creole stories.[5]

Copying down the broken English which he heard among the humbler residents of the Vieux Carré, both white and colored, Cable delighted his readers, but infuriated the aristocratic, upper echelon of Creoles who felt such a characterization of "Creoles" was detrimental to themselves. One of the richest veins of local color Cable discovered was the segment of local society who called themselves "colored Creoles." Such colored Creole landladies as Madame John were a commonplace in New Orleans in the late nineteenth century. No one could deny their existence or the presence of octoroons, quadroons, mulattoes, and griffes in the city.[6] Surreptitious racial mixing was obviously a heritage from slavery days. What white Creoles found startling in Cable's stories was his presentation of such colored Creoles as protagonists. Many of his stories were told from their point of view. They were depicted as complex human beings with emotions and sensitivities which had heretofore been reserved for white heroes and heroines.

---

[4] For Cable's early life see Philip Butcher, *George W. Cable* (New York, 1962), 19–30; Turner, *George W. Cable*, 3–51. His work on the grand jury is discussed in Chapter 7 of this volume.

[5] Coleman, *Historical Sketch Book*, 294.

[6] An octoroon was one-eighth Negro. A quadroon was one-fourth Negro. A mulatto was one-half Negro and a griffe was three-fourths Negro.

His indiscriminate use of the word "Creole" to cover the colored Creoles as well as white French-speaking New Orleanians was the sorest point of all to local whites of French-Spanish background. They felt this word was reserved exclusively for themselves. Grace King, who although not a Creole was one of their major defenders and spokesman, observed that Cable did not understand the Creoles. What was closer to the truth was that Cable's image of what was "Creole" did not coincide with the narrow image that white, upper-class Creoles held to be valid.

Cable's outpouring of Creole stories began in the 1870's. His *Old Creole Days* appeared in 1879; *The Grandissimes* was published in 1880; and *Madame Delphine,* in 1881. *Dr. Sevier,* which dealt with a Charity Hospital doctor's experiences during the Civil War era and is considered one of his finest works, appeared in 1883.[7] Other later works included *The Creoles of Louisiana, Bonaventure,* and *Strange True Stories of Louisiana.* In the two years after *Dr. Sevier* appeared in print, Cable turned to social reform in "The Freedman's Case in Equity" and *The Silent South.* The latter was a collection of his writings on racial discrimination in the South and took its name from Cable's belief that many white southerners like himself favored social justice for Negroes but did not speak out. Cable struck a ragged nerve in his native city and the South as a whole. White antagonism toward him and his family became so bitter after the publication of *The Silent South* that he moved permanently to New England by the end of 1885.[8]

Ironically, in June of 1884 while he was revising a second edition of *Dr. Sevier,* Cable had been interviewed by a *Picayune* reporter about his works of fiction and his interest in civil rights. Cable told the reporter he was convinced that the South was making ethical as well as material progress.[9]

Although Cable continued to write prolifically until the turn of the century, the exile from his native city proved tragically fatal to the caliber of his work. With the exception of *John March,*

---

[7] The character of Dr. Sevier was based on a real person, Dr. D. Warren Brickell. Turner, *George W. Cable,* 160–70.

[8] Arlin Turner (ed.), *The Negro Question* (New York, 1958), 54–131; Turner, *George W. Cable,* 222–23; Butcher, *George W. Cable,* 85–90.

[9] *Daily Picayune,* June 30, 1884.

Southerner (1894) and *The Cavalier* (1901), he produced little
of literary quality. The romantic glow of his early Creole stories
was gone. But its afterglow colored the pages of guidebooks to the
city and articles appearing in such national journals as *Scribner's*,
Harper's and *Century* down to the end of the century.

The first of such guidebooks and still one of the best ever done
on New Orleans was Will Coleman's *Historical Sketch Book*. It
was probably the brain child of Lafcadio Hearn who contributed
at least two of its articles and most likely several others. The publisher, however, also acknowledged contributions and borrowings
from the writings of Charles Gayarré, Judge Alexander Walker,
Charles E. Whitney, Catherine Cole, John and Charles Dimitry,
and Marion Baker, who acted as editor for this work.[10] How the
book came into existence is not too clear, but it seems to have
been included in a package publishing deal between Coleman and
Hearn.

Coleman had been in the machinery business in New Orleans
in the late 1870's and had been drawn into a friendship with the
newcomer Hearn through their mutual love of gourmet food. After the failure of his business in 1880, Coleman moved to New York
City and opened a bookstore. Hearn wrote to him after his work
on Negro patois or "Gombo French" proverbs had been turned
down by Harper's publishing house and asked Coleman to sponsor publication of this work. Coleman wrote back that the market for such a book was negligible. Hearn's reply was an offer to
throw in a collection of Creole recipes which he had collected from
friends in New Orleans, such as young Rudolph Matas and his
wife who entertained Hearn at dinner occasionally. This was more
to Coleman's taste and he agreed. Since the Cotton Centennial
Exposition was also in the preparatory stages, a guidebook was
also planned which was to come out by 1884. It did not appear
until 1885 when the exposition was coming to a close and sold
poorly as a result. Hearn's book of proverbs entitled *Gombo
Zhebes* also found new buyers. But *La Cuisine Creole,* which
Hearn had requested be published anonymously since he felt em-

10 Coleman, *Historical Sketch Book,* see Introduction after title page for list
of contributors; Turner, *George W. Cable,* 198.

barrassed at having his name on a cookbook, was a complete success.[11] Like the *Historical Sketch Book*, which survived its early poor reception to set an example for later guidebooks, *La Cuisine Creole* was a pioneer and precursor of the many cookbooks extolling the glories of Creole cuisine which were to follow it.

So much exaggeration of the peculiarities of Lafcadio Hearn during his New Orleans sojourn has been put into print that it is only through reading some of his many sketches in the *Item*, or his letters to friends such as Henry Krehbiel, or examples of his literary criticism in the *Times-Democrat*, that the modest, tenderhearted, yet tolerant and worldly-wise figure of the man emerges.[12] Although blind in one eye as a result of a childhood accident and with only partial vision in the other, Hearn "saw" much more than most of his contemporaries, and he saw it in a perspective that many of them were not capable of attaining. A lonely wanderer through much of his life, he had been born on the Greek island of Santa Maura, the child of a runaway marriage between an English surgeon-major in the British army and a local Greek girl. After the birth of another son and a move to Dublin, the Hearns ended their marriage. Mrs. Hearn returned to Greece, remarried and never saw her children from her first marriage again. Lafcadio was adopted by an English aunt who took him to Wales to live and wasted little affection on him. The separation from his father and brother was a permanent one. Under such handicaps it was no wonder that he became moody, distrustful of even the most sincere of friends, and too insecure to settle down in one place after he became old enough to be on his own. His wanderlust had taken him from Europe to New York, then on to Cincinnati before he decided to seek the southern climate of New Orleans in 1878.[13]

For the *Item*, his first place of employment, Hearn wrote a series of brief sketches on such subjects as flower-sellers, Creole

11 Tinker, *Lafcadio Hearn's American Days*, 181–83.

12 For an excellent example of a reappraisal of Hearn during his New Orleans sojourn, see Albert Mordell, *Discoveries: Essays on Lafcadio Hearn* (Tokyo, 1964), Chapter 11, 167–77.

13 Elizabeth Bisland, *The Life and Letters of Lafcadio Hearn* (Boston and New York, 1906) I, 3–39, 40–67.

songs, why crabs are boiled alive, the charcoal vendors, local cemeteries and their depressing neglect, the problem of packs of stray dogs roaming the city, the Negro cake and candy peddler, cockroachs and their antics, and the misfortune of having to listen to amateur musicians. He often illustrated the sketches himself with little pen drawings. Humorous, lusty, brimming with a natural vivacity and sometimes a hot indignation, these sketches offer invaluable vignettes of the sights and sounds of Gilded Age New Orleans. A number of them have been reprinted under the title *Creole Sketches,* edited by Charles W. Hutson. Others appear in *Lafcadio Hearn's American Days,* by Edward Larocque Tinker.[14] In addition to his *Item* sketches and his *Gombo Zhebes,* Hearn wrote and published *Chita; A Memory of Last Island* after he left the city. Its plot was centered around the hurricane of 1856 and the results of its devastation on the lives of the survivors at this antebellum Louisiana resort spot.[15]

After Hearn went to work for the *Times-Democrat* in 1881, he often translated the works of French or Spanish writers for his readers, and on both the *Item* and *Times-Democrat* he wrote brilliant book reviews which revealed a genuine flair for literary criticism. Of the local fiction writers and poets whose work he reviewed, Hearn lavished special praise on Cable, on Father Adrien Rouquette, Judge Frank McGloin, Dr. Alfred Mercier, Alice Morris Buckner, and Elizabeth Bisland.[16]

Father Rouquette was a member of an aristocratic Creole family who with his brother Dominique had been educated in France in the early nineteenth century. Both of the Rouquette brothers wrote poetry and were inspired by French romanticism and the works of Chateaubriand. Adrien entered the priesthood and became a missionary to the remnant of the Choctaws located in St. Tammany Parish. By the time Hearn first met and became friends with Father Rouquette or "Chahta-Ima" as he was called by the Indians, the poet-priest had been living among the Indians for

14 Other articles by Hearn are discussed in Mordell, *Discoveries: Essays on Lafcadio Hearn,* Chapter 6, 78–91. Hearn's articles for the *Item* which Mordell researched appeared between June 16, 1878 and December, 1881.
15 Bisland, *The Life and Letters of Lafcadio Hearn,* I, 95–100.
16 Mordell, *Discoveries: Essays on Lafcadio Hearn,* 73.

twenty years and wore long hair and native Choctaw garb, except when saying mass.[17] Hearn was fascinated by the exotic romanticism of this learned priest who loved the simple life in the forest, but occasionally came to the city where he occupied a small, austere room in the Presbytére. Father Rouquette's principal collection of poems was *Les Savanes* dealing with Louisiana subjects. His novel *La Nouvelle Atala,* based on an Indian legend, appeared in 1879 and was discussed in the *Item* by Hearn in these words, "a creation inspired by the Spirit of forest solitudes,—a prose poem melodious as an autumn wind chanting a language, mystic and unwritten, through woods of pine. . . . None but one whose life had been passed in communion with nature and all her moods could have written such a book." [18] As Hearn was quick to discern, Father Rouquette's life and literary work were living examples of French romanticism transplanted to a Louisiana setting and thriving vigorously long after romanticism had ceased to be a vital force in European intellectual circles. After Cable's works on the Creoles began to appear, Father Rouquette was one of the Creoles who bitterly criticized Cable's portrayals and refuted them in the columns of the French daily, *L'Abeille.*

Frank McGloin, whose profession was the law and who served as judge of the state court of appeals in New Orleans, wrote fiction and poetry as an avocation. Deeply religious, Judge McGloin also edited the Catholic publication, the *Holy Family,* which was aimed at family readers and contained material on both religious and civic topics. As an ardent antilottery campaigner, Judge McGloin was one of the first to denounce the lottery through the pages of the *Holy Family.* His work of fiction which won extravagant compliments from Hearn was a novel about southeast Asia called *Norodom, King of Cambodia.*[19] Always enthralled by faraway places, Hearn was delighted with McGloin's novel. Alcée Fortier also noted in an essay on Louisiana literature that Mc-

17 *Biographical and Historical Memoirs of Louisiana,* II, 68–69 (Alcée Fortier wrote the chapter on literature in this book) ; Tinker, *Lafcadio Hearn's American Days,* 138–47.

18 Tinker, *Lafcadio Hearn's American Days,* 145; *Item,* February 25, 1879.

19 Mordell, *Discoveries: Essays on Lafcadio Hearn,* 74; *Biographical and Historical Memoirs of Louisiana,* II, 77, 224–25.

Gloin's imagination was extraordinary in conjuring up the palace gardens and other settings in this book.[20] As in the case of Rouquette, McGloin leaned toward romanticism.

Two of the other local authors whom Hearn praised, a physician Dr. Alfred Mercier, for his *L'Habitation Saint Ybars* and Alice Buchner, for her anonymously published *Towards the Gulf,* dealt with Louisiana subjects and the problem of miscegenation.[21] This was a problem which Hearn understood probably better than most since he had entered into a stormy and short-lived marriage with a mulatto woman in Cincinnati before coming to New Orleans. As in the novels of Mercier and Buchner, Hearn's daring marriage had been doomed by the pressures of society, by state law which did not recognize it as legal, and by the gulf of differences in outlook and background between himself and his wife. They finally parted in bitterness.[22] From Hearn's reviews of these two novels, it seems that they were above average in literary quality and were invaluable for the first-hand picture they gave of Louisiana plantation life in the mid-nineteenth century.

Dr. Mercier had been the prime mover behind the founding of *L'Athénée Louisianais* in 1876, which was a society dedicated to the study of the French language, the publication of local literary works in French, and the preservation of the Creole culture in Louisiana through its journal, the *Comptes Rendus de l'Athénée Louisianais.*[23] He was obviously a writer whose interests lay in controversial social subjects. In addition to miscegenation, he attacked the celibacy of priests in the novel *La Fille du Pretre* and dealt with a crime of infanticide in *Johnelle.* Two other novels, *Le Fou de Palerme* and *Lidia* were simply love stories in the well-worn groove of French romanticism.[24] Fortier calls Dr. Mercier "a master of the creole patois" which he used freely in his book.[25]

20 *Biographical and Historical Memoirs of Louisiana,* II, 77.
21 Mordell, *Discoveries: Essays on Lafcadio Hearn,* 73–74.
22 An account of Hearn's marriage is given in Tinker, *Lafcadio Hearn's American Days,* 27–29.
23 Rightor, *Standard History of New Orleans,* 366–67; 628; *Biographical and Historical Memoirs of Louisiana,* II, 69.
24 *Biographical and Historical Memoirs of Louisiana,* II, 69.
25 *Ibid.*

Thus Mercier, like Cable, combined local color, romanticism and social problems in his writings.

Elizabeth Bisland, who worked on the *Times-Democrat* covering women's meetings and writing articles of feminine interest, produced mixed emotions in her coworker Lafcadio Hearn. He publicly acknowledged her talent in writing poetry which she published under the pseudonym, R. B. L. Dane, and privately admitted her physical attractiveness. But he shrank away from her driving ambition and disarming self-confidence, a quality he sadly lacked. He called her "a girl who reminds me of a hawk,—although her nose is not aquiline—a graceful creature of prey!" [26] Miss Bisland was to gain her fame after she left New Orleans in the late 1880's for New York City. She eventually became associate editor of *Cosmopolitan Magazine* and was most well known for the publicity stunt of traveling around the world in an attempt to beat another woman journalist, Nellie Bly, in shattering the eighty-days travel record of Jules Verne's fictional hero. She lost the around-the-world race, but won a secure place in journalism. Although her friendship with Hearn had flickered bright and low during the years that he drifted in and out of her life in New Orleans and later New York, her most lasting literary achievement was to be the three-volume *Life and Letters of Lafcadio Hearn* published after his death.[27] The letters in this collection reveal many vivid impressions of persons and events in New Orleans during the 1880's.

In addition to Elizabeth Bisland, a number of other women contributed to the literary climate of Gilded Age New Orleans. The most influential was Eliza Nicholson, the petite, poetical proprietor of one of the South's largest daily newspapers, the *Daily Picayune*. Born Eliza Poitevent, the daughter of a lumberman and steamboat builder, she had spent her childhood on a plantation of her uncle and aunt in the piney woods lowlands of Mississippi near the Pearl River.[28] Using the pen name of Pearl Rivers (after

26 Tinker, *Lafcadio Hearn's American Days*, 175.

27 Francis E. Willard and Mary A. Livermore (eds.), *A Woman of the Century, Fourteen Hundred-Seventy Biographical Sketches Accompanied by Portraits of Leading American Women in All Walks of Life* (reprint ed., Detroit, 1967), 86–87.

28 *Ibid.*, 537–38; Dabney, *One Hundred Great Years*, 260–64.

the stream near her childhood home) she became a contributor of poems to the New York *Home Journal* and to New Orleans newspapers. A few years after her graduation from the Amite (Louisiana) Female Seminary, she made a fateful visit to her grandfather in New Orleans, Samuel Potter Russ. In this city she met the owner of the *Daily Picayune,* Colonel Alva Morris Holbrook, who was already familiar with her poems and who now offered the shy young girl of nineteen a job on his paper as literary editor. She accepted despite the horrified protests of family and friends that a newspaper office was no place for a southern gentlewoman.

In 1872 she married Colonel Holbrook. He was sixty-four and she was twenty-three. The young Mrs. Holbrook, according to Thomas Ewing Dabney, the official historian of the *Picayune,* "introduced fiction, fashions, art, and kindred subjects, in a large way, into the paper. She expanded the column of book reviews, and printed the poetry of many writers." The short works of Mark Twain appeared frequently in her columns. The introverted country girl from Mississippi was turning into a gracious woman of letters. But she had ugly experiences as well as happy ones as a result of her marriage. A month after her marriage, she was attacked viciously by her husband's former wife who broke into the Holbrook home, tried to shoot Eliza, and then hit her over the head with a bottle of bay rum. Saved by servants, the young poetess fled next door while her attacker took an ax from the backyard and proceeded to break up the Holbrook furniture until the police arrived.[29] The June-December marriage of the Holbrooks ended in 1876 with the colonel's death. His widow was left with a paper heavily in debt, but a determination to try to manage it herself. During the next few years she faced a constant struggle to keep the paper going. In 1878 she married again—this time the *Picayune*'s business manager, George Nicholson.[30] The Nicholsons during the 1880's put the *Daily Picayune* on a solvent basis once more while keeping it among the ranks of the foremost southern dailies.

Eliza Nicholson, in addition to caring for her two sons Leonard and Yorke from her second marriage, continued to direct and shape

[29] Dabney, *One Hundred Great Years,* 261–64, 265.
[30] Willard and Livermore, *A Woman of the Century,* 537–38.

the character of the *Picayune*. As the carnival season developed
into a fashionable affair in the 1880's, Mrs. Nicholson realized the
importance of society news, accounts of balls, and debutantes and
their parties. The *Picayune* was one of the first southern papers to
report such news. A society bee buzzed in a gossipy column about
the latest trips and accomplishments of New Orleans *haut mon-
de*.[31] By the 1890's there was also a children's page with quaint
brownies and animal drawings which reflected the imagination of
the paper's woman proprietor. The *Picayune* frog which appeared
alongside the weather report also was witness to the delicate sense
of humor of Eliza Nicholson. When the *Times-Democrat* merged
in the 1880's, it recognized the interest Mrs. Nicholson's literary
page had generated among local readers by hiring Lafcadio Hearn
to write articles on books and literary topics. A friendly rivalry
grew up between the two papers over the merits of their respective
literary editors and their translations from French and Spanish
classics.[32]

The major share of Eliza Nicholson's energies went into man-
aging the *Picayune*. As a result, although she was probably the
most gifted of the women who wrote poetry in the state, only one
volume of her poems appeared in print, *Lyrics*, published in
1873.[33] But Eliza Nicholson's personality left an indelible impression upon the intellectual life of New Orleans. She died in
1896 at forty-seven after a brief spell of influenza.[34]

With encouragement from Eliza Nicholson, other local women
writers blossomed out. One woman journalist who began her
newspaper career on the *Picayune* was Martha R. Field, who
wrote under the name of Catherine Cole. A feature writer on the
local scene and editor of the woman's department in the *Picayune*
for years, Mrs. Field made several trips to Europe which she reported on in detail for the paper's Sunday section and covered the
Chicago World's Fair in 1893. She later worked on the *Times-*

31 Dabney, *One Hundred Great Years*, 307. The "society bee" first appeared
on March 16, 1879 in the *Daily Picayune*.
32 Tinker, *Lafcadio Hearn's American Days*, 163–64.
33 Willard and Livermore, *A Woman of the Century*, 538.
34 *Daily Picayune*, February 16, 1896.

Democrat. After her death, a selection of her best articles was collected in *Catherine Cole's Book,* edited by Mrs. Mollie Evelyn Moore Davis.[35]

Mrs. Davis's husband, Major Thomas E. Davis, who had started as a reporter on the *Picayune* in 1879, worked up to editor-in-chief by 1889 and held that post until his death in 1914.[36] A native of Alabama, who spent most of her childhood in Texas where she had begun to write poetry as a teenager like Eliza Nicholson, Mollie Evelyn Moore Davis also became a regular contributor to the pages of the paper her husband edited. In addition to verse, she did a series of local sketches called the "Keren-happoch Papers." These attracted the interest of national magazines looking for local color similar to Cable's stories. Mrs. Davis soon broadened her audience to include the readers of *Harper's Magazine* and almost every leading periodical in the country. Her most memorable collection of stories in book form was *In War Times at La Rose Blanche* which recalled bittersweet memories of her childhood in Texas during the Civil War.[37] Another protégé of Mrs. Nicholson was Mrs. Elizabeth M. Gilmer whose first article appeared in the *Picayune* in 1887. By 1895 she was a full-time *Picayune* staff member, under the name which would make her world famous as a love-lorn advisor—Dorothy Dix.[38]

Other local women who followed the Genteel Tradition of literature in the late nineteenth century to recount the memories of their childhood on a southern plantation, to write local color stories on New Orleans, or to compose poetry about nature or the Civil War and its heroes were Julie K. Wetherill Baker, Ruth McEnery Stuart, Mary Ashley Townsend, and Mrs. Cecelia Viets Jamison. Mrs. Baker was the wife of Marion Baker, literary editor of the *Times-Democrat.* After Hearn left New Orleans for the West Indies in 1887, she frequently wrote book reviews and literary articles for her husband's literary page. But she also contributed arti-

35 Dabney, *One Hundred Great Years,* 306; Rightor, *Standard History of New Orleans,* 380.

36 Dabney, *One Hundred Great Years,* 305–306.

37 Rightor, *Standard History of New Orleans,* 377; *Biographical and Historical Memoirs of Louisiana,* II, 75.

38 Dabney, *One Hundred Great Years,* 306–307.

cles filled with subtle irony to such publications as *Lippincott's*.[39]
Ruth McEnery Stuart wrote about Louisiana plantation life and
was praised by Joel Chandler Harris for her knowledge and skill-
ful use of Negro dialect. A native of Avoyelles Parish which offered
the background for many of her stories, Mrs. Stuart began writing
after her husband's death when she moved to New Orleans. During the 1880's she began to make a national reputation through
magazine articles. By 1892 she moved to New York where she wrote
mainly for *Harper's Bazaar* and served for a brief period as acting
editor of that publication while editor Margaret Sangster was in
Europe. Her collected works include *A Golden Wedding and Other
Tales, Carlotta's Intended and Other Stories, Solomon Crow's
Christmas Pockets and Others, In Simpkinville,* and her most en-
during work which has become a juvenile classic, *The Story of
Babette*.[40]

Mary Ashley Townsend, who came to New Orleans from her
native state of New York as a bride in 1856, was a society leader
and one of the Crescent City's most brilliant hostesses in addition
to being a pioneer among the flock of local women writers whose
works appeared in local papers and national magazines. Writing
poetry under the name of Xariffa, she produced several collections of poems including *Xariffa's Poems, Down the Bayou and
Other Poems,* and *Distaff and Spindle*.[41] An active participant in
carnival festivities, Mrs. Townsend enjoyed the position of poet
laureate to Rex, king of the Mardi Gras. For her services in 1873,
the second year of the Rex organization, she received a butt of
wine.[42] In 1881 she was the official correspondent of the *Daily
Picayune* on a trip to Mexico.[43] One of her family's friends and a

39 John Smith Kendall, "Old Days on the Times-Democrat," *Louisiana
Historical Quarterly,* XXXIII (July, 1950), 422; *Biographical and Historical
Memoirs of Louisiana,* II, 76; Rightor, *Standard History of New Orleans,* 379.

40 Rightor, *Standard History of New Orleans,* 378; Davis, *Louisiana: A Narrative History,* 312.

41 Rightor, *Standard History of New Orleans,* 376.

42 Rex, King of Carnival to Xariffa, January 1, 1874, in Mary Ashley Townsend Papers, Special Collections Division, Howard-Tilton Memorial Library,
Tulane University.

43 Official letter of certification as *Picayune* correspondent signed by George
Nicholson, December 3, 1881, in Mary Ashley Townsend Collection, Special
Collections Division, Howard-Tilton Memorial Library, Tulane University.

fellow-poet who corresponded with Mrs. Townsend was Oliver Wendell Holmes.[44]

Another woman who came to New Orleans after her marriage in 1879 and gained a national reputation as a writer of children's fiction was Canadian-born Cecelia Viets Jamison. Many of her short stories and novels appeared in serial form in *St. Nicholas Magazine*. She used the Vieux Carré, the exotic sights and sounds of the levee, and the desolate stretches of swamp on the outskirts of the city as background for her children's books, *Lady Jane* and *Toinette's Philip* which are still widely read.[45]

Probably the most penetrating interpreter of the character and personality of the Creole woman was Kate Chopin. Her stories depict not only the sheltered girlhood of the Creole belles, but the witty, worldly-wise conversational powers of young Creole matrons, their "entire lack of prudery," and their greatest virtue— a complete, self-sacrificing loyalty to their families. A native of St. Louis, Mrs. Chopin married Oscar Chopin in 1870 and lived for ten years in New Orleans where her husband was a cotton factor and commission merchant. When the Chopin business failed in 1880, the family moved to Cloutierville, Chopin's hometown, where they occupied one of his properties and ran a general store. From the combination of experiences in New Orleans (with summers spent at Grand Isle) and among the planters and Chopin relations in Natchitoches Parish, Kate stored up a reservoir of character sketches. These she put down on paper after her husband's death in 1882 and her return to her hometown of St. Louis as a widow with six children who was in need of extra income. She wrote numerous stories, articles, poems, and two novels, *At Fault* and *The Awakening*. Her most well-known works are collections of short stories dealing with Louisiana, *Bayou Folk* and *A Night in Acadie*. The Creole woman as Mrs. Chopin had known her in New Orleans is probably best displayed in *The Awakening*.[46]

44 Oliver Wendell Holmes to Mary Ashley Townsend, July 17, 1888, in Mary Ashley Townsend Collection, Special Collections Division, Howard-Tilton Memorial Library, Tulane University.

45 Rightor, *Standard History of New Orleans*, 378–79.

46 Marie Fletcher, "The Southern Woman in the Fiction of Kate Chopin," *Louisiana History*, VII (Spring, 1966), 117–32.

By the last twenty years of the nineteenth century, the painful ordeal of the Civil War was beginning to be translated into print. In the 1870's when a Scottish visitor, David Macrae, called on General Beauregard with several letters of introduction from former Confederate comrades, the general received him cordially and discussed the problem of chronicling the South's side of the recent struggle. Beauregard told Macrae with regret that "the world would never get much more than the Northern side of the war. The North had possession of all materials, and could do with them what it liked." [47] A century later this statement seems ironic. But to Beauregard's generation it was a nagging fear which they tried to put to rest by writing wartime memoirs and biographies. In recalling the events of the Civil War in print, former Confederate generals and officials, or their biographers, often started a small paper war of their own. Beauregard took issue with published statements about himself made by Jefferson Davis in his *Rise and Fall of the Confederate Government* and by Tulane president William Preston Johnston, who wrote a biography of his father, Albert Sidney Johnston. Although he had been trying to write his memoirs for years, it was probably the irritant of the Davis and Johnston books which spurred Beauregard to turn his papers over to General Alfred Roman who was to write an account of Beauregard's career. The final product of this collaboration was *The Military Operations of General Beauregard* which appeared in two volumes in 1884. According to Beauregard biographer T. Harry Williams, Beauregard was actually the author of this work. Roman, also did ghost writing for Beauregard on several national magazine articles dealing with Civil War battles.[48] Other Civil War histories by local writers included Napier Bartlett's *Military Record of Louisiana* and *A Soldier's Story of the War,* and General William Miller Owen's *In Camp and Battle with the Washington Artillery.* Mrs. Eliza Ripley described the troubles of a Louisiana family exiled during the Civil War in *From Flag to Flag*

[47] David Macrae, *The Americans At Home, Pen-and-Ink Sketches of American Men, Manners, and Institutions* (Glasgow, 1885) , 312–13.
[48] *Biographical and Historical Memoirs of Louisiana,* II, 70, 72; Williams, *P. G. T. Beauregard,* 306–18.

and later wrote *Social Life in Old New Orleans*, one of the best accounts of early Crescent City life in existence.

Historical writing by the end of the nineteenth century in New Orleans was still dominated by the presence and influence of Charles Gayarré, the father of Louisiana history whose lifespan, 1805–95, bridged the century. Such younger historians as John Ficklen and Alcée Fortier, both Tulane faculty members whose major historical works on Louisiana were produced after the turn of the century, acknowledge the trail-blazing influence of Gayarré.

The son of Carlos Gayarré and the youngest daughter of sugar planter Étienne de Boré, Gayarré had listened to the sound of cannon coming from the Chalmette battlefield during the Battle of New Orleans as a 10-year-old boy on his grandfather's plantation. Later he met General Andrew Jackson when that returning hero had visited Étienne de Boré.[49] Raised in wealth and Creole privilege as a member of one of the first families of Louisiana, Gayarré's youth was precocious. After studying law in Philadelphia, he returned to New Orleans, was admitted to the bar in 1829, and elected to the lower house of the state legislature in 1830. He later served as state assistant attorney-general and a judge of the City Court in New Orleans. In 1835, just three days after his thirtieth birthday made him eligible to serve in the United States Senate, he was elected to that body. But ill health forced him to decline this position. He went instead to France seeking medical treatment for asthma, which was to stay with him the rest of his life. In later years he also developed emphysema as a result of the strain of asthma attacks upon his lungs. Although Gayarré's thirteen years in Europe did not cure his asthma, it did provide him with first-hand knowledge of European culture and access to documents in the French archives dealing with Louisiana history. He laboriously copied many of these and began writing his first volume of *Histoire de la Louisiane*.[50]

After his return to Louisiana in 1843, he again served in the leg-

49 Grace King, "Charles Gayarré, A Biographical Sketch," *Louisiana Historical Quarterly*, XXXIII (April, 1950) , 159–69.
50 *Ibid.*, 170–75; Fortier, *Louisiana*, I, 464–65; Rudolph Matas, "An Evening with Gayarré," *Louisiana Historical Quarterly*, XXXIII (April, 1950) , 290.

islature, and was appointed secretary of state, a job he held until 1850. During the 1850's he continued the writing of his multi-volume history of the state, feuded with the Democratic Party, flirted briefly with the Know Nothings, and experienced what he came to believe had been the greatest lost opportunity of his life— a chance to be appointed United States minister to Spain by President Franklin Pierce. The appointment would have meant that Gayarré could have delved into the colonial archives of the Spanish government and copied valuable documents on Louisiana. Another Louisianian, Pierre Soulé, got the appointment instead. This was to foreshadow a host of disappointments over the loss of both federal and state positions that Gayarré applied for in vain after the Civil War which wiped out his personal fortune. By 1866 his three-volume *Histoire de la Louisiane* was complete in French. In 1879 it was reissued in an English translation, *The History of Louisiana,* which Gayarré had rewritten and expanded to four volumes, although by now in his seventies.[51]

Hearn in reviewing the English translation found magic in the Creole historian's pen. "Descriptions of manners and customs, analyses of character, studies of habits and dresses, presentations of ancient documents and long-buried correspondence, . . . lend a fascinating power to this history of Louisiana which very few American works possess," Hearn wrote.[52] These words were probably sweet to the ears of Gayarré who had faced nothing but genteel poverty and bitter disappointment since the Civil War. But he was too old to repeat the epic job of another history in this vein. It was to remain his magnum opus. By the late 1870's when Grace King as a young woman had come to know and love "Judge" Gayarré and his wife as if they were a second set of grandparents, Gayarré was reduced to writing hack articles which were frequently rejected. He did a promotional tract for the Louisiana Lottery, *The Cornucopia of Old, the Lottery Wheel of the New* in 1877. The lottery thoughtfully sent over two small wheels and two boys to operate them when the Gayarrés were forced by financial nec-

51 King, "Charles Gayarré," 177–86; Rightor, *Standard History of New Orleans,* 364; on Gayarré's connection with the Know Nothings see Soulé, *The Know Nothing Party in New Orleans,* 66–67.
52 Mordell, *Discoveries: Essays on Lafcadio Hearn,* 72–73.

essity to hold a lottery with their remaining heirlooms and paintings as prizes.[53] For a brief period in the 1870's, Gayarré tried his hand at historical romances, producing one on Aubert Dubayet, a Louisianian who had participated in both the American and French Revolutions. *Aubert Dubayet or The Two Sister Republics* reflects the disillusionment of Gayarré with democracy.[54] His own ideas of democracy had been shaped in the age of John C. Calhoun and were aristocratic—akin to Calhoun's notion of a democratic republic set atop a slave base. When the Civil War had turned his world upside down, Gayarré had reacted with deep hatred to the new order of "Reconstruction democracy" which he saw about him. He wrote to one friend during the years of the Black and Tan legislature in Louisiana that ancient Greece had been ruled by its Solons, but Louisianians had Sambo for a ruler.[55] When George W. Cable's works on the Creoles began to appear, Gayarré's own memories of the heroic past of which "just yesterday" he had been a part prompted him to dispute Cable's Creole characterizations in a magazine article, "The Creoles of History and the Creoles of Romance." Gayarré lived on to 1895, dying at the age of ninety in a modest little house on Prieur and Kerlerec streets.[56]

The grand tradition of panoramic history and documentary writing which Gayarré had set was carried on by the sensitive young woman whose family had almost been a part of the Gayarré household, Grace King. In her *Memories of a Southern Woman of Letters,* Miss King explains how an argument over Cable's interpretation of Creoles with a visiting northern editor, Richard Watson Gilder, had started her on a literary career. The editor had told her bluntly, "If you are not satisfied with Cable's work why

53 Herbert H. Lang, "Charles Gayarré and the Philosophy of Progress," *Louisiana History,* III (Summer, 1962) , 258–59; Grace King, *Memories of a Southern Woman of Letters* (New York 1932) , 45.

54 Lang, "Charles Gayarré and the Philosophy of Progress," 260–61.

55 Charles Gayarré to Evert A. Duyckinck, December 18, 1872 in "Some Letters of Charles Gayarré," *Louisiana Historical Quarterly,* XXXIII (April, 1950) , 247–49.

56 On Gayarré's dispute with Cable see Tinker, *Creole City,* Chapter 10, 208–22. On Gayarré's last years see John Smith Kendall, "The Last Days of Charles Gayarré," *Louisiana Historical Quarterly,* XV (July, 1932) , 359–75.

don't you write something yourself? [57] This gauntlet was picked up by Grace King and resulted in first a career of short story and novel writing, and then a turn to history—which was to be her best field. Beginning with "Monsieur Motte," published in the *New Princeton Review* in 1886, she wrote delightful, nostalgic stories of plantation days, of white families and their Negro servants told from the viewpoint of a southern white woman remembering her childhood. Her writing career was to span a period of the next forty years. Her works of fiction published in the 1890's were *Tales of a Time and Place,* about New Orleans after the Civil War, and *Balcony Stories,* short sketches in which she presented her version of Creole life. Her historical works during this decade included *Jean Baptiste le Moyne, Sieur de Bienville; A History of Louisiana* (a school textbook written in collaboration with John Ficklen of Tulane) ; *New Orleans, the Place and the People,* one of her best books; and *De Soto and His Men in the Land of Florida.*

The decades after the Civil War saw a decline in the literary fortunes and production of colored Creoles who had produced a coterie of writers and poets before 1860. The movement of some out of the state or into politics instead of literature accounted for part of this decline. The use of music as an artistic expression among others took the place of the written page. Also, French was fast being discarded by the end of the 1890's by many younger people, both white and colored in New Orleans. One of the men who tried to keep the French tradition of the colored Creoles alive was Rodolphe L. Desdunes who laboriously compiled information on the various colored Creole writers, artists, and philanthropists in nineteenth century Louisiana and finally published the results of his research in the early twentieth century in *Nos Hommes et Notre Notre Histoire.*[58]

Literature produced by New Orleanians in the Gilded Age had a number of common denominators. It was often spiced with romanticism of the French school. But French as a vehicle for writers declined by the end of the century. It leaned overwhelmingly

---

[57] King, *Memories of a Southern Woman of Letters,* 59–60.
[58] Rousseve, *The Negro in Louisiana,* 151–64.

upon local color materials for its sources—indeed this was a national trend after the Civil War to turn to dialect and quaint, local customs—but New Orleans, with a more exotic setting and cultural milieu than most American cities, was especially suitable to this treatment. When it reflected social problems, the race issue was the one taken up most often. Following the Genteel Tradition of writing then in vogue, more women appeared in print than ever before with ephemeral poetry and their reminiscences of the "Old South" before and during the Civil War. Some of these reminiscences such as Eliza Ripley's *Social Life in Old New Orleans* were to become prime sources for cultural historians. Civil War military histories and memoirs also began to appear. But earlier local history continued to be dominated by the style and interpretations of Charles Gayarré. The controversy over what constituted "Creole" society which Cable had generated was the one exception to this rule. Cable indeed is the key to the entire literary image of New Orleans in the Gilded Age. He began the trend in local color writing which was picked up by local and national writers and by the end of the century had popularized the "romantic old New Orleans" of the tourists. He sparked the one literary and historical argument of the generation—over the identity of the Creoles. Ironically, Grace King who was wholeheartedly opposed to Cable's interpretation of the word "Creole," might never have written a line without the galling challenge of Cable's success.

In the same period after the Civil War when New Orleans began to attract tourists who had read of its romantic history, its temperate climate and delicious cuisine in some current book or magazine, the phenomenal growth of the carnival celebration culminating in Mardi Gras produced a seasonal tourist boom for the Crescent City. The Latin traditions of carnival festivities before Lent could be found in New Orleans as far back as its earliest days when masked balls and merrymaking maskers in the streets enlivened colonial Mardi Gras. The balls and maskers multiplied between the 1830's and 1850's, but rowdiness often spoiled the fun. Some maskers carried bags of flour with which to douse passersby. Sometimes, less good-humored celebrants substituted lime for flour—a nuisance which required the city authorities to forbid such practices. Fighting, drunkenness, and even murder gave Mardi Gras a bad name by the 1850's. An organized marching parade had taken place as early as 1827, and in the 1830's such yearly spectacles on Mardi Gras were staged by a Creole group, the Bedouins. But it was not until 1857 that New Orleans saw its first night parade, with two floats staged by a group of Americans who had caught the Creole carnival fever. The Mistick Krewe of Comus, with its socially prominent krewe which kept strict secrecy in regard to their king and officials, rolled through the city streets on floats illuminated by flambeau torches, and afterward staged a ball and supper, set the pattern for all other carnival organizations which were to follow.[59]

The Civil War dampened carnival festivities and it was not until the postwar period that the cult of carnival picked up its momentum and began to enlarge its traditions. In 1870 a new krewe, the Twelfth Night Revelers, staged a parade of eighteen floats and their first ball.

Rex, king of carnival and arbitor of Mardi Gras day festivities, came into existence in 1872 as a result of a Mardi Gras visit to New Orleans by the Grand Duke Alexis of Russia. Fearful that the carpetbag municipal government would not properly welcome such a renowned visitor, a group of local businessmen quickly organized a daytime parade. Charles T. Howard was the first contributor to their fund and took an active part in the organization in subsequent years. He was Rex in 1877, the first year the krewe displayed papier-mache floats in its parade. His daughter, Annie Howard, was queen in 1884, and his son Frank T. Howard reigned as Rex in 1895. The theme song of Rex and of Mardi Gras, "If Ever I Cease to Love," was a comic stage song made popular by performer Lydia Thompson whose presence in New Orleans was one of the attractions which drew the Russian grand duke to the city at this time. It was played by bands participating in Rex's first Mardi Gras parade and has been ever since. On horseback, the king and his krewe led a parade of maskers and a gaily decorated live Boeuf Gras followed by advertising wagons and carriages of gay celebrants. Thousands participated in the impromptu parade.

59 Laurraine Goreau, "Mardi Gras," in Carter, *The Past As Prelude: New Orleans, 1718-1968,* 342–51; Thomas DiPalma, *New Orleans Carnival and Its Climax, Mardi Gras* (New Orleans 1953), 46; Coleman, *Historical Sketch Book,* 210–12.

No ball was held afterward and there was no queen the first year. But the Grand Duke Alexis was delighted with the parade which was to become an annual event destined to grow into the greatest Mardi Gras spectacle in the world.[60] The second year of the Rex organization a ball was held to which the public was invited. Rex chose his queen at random from the ladies in the audience, selecting Mrs. Walker Fearn who lamented that she had come in a black dress and bonnet. The custom of selecting a debutante as Rex's queen began in 1874 when Margaret Maginnis was chosen. That year Rex also made a courtesy call on Comus which was to become traditional.[61] Floats did not play the dominant part in Rex's parades until the 1880's. By then the advertising vans and idle marchers had been deleted. By this time also other carnival organizations had come into existence. Those who offered night parades as well as balls included Comus, Momus, and Proteus. Two daytime parading organizations who followed Rex and usually chose a broad satirical theme for their parades were the Independent Order of the Moon and the Phunny Phorty Phellows. As a rule, most carnival organizations chose mythological or historical themes. But carpetbag politics during the troubled 1870's prompted two famous parades which ridiculed the carpetbaggers and the Republicans, the Comus parade of 1873 whose theme was "The Missing Links to Darwin's Origin of the Species," and the Momus parade of 1877 which illustrated scenes from "Hades—a Dream of Momus." Even President Ulysses S. Grant was satirized in this parade.[62] In 1882 the Independent Order of the Moon poked good-natured fun at the first Shakspeare administration. One of their most popular floats depicted the City Hall's war against loose goats in the city streets and squares. It showed Mayor Shakspeare walking up the steps of City Hall as a goat nimbly pulled a handkerchief out of his back pocket.[63] As time passed, political satire was dropped and general social comment took its place. In 1896 the Phunny Phorty Phel-

[60] Arthur Burton LaCour, *New Orleans Masquerade, Chronicles of Carnival* (New Orleans, 1952) , 40–45.

[61] *Ibid.,* 44–48.

[62] Goreau, "Mardi Gras," in Carter, *The Past as Prelude: New Orleans: 1718–1968,* 352–53; Tinker, *Creole City,* 325–30; Coleman, *Historical Sketch Book,* 217.

[63] *Daily Picayune,* February 22, 1882.

lows satirized such topics as the "New Woman" pictured in bloomers with a bicycle, the Salvation Army's fight against liquor, the free silver fad then sweeping the country and American imitation of English styles.[64] Mayor Shakspeare made Mardi Gras history in 1882 by reigning as Rex while he was still mayor. His queen was Frances Isabel Morris, the daughter of John A. Morris. The custom of a supper for the royal couple after the ball was begun that year with the affair being held at the Morris mansion.[65]

By the 1890's new carnival organizations which were to become a permanent part of the season began to crowd the pre-Lenten social calendar. They included the Atlanteans, Nereus, the Elves of Oberon, and Mithras. Other social groups staging parades or balls arose and disappeared with almost every carnival season. One of the most unusual was the knights of Electra sponsored by the Edison Electric Company which was to feature electric lights on its floats. This was in 1889, the year Canal Street got electric lighting. Rain and bad weather "short-circuited" the parade and an insufficient number of mules were available to pull the heavy dynamos needed on a subsequent night. Instead of an electrical display on floats, local citizens had to be satisfied by the electric lighting display along Canal Street which lighted up mock figures of carnival characters. In 1900 the krewe of Nereus tried staging a parade on electric streetcars. But the cars became too widely separated, and this innovation was never tried again.[66]

Although in the 1870's spectators at carnival balls did not always adhere to the instructions on invitations that ladies wear formal dresses and gentlemen must attend in full-dress attire, by the 1890's rigid rules had been set down about this and other protocol associated with carnival balls. The call-out section was established by then. No one was allowed to re-enter a ball if he or she left after it began. Elaborate invitations and programs which resembled valentines were in vogue. Favors, such as pins, fans, or scarves were given to those ladies honored by call-out invitations to dance with krewe members. Queens and their maids were chosen almost exclusively from the current debutante circle. Occa-

64 *Daily Picayune*, February 19, 1896.
65 LaCour, *New Orleans Masquerade*, 49–50, 56.
66 *Ibid.*, 94, 198–99.

sionally the daughters of Confederate heroes were honored by inclusion in the carnival courts. Jefferson Davis's daughter, Varina "Winnie" Davis was queen of Momus in 1883 and queen of Comus in 1892. In 1884 Comus selected a queen for the first time by choosing Mildred Lee, the daughter of Robert E. Lee, as his dancing partner. Mildred's sister Mary Lee, Varina Davis, Nannie Hill, daughter of Ambrose P. Hill, and Julia Jackson, daughter of General Thomas "Stonewall" Jackson, were her maids of honor. Both Jefferson Davis and General Hill were in the audience to enjoy the Comus spectacle.[67] By the 1890's local talent was beginning to take over the designing and making of floats, and many of the costumes and decorations for the balls' tableaus which had formerly been ordered from Europe. The French Opera House and the Grand Opera House were the scenes of the balls of Momus, Proteus, and Comus. Rex held sway Mardi Gras night at the Washington Artillery Hall.[68]

Since some of the parading carnival organizations let several carnival seasons pass by without staging parades, there was occasional confusion when they attempted to return to their original night with flambeau-lit display. The most famous of these incidents was the return of Comus's night parade on Mardi Gras in 1890. Proteus, who had this night every year since 1886, refused to step aside. The two parades went on as scheduled and met on Canal Street where the Proteus parade was forced to wait for Comus to pass by before it could turn into Bourbon Street and proceed to the French Opera House. Tempers flared between the arguing Comus and Proteus officials that night on Canal Street, and the next year the two organizations continued their rivalry by parading and holding balls on Mardi Gras night. The exorbitant price which Proteus was forced to pay for the French Opera House because of the Comus competition was the final dash of harsh reality which was needed to end the petty rivalry. By 1893 the parade of Proteus returned to its original Monday night before Mardi Gras.[69]

The New Orleans carnival season as an attraction to others be-

67 *Ibid.*, 19–20, 67–68.
68 A detailed discussion of behind the scenes planning and building of parade floats is given in Coleman, *Historical Sketch Book*, 220–22.
69 Tinker, *Creole City*, 332–33; LaCour, *New Orleans Masquerade*, 19–20.

sides the local population was recognized by the 1880's. National magazines sent down reporters to cover its festivities or solicited articles from writers on the scene. English writer George A. H. Sala wrote in detail on the Crescent City carnival for a London newspaper as early as 1880. Later with lavish illustrations the material appeared as part of a book, *America Revisited.* Its drawings remain some of the best early depictions of parades, balls, dens where floats were constructed, and costumes worn by ordinary maskers on Mardi Gras.[70]

The carnival season of 1896, two months before the end of Mayor Fitzpatrick's term of office came to an end, was the biggest and brightest ever experienced by the city up to that time. It illustrates how phenomenally carnival festivities had grown since 1872 and the extent to which it had become a major drawing card for tourists. The *Daily Picayune* pointed out on February 16, two days before Mardi Gras, that the carnival season had grown until it extended in 1896 from January 6, the date of the Twelfth Night Revelers' ball down to Mardi Gras itself. During this period numerous balls were held by clubs and fraternal orders in addition to those of the major krewes.[71]

Since this was a leap year, a group of ladies had combined their resources to stage a ladies' ball, the first of its kind, on January 10 at the French Opera House. The group called themselves Les Mysterieuses and selected as their king, William E. Stauffer. The queen's identity naturally remained a secret. This innovation of a feminine krewe was so popular that it was repeated in 1900, the next leap year. It set the precedent for the other feminine carnival clubs that would come into being in the twentieth century.[72]

The weekend before Mardi Gras saw a hectic scramble of tourists arriving by train and steamboat to haggle for the few hotel rooms still available. Train facilities were taxed to the limit. Excursion parties, some of them occupying an entire train or portions of one, rolled into New Orleans from Chicago, Philadelphia, and Boston. The Northeastern railroad's local office estimated that its

[70] Carnival illustrations are in Sala, *America Revisited,* Chapters 6 and 7, 74–101.
[71] *Daily Picayune,* February 16, 1896.
[72] LaCour, *New Orleans Masquerade,* 199.

line alone had brought into the city ten thousand persons during the weekend before Mardi Gras. During the evening of February 15, eight special trains pulled into the Morgan line depot bearing carnival visitors. This was in addition to the many arriving on its regularly scheduled trains. This heavy railroad traffic was repeated on the Illinois Central and Louisville and Nashville lines.

Railroad executives were as carnival conscious as the ordinary tourist. The papers reported the arrival of private railroad cars bearing such dignitaries as Stuyvesant Fish, president of the Illinois Central railroad, Henry Bradley Plant of the Plant railroad system, and a Mr. L. Moloy, superintendent of the Wyoming branch of the Union Pacific. Mr. Moloy was dumbfounded at the crowds which turned out for night parades in the week before Mardi Gras. "Why, to take a ride through your streets," he said, "one would be led to believe that you were getting ready down here for a presidential inauguration." Along the Mississippi levee, steamboats were also arriving with carnival visitors, mainly from points along bayous and small rivers in Louisiana. Many of these would use their staterooms aboard the boats as living quarters during their holiday.[73] They were luckier than most guests arriving in the city without reservations.

Merchants in the city took full advantage of the expanded potential of customers at their doors. Special displays in their windows were designed to entice the visitors. Jewelry and clothing establishments reported after the carnival season of 1896 that they had done 25 to 50 percent more business during the week before Mardi Gras. Local manufacturers of cigars and cigarettes reported a 20 percent rise in the demand for their products by local distributors. Even Grunewald's music house reported that they had sold so many pianos and other musical instruments to visitors that it would take weeks to ship them out-of-town to the purchasers.[74] The seasonal business of costume rentals advertised in bold face type in the papers. One such ad which was typical offered "a fine assortment of costumes such as kings, princes, Venetians, courtiers, Romeos, Hamlets, Marquises, pages, Spanish clowns, monkeys,

73 *Daily Picayune*, February 17, 18, 1896.
74 *Ibid.*, February 27, 28, 1896.

and all sorts of character disguises; masks and dominoes of fine silk; wigs and beards to hire." This costume shop was operated by Mrs. C. F. Snell at 241 Bourbon Street.[75]

For those who wished to participate in carnival, as well as look on, the steamer *Teche* advertised for fifty cents per person a round-trip cruise on the Mississippi from Canal Street down to Chalmette landing and back. This trip was scheduled on the Monday before Mardi Gras when Rex would arrive via boat and be escorted by a military guard of honor to the City Hall to receive the keys of the city from the mayor. The *Teche* would join the Rex flotilla at Chalmette and accompany the "royal yacht" back upstream to the foot of Canal Street.[76]

Mardi Gras, 1896, saw record crowds along Canal Street and the intersecting streets. While there were plenty of clowns, devils, Indians, burlesque firemen, Chinese, and sham soldiers, a striking new note among the maskers' costumes was the surprising number of young girls in bloomers. Marching societies such as the Jefferson City Buzzards and the What's Up marching group put on impromptu parades. The What's Up party had its own band and went around to each of the newspaper offices serenading the working press. Across the river in Gretna, a hamlet on the outskirts of New Orleans, the Gretna Cyclones, a Negro marching society, also paraded in costume with a brass band. As on other Mardi Gras holidays, there were some outstanding, eye-popping costumes— one masker calling himself Klapper the Great was covered with links of sausages from head to foot.

Bags of hot roasted peanuts, cotton candy, pralines, rice cakes— all these delicacies were available from vendors who had stationed themselves on strategic corners shortly after dawn. Most Crescent City natives came to the heart of the city for Mardi Gras on streetcars. A *Picayune* reporter estimated that there were 225 electric streetcars on the Canal Street run alone and about 118 on the St. Charles to Carrollton line. In addition, dozens of other streetcar lines, some of them using the slower but still reliable power of

75 *Ibid.*, February 16, 1896.
76 *Ibid.*, *Times–Democrat*, February 16, 1896.

mules, struggled to bring the holiday crowds to Canal Street or its vicinity.[77]

The theme of the 1896 Rex parade was "Heavenly Bodies" with floats depicting the various planets and stars and their relation to the zodiac. Rex was Charles Janvier. His queen was Arthemise Baldwin, daughter of Albert Baldwin who had reigned as Rex in 1884. At the invitation of the Rex organization, the Phunny Phorty Phellows, who had not paraded since 1885, revived the tradition of following Rex with a parade in 1896.[78]

According to the police, it had been an orderly Mardi Gras. Police Chief Dexter Gaster commended his force on their handling of the crowds and of the arrests they had made. The main police problem had been pickpockets. One suspect was arrested when he tried to lift the wallet of a detective. Crowded streetcars were particularly fertile fields for such petty thieves. Their favorite method of operation was to wait until the streetcar stopped to pick up or let off passengers. They would grab the change purse of a passenger about to pay his or her fare and jump out of the car before anyone could stop them. The only serious crimes of the day were two murders which the police did not seem to feel especially attributable to Mardi Gras.

For weeks after the 1896 carnival season ended, the local newspapers continued to run occasional stories and editorials on its success, lingering over its commercial implication for the city. The national image of New Orleans as the romantic city of the Creoles and of carnival merriment and Mardi Gras had developed remarkably in the generation since 1872. In no small measure, the pen of Cable and the scepter of Rex were the "magic wands" responsible for this transformation.

77 *Daily Picayune*, February 19, 1896; *Times–Democrat*, February 19, 1896.
78 *Daily Picayune*, February 19, 1896; *Times–Democrat*, February 19, 1896.

EPILOGUE TO AN ERA

EIGHT DAYS AFTER Mardi Gras in 1896, banker Charles Janvier, who had reigned over the city that year as a proper, nonpartisan, good-humored Rex, turned back to serious, everyday life and assumed the role of reformer. On February 26, 1896, a lengthy statement appeared in the daily papers signed by Janvier in his capacity as president of the Citizens League, the political offspring of the Citizens Protective Association which had gathered evidence against the Boodle Council and tried to impeach Mayor Fitzpatrick. Janvier's statement called the incumbent Fitzpatrick administration selfish, corrupt, brazen, and inspired by Ring rule. It called for a change in these words: "We must have a new city charter under which positions of responsibility and trust shall command salaries commensurate with their exacting duties and provide safeguards to protect the honest employees of the city against the capricious domination and grinding tyranny of the ward boss. We must have laws giving to New Orleans a clean registration and guaranteeing a free expression of the public will—to attain these ends periodical revolutions are no longer to be endured." [1]

With this opening blast the president of the Citizens League served notice on City Hall that a new era was around the corner— one stirred by Populist emotions and Progressive-minded reforms for municipal government. No longer were self-styled reformers interested only in balancing the city budget and replacing Ring stalwarts with businessmen in municipal executive posts. Against

[1] *Daily Picayune*, February 26, 1896; *Times-Democrat*, February 26, 1896.

312

a national background of Populist agitation for the Omaha Platform, New Orleanians began to speak of voting reforms, particularly the Australian ballot. The Citizens Leaguers were in accord with the Populists and National Republicans (the lily white faction of Louisiana Republicanism dominated by sugar cane planters) in calling for an end to corruption in city and state elections.[2]

Between the end of February and election day, April 21, 1896, the Citizens League tried to remove fraudulent names from the Orleans Parish registration books by canvassing the city. This maneuver was unsuccessful and earned them the wrath of Registrar of Voters Colonel Frank C. Zacharie.[3] They also tried, again unsuccessfully, to ally with incumbent governor, Murphy J. Foster, in his bid for reelection.[4] But the governor shied away from the New Orleans reformers and gave his support to the Ring. The Citizens League platform and ticket were backed by the National Republicans, while the Regular Republicans supported the Ring.[5]

To further confuse the situation, the National Republicans had drafted a Fusion state ticket with the Populists to run against Foster. The Regular Republicans, after a bitter fight in a separate state nominating convention, endorsed the Fusion state ticket.[6] But it was obviously a National Republican dominated slate of candidates. Governor Foster thus saw looming up in opposition to him the Republicans, with a coterie of former Democrats pulling the strings as National Republicans; the Populists, whose strength was an unknown quantity, and the reformers in New Orleans, who after being rebuffed by him, unofficially endorsed the Fusion ticket of the Republicans and Populists. In addition to a slate of municipal candidates, the Citizens League also offered candidates for legislative seats. Its determination to secure the passage of a new city charter by the legislature prompted this action. Remembering the rejection of the charter drafted by the commercial exchanges

2 Background on the National Republicans' formation is in Philip D. Uzee, "The Republican Party in the Louisiana Election of 1896," *Louisiana History*, II (Summer, 1961) , 332–34.

3 *Daily Picayune*, February 25, 1896.

4 *Ibid.*, March 4, 16, 1896.

5 Uzee, "The Republican Party in the Louisiana Election of 1896," 339.

6 *Ibid.*, 336–37.

in 1882, when it was introduced into the legislature where the New Orleans representatives were overwhelmingly Ring affiliates, Citizens League reformers meant to vie with the Ring and the governor for legislative as well as municipal power.

In these circumstances, the governor wanted the municipal ticket of the Ring to be as strong and appealing as possible. The *Daily Picayune* reported on February 26 that he had rejected the desire of Mayor Fitzpatrick to run for a second term.[7] The elimination of the mayor as a possible Ring nominee for reelection was not definite, however, until March 4.[8] Several men were discussed in the newspapers as the possible Ring mayoral choice. Colonel William G. Vincent, who had been a political ally of Governor Foster as president of the Anti-Lottery League, was one of them. But he tactfully removed himself from the race by telling a reporter that if offered the nomination he would decline since he felt committed already to his work on the board of commissioners of Charity Hospital and in other charitable organizations.[9] On March 23, the Citizens League ended its search for a mayoral candidate when Walter C. Flower, New Orleans attorney and former businessman, accepted their nomination. His candidacy was enthusiastically received by the press and made it more imperative than ever that the Ring settle on a respected community leader to head their slate. A scant two weeks before the election of 1896 their ticket was finally drawn up with Congressman Charles F. Buck as the Ring candidate for mayor.[10] No one could deny that Congressman Buck was a formidable opponent for Flower.

Buck was a German immigrant who at the age of twelve had lost his parents in a yellow fever epidemic shortly after arriving in New Orleans in 1853. He had managed, nevertheless, to get an education, study law, work in the office of the renowned Christian Roselius, and find time for amateur theatrics and even a brief career as a professional actor, before becoming city attorney at twenty-seven. A brilliant speaker, he had full command of Ger-

7 *Daily Picayune,* February 26, 1896.

8 *Ibid.,* March 4, 1896.

9 *Ibid.,* March 5, 1896.

10 *Ibid.,* March 23, 31, April 8, 1896; *Times–Democrat,* March 23, April 8, 1896; *Item,* March 23, April 8, 1896.

man, French, and English. In addition to his love for drama, especially Shakespearian plays (on which he was an authority), Buck found time for chess and fencing, membership in the local German Turn-Verein, the Germania Lodge, and the Masons. At the time he was nominated on the regular Democratic city ticket for mayor, he was just beginning a term as congressman from the Second Congressional District.[11]

Although the Ring's mayoral candidate was as respectable and emminent as that of its reformer opposition, morale among the Ring faithful deteriorated as election day drew closer. Shaken by the lottery fight in 1892, the regular Democratic ranks had thinned noticeably as a result of the scandals during the Fitzpatrick regime. Those who had remained faithful had done so usually out of loyalty or expediency which tied them to John Fitzpatrick. When this last dynamic figure of the Ring was pushed aside for renomination as mayor in favor of Buck, a man with an untarnished image, even the Fitzpatrick followers lost heart to work for a Ring victory. Such a Ring boss as former Mayor Guillotte joined the Citizens League and even marched in a political parade in his home territory, the Ninth Ward, carrying a banner calling for the end of Ring rule.[12] The Ring was still capable of performing some of its old tricks, however. Five days before the election it was accused by the *Daily Picayune* of setting up an office for the specific purpose of buying Negro votes at $12.50 a vote.[13]

Election day was tense but quiet in the city. The results of the voting gave victory to Flower. He received 23,345 votes to Buck's 17,295.[14] This defeat of the Ring had been a foregone conclusion among astute observers of city politics. On the state level, Foster won, claiming 116,216 votes to 90,138 for his Fusion opponent, John N. Pharr.[15] The Fusionists were convinced mass frauds had occurred in the alluvial Mississippi River parishes with large Negro registrations, since these areas had gone overwhelmingly for Foster. The Democrats, they claimed, had simply stuffed

---

11 Nau, *The German People of New Orleans*, 129–30.
12 *Daily Picayune*, March 25, 1896.
13 Uzee, "The Republican Party in the Louisiana Election of 1896," 339.
14 Campbell, *Manual of the City of New Orleans*, 33–43.
15 Romero, "The Political Career of Murphy James Foster," reprint, 109.

the ballot boxes with stolen Negro votes. By the time the new legislature met on May 14, a compromise agreement had been worked out between the various political factions in the state as to what action by the Democrats would be necessary to keep the Fusionists from challenging the election in earnest. (The Fusionists reserved the right to offer a token challenge to the election in the legislature.) The compromise called for accepting Foster's election in return for which the governor's new administration would agree to support a new election law including the Australian ballot and to call a constitutional convention. The major purpose of the convention would be to eliminate Negro suffrage in the state. Although the Citizens League wooed Negro voters just like the Ring, it had been the go-between in arranging this compromise.[16] The Citizens League not only captured the mayor's office and almost all of the municipal offices in 1896, but also sent enough legislators to the State Capitol to hold the balance of power between the Fusionists and the Foster Democrats. This put its organization in the perfect position to draft and put through the legislature a new city charter for New Orleans along lines which followed the precepts of the national Municipal Reform League.

This charter cut the council to seventeen, who were to receive salaries and were severely limited in the granting of contracts and franchises. It gave the mayor the power to appoint the commissioners of public works and of public buildings, the two former strongholds of Ring bossism, and it set up a Civil Service Board to classify and supervise many city jobs.[17] The election of 1896 and passage of the 1896 city charter, which would go into effect in 1900, spelled the end of the old Ring. With Mealey dead, Burke in exile, Guillotte a defector to reform, and Fitzpatrick's forces routed, it fell apart. Reorganized the following year, it had new faces, new objectives, and a new name, the Choctaw Club, which

16 Uzee, "The Republican Party in the Louisiana Election of 1896," 342–43. On connections of Citizens League with Negro voters, see mention of Negro public mass meetings held in New Orleans to pledge support for Citizens League in Henry C. Dethloff and Robert R. Jones, "Race Relations in Louisiana, 1877–98," *Louisiana History*, IX (Fall, 1968), 310–11.
17 Flynn, *Flynn's Digest*, xx–xlvi, li–liii, lv, lix, lx–lxiv.

was to come to power in the early twentieth century under Martin Behrman.

When Fitzpatrick left the mayor's office in 1896, therefore, an entire era of Crescent City politics came to an end. It had been a raucous, corrupt, debt-ridden age. Reaching manhood during Reconstruction, Fitzpatrick's generation had learned to live by its wits; honor meant loyalty to one's associates, not theoretical honesty. It was all right to cheat the other side, since they were all "scoundrels" and Republicans anyway. The greatest virtue in the demoralized, poverty-stricken city of the 1870's had been charity. To be willing to share with the less fortunate at a time when none had too much, except the "thieving carpetbaggers" in the State House, was considered the greatest deed any citizen could perform. This is perhaps why the benevolence of Irish-immigrant bakery owner Margaret Haughery was remembered after her death in 1881 by the erection of the first statue in America to a woman. It was also one of Fitzpatrick's chief attractions for the lower classes. He was without a doubt one of the most generous men of his time where the poor were concerned. His hiring of more men than necessary in the Department of Public Works and his fierce loyalty to his councilmen were also accepted rules in the game of politics as his side played it.

By any set of standards Fitzpatrick has to be classed as an outstanding man. His intelligence, drive, and colorful personality always had a definite effect–people loved him or hated him, but were never indifferent. Although he was a professional, he could not be called a callous politician, nor in retrospect a selfishly dishonest one–however poor his judgment may have been in trusting associates. Proof of this last point came at the closing of his public career, when he became tax collector of the First District. Through his deputy's dishonesty the state lost $116,000. Fitzpatrick's bond was responsible for the deputy up to the sum of $30,000. But the former mayor insisted upon paying back the entire amount, although he had not been implicated in its loss and could not have been forced to replace it. His personal fortune was almost wiped out as a result.[18] If he had been the hero in a Gilded Age dime

18 On the incident involving the tax collection scandal, see Kendall, *History of New Orleans*, II, 516; Fitzpatrick's obituary in *Times–Picayune*, April 8, 1919.

novel, he could not have had a more dramatic closing scene.

Not only did 1896 mark the end of the Ring and its style of paternal bossism, but it spelled political oblivion for Negroes. In New Orleans throughout the Gilded Age, both regulars and reformers had catered to the Negro vote. But by the 1890's a hardening of white racial prejudices had set in all over the state. In 1890 the Louisiana legislature passed its first Jim Crow law requiring separate seating of whites and Negroes on railroads. By 1894 this was augmented by another law stipulating the segregation of the races in railroad stations. That same year a law outlawing miscegenation was passed. Similar measures had been defeated in 1880 and 1888.[19]

The crucial United States Supreme Court case of *Plessy* vs. *Ferguson*, which upheld Louisiana's separate railroad coach law, was handed down in 1896. This opened the door to a host of similar Jim Crow legislation in Louisiana and the rest of the South. That same year the compromise over Foster's election set the seal of doom on Negro suffrage in Louisiana. The constitutional convention it had promised was held in 1898. The literacy and property-owning qualifications written into the 1898 Louisiana constitution removed the bulk of Negroes from the state's registration rolls. In Louisiana in 1888 there were 128,150 Negro registered voters. By 1900 under the new state constitution, they numbered only 5,320. [20] In the sphere of public education de facto racial segregation had existed in New Orleans schools and those in the rest of the state since the end of Reconstruction. It finally became law in the 1898 state constitution.[21]

Economically the city expanded its opportunities in many directions between 1880 and 1896. The jetties built at the outset of

[19] Dethloff and Jones, "Race Relations in Louisiana, 1877–98," 315–16; Germaine A. Reed, "Race Legislation in Louisiana, 1864–1920," *Louisiana History*, VI (Fall, 1965) , 383.

[20] Reed, "Race Legislation in Louisiana," 391–92; *Select Speeches of the Hon. Randall Lee Gibson, of Louisiana, Delivered in the Senate of the United States, 1888–1891*, II (Washington, 1891) , 80–81; Dethloff and Jones, "Race Relations in Louisiana, 1877–98," 316. The new voter registration article of the 1898 Louisiana constitution was of such widespread interest to the public that the *Item* printed the entire Article 197 in its 1899 almanac. *Item Almanac and Political Register for 1899* (New Orleans, 1899) , 35–37.

[21] Dethloff and Jones, "Race Relations in Louisiana, 1877–98," 318; Reed, "Race Legislation in Louisiana," 385–86.

the period allowed oceangoing ships to enter the river and reach New Orleans. The fear of being locked in by silt deposits at the Mississippi's mouth was overcome. This Gilded Age period also saw the rise of commercial organizations such as the Cotton Exchange, the Produce Exchange, the Maritime Union and the Board of Trade, and the appearance of labor unions such as the Knights of Labor and the American Federation of Labor.

In general terms, a number of key changes took place. The bulk of products coming to the port of New Orleans from the interior shifted from river to rail transportation. Business began to be carried on largely through the newly organized exchanges. Much of the cargo passing through the port went from railroad cars directly into the holds of ships—cotton was the biggest example. Exports came to be carried mainly in foreign vessels. New trends in trade included the rising fruit trade with South America, which was developed by Italian immigrants who settled in the city, and the rapid growth of the grain trade brought to the city via railroad boxcars from the Far West. By 1896 New Orleans was the third largest grain port in the United States.[22]

The *Times-Democrat Almanac for 1896* gives a statistical account of the growth of the city between 1880 and the beginning of 1896. Total commerce had increased 12.1 percent; railroad tonnage rose 691.9 percent; value of products handled by railroads went up 119.8 percent; the coastwise trade increased 96.5 percent and ocean-going trade rose 47.4 percent. In finance, city assessments rose 54.4 percent, while taxation decreased 18.3 percent per person. Real estate sales went up 111.5 percent, and expenditures for public improvements showed a 259.8 percent increase. The number of banks in New Orleans rose from eleven in 1880 to nineteen by 1896, a 72.7 percent gain. The capital and surplus funds in city banks also increased 58.4 percent between these two dates. In 1880 there had been no savings banks or homestead associations in New Orleans. By the end of 1895 there were four of the former and twenty-four of the latter. Although New Orleans remained predominantly a commercial center, its manufacturing establishments by 1896 had expanded 402.7 percent over those in

22 Rightor, *Standard History of New Orleans*, 576–77; George E. Cunningham, "The Italian, A Hindrance to White Solidarity in Louisiana, 1890–1898," *Journal of Negro History*, L (January, 1965), 24.

1880. The average wage earned by a New Orleans laborer had gone up 95.6 percent in this same period. In terms of yearly income, the average New Orleanian had received about $272.73 a year in 1880, which by the beginning of 1896 rose to $434.72. [23]

Despite the bossism of the Ring, the violence of politicians and city employees, the corrupting influence of the lottery, and the general poverty and debt of the city government in the early 1880's, by 1896 the city's two debt settlements had put its operations on a solvent basis and made possible the beginnings of modest internal improvements. The city wharves which had been under private contract throughout the period were transferred to the jurisdiction of a state agency, the Commission for the Port of New Orleans, or the Dock Board, created by the legislature in 1896. The board began its preparations for wharf operations immediately. But the actual takeover did not occur until the private wharf lease ran out in 1901. The creation of the Dock Board marks the beginning of the modern era in the history of New Orleans port. The limits of the port were also extended in 1896 to include portions of Jefferson and St. Bernard parishes along the river. [24]

New Orleans cultural development was quite marked in certain areas. The establishment of Tulane University and Newcomb College stimulated the intellectual climate of the city and laid the groundwork for their complex expansion in the next half century. In literature Gilded Age New Orleans saw a generation of local colorists arise with Cable as their prophet without honor in his own land. The French language as a written and spoken everyday language in the Crescent City declined slowly but relentlessly during this period. Always musically rich in both opera and dance hall offerings, the city spawned an exciting new music, jazz, which was half-black, half-white, sometimes sad and sometimes joyful, but always close to the people whose polyglot lives it reflected. The celebration of Mardi Gras by 1896 had become a universal people's holiday as well as a prime tourist attraction and the climax of the city's most brilliant social season.

To someone who had not seen the city since its ragged Recon-

[23] *Times–Democrat Almanac for 1896*, p. 16.
[24] James P. Baughman, "Gateway to the Americas," in Carter (ed.), *The Past As Prelude: New Orleans, 1718–1968*, 271–74.

struction days, the sight of New Orleans bedecked with yellow, green, and purple bunting for the 1896 Mardi Gras was an inspiring sight. It summed up the great changes materially and psychologically which had come to the city's population in two decades. Senator Nelson Aldrich, recalling his visit to the Crescent City in 1876, put it in his usual succinct fashion: "New Orleans has improved marvelously since I was here twenty years ago. Then you had only mule cars, your buildings were not so tall as they now are and your streets not so clean nor well paved. There seems to be a great deal of business and life here, and from what I have heard recently the commercial aspects of the city are most flattering to its growth and development." [25]

The year 1896 was a watershed in local history. It marked the end of an era which may be said to have started with the first Shakspeare administration. It had been an era suspended between the chaos of Reconstruction and the Progressive Era of Martin Behrman; an era in which municipal affairs often stood still, sometimes slipped backward, and progressed forward only slowly, painfully by inches. Most of the principal players in the gaslight drama of Gilded Age New Orleans had left the stage by 1896. Patrick Mealey, Charles T. Howard, John A. Morris, David Hennessy, General P. G. T. Beauregard, Charles Gayarré, Father Rouquette, and Eliza Nicholson were dead. Shakspeare died that year also. Two such vastly different men as E. A. Burke and George W. Cable had both gone into self-imposed exile after feeling the wrath of New Orleanians directed at them. Fitzpatrick retired from the mayor's office, disheartened over the scandals which had sent several members of his administration to prison and destroyed the political organization which the reformers branded a brazen Ring, but which he had loved and worked for since his youth.

Around the corner of the twentieth century lay radical changes in the conquest of yellow fever, the eradication of smallpox, proper drainage, a sewerage system, water purification, and improved port facilities. It was the city that reformers, reporters, and Ring politicians of Fitzpatrick's generation had dreamed and talked about. But few of them lived to see the dream's fulfillment.

25 *Daily Picayune*, February 18, 1896.

Appendix

The information in this section is taken from *Administrations of the Mayors of New Orleans, 1803–1936*. Typescript compiled and edited by Works Progress Administration. New Orleans, 1940. In New Orleans Public Library.

Shakspeare Administration
(1880–1882)

Mayor: Joseph A. Shakspeare

Administrator of Water Works
    and Public Buildings: ....J. Valsin Guillotte
Administrator of Finance: ....Blayney T. Walshe
Administrator of Improvements: ....John Fitzpatrick
Administrator of Police: ....Patrick Mealey
Administrator of Accounts: ....William E. Huger
Administrator of Assessments: ....George Delamore
Administrator of Commerce: ....William Fagan
    City Attorney: ....Charles F. Buck
    City Notary: ....Samuel Flower
    City Surveyor: ....Daniel M. Brosnan
    Coroner: ....Dr. J. C. Beard
    Police Chief: ....Thomas N. Boylan
    Fire Chief: ....*Thomas O'Connor

* O'Connor was actually the chief engineer of the Firemen's Charitable Association which contracted with the city to fight municipal fires.

323

Behan Administration
(1882–1884)

Mayor: William J. Behan

Commissioner of Police and
    Public Buildings: ....Patrick Mealey
Commissioner of Public Works: ....John Fitzpatrick
Treasurer: ....Blayney T. Walshe
Comptroller: ....J. Valsin Guillotte
    City Attorney: ....Charles F. Buck
    City Surveyor: ....Daniel M. Brosnan
    City Notary: ....Joseph D. Taylor
    Coroner: ....Dr. Yves R. LeMonnier
    Police Chief: ....Richard B. Rowley
    Fire Chief ....Thomas O'Connor

Councilmen

Edward Booth	R. H. Benners
Charles A. Butler	H. Albert
H. L. Frantz	S. Patorno
F. Lauer	L. A. Burthe
N. Amann	Thomas Ryan
B. O. S. Rayne	A. D. Saucier
L. Nael	J. N. Hardy
A. J. Fitzpatrick	J. Lusk
Phil J. Rielly	H. C. Miller
M. D. Lagan	Z. Dowty
William Conway	William Graner
Hugh McManus	W. J. McGeehan
T. D. Semmes	P. Kaiser
W. J. Grady	Otto Thoman
Peter Blaise	A. J. Michaelis
C. Howard	C. Henshart

While the council was made up of thirty men, two were replaced. Therefore, thirty-two names are given here.

Guillotte Administration
(1884–1888)

Mayor: J. Valsin Guillotte

Commissioner of Police and
   Public Buildings: ....Patrick Mealey
Commissioner of Public Works: ....John Fitzpatrick
Treasurer: ....Isaac W. Patton
Comptroller: ....Joseph N. Hardy
   City Attorney: ....Walter S. Rogers
   City Notary: ....Joseph D. Taylor
   Coroner: ....Dr. James S. Finney
   City Surveyor: ....Daniel M. Brosnan
   Police Chief: ....Zach Bachemin
   Fire Chief: ....Thomas O'Connor

Councilmen

James B. Prague ....Thomas Carey
N. Amann ....D. M. Kilpatrick
A. Prados, Jr. ....T. H. Ryan
E. Baumann ....E. L. Israel
J. P. Stoulig..Louis Zeller
James A. Brennan ....A. C. Winn
Peter Farrell ....Christy McCarthy
H. C. Miller ....John E. Sliger
M. Carroll ....G. Devron
Edward S. Maunsell ....A. D. Saucier
A. Patorno ....Joseph Garidel
V. Mauberret ....Henry Albert
Hugh McManus ....George H. Lord
Henry Lehman ....W. H. Moon
Pat Mullen ....Edward Burke
George Huhner M.D. ....B. T. Walshe

Shakspeare Administration
(1888–1892)

Mayor: Joseph A. Shakspeare

Commissioner of Police and
  Public Buildings: ....Thomas Agnew
Commissioner of Public Works: ....Pierre G. T. Beauregard, re-
    signed and was succeeded by
    Edgar T. Leche
Treasurer: ....Joseph N. Hardy
Comptroller: ....Otto Thoman
  City Attorney: ....Carleton Hunt
  City Notary: ....Joseph D. Taylor
  Coroner: ....Dr. Yves R. LeMonnier
  City Surveyor: ....Benjamin M. Harrod
  Police Chief: ....*David C. Hennessy, suc-
    ceeded by Dexter S. Gaster
  Fire Chief: ....Thomas O'Connor

Councilmen

Robert Aitken	W. I. Hodgson
T. A. Beck	W. E. Hunter
A. Brittin	L. A. Hymel
A. Borman	George L'Hote
Charles F. Claiborne	C. L. Keppler
J. G. Clark	Arthur Lambert
Frank A. Daniels	A. C. Landry
A. DeLavigne	William Lynd, Jr.
Alex K. Finlay	M. J. McAdam
George H. Dunbar	A. R. Moulin
Henry Haag	James B. Prague
Frank M. Hall	J. R. S. Selleck
George Hauer	George W. Stockton
A. H. Hannemann	Louis T. Stoulig
Philip Hirsch	J. B. Woods

* John Journe served as temporary acting police chief from the time of Hennessy's assassination in October, 1890, until Gaster's appointment in January, 1891.

Fitzpatrick Administration
(1892–1896)

Mayor: John Fitzpatrick

Commissioner of Police and
    Public Building: ....C. Taylor Gauche
Commissioner of Public Works: ....Peter Farrell
Treasurer: ....Charles W. Schenck
Comptroller: ....Charles R. Kennedy
    City Attorney: ....Emmanuel A. O'Sullivan
    City Notary: ....Joseph D. Taylor
    Coroner: ....Dr. George B. Lawrason
                                 Dr. Charles L. Seeman
    City Engineer: ....Linus W. Brown
    Police Chief: ....Dexter S. Gaster
    Fire Chief: ....Thomas O'Connor

Councilmen

J. T. Callahan	L. Cucullu
Samuel Gautier	N. Dudoussat
Louis O. Desforges	L. B. Miro
William A. Brand	Louis Knop
Alex Barras	E. J. Louapre
C. E. Murray	F. B. Thriffley
Henry Pohlman	John M. Clarke
Charles Dickson	Charles Noel
Maurice Kenny	Jacob Boes
Irwin Jamison	John Schlumbrecht
Thomas Haley	Dan A. Meyer
William J. Kane	Peter Doerr
Samuel T. Gateley	Peter B. Caulfield
Charles A. Desporte	Charles Wirth
Charles Louque	Adam Lorch
J. J. Hannafy	Henry Harmeyer
	George Foster

Bibliography

PRIMARY MATERIALS

Archival

In Archives of the City of New Orleans,
New Orleans Public Library

Administrations of the Mayors of New Orleans, 1803–1936. Typescript compiled and edited by Works Progress Administration. New Orleans, 1940.

Biographies of the Mayors of New Orleans, 1803–1936. Typescript compiled and edited by Works Progress Administration. New Orleans, 1940. (This is a version of the preceding manuscript.)

City Ordinances, No. 4280 Administration Series in the Year 1878 through No. 7336 Council Series in the Year 1887. (Clippings from the *Official Journal of the City Council of New Orleans* in a ledger book.)

Department of Improvements Record Book of Bridge Gangs and Repairs to Bridges, 1881–83.

Francis P. Burns to the Commissioners of the McDonogh Fund, June 24, 1925. (In Commissioners of the McDonogh Fund Folder.)

Ledger Book of Treasurer, Public Schools, City of New Orleans, 1873–84.

Letter Book No. 7. Mayor's Office: 1891–92. (Letters of Joseph A. Shakspeare during his second term as mayor of New Orleans.)

Letter Book of Administrator of Department of Improvements of the City of New Orleans, 1881–83.

Minute Book, Commissioner of the John McDonogh School Fund. Typescript.

Minutes of the City Council of New Orleans, July 20, 1880–March 31, 1881.

Receipts for Petitions and Protests Acted Upon by Departments and Committees, 1882–83 (of the municipal government of New Orleans).
Record of Entries and Releases, [New Orleans] City Insane Asylum, September 1, 1872–September 1, 1882. 2 volumes.

In Special Collections Division, Howard-Tilton Memorial Library, Tulane University

Pierre G. T. Beauregard, Manuscripts.
George Washington Cable, Collection.
Minute Book, Orleans Steam Fire Engine Company, No. 21, 1881–92.
Jacotot, Prosper, "Voyage d'un ouvrier dans la vallée du Mississippi de Saint Louis á la Nouvelle Orleáns, 1877." Translated from French by S. Fucich and Mrs. F. Peterson. (Typescript).
Mary Ashley Townsend, Papers.

In Department of Archives and Manuscripts, Louisiana State University

E. John Ellis, Collection.
Thomas C. W. Ellis, (and family), Collection.

Public Documents

1. Municipal Documents

Amended Charter of the City of New Orleans. New Orleans, 1871.
Annual Reports of the Board of Police Commissioners. New Orleans, 1899.
Annual Report of the Board of Commissioners of Prisons and Asylums of New Orleans, Louisiana, November 1, 1898. New Orleans, 1898.
Annual Report of the Board of Directors of Public Schools for the Parish of Orleans, December, 1895. New Orleans, 1895.
Brown, Henry C. (city surveyor). *Report on the Drainage, Sewerage and Health of the City of New Orleans.* New Orleans, 1879.
Charter of the City of New Orleans and the Laws Relative to the City Debt adopted at the Regular Session of the General Assembly of the State of Louisiana. New Orleans, 1882.
Eighteenth Semi-annual Report, New Orleans Sewerage, Water and Drainage Board. New Orleans, 1908.
Fitzpatrick, John. *Mayor's Message to the City Council of the City of New Orleans.* New Orleans, 1892 and 1894.
Flynn, J. G. *Flynn's Digest of the City Ordinances Together with the Constitutional Provisions, Acts of the General Assembly and Deci-*

sions of the Courts Relative to the Government of the City of New Orleans. New Orleans, 1896.

Jeffrey, Edward T. *Remarks of E. T. Jeffrey before the City Council of New Orleans on the Extent of Illinois Central and its Bearing on the Prosperity and Commerce of New Orleans.* New Orleans, 1889.

Jewell, Edwin L. (ed.). *Charter of the City of New Orleans, 1882, Annotated and Indexed.* New Orleans, 1882.

———— (comp.). *Jewell's Digest of the City Ordinances Together with the Constitutional Provisions, Acts of the General Assembly and Decisions of the Courts Relative to the Government of the City of New Orleans.* New Orleans, 1882.

Report of Board of Managers, Touro-Shakspeare Almshouse, Being a Report and Inventory of Improvements made during the Period 1901–1908. New Orleans, 1908.

Report of the Board of Commissioners of the McDonogh School Fund, from January 1, 1881 to December 31, 1881. New Orleans, 1882.

Report of the Board of Commissioners of the McDonogh School Fund, from January 1, 1892 to December 31, 1895. New Orleans, 1896.

Report of the Board of Commissioners of the McDonogh School Fund, from January 1, 1896 to December 31, 1899. New Orleans, 1900.

Report of the Chief Superintendent of Public Schools to the Board of Directors of the Public Schools, January, 1886. New Orleans, 1886.

Report of the Drainage of the City of New Orleans by the Advisory Board (appointed by Ordinance No. 8327, Adopted by the City Council, November 24, 1893). New Orleans, 1895.

Rogers, William C. *Report of the Chief Superintendent of the Public Schools of New Orleans, Louisiana, to the Board of School Directors.* New Orleans, 1884.

Statement of the Bonded and Floating Indebtedness of the City of New Orleans. Report of the Committee of City Debt to the Honorable City Council. New Orleans, 1882.

Weston, R. S. *Sewerage and Water Board Report on Water Purification Investigation and on Plans proposed for Sewerage and Water Works Systems.* New Orleans, 1903.

2. State Documents

Acts Passed by the General Assembly of the State of Louisiana, at the First Session of the First Legislature, Begun and Held in the City of New Orleans, June 29, 1868. New Orleans, 1868.

Acts Passed by the General Assembly, State of Louisiana, Regular Session, 1882. Baton Rouge, 1882.

Acts Passed by the General Assembly, State of Louisiana, Regular Session, 1890. Baton Rouge, 1890.

Acts Passed by the General Assembly, State of Louisiana, Regular Session, 1894. Baton Rouge, 1894.

Acts Passed by the General Assembly, State of Louisiana, Regular Session, 1896. Baton Rouge, 1896.

Acts Passed by the General Assembly, State of Louisiana, Regular Session, 1898. Baton Rouge, 1898.

Acts Passed by the General Assembly, State of Louisiana, Regular Session, 1900. Baton Rouge, 1900.

Election Laws of Louisiana. New Orleans, 1884.

Jones, Joseph. *Quarantine and Sanitary Operations of the Board of Health of the State of Louisiana during 1880, 1881, 1882,* and *1883 (Introduction to the Annual Report of the Board of Health to the General Assembly of the State of Louisiana, 1883–1884).* Baton Rouge, 1884.

Louisiana Board of Health Biennial Report, 1890–1891.

Louisiana Board of Health Report for the Year 1884–1885.

3. Federal Documents

Abstract of the Twelfth Census. Washington, 1904.

"Biographical Directory of the American Congress, 1774–1961," *House Documents,* 85th Cong., 2nd sess., No. 442.

Compendium of the Eleventh Census. Part 2. Washington, 1894.

Congressional Record, 48th Cong., 1st Sess.

Department of Commerce, United States Bureau of the Census, Samuel L. Rogers, Director, *Negro Population, 1790–1915.* Washington, 1918.

Eleventh Census, Vital Statistics, Cities of 100,000 Population and Upward: Part 2. Washington, 1896.

Fish, Stuyvesant. *Statement to the Committee of the House of Representatives on Rivers and Harbors Relating to the Foreign Commerce of the United States Before and After the Civil War Through the Port of New Orleans, March 6, 1900.* New Orleans, 1900.

———. *Statement to the United States Industrial Commission (Relative to the Great Central Basin Drained by the Mississippi River and New Orleans the Seaport of that Basin), October, 1899.* New Orleans, 1899.

Kennedy, Joseph C. G. (comp.). Superintendent of Census, *Population of the United States in 1860; Compiled from the Original Returns of the Eighth Census under the Direction of the Secretary of the Interior.* Washington, 1864.

Memorial Addresses on the Life and Character of Samuel D. McEnery, Delivered in the Senate and House of Representatives of the United States, Sixty-First Congress, Third Session. Washington, 1911.

Report of Statistics of Churches in the United States at the Eleventh Census, 1890. Washington, 1894.

Report of the Commissioner of Education, 1888–1889. II. Washington, 1891.

Report on the Manufactures of the United States at the Tenth Census. Washington, 1883.

Statistics of the Population of the United States at the Tenth Census (June 1, 1880): Embracing Extended Tables of the Population of States, Counties and Minor Civil Divisions, with Distinction of Race, Sex, Age, Nativity, and Occupations, I. Washington, 1883.

Twelfth Census of the United States Taken in the Year 1900, I, Part 1. Washington, 1901.

Waring, George E., and George W. Cable. "History and Present Condition of New Orleans, Louisiana," *Tenth Census, Report on the Social Statistics of Cities,* XIX, Part 2. Washington, 1887.

4. Legal Documents

Cases Argued and Decided in the Supreme Court of the United States, (In 118, 119, 120, 121, 122, U.S.). Reprint. Rochester, N.Y., 1958.

Cases Argued and Decided in the Supreme Court of the United States, (In 143, 144, 145, 146, U.S.). Reprint. Rochester, N.Y., 1920.

Civil District Court, Parish of Orleans, Division E. *The State of Louisiana versus the New Orleans Water Works Company. Printed Compilation of Pleadings.* New Orleans, n.d.

Civil District Court, Parish of Orleans, Division E, No. 58,345. *The State of Louisiana versus the New Orleans Water Works Company. Defendant's Reply to the Brief of the State by J. R. Beckwith of Counsel for Defendant.* New Orleans, n.d.

Civil District Court, Parish of Orleans, No. 58,345. *The State of Louisiana versus the New Orleans Water Works Company. Defendant's Reply, J. R. Beckwith, Farrar, Jones & Krutschnitt, E. Howard McCaleb, Counsel for Defendant.* New Orleans, n.d.

Louisiana Annual Reports, XXXVI. Baton Rouge, 1884.

Reports of Cases Argued and Determined in the Supreme Court of Louisiana, XXXXI. (Reprint of XXXIV of *Louisiana Annual Reports*). St. Paul, 1907.

Reports of Cases Argued and Determined in the Supreme Court of Lou-

isiana, XXXIX. (Reprint of XXXII of *Louisiana Annual Reports*). St. Paul, 1908.

State of Louisiana, Parish of Orleans, Civil District Court, Division B, No. 43,762. *State Ex. Rel. Charles A. Butler, District Attorney vs. John Fitzpatrick, Mayor, Argument of Counsel for Citizens in the Proceedings asking for a Removal of Mayor of New Orleans.* New Orleans, 1895.

Supreme Court of Louisiana, No. 13,701. *State of Louisiana, Appellant versus the New Orleans Water Works Company, Appelle. The City of New Orleans, Intervenor. Appeal from the Civil District Court for the Parish of Orleans.* New Orleans, n.d.

Supreme Court of Louisiana, No. 13,701. *State of Louisiana, Appellant* versus the New Orleans Water Works Company, Appelle. The City *of New Orleans, Intervenor. Appeal from the Civil District Court for the Parish of Orleans. Reply to Supplement Brief of Appellant by Counsel for Appelle.* New Orleans, n.d.

City Guides and Directories

Coleman, Will H. (comp. and pub.) . *Historical Sketch Book and Guide to New Orleans and Environs with Map. Illustrated with Many Original Engravings and Containing Exhaustive Accounts of the Traditions, Historical Legends, and Remarkable Localities of the Creole City.* New York, 1885.

Fairall, Herbert S., *The World's Industrial and Cotton Centennial Exposition, New Orleans, 1884–1885.* Iowa City, 1885.

Item Almanac for 1897. New Orleans, 1897.

Item Almanac and Political Register for 1899. New Orleans, 1899.

Louisiana Telephone Company List of Subscribers, New Orleans Telephone Exchange. New Orleans, April, 1881.

Soards, Lon (comp.) . *Soards' New Orleans City Directory* (for the years 1874–96.) . New Orleans, 1874–96.

Times-Democrat Almanac for 1896. New Orleans, January, 1896.

Visitors' Guide to the World's Industrial and Cotton Centennial. New Orleans, 1884.

Visitor's Handbook of New Orleans. New Orleans, 1884.

Waldo, J. C. *Visitors' Guide to New Orleans.* New Orleans, 1879.

Zacharie, James S. *New Orleans Guide: With Descriptions of Routes to New Orleans, Sights of the City Arranged Alphabetically, and other Information Useful to Travellers; also, Outline of the History of Louisiana.* New Orleans, 1885.

Newspapers

London *Daily Telegraph*, 1880 and 1885, scattered dates.
New Orleans *Daily Democrat*, 1880–81.
New Orleans *Daily Picayune*, 1880–1900.
New Orleans *Daily Item*, 1880–96.
New Orleans *Daily States*, 1883–92.
New Orleans *Daily Times*, 1881.
New Orleans *Mascot, An Independent Journal of the Day*, 1882–94.
New Orleans *Tax Payers' Organ and Journal of Reform*, 1882.
New Orleans *Times-Democrat*, December, 1881–96.
Public Opinion (published weekly by the Public Opinion Company).
    Excerpts from newspapers on the lynching of the Italians. Washington and New York, March 21, 1891, pp. 561–65.
Washington *Post*, 1883.

Miscellaneous

Annual Reports of the Water Works Company. New Orleans, 1879–98.
Earl, G. G. *Proceedings of the Thirtieth Annual Convention of American Water Works Association*. New Orleans, 1910.
Final Report of the Citizens' Central Storm Relief Committee. New Orleans, 1894.
Frank McGloin Papers, Anti-Lottery League, 1890–92. (Bound collection of articles and legal papers on the lottery in New Orleans Public Library.)
First Annual Report of the Charity Organization Society of New Orleans, Louisiana, From December 1st, 1896 to December 31st, 1897. New Orleans, 1896.
Hecht, R. S. *Municipal Finances of New Orleans, 1860–1916*. (Address delivered by R. S. Hecht, vice-president of the Hibernia Bank and Trust Company before Tulane Society of Economics.) New Orleans, 1916.
Holt, Joseph *The Sanitary Relief of New Orleans: A Paper Read Before the New Orleans Medical and Surgical Association, October 31, 1885*. New Orleans, 1886.
Layton, Thomas, W. P. Brewster, E. T. Shepard, and Joseph Holt. *Report on Milk and Dairies in the City of New Orleans, Presented to the New Orleans Medical and Surgical Association . . . July 5, 1879*. New Orleans, 1879.

Map of the City of New Orleans. (Printed by M. F. Dunn and Brother in New Orleans, 1884–85, for Staub, News Dealer, Goldthwaite's Book Store, Canal and Exchange Place.)

Memorial of the Committee of One Hundred to the General Assembly of the State of Louisiana. New Orleans, 1886.

Official Text-Book and Programmes of the Twenty-Sixth Saengerfest of the North American Saengerbund. New Orleans, 1890.

Petition in Behalf of State Medicine to the General Assembly of the State of Louisiana (by the Louisiana State Medical Society, New Orleans Medical and Surgical Association). New Orleans, 1883.

Proceedings of the Orleans Parish Medical Society, New Orleans, 1897. New Orleans, 1898.

Select Speeches of the Hon. Randall Lee Gibson of Louisiana, Delivered in the Senate of the United States, 1888–1891. II. Washington, 1891.

SECONDARY MATERIAL

Books

A Near Century of Gas in New Orleans. New Orleans, 1926.

Asbury, Herbert. *Sucker's Progress, An Informal History of Gambling in America from the Colonies to Canfield.* New York, 1938.

———. *The French Quarter, An Informal History of the New Orleans Underworld.* Garden City, 1938.

Baughman, James P. *Charles Morgan and the Development of Southern Transportation.* Nashville, 1968.

Beard, Charles A. and Mary R. *The Rise of American Civilization.* 2 vols. New York, 1927.

Behrman, Martin. *The History of Three Public Utilities—Sewerage, Water, and Drainage and their Influence upon the Health and Progress of a Big City.* New Orleans, 1914.

Bevan, Evelyn C. *City Subsidies to Private Charitable Agencies in New Orleans: The History and Present Status, 1824–1933.* New Orleans, 1934.

Biographical and Historical Memoirs of Louisiana. 2 vols. Chicago, 1892.

Bisland, Elizabeth. *The Life and Letters of Lafcadio Hearn.* 3 vols. Boston and New York, 1906.

Blain, Hugh M. *A Near Century of Public Service in New Orleans.* New Orleans, 1927.

Blesh, Rudi, and Harriet Janis. *They All Played Ragtime.* New York, 1966.

Boyle, James E. *Cotton and the New Orleans Cotton Exchange: A Century of Commercial Evolution.* Garden City, 1934.

Bruce, Philip A. *The Rise of the New South.* Philadelphia, 1905.

Burlingame, Roger. *Engines of Democracy: Inventions and Society in Mature America.* New York, 1940.

Butcher, Philip. *George W. Cable.* New York, 1962.

Cable, George W. *The Creoles of Louisiana.* New York, 1910.

Campbell, T. W. (comp.). *Manual of the City of New Orleans.* New Orleans, 1901.

Capers, Gerald M., Jr. *The Biography of a River Town (Memphis: Its Heroic Age).* Chapel Hill, 1939.

———. *Occupied City: New Orleans Under the Federals, 1862–1865.* Lexington, 1965.

Carter, Hodding (ed.). *The Past as Prelude: New Orleans, 1718–1968.* New Orleans, 1968.

Cash, Wilbur J. *The Mind of the South.* Garden City, 1956.

Caskey, W. M. *Secession and Restoration in Louisiana.* Baton Rouge, 1938.

Chaillé, Stanford E. *Life and Death-Rates: New Orleans and other Cities Compared.* New Orleans, 1888.

———. *Small-Pox and Vaccination.* New Orleans Auxiliary Sanitary Association publication, 1883.

Chambers, Henry E. *A History of Louisiana: Wilderness, Colony, Province, Territory, State, People.* 3 vols. Chicago and New York, 1925.

Clement, W. E. *Over a Half Century of Electricity and Gas Industry.* New Orleans, 1947.

Dabney, Thomas E. *The Indestructible City (The Story of New Orleans' Amazing Battle with Nature, and How, in Over-Coming the Obstacles with which It was Faced, It Has Set a Superb Record of Progress and Development).* New Orleans, n. d.

———. *One Hundred Great Years: The Story of the Times-Picayune from its Founding to 1920.* Baton Rouge, 1944.

Davis, Edwin Adams. *Louisiana: A Narrative History.* Baton Rouge, 1965.

De Santis, Vincent P. *Republicans Face the Southern Question: The New Departure Years, 1877–1897.* Baltimore, 1959.

Di Palma, Thomas. *New Orleans Carnival and Its Climax, Mardi Gras.* New Orleans, 1953.

338   Bibliography

Duffy, John (ed.). *The Rudolph Matas History of Medicine in Louisiana.* 2 vols. Baton Rouge, 1962.

Dyer, John P. *Tulane: The Biography of a University, 1834–1865.* New York, 1966.

Engelhardt, George. *The City of New Orleans.* New Orleans, 1894.

Faulkner, Harold U. *Politics, Reform and Expansion, 1890–1900.* New York, 1959.

Ficklen, J. R. *History of Reconstruction in Louisiana.* Baltimore, 1910.

Fortier, Alcée. *History of Louisiana.* 4 vols. New York, 1904.

——. *Louisiana (Comprising Sketches of Parishes, Town, Events, Institutions and Persons, Arranged in Cyclopedic Form).* 3 vols. Madison, Wis., 1914.

Ginger, Ray. *Altgeld's America: The Lincoln Ideal Versus Changing Realities.* New York, 1958.

Gosnell, H. F. *Boss Platt and the New York Machine.* Chicago, 1924.

Hamlin, Walter. *A History of the Courts in the Parish of Orleans.* New Orleans, 1950.

Hennick, Louis C. and E. Harper Charlton. *Louisiana: Street and Interurban Railways.* Shreveport, 1962.

——. *The Streetcars of New Orleans, 1831–1965.* Shreveport, 1965.

Herring, H. S. *History of the New Orleans Board of Trade, Limited, 1880–1930.* New Orleans, 1930.

History of the New Orleans Police Department, Benefit of the Police Mutual Benevolent Association of New Orleans. New Orleans, 1900.

Holt, Dr. Joseph. *The Sanitary Protection of New Orleans, Municipal and Maritime, Reprint from The Sanitarian.* January, 1886.

Howe, William W. "Municipal History of New Orleans" (volume VII, Herbert B. Adams, ed., *Johns Hopkins University Studies in Historical and Political Science*). Baltimore, 1889, pp. 155–87.

Jewell, Edwin L. (ed. and comp.). *Jewell's Crescent City Illustrated (The Commercial, Social, Political and General History of New Orleans including Biographical Sketches of its Distinguished Citizens).* New Orleans, 1874.

Johnson, Thomas C. *The Life and Letters of Benjamin Morgan Palmer.* Richmond, 1906.

Kendall, John S. *History of New Orleans.* 3 vols. New York, 1922.

Key, V. O., Jr. *Southern Politics in State and Nation.* New York, 1949.

King, Grace. *Memoirs of a Southern Woman of Letters.* New York, 1932.

——. *New Orleans: the Place and the People.* New York, 1907.

Kmen, Henry A. *Music in New Orleans: The Formative Years, 1791–1841.* Baton Rouge, 1966.

Kreeger, Maurice B. *I Remember When.* New Orleans, 1955.

LaCour, Arthur Burton. *New Orleans Masquerade, Chronicles of Carnival.* New Orleans, 1952.

Land, John E. *Pen Illustrations of New Orleans, 1881-1882.* New Orleans, 1882.

Landauer, A. J. R. *Resources and Industries of the State of Louisiana Together with a General Review of the Trade of New Orleans.* New Orleans, 1883.

Longstreet, Stephen. *Sportin' House: A History of the New Orleans Sinners and the Birth of Jazz.* Los Angeles, 1965.

Lonn, Ella. *Reconstruction in Louisiana After 1868.* New York and London, 1918.

Macrae, David. *The Americans At Home, Pen-and-Ink Sketches of American Men, Manners, and Institutions.* Glasgow, 1885.

Malone, Dumas (ed.). *Dictionary of American Biography.* New York, 1931.

McGinty, Garnie. *Louisiana Redeemed: The Overthrow of Carpetbag Rule, 1876-1880.* New Orleans, 1941.

McNeill, George E. (ed.). *The Labor Movement: The Problem of Today.* Boston, 1886.

Miller, William D. *Memphis During the Progressive Era, 1900-1917.* Memphis, 1957.

Mordell, Albert. *Discoveries: Essays on Lafcadio Hearn.* Tokyo, 1964.

Morison, Samuel E. and Henry S. Commager. *The Growth of the American Republic.* 2 vols. New York, 1956.

Morrison, Andrew. *Industries of New Orleans: Her Rank, Resources, Advantages, Trade, Commerce and Manufactures, Conditions of the Past, Present and Future, Representative Industrial Institutions, Historical, Descriptive and Statistical.* New Orleans, 1885.

————. *New Orleans, Her Relation to the New South.* New Orleans, n.d. but probably 1883.

Mumford, Lewis. *The Culture of Cities.* New York, 1938.

National Cyclopaedia of American Biography. New York, 1907.

Nau, John Frederick. *The German People of New Orleans, 1850-1900.* Leiden, 1958.

New Orleans City Guide. Written and compiled by the Federal Writers' Project of the Works Progress Administration for the City of New Orleans. Boston, 1938.

New Orleans of 1894. Reprinted from the annual commercial edition of the *Daily Picayune,* September 1, 1894, and published by the Young Men's Business League. New Orleans, 1894.

O'Connor, Thomas (ed.). *History of the Fire Department of New Orleans: From the Earliest Days to the Present Time, Including the Original Volunteer Department, the Fireman's Charitable Association, and the Paid Department down to 1895.* New Orleans, 1895.

Patton, G. Farrar. *History and Work of the Louisiana State Board of Health.* New Orleans, 1904.

Pierce, Bessie Louise. *A History of Chicago.* 3 vols. New York, 1957.

Progressive New Orleans. New Orleans, 1894.

Reynolds, George. *Machine Politics in New Orleans, 1897–1926.* New York. 1936.

Rightor, Henry (ed.). *Standard History of New Orleans, Louisiana.* Chicago, 1900.

Roberts, W. Adolphe. *Lake Pontchartrain.* Indianapolis and New York, 1946.

Robinson, Lura. *It's An Old New Orleans Custom.* New York, 1948.

Rose, Al and Edmond Souchon. *New Orleans Jazz: A Family Album.* Baton Rouge, 1967.

Rothman, Edwin, Edgar Rosenthal, Emma L. Bowman, and Leigh B. Hebb. *Philadelphia Government, 1956.* Bureau of Municipal Research and Pennsylvania Economy League, Eastern Division. Philadelphia, 1956.

Rousseve, Charles T. *The Negro in Louisiana, Aspects of His History and His Literature.* New Orleans, 1937.

Sala, George Augustus Henry. *America Revisited.* London, 1883.

Samuel, Ray, Leonard V. Huber, and Warren Ogden. *Tales of the Mississippi.* New York, 1955.

Saxon, Lyle, Robert Tallant, and Edward Dreyer (comp.). *Gumbo Ya-Ya.* Cambridge, 1945.

Schlesinger, Arthur M. *The Rise of the City, 1878–1898.* New York, 1933.

Shaw, Frederick. *The History of the New York City Legislature.* New York, 1954.

Shugg, Roger W. *Origins of Class Struggle in Louisiana: A Social History of White Farmers and Laborers during Slavery and After, 1840–1875.* Baton Rouge, 1939.

Sights and Sounds Along the Sunset Route. New York, 1885.

Simkins, Francis B. *The South, Old and New: A History, 1820–1947.* New York, 1948.

Stewart, Frank Mann. *A Half Century of Municipal Reform.* Berkeley and Los Angeles, 1950.

Telephone Conditions in New Orleans, Louisiana, Being a Report Presented by a Special Committee of the New Orleans Board of Trade Approved April 8th, 1908. New Orleans, 1908.

The Louisiana State Lottery Company, Examined and Exposed. New Orleans, 1889.

The Mechanics, Dealers and Lumbermen's Exchange: Its Imprint and Purposes, New Orleans Souvenir. New Orleans, 1895.

Tinker, Edward Larocque. *Creole City: Its Past and Its People.* New York, 1953.

————. *Lafcadio Hearn's American Days.* New York, 1924.

Tolman, William Howe. *Municipal Reform Movements in the United States.* New York and Chicago, 1895.

Tracey, Francis. *Startling Confession of Henri Romani, the King of the Mafia.* Philadelphia, 1891.

Turner, Arlin. *George W. Cable, A Biography.* Durham, 1956.

————. (ed.) . *The Negro Question.* New York, 1958.

Twain, Mark, and Charles D. Warner. *The Gilded Age.* 2 vols. Hartford, 1874.

Twain, Mark. *Life on the Mississippi.* New ed. New York, 1960.

Tyler, Alice F. *The Foreign Policy of James G. Blaine.* Minneapolis, 1927.

Vance, Rupert B. and Nicholas J. Demerath (eds.) . *The Urban South.* Chapel Hill, 1954.

Warmoth, Henry Clay, *War, Politics and Reconstruction: Stormy Days in Louisiana.* New York, 1930.

Who Was Who in America, 1897–1942. Chicago, 1942.

Williard, Francis E. and Mary A. Livermore (eds.) . *A Woman of the Century, Fourteen Hundred-Seventy Biographical Sketches Accompanied by Portraits of Leading American Women in All Walks of Life.* Reprint. Detroit, 1967.

Williams, Martin. *Jazz Masters of New Orleans.* New York and London, 1967.

Williams, T. Harry. *P. G. T. Beauregard: Napoleon in Gray.* Baton Rouge, 1955.

Woodward, C. Vann. *Origins of the New South, 1877–1913.* Baton Rouge, 1951. Vol IX, Wendell H. Stephenson and E. Merton Coulter (eds.) , *A History of the South.* 10 vols.; Baton Rouge, 1949——.

————. *Reunion and Reaction.* Garden City, N. Y. 1956.

————. *The Strange Career of Jim Crow.* New York, 1957.

[Wright, Emily,]. *From the Lakes to the Gulf.* n.p., 1884.

Articles

Adams, William H. "New Orleans as the National Center of Boxing," *Louisiana Historical Quarterly,* XXXIX (January, 1956) , 92–112.

Alwes, Berthold C. "The History of the Louisiana State Lottery Company," *Louisiana Historical Quarterly,* XXVII (October, 1944), 964–1118.

Baughman, James P. "The Evolution of Rail-Water Systems of Transportation in the Gulf Southwest, 1836–1890," *Journal of Southern History,* XXXIV (August, 1968) , 357–81.

Brockway, Z. R. "Needed Reform in Prison Management," *North American Review,* CXXXVII (July, 1883) , 40–48.

Buel, Clarence C. "The Degradation of a State: or, the Charitable Career of the Louisiana Lottery," *Century Illustrated Monthly,* XLIII (1892) , 618–32.

Chenault, William W. and Robert C. Reinders. "The Northern-Born Community of New Orleans in the 1850's," *Journal of American History,* LI (September, 1964) , 232–47.

Cunningham, George E. "The Italian, A Hindrance to White Solidarity in Louisiana, 1890–1898," *Journal of Negro History,* L (January, 1965) , 22–36.

Dethloff, Henry. "The Alliance and the Lottery: Farmers Try for the Sweepstakes," *Louisiana History,* VI (Spring, 1965) , 141–59.

———. and Robert R. Jones. "Race Relations in Louisiana, 1877–98," *Louisiana History,* IX (Fall, 1968) , 301–323.

Dixon, Richard R. "Milneburg Joys," New Orleans *Roosevelt Review,* XXV (October, 1962) , 9–20.

East, Dennis, II. "Health and Wealth: Goals of the New Orleans Public Health Movement, 1879–84," *Louisiana History,* IX, (Summer, 1968) , 245–75.

Fletcher, Marie. "The Southern Woman in the Fiction of Kate Chopin," *Louisiana History,* VII (Spring, 1966) , 117–32.

[Godkin, E. L.] "The Italian Trouble," *The Nation (a Weekly Journal Devoted to Politics, Literature, Science, and Art),* LII (April, 9, 1891) , 294.

———. "The New Orleans Massacre," *The Nation,* LII (March 19, 1891) , 232.

———. "Why Capital Does Not Flow into the South," *The Nation,* XXXV (December, 1882) , 501.

Going, Allen J. "The South and the Blair Education Bill," *Mississippi*

Valley Historical Review, XLIV (September, 1957), 267–90.

Gonzales, John Edmond. "William Pitt Kellogg, Reconstruction Governor of Louisiana, 1873–1877," *Louisiana Historical Quarterly,* XXIX (April, 1946), 394–495.

Harris, L. M. "The Creoles of New Orleans," *Southern Collegian,* XXX (January, 1898), 196–212.

Heaton, Augustus G. "A Winter in New Orleans, 1891–'92," *The Nutshell,* XVI (April–June, 1930), 1–3.

Hester, Henry. "Cotton," *Manufacturer's Record,* XXIX (July 17, 1896), 3–5.

Hunt, Belle. "New Orleans, Yesterday and Today," *Frank Leslie's Popular Monthly,* XXXI (June, 1891), 641–55.

"Industrial Growth in the Southern States," *The Saturday Review of Politics, Literature, Science and Art,* LIX (March 7, 1885), 313–14.

[Jackson, Joy.] "Help to Help Themselves," *Dixie Roto Magazine,* New Orleans *Times-Picayune,* November 11, 1956.

———. "How They Erected Lee's Statute the First Time," *Dixie Roto Magazine,* New Orleans *Times-Picayune,* January 18, 1953.

———. "When All Saints' Day Saw the Fashion Parade," *Dixie Roto Magazine,* New Orleans *Times-Picayune,* October 28, 1951.

Kasson, John A. "Municipal Reform," *North American Review,* CXXXVII (September, 1883), 218–30.

Kendall, John S. "Journalism in New Orleans Between 1880 and 1900," *Louisiana Historical Quarterly,* VIII (October, 1925), 557–73.

———. "Old Days on the Times-Democrat," *Louisiana Historical Quarterly,* XXXIII (October, 1950), 406–29.

———. "Old-Time New Orleans Police Reporters and Reporting," *Louisiana Historical Quarterly,* XXVIII (January, 1946), 43–58.

———. "The Last Days of Charles Gayarré," *Louisiana Historical Quarterly,* XV (July, 1932), 359–75.

———. "Who Killa De Chief," *Louisiana Historical Quarterly,* XXII (April, 1939), 492–530.

King, Grace. "Charles Gayarré, A Biographical Sketch," *Louisiana Historical Quarterly,* XXXIII (April, 1950), 159–88.

———. "The Higher Life of New Orleans," *Outlook,* LIII (1896), 754–61.

Lang, Herbert H. "Charles Gayarré and the Philosophy of Progress," *Louisiana History,* III (Summer, 1962), 251–61.

Lathrop, Barnes F. (ed.). "An Autobiography of Francis T. Nicholls, 1834–1881," *Louisiana Historical Quarterly,* XVII (April, 1934), 246–67.

Lowrey, Walter M. "The Engineers and the Mississippi," *Louisiana History*, V (Summer, 1964) , 233–55.

"Mafia and What Led to the Lynching," *Harper's Weekly*, XXXV (March 28, 1891) , 225–27.

Matas, Rudolph. "An Evening With Gayarré," *Louisiana Historical Quarterly*, XXXIII (April, 1950) , 269–93.

McGinty, Garnie W. "The Louisiana Lottery Company," *Southwestern Social Science Quarterly*, XX (March, 1940) , 329–47.

Mitchell, Harry A. "The Development of New Orleans as a Wholesale Center," *Louisiana Historical Quarterly*, XXVII (October, 1944) , 933–63.

O'Connor, Stella. "The Charity Hospital at New Orleans: An Administrative and Financial History," *Louisiana Historical Quarterly*, XXXI (January, 1948) , 5–109.

Paul, Rodman W. "The Wheat Trade between California and the United Kingdom," *Mississippi Valley Historical Review*, XLV (December, 1958) , 391–412.

Reed, Germaine A. "Race Legislation in Louisiana, 1864–1920," *Louisiana History*, VI (Fall, 1965) , 379–92.

Reed, Merl E. "Government Investment and Economic Growth: Louisiana's Ante Bellum Railroads," *Journal of Southern History*, XXVIII (May, 1962) , 183–201.

Reynolds, Donald E. "The New Orleans Riot of 1866, Reconsidered," *Louisiana History*, V (1964) , 5–27.

Romero, Sidney James, Jr. "The Political Career of Murphy James Foster, Governor of Louisiana, 1892–1900," reprint from *Louisiana Historical Quarterly*, XXVIII (October, 1945) , 3–117.

Rothstein, Morton. "America in the International Rivalry for the British Wheat Market, 1860–1914," *Mississippi Valley Historical Review*, XLVII (December, 1960) , 401–18.

Seeger, Ferdinand. "Jobs in Cities," *North American Review*, CXLIII (July, 1886) , 87–95.

Shugg, Roger W. "The General Strike of 1892," *Louisiana Historical Quarterly*, XXI (April, 1938) , 545–60.

"Some Letters of Charles Gayarré," *Louisiana Historical Quarterly*, XXXIII (April, 1950) , 223–54.

Somers, Dale A. "A City on Wheels: The Bicycle Era in New Orleans," *Louisiana History*, VIII (Summer, 1967) , 219–38.

Standish, Hal. "Fred Fearnot in New Orleans, or Up Against the Mafia," *Work and Win, An Interesting Weekly For the Young* (February 13, 1903) , 1–28.

Taylor, Joe Gray. "New Orleans and Reconstruction," *Louisiana History,* IX (Summer, 1968) , 189–208.

"The Mafia," *The Illustrated American,* I, No. III (November 8, 1890) , 327–35.

"The Mafia," *The Nation,* LII (April 9, 1891) , 291.

Tregle, Joseph G., Jr. "Early New Orleans Society: A Reappraisal," *Journal of Southern History,* XVIII (February, 1952) , 20–36.

Turner, Arlin. "George W. Cable's Beginnings as a Reformer," *Journal of Southern History,* XVII (May, 1951) , 135–61.

Uzee, Philip D. "The Republican Party in the Louisiana Election of 1896," *Louisiana History,* II (Summer, 1961) , 332–34.

Waring, George E., Jr. "Sanitary Drainage," *North American Review,* CXXXVII (July, 1883) , 57–67.

White, Charles Henry. "New Orleans," *Harper's Monthly Magazine,* CXIV (December, 1906) , 121–30.

Wiggins, Richard H. "The Louisiana Press and the Lottery," *Louisiana Historical Quarterly,* XXXI (July, 1948) , 716–844.

Theses and Dissertations

Babin, Claude. "The Economic Expansion of New Orleans Before the Civil War." Ph.D dissertation, Tulane University, 1954.

Behrend, Elsa L. "The New Orleans Public School System Since the Civil War." M.A. thesis, Tulane University, 1931.

Eagleson, Dorothy Rose. "Some Aspects of the Social Life of the New Orleans Negro in the 1880's." M.A. thesis, Tulane University, 1961.

Hardy, D. Clive. "World's Industrial and Cotton Centennial Exposition and the New South, 1884–85." M.A. thesis, Tulane University, 1964.

Hicks, Walter S. "The Decline of the Bourbon Democracy in New Orleans." M.A. thesis, Tulane University, 1926.

Klein, Esther B. "The Contributions of William O. Rogers to Education in New Orleans," M.A. thesis, Tulane University, 1942.

Maden, Ann. "Popular Sports in New Orleans, 1890–1900." M.A. thesis, Tulane University, 1956.

Manint, Helen Arthur. "A History of the New Orleans Public Library and Howard Memorial Library. M.A. thesis, Tulane University, 1942.

Marks, Janey. "The Industrial Development of New Orleans Since 1865." M.A. thesis, Tulane University, 1924.

Odum, Edwin Dale. "Louisiana Railroads, 1830–1880: A Study of State and Local Aid." Ph.D dissertation, Tulane University, 1961.

Ozenovich, Steve J. "The Development of Public Secondary Education in New Orleans, 1877–1914." M.A. thesis, Tulane University, 1940.

Parsons, Virginia. "A Study of the Activities of the Louisiana Board of Health From 1855 to 1898 in Reference to Quarantine." M.A. thesis, Tulane University, 1932.

Pearce, Arthur Raymond. "The Rise and Decline of Labor in New Orleans." M.A. thesis, Tulane University, 1938.

Pearson, Edna Mae. "History of Public School Education in Louisiana from 1870 to the Present Time as Influenced by Social and Economic Conditions." M.A. thesis, Tulane University, 1931.

Phillips, William J. "Study of Building and Loan Associations in New Orleans: Early History and Development and their Present Financial Condition." M.A. thesis, Tulane University, 1933.

Porter, Alice T. "An Economic View of Ante-Bellum New Orleans, 1845–1860." M.A. thesis, Tulane University, 1942.

Robert, Mary Elizabeth Phillips. "The Background of Negro Disfranchisement in Louisiana." M.A. thesis, Tulane University, 1932.

Rosenberg, Malcolm Francis. "The Orleans Parish Public Schools under the Superintendency of Nicholas Bauer." Ph.D. dissertation, Louisiana State University, 1963.

Soulé, Leon. "The Creole-American Struggle in New Orleans, 1850–1862." M.A. thesis, Tulane University, 1955.

Stock, Paul R. "Historical Background to the Present Activities of the Board of Health to the City of New Orleans." M.A. thesis, Tulane University, 1932.

Subat, Albert P. "The Superintendency of the Public Schools of Orleans Parish, 1862–1910." M.A. thesis, Tulane University, 1947.

Tucker, Robert Cinnamond. "The Life and Public Service of E. John Ellis." M.A. thesis, Louisiana State University, 1941.

Vegas, Vera M. "The Populist Party in Louisiana." M.A. thesis, Tulane University, 1942.

Walker, David Allan. "A History of Commerce and Navigation on the Lower Mississippi River, 1803–1840." M.A. thesis, Louisiana State University, 1965.

White, John Tobin. "The History of the Louisiana State Lottery." M.A. thesis, Tulane University, 1939.

Williams, Margaret M. "An Outline of Public School Politics in Louisiana Since the Civil War." M.A. thesis, Tulane University, 1939.

Williams, Robert Webb, Jr. "Martin Behrman: Mayor and Political Boss of New Orleans, 1904–1926." M.A. thesis, Tulane University, 1952.

Index

Adams, Thomas Scott, 130, 131
Aldermanic Council: advantages for
Ring, 47–48; escapades of, 48; description of, 76–77; actions during
Guillotte administration, 89–90;
Maurice Hart's influence on, 108
Algiers, La., 9, 19, 164
All Saints Day, description of, 3–4
Almshouse: construction and opening of, 192–93; renamed Touro-
Shakspeare Almshouse, 193
American Exposition, 93, 204. *See also*
Cotton Centennial Exposition
Anchor Line, 219
Anderson, Tom, 254
Anti-Lottery League: founded, 126;
rally at Grand Opera House, 129–30;
convention in Baton Rouge, 130;
mentioned, 128, 133, 135, 280, 314
Arlington, Josie, 254
Audubon Golf Club, 267
Audubon Park, 267. *See also* Upper
City Park
Auxiliary Sanitary Association, 4, 102,
128, 148, 154, 155, 172, 173, 174, 241

Baer, Clara, 260
Baker, Julie K. Wetherill, 295
Baker, Marion, 287, 295
Baker, Page, 252n
Baldwin, Albert, 121, 311
Banks: connected with Louisiana State
Lottery Company, 121; statistics on,
217

Bartlett, Napier, 298
Battle of September 14: description of,
28–29; influence on Gilded Age politics, 29, 30, 31; and Liberty Place
monument, 75; mentioned, 39, 51
Beauregard, Pierre G. T., 63, 96, 98,
113, 114, 118, 122, 157, 298, 321
Beauregard Square. *See* Congo Square
Behan, William J.: as candidate for
mayor, 74–75; inauguration of 75–
76; background of, 77–78; controversial appointment of police chief, 78–
79; attempts to solve problem of
irregular pay to city employees, 79–
81; mentioned, 31, 36, 52, 82, 83, 84,
85, 86, 88, 90, 95, 192, 234, 238
Behrman, Martin, 54, 317, 321
Bicycles, and street surfacing, 159. *See
also* Sports
Bidwell, David, 23
Bisland, Elizabeth, 289, 292
Bloomer Girls, 263
Board of Assessors, 97–98
Board of Commissioners of McDonogh
Fund, 196
Board of Commissioners of Port of
New Orleans, 219. *See also* Dock
Board
Board of Education, State, 195
Board of Fire Commissioners, 106
Board of Health, Louisiana, 51, 153,
158, 170, 171, 172, 173, 174, 175, 176,
177, 178, 179, 180, 181, 182, 183, 203

230, 263; 1880 to 1896, increase of, 319–20

Committee of One Hundred, 93, 94, 241

Committee of Public Safety, 240

Comite des Citoyens, 25

Comus, Mistick Krewe of, 304, 305, 307

Confederate Memorial Hall, 122

Congo Square, 274, 275

Conrad, Paul, 118

Cotton: receipts, 5, 213; founding of Cotton Exchange, 215; Hester reports on, 215, 216, 231; sale of futures in, 216; problem of through cotton, 230; mentioned, 209, 213

Cotton Centennial Exposition: description of, 204–206; mentioned, 7, 9, 41, 42, 48, 82, 84, 87–88, 92–93, 145, 166, 246, 261, 268, 279, 287. *See also* American Exposition

Cotton Exchange: views on city charter of 1882, p. 46; founded, 215; mentioned, 164, 188–89, 217, 319

Cotton terminal, 220

Creole controversy, 14–15, 285, 286, 290, 301

Creoles, 14–15, 18, 178, 203, 284, 285, 286, 297, 301; Negro, 276, 277, 285, 302

Crescent City Jockey Club, 269

Crescent Democratic Club, 54

Crime and vice: gambling, 63, 234, 235, 253–54; among politicians, 90, 91, 236, 237; "Cap" Murphy murder, 91–92; confidence men, 234; juvenile delinquents, 234; dope addiction, 235; criminal gangs, 236; labor strike violence, 237, vigilante groups to combat spread of, 240–41; and Mafia, 245; Devereaux murder, 246; Hennessy investigates Matrangas and associates, 247; Hennessy murder, 248; illegal lotteries, 253; prostitution and Storyville, 254–55; and Mardi Gras, 311

Dairies, conditions of, 179–80

Dane, R. B. L. *See* Bisland, Elizabeth

Dauphin, Maximilien, 118, 122, 125

Davey, Robert C., 50, 96–97, 134

Davis, Jefferson, 298, 307

Davis, Mollie Evelyn Moore, 295

Davis, Varina "Winnie," 307

Delamore, George, 59, 102

Democratic (Conservative) Party: holds first white primary in state, 132; split over lottery issue, 132–35; mentioned, 74, 79, 86, 87, 91, 95, 96, 109, 111, 225, 300

Denegre, Walter, 249

Denis, Jules, 36

Desdunes, Rodolphe L., 302

Devereaux, Thomas, 65–66, 245, 246, 248

Disease: yellow fever, 4, 153, 170, 175, 177, 178, 209; sources of, 147, 154, 179; ordinances on, 178–79; smallpox, 182–83; typhoid, 182–83; and death rates, 182, 183, 184, 185; mentioned, 21

Dix, Dorothy, 295

Dock Board, 220, 320. *See also* Board of Commissioners of the Port of New Orleans

Drainage: connection to sewerage and water, 147; system in 1880's, pp. 148–49; plans for, 150–52; topographical survey of city, 151–52; new system of, 512; Advisory Board on, 152

Drinking water: sources, 154; problems during droughts, 154; purification of, 155n; mentioned, 145

Drugs: regulation of, 180–81

Eads, James B., 5, 209, 210

Early, Jubal A., 63, 113, 114, 122, 123

Easton, Warren, 197

Education: funds for, 195, 196; Blair Bill, 196–97; teachers' salaries, 197; schools' shutdown, 197–98; institutions of higher learning, 201–202; illiteracy rates, 201–202

Elections: and electoral returns, 57, 75, 86, 96, 134, 315; set by 1882 charter, 66; attempts at reform of, 94; and vigilante action, 96

Electra, Knights of, 306

Electricity: Mark Twain comments

ty, 132–35; moves to Honduras, 134–35; mentioned, 16, 50, 52, 63, 64, 110, 111, 206, 253, 258, 300
Louisiana State Railroad Commission, 217
Louisiana State University, 268
Lower City Park, 160–61, 261
Lyceum Library, 202

McDonogh Fund, 195, 196
McEnery, John, 28–29
McEnery, Samuel D., 49, 50, 110, 130, 132, 134, 187, 289, 290, 291
McGloin, Frank, 289
Madame John's Legacy, 284
Mafia, 18, 245
Marine Hospital Service, 174
Maritime Association, 217
Marks, Isaac, 106
Matas, Rudolph, 186, 287
Mayor's Charity Fund, 194
Mealey, Patrick, 38, 44, 46, 58, 64, 66, 74, 79, 84, 85, 87, 95, 225, 236, 237, 316, 321
Mercier, Alfred, 289, 291, 292
Milneburg, 24, 278
Morris, Frances Isabel, 306
Morris, John A., 116, 117, 118–19, 119n, 123, 126, 127, 128, 132, 134, 269, 306, 321

Negroes: in New Orleans' population, 19–20; in politics, 20; relations with whites 20–21; churches of, 25–26; in Louisiana population in 1880, p. 33; and municipal elections, 33; disfranchisement of, 33–34, 316, 318; and Shakspeare's patronage, 109–10; as flood victims, 150; death rate of, 183; illiteracy of, 196, 197, 201, 202; school population of, 199; sugarcane strike by, 224–25; relation with white laborers, 226, 230; 1881 strike violence of, 237; voodoo ceremonies, 254–55, 275–76; Congo Square dancing, 274; dance halls, 274–75; plantation dancing, 275; works songs, 276, 277; brass bands, 279; Lincoln Park, 279; French-speaking, 285; Gretna Cyclones, a carnival march-

ing society of, 310; Ring accused of offering to buy votes of, 315; 1896 alleged voting irregularities of, 315–16; public school segregation of, 318; decline in registered voters among, 318; Jim Crow laws affecting, 318
Nereus, Krewe of, 306
New Basin Canal, 151, 219
Newcomb College, 202, 259, 260, 261, 263, 320
New Louisiana Jockey Club, 267–69
New Orleans Clearing House Association, 217–18
New Orleans Conference of Charities, 194
New Orleans *Daily Item,* purchased by Dominick C. O'Malley, 252n
New Orleans *Daily Picayune:* demanded nullification of 1884 election, 86; as booster of Blair bill, 196; Eliza Nicholson's connection with, 292–94; rivalry with *Times-Democrat* over literary pages, 294
New Orleans *Daily States,* sued by mayor, 142
New Orleans *Democrat:* antilottery sentiment of, 115, 120; acquired by Burke and lottery interests, 40–41, 120
New Orleans *Mascot, An Independent Journal of the Day:* weekly, 18; and injunction incident, 68–71; Robert Brewster killed in attack on editor of, 91
New Orleans *Times-Democrat,* consolidation of, 41
New Orleans Medical and Surgical Association, 179
New Orleans Public Service, Incorporated, 167
Newspapers, in city, 26, 27
Nicholls, Francis T., 39, 42, 49, 50, 71, 100, 119, 120, 125, 126, 127, 128, 131n, 133, 135, 186, 271
Nicholson, Eliza: background of, 292–93; as publisher of *Daily Picayune,* 293–94; mentioned, 16, 134, 292, 321
Nicholson, George, 293